THE OXFORD BOOK OF
Canadian Political Anecdotes

THE OXFORD BOOK OF
Canadian Political Anecdotes

Edited by Jack McLeod
with Cynthia M. Smith, Associate Editor

Toronto Oxford New York
OXFORD UNIVERSITY PRESS

Oxford University Press, 70 Wynford Drive, Don Mills, Ontario, M3C 1J9

Toronto   Oxford   New York   Delhi   Bombay   Calcutta   Madras   Karachi
Petaling Jaya   Singapore   Hong Kong   Tokyo   Nairobi   Dar es Salaam
Cape Town   Melbourne   Auckland

and associated companies in
Berlin   Ibadan

Canadian Cataloguing in Publication Data

Main entry under title:

The Oxford book of Canadian political anecdotes

ISBN 0-19-540667-2 (bound). – ISBN 0-19-540812-8 (pbk.)

1. Canada – Politics and government – Anecdotes.
I. McLeod, Jack, 1932-   .   II. Smith, Cynthia M.

FC173.095 1988   971   C88-094622-9
F1008.4.095 1988

1 2 3 4 5 6 – 4 3 2 1 0

For
Adrienne, Andrew, and Heather

CONTENTS

INTRODUCTION

The political game is a great one to play. It is exciting even to watch; it brings with it disappointments and frustrations, but there are compensations in the acquaintances it brings, the friendships formed, and in the knowledge acquired of humanity, sometimes at its worst, more often at its best.

C.G. (CHUBBY) POWER, *A Party Politician*

Among other things, man is a story-teller. Whether around the fire in the mouth of the cave, in the parliamentary lobbies, on the hustings, or between the covers of history books and memoirs, there can be charm and wonder in the stories told. An anecdote, essentially a brief self-contained story, is often a valuable source of historical truth, augmenting our understanding and pleasure. Not all of us are interested in political philosophy or constitutional law, but we all respond to a good tale well told, and the quirks and foibles of personality such stories reveal can be fascinating. Quotes and jokes by or about political personalities may be memorable, but the special flavour of a genuine anecdote frequently provides an added dimension of insight, perspective, or amusement.

Boswell's *Life of Johnson* is full of anecdotes, and Dr Johnson himself in the later editions of his *Dictionary* defined the anecdote as a 'biographical incident; a minute passage of private life'. As editors we have borne that in mind, as well as the more recent *Oxford English Dictionary* definition: 'the narrative of a detached incident, or of a single event, told as being in itself interesting or striking'. For this book we have selected material, however defined, that we found biographically illuminating.

Our focus is on the national political scene. Although we have included glimpses of politicians and events in the provincial and even the municipal arenas, most of the attention here goes to players on the national stage. Inevitably such major figures as Sir John A. Macdonald, Sir Wilfrid Laurier, John Diefenbaker, and Pierre Trudeau command large shares of these pages. Our attempt has been to assemble not only representative samplings of these notables but also to include, in a characteristically eclectic and balanced Canadian manner, representations of politicians who reflect our regional and multicultural diversities: maritimers and westerners, Francophones and Anglophones, women and men, prime ministers and back-benchers, practitioners and commentators, historians and political journalists. In casting such an inclusive net, we believe we have caught some rare as well as some familiar examples of the nation's rich and varied public life.

Our difficulty was not in discovering material to include, but in deciding what to exclude. After the first of our two years as collectors of anecdotes, we faced the danger of presenting an impossibly thick, unwieldy (and expensive) tome of 800 or more pages. Arbitrary and sometimes painful decisions had to be made on what to slash. Kind correspondents and contributors, in addition to the surfeit of printed sources, made the task of selection even more perplexing. We received many letters and read more than four hundred biographies, autobiographies, articles, histories, and memoirs before beginning to carve the intimidating mass of material down to manageable dimensions. Ruefully we acknowledge that the stories we were obliged to omit could fill at least another two books—as, in the fullness of time, they may. Not every person or every taste could possibly be accommodated and, as every anthologist expects, readers' disappointments over exclusions will be as keen as their satisfaction with what was retained. The implacable requirements of space and balance were stern, but we are confident that the tough process of selection has yielded interesting results.

Some readers will already be familiar with the tradition within which this book appears. The Oxford University Press has published volumes of anecdotes on subjects literary, legal, and military as well as political. The British *Political Anecdotes* (1986), edited by Paul Johnson, and the American *Presidential Anecdotes* (1981), edited by Paul F. Boller, have given pleasure to many. A Canadian contribution to this series may provide interesting points of comparison.

Graceful and witty repartee may not be as striking a characteristic of our political life as it is of the British. If we go no further than the example of Sir Winston Churchill, it is difficult to find close parallels in our politics to Winnie's exchange with Bessie Braddock, a formidable Socialist MP:

'Winston, you're drunk.'
Churchill replied: 'Bessie, you're ugly, and tomorrow I'll be sober but you'll still be ugly.'

Or to his sharp clash with Lady Astor:

'If you were my husband, I'd poison your wine.'
'And if I were your husband,' Winston retorted, 'I'd drink it.'

The lambent style of a John F. Kennedy is not much in evidence on this side of the border. JFK once gave a friend a silver beer mug bearing this inscription:

'There are three things which are real;
God, human folly and laughter.
The first two are beyond our comprehension
So we must do what we can with the third.'

The Canadian manner is different. Although lacking the debating snap of the Oxford Union or the élitist polish of Harvard Yard, our leaders have seldom been deficient in brains or fortitude. Many, even quite recently, have been close to the earthy experience of pioneering and settlement, for Canada had a later start. It is useful to remember that by, say, the 1780s British politics was graced by William Pitt and Edmund Burke, and the Americans had produced

Benjamin Franklin and Thomas Jefferson, while Canadian public life was more notable for colonial governors, Loyalist immigrants, and fur traders. What is remarkable in our history is how impressively our politicians grappled with adversities and leapt forward to solid achievements in so short a time. Self-deprecating glances over our shoulders at the British or Americans are not usually realistic and Canadians have little to fear from invidious comparisons. Surely it would be idle to contend that George Washington was a more complex or interesting man than Sir John A. Macdonald, that Lincoln's tactics or oratory were more sophisticated than Sir Wilfrid Laurier's, or that Ronald Reagan's cue cards and astrology are more fascinating than the subtlety and spiritualism of Mackenzie King. On balance, what is most impressive about our politicians is their depth of character and their mettle.

And their humour. It was not our intention to compile a collection that would emphasize the comic; however, appealing stories of wit and humour kept pressing on us. As Dr Johnson observed, 'I have tried in my time to be a philosopher, but cheerfulness kept breaking in.' When beyond the call of Mr Speaker, at least, Canadian politicians have been a surprisingly jovial lot. Their wit is often salty and ribald, but so persistent and whimsical as to enliven our national story and demand inclusion here.

This is not in any way intended to trivialize the importance and centrality of politicians to our country's existence. The distinguished historian Donald Creighton once lamented 'the dominance of politics over nearly every aspect of Canadian life'. In the absence of the normal bonds of common origins, linguistic unity, or shared founding myths, it sometimes seems that (apart from sports) only politics and political structures hold us together. Politics, says Jeffrey Simpson, 'is like an endless river winding its way through the nation's psychological terrain'.

While we do not pretend that a collection of anecdotes reveals the sweep of history, it is noteworthy how many of the issues keep recurring, how the main political preoccupations of the past re-emerge in the present. Insistently repeated themes reflected here include questions of language, separate schools, tariffs and free trade, regionalism, immigration, and the relationships—sometimes tense, often cozy—between business and government. *Plus ça change. . .*

What does change throughout these pages, implicitly but strikingly, is the technology of politics. From the 'manly practice' of declaring one's vote in public, with the counting of heads often accompanied by the breaking of heads, by 1874 we had moved to the secret ballot. The telephone came to Ottawa only during the administration of Alexander Mackenzie, and when Laurier became Liberal leader in 1887 he jumped eagerly at his party's offer to relieve the burden of his correspondence with not merely a secretary but also a typewriter. Campaigning in the nineteenth century principally meant powerful use of the unassisted voice in meeting halls, political picnics, and *assemblées contradictoires*, and the partisan newspaper was the main source of public information at least until R.B. Bennett took to the radio to explain his 'New Deal' in 1935. The election of 1968 may have been the last time parties would risk emphasis on mass rallies with rock bands in hockey stadia or shopping plazas. Television, which so greatly assisted John Diefenbaker's campaign of 1957, quickly became king. Now TV dominates leadership conventions, the nightly news, image-making through the thirty-second film clip, and even Question Period in the House of Commons. If the abiding issues change slowly, the technology that conveys them has changed dramatically.

We have presented our selections in chronological sequence to suggest the changing times. When an important person's career has spanned several decades we have tried to choose the most appropriate niche. Given that stories about Mackenzie King, for example, date from the 1890s to the 1940s, we gave him—as well as Sir John A.—two separate positions in the book bracketing his time, and in this way we intend that the reader will see a sensible historical flow.

Technology and chronology aside, the main utility of this book may be to suggest the immutable qualities of human foibles and human nature, which not even the greatest politicians can transcend. It is curious how the unbuttoned frailties of Robert Baldwin and George Brown, of Macdonald and Blake and Borden, make them come alive, seem more real; anecdotal glimpses let them reappear not as historical monuments but as sympathetic flesh and blood, almost contemporary acquaintances who laughed and suffered as we do, reassuringly mortal and vulnerable. We are indebted to them, but connected to them across the gulf of time. As the German historian Leopold von Ranke puts it: 'All generations are equidistant from eternity.'

During the course of this project we have received more help from more sources than we can adequately acknowledge. Years ago we learned from friends and mentors including professors Norman Ward, Roger Graham, Donald Creighton, and Maurice Careless that the motherlode of Canadian political history was immensely rich if care were taken to mine it. The Honourable Eugene Forsey, with characteristic warmth and incisiveness, granted a long interview that provided many nuggets and pointed to other happy discoveries. Mr Marc Bosc, an historian with the Bourinot Project, Office of the Clerk, House of Commons, Ottawa, contributed a number of items (pp. 31–2, 32–3, 43, 53 [centre], 55, 64 [top], 68–70, 73–4, 74–5), particularly from the journalistic scrapbooks of Fred Cook in the National Archives of Canada. Janice Tyrwhitt provided stories from her *Reader's Digest* articles and from her personal interview files (pp. 105–6, 156–7). Useful anecdotes arrived in the mail from innumerable contributors, notably professors John Wilson, University of Waterloo (pp. 113, 123, 130, 234); Garth Stevenson, Brock University (pp. 124, 235); Norman M. Ward, University of Saskatchewan (p. 99); Paul Aird, University of Toronto (pp. 244–5); Graham Parker, Osgoode Hall, York University (pp. 126–7); F.G. Hulmes, University of Alberta (pp. 113 [top], 121–2, 131–2, 177–8); R.S. Blair, University of Toronto (pp. 67–8); and Richard Gregor, University of Toronto (pp. 129–30); Jim Coutts (p. 156); K.D.

Doolittle (p. 131); Robert Fulford (p. 194); Dr Wilfrid I. Smith (pp. 173–4); and Peter Warren (p. 223).

The efficient staff and the resources of the Robarts Library, University of Toronto, proved invaluable. Our special thanks go to a bright and brisk student of history and of library science, Ms Vivian O'Hara Lewis, who worked for a year as research assistant, diligently tracking down sources and alertly spotting stories that have added a great deal to this volume.

We are very much obliged to Richard Teleky of Oxford University Press, Canada, for the initiation of this project, and to him, Phyllis Wilson, and Sally Livingston for assisting and sustaining us through the arduous process of seeing a difficult manuscript into print.

As we round off these pages it is impossible to resist quoting Sir John Willison's account of one Mr Tooley, a venerable and respected Member of the Ontario Legislature in the 1880s who did not always find it easy to devote his full attention to the flow of public business in the House—underlining the inescapable fact that, with the best of intentions, political (and even editorial) lapses do occur:

> Once Mr Tooley . . . fell asleep and gently slid from his chair to the floor. Mr Tooley opened his eyes, seemed to be wholly unimpressed by the incident, arose slowly and deliberately reseated himself, and as Mr John Lewis said in *The Globe*, 'gravely resumed his legislative duties'.

J.T.McL.
C.M.S.

SAMUEL DE CHAMPLAIN

Explorer and cartographer Samuel de Champlain was the founder of New France and its governor from 1608 to 1635.

When Samuel Champlain in 1603 sailed up the St Lawrence river and agreed to support the Algonkian Indians at Tadoussac against the aggression of the Iroquois, he could not foresee that the petty strife between those two apparently insignificant hordes of 'savages' would one day decide the fate of New France and of the vast territory that stretched for an unknown distance to the west. At the time no other choice lay open to him. The migratory Algonkians and their allies, the Hurons, controlled most of the territory which he hoped to explore, possessed the best means—birch-bark canoes and snow-shoes—of travelling through that territory, and supplied the furs from which he hoped to finance his explorations. Of the Iroquois to the southward he knew little except that they practised agriculture, built permanent or semi-permanent villages, and were far less rich in the furs which at that time seemed to be the most important of the country's natural resources. Had Champlain, like his predecessor Cartier, encountered first Iroquois on the St Lawrence river and discovered their military strength and genius for political organization, France might to-day be the dominant power in North America. But fate decreed that the hostility of a few thousand Indians should check the expansion of the new colony and determine the course of history.

Diamond Jenness, *The Indians of Canada*, 1932

EARLY DEMOCRACY

An anthropologist describes the democracy of the Iroquoians.

On the whole, public opinion and the knowledge that the entire village would be held responsible for wrong-doing seem to have proved adequate safeguards, and the domestic life of the Iroquoians was probably no less peaceful than our own. Theft was comparatively rare, for land was the property of the community, surplus food was commonly shared with needier neighbours, the long bark dwelling belonged to the maternal family, and personal property like the tools and weapons of the men, the household goods and utensils of the women, were so easily replaced that they possessed little value. Practically the only objects open to theft were the strings of wampum beads that served both as

I

ornaments and currency; but such was the community spirit of the Iroquoians, so little did they esteem individual wealth, that a multitude of beads brought neither honour nor profit except so far as it gave the owner an opportunity to display his liberality by lavish contributions to the public coffers.

The Iroquoians were a very democratic people. Their chiefs differed in no way from the rank and file, but depended solely on skill and valour in battle, dignity of bearing and eloquence to maintain their prestige and influence. Captives, when not sacrificed, were adopted into the families, given Iroquoian wives, and regarded as citizens of full standing. There were no strata in society. . . .

                                                                      Ibid.

JEAN DE BRÉBEUF

A leading Jesuit missionary in New France, Jean de Brébeuf (1593–1649) was martyred at Saint-Ignace when the Iroquois raided the mission. His writings, included in R.G. Thwaits, The Jesuit Relations *(73 volumes), are an important source of our knowledge of the Hurons.*

About the month of December, the snow began to lie on the ground and the savages settled down into the village. For, during the whole Summer and Autumn, they are for the most part either in their rural cabins, taking care of their crops, or on the lake fishing, or trading; which makes it not a little inconvenient to instruct them. Seeing them, therefore, thus gathered together at the beginning of this year, we resolved to preach publicly to all, and to acquaint them with the reason of our coming into their Country, which is not for their furs, but to declare to them the true God and his son, Jesus Christ, the universal Saviour of our souls.

The usual method that we follow is this: We call together the people by the help of the Captain of the village, who assembles them all in our house as in Council, or perhaps by the sound of the bell. I use the surplice and the square cap, to give more majesty to my appearance. At the beginning we chant on our knees the *Pater noster*, translated into Huron verse. Father Daniel, as its author, chants a couplet alone, and then we all together chant it again; and those among the Hurons, principally the little ones, who already know it, take pleasure in chanting it with us. That done, when every one is seated, I rise and make the sign of the Cross for all; then, having recapitulated what I said last time, I explain something new. After that we question the young children and the girls, giving a little bead of glass or porcelain to those who deserve it. The parents are very glad to see their children answer well and carry off some little prize, of which they render themselves worthy by the care they take to come privately to get instruction. On our part, to arouse their emulation, we have each lesson retraced by our two little French boys, who question each other,— which transports the Savages with admiration. Finally the whole is concluded by the talk of the Old Men, who propound their difficulties, and sometimes make me listen in my turn to the statement of their belief.

Two things among others have aided us very much in the little we have been able to do here, by the grace of our Lord; the first is, as I have already said, the good health that God has granted us in the midst of sickness so general and so widespread. The second is the temporal assistance we have rendered to the sick. Having brought for ourselves some few delicacies, we shared them with them, giving to one a few prunes, and to another a few raisins, to others something else. The poor people came from great distances to get their share. Our French servants having succeeded very well in hunting, during the Autumn, we carried portions of game to all the sick. That chiefly won their hearts, as they were dying, having neither flesh nor fish to season their sagamité.

The Jesuit Relations and Allied Documents (1635), ed. S.R. Mealing

MARIE DE L'INCARNATION

The founder of an Ursuline convent in Québec, Mère Marie (1599–1672) knew almost everything of importance that went on in New France and commented perceptively in voluminous letters that tell us much about life in the colony.

The hundred girls that the King sent this year have just arrived and already almost all of them are married. He will send two hundred more next year and still others in proportion in the years to come. He is also sending men to supply the needs of the marriages, and this year fully five hundred have come, not to speak of the men that make up the army. In consequence, it is an astonishing thing to see how the country becomes peopled and multiplies. It is said that His Majesty intends to spare nothing, being urged to this by the seigneurs that are here, who find the country and living here delightful in comparison with the West Indies whence they come, where the heat is so extreme one can scarcely live. Those countries are rich because of the sugar and tobacco taken from them, but it is impossible to grow wheat there, and their bread is made of a certain root that necessity forces them to subsist on. But here wheat, vegetables, and all sort of cereals grow in abundance. The soil is excellent for wheat and, the more the woods are stripped from it, the more fertile and bounteous it becomes. Its fertility was very apparent this year because, the army's flour having spoiled on the ocean, enough wheat was found here to supply their needs without harming the provision of the habitants.

However this bounteousness does not prevent there being a great many poor folk here; the reason is that, when a family commences to make a habitation, it needs two or three years before it has enough to feed itself, not to speak of clothing, furniture, and an infinite number of little things necessary for the maintenance of a house; but when these first difficulties are past, they begin

to live comfortably and, if they have guidance, they become rich with time—
or as much so as is possible in a new country such as this. In the beginning
they live on their cereals and vegetables and on wild game, which is plentiful
in winter. To obtain clothing and other household utensils, they make roofing
planks and cut timber, which they sell at a high price. When they have thus
obtained all their necessities, they begin to trade and in this way advance little
by little. . . .

I told you in another letter that part of the army has gone on ahead to get
control of the river of the Iroquois [Richelieu] and build forts on its banks in
the most advantageous places. To this I shall add that our Christian Algonkins
have gone to camp with their families under protection of the forts and those
that guard them. They are hunting where their enemies were accustomed to
do so and obtain the greater part of their pelts. Their hunt is so bounteous
that it is said they take more than a hundred beaver each day, not to speak of
moose and other wild beasts.

In this the French and the Savages help one another. The French defend the
Savages, and the Savages provide food for the French by the flesh of the beasts
they kill, after they have removed the skins, which they take to the storehouses
of the country. Monsieur de Tracy told me a few days ago that he had informed
the King of all this and also the other advantages there are in making war upon
the sworn enemy of our Faith.

Word from New France: The Selected Letters of Marie de l'Incarnation (1665),
trans. and ed., Joyce Marshall

FRANÇOIS BIGOT

*The Colonial Minister of France, Berryer, wrote in 1759 to François Bigot, Intendant
of New France, providing an early example of public money sticking to private fingers.*

'The ship "Britannia",' wrote the Minister, Berryer, 'laden with goods such as
are wanted in the colony, was captured by a privateer from St Malo, and
brought into Quebec. You sold the whole cargo for eight hundred thousand
francs. The purchasers made a profit of two millions. You bought back a part
for the King at one million, or two hundred thousand more than the price
which you sold the whole. With conduct like this it is no wonder that the
expenses of the colony become insupportable. The amount of your drafts on
the treasury is frightful. The fortunes of your subordinates throw suspicion on
your administration.' And in another letter on the same day: 'How could it
happen that the small-pox among the Indians cost the King a million francs?
What does this expense mean? Who is answerable for it? Is it the officers who
command the posts, or is it the storekeepers? You give me no particulars. What
has become of the immense quantity of provisions sent to Canada last year? I
am forced to conclude that the King's stores are set down as consumed from

the moment they arrive, and then sold to His Majesty at exorbitant prices. Thus the King buys stores in France, and then buys them again in Canada. I no longer wonder at the immense fortunes made in the colony.'

Francis Parkman, *Montcalm and Wolff*, 1962

An old lady by the name of Descarrières had a store of lively anecdotes from the old days. Despite her eighty years, she was subject to that vanity which even old women cling to, and loved to tell a story that proved she had been pretty in her youth, although one would never have guessed it when I knew her. Knowing her weakness, all her friends made a point of saying often, 'Madame Descarrières, you must have known Intendant Bigot?' The old dowager would preen herself and tell her tale, always in the same words.

'The intendant, Monsieur Bigot, was a most courtly man. When I was presented to him at the age of eighteen, he kissed me as was the custom for coming-out presentations, both at the intendant's palace and the Château Saint-Louis. Then he clasped me around the waist with four fingers (I was so slim then that the fingers met) and exclaimed, "What a gorgeous handful of brunette!" I had light brown hair, you see.'

She told how, during the siege of Quebec, the same intendant had a dish of roast horse served at his table, which was always sumptuously laid in spite of the lack of food. Everyone agreed that this was to give an encouraging example to the rest, although he didn't eat it himself.

A Man of Sentiment: The Memoirs of Philippe-Joseph Aubert de Gaspé, trans. Jane Brierley, 1988

LIEUTENANT GOVERNOR JOHN WENTWORTH

The Governor of New Hampshire after 1766, Wentworth (1737–1820) found himself on the losing side of the American Revolution and removed to Halifax. He was Lieutenant-Governor of Nova Scotia from 1792 until 1808.

Halifax was full of naughty women, ranging all the way from the unwashed sluts of Barrack Street to the elegant wife of Mr John Wentworth, and Billy [Prince William, son of George III] knew them all. His favourite evening amusement was a tour of the town's bawdyhouses accompanied by Dyott and one or two other debauched young gentlemen of the service, who made sure that the daughters of joy staged a command performance for the prince—'some very pretty scenes', as Dyott tittered in his reminiscences.

More than once William must have gone straight from these pretty scenes to the arms of pretty Mrs Wentworth, a fact of which she was doubtless aware, although it does not seem to have offended her in the least. Frances Wentworth at this time was forty-two, a little past her bloom but still slender, vivacious, adept, and experienced in the arts of the drawing room and the bedchamber— and still very much the clever and ambitious wife of plodding John. How much her liaison with Prince William was induced by passion and how much by womanly calculation it is impossible to say. Certainly she played her part well, with John's obvious knowledge and consent. Whenever the prince was in town Mr Wentworth conveniently left for the country to pursue his duties as Sur- veyor-General of the King's Woods; and while John strode the forest clearings levying fees upon the reluctant settlers his lady exerted her shapely self with no less purpose for the pleasure of their royal guest.

All this made scandal in the more sober circle of Halifax society. Indeed many ladies would not call on Mrs Wentworth, much less admit her to their drawing rooms; and Prince Billy, a snob at heart, took care not to be seen in the same carriage with her. But beauty and patience conquer all things, and Frances Wentworth had a sweet revenge. In 1791 she and John sailed for England to visit their sixteen-year-old son, a student at Westminster. While they were there, old Lieutenant Governor Parr died at Halifax in an apoplectic fit. The news sped across the sea—and Opportunity appeared at the Went- worths' lodging with a thunderous knock.

Frances had lost no time in renewing her acquaintance with Prince William, now Duke of Clarence. At forty-six this provincial Ninon de Lenclos had lost little of her charm and none of her ability to please; and for his part William, while deep in his amour with the coarse and jolly Mrs Jordan, was not averse to re-tasting a remembered pleasure from across the sea. Always generous for favours received, he exerted himself on her behalf. In certain quarters his influence had weight. Added to the exertions of the Rockinghams and other powerful friends of the Wentworths it had the desired effect. An irreverent young Haligonian visiting in London at this time wrote home to Nova Scotia: 'I wrote my friend Paine a few days back, since which inform him that his friend Wentworth has succeeded to the Government of Nova Scotia, and Madam had the honour of kissing our gracious sovereign's hand. Previous to her departure the Duke of C—e presented her with a Damask Sopha accom- modated with four well-stuffed pillows, and she tried the length of it on the Queen's birthday.'

With or without the sofa, but with His Majesty's commission in John's traveling case, in April 1792 the new lieutenant governor and his lady sailed for home in HMS *Hussar*, and five weeks later they were greeted by a salute of fifteen guns from the Halifax batteries and escorted to Government House by a delegation of magistrates and army officers. On the following day Went- worth was sworn into office, and the boom of the cannon ranged along the upper side of Grande Parade announced his inauguration to the harbour hills.

Thomas H. Raddall, Halifax: Warden of the North, 1965

RICHARD J. UNIACKE

Speaker of the Nova Scotia legislature from 1789 to 1793, Richard J. Uniacke (1753–1830) was Attorney General after 1797.

The arrival in 1794 of Edward, Duke of Kent, the fourth son of George III, as commander of the troops in Nova Scotia and New Brunswick, gave to Halifax society a sense of the *beau monde* that was long remembered. The future father of Queen Victoria, with his mistress Julie St Laurent, entertained and was entertained with such lavishness that the six years of his stay became known as the 'golden age' of Nova Scotia. . . .

A martinet with a strong sense of decorum and propriety, he soon imposed a high moral tone on a garrison and a society where gambling and drunkenness had been only too common. He was careful always to bestow his favour impartially . . . and as a token of his regard for Uniacke the Duke gave him two Louis XVI chairs, one of which is on display today in the drawing room of Mount Uniacke. . . .

Shortly after the Duke's arrival, Uniacke was promoted to lieutenant colonel and raised a new battalion of militia, the 8th Battalion. . . . If Prince Edward had a high opinion of Uniacke's military abilities, he was soon disabused. During a military review on the King's birthday, the Duke requested Uniacke to put his battalion through a few movements. He replied, 'If your Royal Highness only knew how much trouble I have had in getting them into line, you would never ask me to break it.'

Brian Cuthbertson, The Old Attorney General, 1980

FRANÇOIS-MARIE-THOMAS DE LORIMIER

Associated with Louis-Joseph Papineau as a 'brigadier general' in the rebellion of 1837 in Lower Canada, de Lorimier was convicted of high treason and hanged in 1839. His last letter was to his son.

I die without remorse; in the insurrection I only desired the well-being and independence of my country. My views and my actions were sincere and were innocent of any of the crimes which dishonor mankind, and which are only too common when released passions boil up. For seventeen or eighteen years I have taken an active part in every movement, and always with conviction and sincerity. . . . My efforts have been for the independence of my compatriots. To this day we have been unsuccessful. Death has already decimated us. Many groan in bondage. Many are in exile, their property destroyed, their families abandoned without resources at the mercy of the Canadian winter. In spite of so many mishaps, my heart still keeps its courage and its hopes for the future; my children and my friends will see better days. Looking tranquilly ahead, I am sure that they will win freedom. That is what fills me with joy when all around me is sorrow and desolation. The wounds of my country will heal after the turmoil of anarchy and bloody revolution. Peaceful Canadians will see happiness and liberty born again on the banks of the St. Lawrence. Everything works towards this end, even these very executions; the blood and the tears poured on the altar of liberty are watering the tree which will bear the two-starred flag of the Canadas. I leave behind me children whose only heritage is the memory of my misfortune. Poor orphans, it is you who are to be pitied, you whom the bloody and arbitrary hand of the law strikes through my death. You will have no gentle and affectionate memories of happy days with your father. When you are old enough to reflect, you will see in your father a man who has paid on the scaffold for actions such as have immortalized other happier men. The only crime of your father was his failure.

D. DE LORIMIER

1838

Quoted in Margaret Fairley, *Spirit of Canadian Democracy*, n.d. [1946?]

WILLIAM LYON MACKENZIE

Grandfather of W.L. Mackenzie King, William Lyon Mackenzie led the 1837 Rebellion in Upper Canada against the Family Compact. Samuel Thompson's Reminiscences *provides an early glimpse of the young Mackenzie.*

In 1820, on his first arrival in Montreal from Scotland, he got an engagement as chainbearer on the survey of the Lachine canal. A few days afterwards, the surveying party, as usual at noon, sat down on a grassy bank to eat their dinner. They had been thus occupied for half an hour, and were getting ready for a smoke, when the new chain-bearer suddenly jumped up with an exclamation, 'Now, boys, time for work! we mustn't waste the government's money!' The consequence of which ill-timed outburst was his prompt dismissal from the service.

Samuel Thompson, *Reminiscences of a Canadian Pioneer*, 1884

It is hard to imagine him sitting still. You had best see him at work, at which, in one way or another, he spent almost every hour of the day and night. In a small plain structure built a generation earlier for Dr Baldwin's family, and situated on the Bay just a few blocks from St James', Mackenzie kept house, newspaper office, editorial room, printing press, and bookstore all together. . . . Over the door a small sign announced 'The Colonial Advocate, Wm. Lyon Mackenzie Editor & Prop.' Inside it was dim and smelt of printer's ink. Long after his apprentices had finished their work and departed, Mackenzie could still be found there, proof-reading perhaps, writing out an editorial or, if he was rushed, cramming the words right into the type case as they came to mind.

He was only five foot six and looked smaller because of a slight, wiry build and a large head and high brow. The prominence of chin, and the lips pressed together like a vise suggested a will that would not be broken. One observer particularly remembered the 'keen, restless, piercing blue eyes which, when they met your gaze at all, seemed to read your innermost thoughts.' His features announced plainly that he was honest through and through, and uncomfortably suggested that if you did not agree with their owner, you must be *dis*honest or something worse. He had lost his hair from a fever and covered his baldness with a loose, flame-red wig which in moments of jubilation he used to toss at a friend or hurl to the floor.

William Kilbourn, *The Firebrand*, 1960

On Sunday, the 3rd, we heard that armed men were assembling at the Holland Landing and Newmarket to attack the city, and that lists of houses to be burned by them were in the hands of their leaders; that Samuel Lount, blacksmith, had been manufacturing pikes at the Landing for their use; that two or three persons had been warned by friends in the secret to sell their houses, or to leave the city, or to look for startling changes of some sort. Then it was known that a quantity of arms and a couple of cannon were being brought from the garrison, and stored in the covered way under the old City Hall. Every idle report was eagerly caught up, and magnified a hundred-fold. But the burthen of all invariably was, an expected invasion by the Yankees to drive all loyalists from Canada. In this way rumour followed rumour, all business ceased, and everybody listened anxiously for the next alarm. At length it came in earnest. At eleven o'clock on Monday night, the 4th of December, every bell in the city was set ringing, occasional gun-shots were fired, by accident as it turned out, but none the less startling to nervous people; a confused murmur arose in the streets, becoming louder every minute; presently the sound of a horse's hoofs was heard, echoing loudly along Yonge Street. With others I hurried out, and found at Ridout's corner a horseman, who proved to be Alderman John Powell, who told his breathless listeners, how he had been stopped beyond the Yonge Street toll-gate, two miles out, by Mackenzie and Anderson at the head of a number of rebels in arms; how he had shot Anderson and missed Mackenzie; how he had dodged behind a log when pursued; and had finally got into town by the College Avenue.

There was but little sleep in Toronto that night, and next day everything was uproar and excitement, heightened by the news that Col. Moodie, of Richmond Hill, a retired officer of the army, who was determined to force his way through the armed bodies of rebels, to bring tidings of the rising to the Government in Toronto, had been shot down and inhumanly left to bleed to death at Montgomery's tavern. The flames and smoke from Dr Horne's house at Rosedale, were visible all over the city; it had been fired in the presence of

Mackenzie in person, in retaliation, it was said, for the refusal of discount by the Bank of Upper Canada, of which Dr Horne was teller. The ruins of the still-burning buildings were visited by hundreds of citizens, and added greatly to the excitement and exasperation of the hour. By-and-by it became known that Mr Robert Baldwin and Dr John Rolph had been sent, with a flag of truce, to learn the wants of the insurgents. Many citizens accompanied the party at a little distance. A flag of truce was in itself a delightful novelty, and the street urchins cheered vociferously, scudding away at the smallest alarm. Arrived at the toll-gate, there were waiting outside Mackenzie, Lount, Gibson, Fletcher, and other leaders, with a couple of hundred of their men. In reply to the Lieutenant-Governor's message of inquiry, as to what was wanted, the answer was, 'Independence, and a convention to arrange details', which rather compendious demand, being reported to Sir Francis, was at once rejected. So there was nothing for it but to fight.

Samuel Thompson, *Reminiscences of a Canadian Pioneer*, 1884

JOHN STRACHAN

An Anglican bishop and educator, founder of Ontario's school system and of King's College (1827; later the core of the University of Toronto) Strachan was a leading member of the Family Compact against which William Lyon Mackenzie had rebelled. When the Reformers secularized King's College and the Clergy Reserves, Strachan responded by opening Trinity College in 1852.

[Strachan to Cartwright, 24 May 1844] Is it to be expected that the members of the Church of England in this country can feel satisfied with a government which can find £500 per annum for a Romish Bishop of Kingston without difficulty, and one thousand pounds per annum for another in Lower Canada, and nothing for the Bishop of the national church. Such injustice can never prosper. Had I voted with Lord Sydenham, £2000 a year would have been forthcoming from the day of my consecration; but I choose rather to sell half my garden and my property bit by bit to keep up the dignity and enable me to discharge the duties of my high station.

   [Strachan to Hawkins, 1 December 1847] This has been a sad year for Canada. The great emigration from Ireland of about one hundred thousand souls consisted of persons who were sick or . . . became sick before they embarked. Of this number about thirty-four thousand, or more than one-third, were pushed forward to Toronto, bringing with them the ship fever or rather the pestilence which was carried off many of our inhabitants when charity induced them to minister to the necessities of these unhappy strangers. Two of my clergy were taken ill. Two of our best physicians have been taken from us; but almost all of them have been ill. . . . This town has during the whole season resembled a lazar house, for we have had from seven hundred to one thousand sick continually in the hospitals. What adds greatly to the calamity, the poor emigrants who survive are seldom able or disposed to be industrious. Many are old and feeble and totally incapable of work; many are children not yet old enough to be useful; and a large proportion of them who are able to do something are so awkward and ignorant of the methods of the country . . . [that] they are unwilling to labour; and some absolutely refuse and tell us plainly that they never have been accustomed to continued labour, and that they will not labour. The city is in great confusion from this heavy visitation; and, although government is doing what it can and private charity exerting itself to the utmost, there will be during our long and severe winter such a frightful amount of misery as cannot be contemplated without consternation.

John Strachan: Documents and Opinions, ed. J.L.H. Henderson, 1969

EGERTON RYERSON

A Methodist minister and a moderate Liberal-Conservative, Egerton Ryerson was Superintendent of Education for Canada West (Ontario) from 1844 to 1876. From time to time, he had some brisk differences of opinion with the Grit leader and editor of The Globe, *George Brown.*

March 24, 1868, EGERTON RYERSON, Toronto, to the HON. GEORGE BROWN.

I desire, on this the 65th anniversary of my birth, to assure you of my hearty forgiveness of the personal wrongs which, I think, you have done me in past years, & of my forgetfulness of them so far, at least, as involves the least unkindness & unfriendliness of feeling.

To express free & independent opinions on the public acts of public men, to animadvert severely upon them when considered censurable, is both the right & duty of the press; nor have I ever been discourteous, or felt any animosity towards those who have censured my official acts, or denounced my opinions. Had I considered that you had done nothing more in regard to myself, I should have felt & acted differently from what I have done in regard to you—the only public man in Canada with whom I have not been on speaking & personally friendly terms. But while I wish in no way to influence your judgment & proceedings in relation to myself, I beg to say that I cherish no other than feelings of good will with which I hope to (as I soon must) stand before the Judge of all the earth—imploring as well as granting forgiveness for all the wrong deeds done in the body.

March 24, 1868, GEO. BROWN, Toronto, to THE REVD DR RYERSON.

I have received your letter of this day & note its contents.

I am entirely unconscious of any 'personal wrong' ever done you by me, and had no thought of receiving 'forgiveness' at your hands.

What I have said or written of your public conduct or writings has been dictated solely by a sense of public duty, and has never, I feel confident, exceeded the bounds of legitimate criticism, in view of all attendant circumstances. What has been written of you by others in the columns of the *Globe* newspaper, so far as I have observed, has been always restrained within the limits of fair criticism toward one holding a position of public trust.

As to your personal attacks on myself—those who pursue the fearless course as a politician and public Journalist that I have done for a quarter of a century, cannot expect to escape abuse & misrepresentation; and assuredly your assaults have never affected my course toward you in the slightest degree. Your series of letters printed in the Leader newspaper some years ago, were not, I am told, conceived in a very Christian spirit—but I was ill at the time they were published and have never read them. Your dragging my name into your controversy with the messrs. Campbell—in a matter with which I had no personal concern whatever—was one of those devices, unhappily too often resorted to in political squabbles to be capable of exciting more than momentary indignation.

(Appended—Though the foregoing letter is dated the 24th of March, it was not mailed & sent to me through the Post Office until the 11th of April. E.R.)

April 13, 1868, EGERTON RYERSON, Toronto, to THE HON. GEORGE BROWN, Toronto.

Your note of the 24th ult. did not reach me until Saturday Evening—night before last.

I wrote my note of that date with the view of forgetting, rather than reviving the recollection of past discussions.

I never objected to the severest criticisms of my 'public conduct or writings'. My remarks had sole reference to your 'personal attacks' & 'assaults', made over your own name, & involving all that was dear to me as a man & a father, as well as a Christian—'personal attacks' & 'assaults' to which my letters in the Leader referred to by you, & which you had engaged to insert in the Globe but afterwards refused, were a reply; in the course of which I convicted you not only of many misstatements, but of seven distinct forgeries—you, by additions, professing to quote from me in seven instances the very reverse of what I had written, & your having done all this to sustain your 'personal attacks' & 'assaults' upon me.

Besides this, on at least two subsequent occasions, you charged me with what involved an imputation of dishonesty; & when I transmitted to you copies of official correspondence relating to the subject of your allegations, & refuting them, you refused to insert it in the Globe, & left your false accusations unretracted to this day.

It was to such 'personal attacks' & 'assaults' on your part against me, & not to any legitimate criticisms upon my 'public conduct or writings', that I referred in my letter of the 24th ult.

I admit the general fairness of the Globe towards me during the last few months; but that does not alter the character of your former 'personal attacks'

& 'assaults' upon me, & to which alone what you call my 'personal attacks' & 'assaults' upon you were but defensive replies & rejoinders.

I certainly have no reason to be dissatisfied with the results of such 'personal attacks' & replies, notwithstanding your great advantage in having a powerful press at your disposal; & I am prepared for the future as I have been for the past, though I wish, if possible, to live peaceably with all men.

Egerton Ryerson: His Life and Letters, ed. C.B. Sissons, 1937

JOSEPH HOWE

'The Tribune of Nova Scotia', Joseph Howe achieved Responsible Government for his colony in 1848, served as its Premier from 1860 to 1863, and although initially opposed to Confederation, was a member of Sir John A.'s cabinet from 1869 to 1873.

Howe's rough handling of the official faction had aroused strong resentment among its members, all the more so because his success in the Assembly was exceeding all expectations. He soon realized that he would have to fight a duel with one of them or lose face. A letter to his half-sister dated May 24, 1840, described his encounter with John C. Halliburton, son of the Chief Justice, on March 14.

> Nobody but himself could exactly understand the requirements of my position, and constituted as society is, the almost imperative necessity there was for my taking the step. . . . For my part I hate and detest duelling as much as you do—as much as anybody can—a person who engages in it lightly must be a fool—he who is fond of it must be a villain. It is a remnant of a barbarous age, which civilization is slowly but steadily driving away, but yet it is not worn out. . . . My own belief is that there are situations which try the moral courage more severely than duelling. So far as my experience goes, I would rather stand a shot, than go through the 'rescinding of the Resolutions', 'the Libel trial', or the moving the 'Address of Censure'. On either or all of these occasions there was more at stake than a limb, so far as I was concerned, more than a life as regarded the Country, and I suffered a thousand times more, than on the morning, I went out with Halliburton. . . . I had been long impressed with the conviction it would have to be done with somebody, at some time—and had balanced the pros and cons and regarded the matter as settled. So long as the party I opposed possessed all the legislative influence they did not much mind my scribbling in the Newspapers—when I got into the House they anticipated that *a failure* there would weaken my influence as a political writer, and believing I would fail were rather glad than sorry. When however, they found I not only held my own against the best of them, but was fast combining and securing a majority upon principles striking at the root of their monopoly, they tried the effect of wheedling, and that failing, resorted to intimidation. . . .
>
> [On several occasions a duel was averted.] Thus stood matters when Halliburton's missive came. To him I could not object. Though younger than I, and

having neither any family nor political party depending upon him, still he was in the situation of a gentleman, and had a right to make the demand. . . . Feeling assured that he could not draw back, and that if I did, it would subject me to repeated annoyances from others, and perhaps either weaken my position as a public man or compel me to shoot some fellow at last, I selected a friend [Huntington] whom I knew would go through with it if necessary. He did his best to prevent it, but the thing had to be done, and 'all is well that ends well'. I never intended to fire at him and would not for Ten Thousand Pounds—all that was necessary for me was to let them see that the Reformers could teach them a lesson of coolness and moderation, and cared as little for the pistols, if anything was to be got by fighting. . . . Politically, there were strong temptations [to fight this duel], and among them the one which I know you will prize the highest was the perfect independence I secured—to explain or apologize—to fight or refuse, in future. A proof of the advantage gained in this respect was shown a fortnight ago. Sir Rupert D. George [the Provincial Secretary], being annoyed at a passage in the first letter to the Solicitor General, sent John Spry Morris to me with a challenge—my answer was that 'never having had any personal quarrel with Sir Rupert, I should not fire at him if I went out, and that having no great fancy for being shot at, by every public officer whose intellect I might happen to compare with his emoluments, I begged leave to decline.' This I could not have done had he come first, but now the honour was not equal to the risk— nothing was to be gained either for myself or my cause—they got laughed at and nobody blamed me.

Joseph Howe Papers [National Archives of Canada, VI]. Quoted in Joseph Howe: Voice of Nova Scotia, ed. J. Murray Beck, 1964

George Johnson, writing the life of Joseph Howe around the turn of the century, supplied the Reverend George Grant, Principal of Queens, with an account of Howe in Lunenburg from a 'Dutch' woman that Howe knew. 'Oh! yes Mr Howe is just the nicest man I ever knew. No nonsense about him. He's just one of ourselves. He stands up with his back to the fire, puts his hands under his coat-tails and breaks wind (that's not the word she used) like one of the family.'

Peter B. Waite, Canada 1874–1896, 1971

OTTAWA

Ottawa was chosen the capital city of the United Province of Canada in 1857, and of the new Dominion in 1867.

No one in administrative circles really imagined that Queen Victoria or the Colonial Secretary, Labouchère, would attempt to make an independent choice in a matter which required so much local knowledge, and a matter in which such knowledge was sadly lacking in England, to judge by a ponderous pronouncement from the London *Times* in favour of Montreal, based on the assumption that Montreal was in Upper Canada! The decision was really made on the advice of Sir Edmund Head, acting with what degree of independence it is not possible now to say. By whomsoever made, the choice has been ratified by the judgement of succeeding years as a wise one. Ottawa was still 'a backwoods village', but its position on the border line between Upper and Lower Canada made it to some extent a compromise and its distance from the United States border increased its military security.

Oscar Douglas Skelton, *The Life and Times of Sir Alexander Tilloch Galt*, 1920

ROBERT BALDWIN

A prominent Reformer of Upper Canada, Robert Baldwin was co-premier with L.H. LaFontaine from 1842 to 1843 and 1848 to 1851. Married in 1827 and a widower in 1836, Baldwin left the most remarkable ante-mortem instructions of any Canadian politician.

Throughout the last years of his life, and possibly even before that, Robert Baldwin carried in his waistcoat pocket a terse, forcefully written memorandum:

> that in case it be God's will that I should be taken away suddenly . . . that I may not be interred without my last injunction as to the operation mentioned being scrupulously complied with. And I earnestly entreat of those who may be about me when I die, both Physicians and others, that for the love of God, as an act of Christian charity, and by the solemn recollection that they may one day have themselves a dying request to make to others, they will not on any account whatever permit my being enclosed in my coffin before that performance of this last solemn injunction. And that if from this memorandum not having been found in time, or other accident I may have been interred without this request having been attended to they will see that I am disinterred for the purpose of complying with it, that so under no circumstance may my body be finally left to its repose in the grave till such operation has been performed upon it. And may the blessing of God rest with those who shall make it their business to see this my request. . . .

It was January 1859. Robert Baldwin, statesman, father of responsible government, had been dead for a month. His body lay in the crypt on his family estate, Spadina, in Toronto's Yorkville suburb. Four men gathered in the vault to honour, belatedly, the antemortem instructions of the dead reform leader. Dr James Richardson took a scalpel and approached the reopened coffin. Following Baldwin's injunction, Richardson made 'an incision . . . into the cavity of the Abdomen extending through the two upper thirds of the Linea alba'. Robert Baldwin was now complete, gone to eternity bearing the same surgical wound as his beloved wife Eliza—the scar of a Caesarian section.

' "The waste that lies before me": The Public and the Private Worlds of Robert Baldwin', eds Michael S. Cross and Robert L. Fraser, in *Historical Papers*, 1983

CHARLES CONNELL

Charles Connell was Post Master General of New Brunswick during the 1850s.

During the spring of 1860 circumstances occurred which led to the resignation of the Post Master General, Hon. Charles Connell. The Legislature having adopted the decimal system of currency in the place of the pounds, shillings, and pence which had been the currency of the Province since its foundation, in March, 1860, Mr Connell was authorized to obtain a new set of postage stamps of the denominations required for use in the postal service of the Province. No person at that time thought that a political crisis would arise out of this order, but it appears that Mr Connell, guided by the example of Presidents and Post Masters General of the United States, had made up his mind that instead of the likeness of the Queen, which had been upon all the old postage stamps of the Province, the five cent stamp, the one which would be most in use, should bear the impress of his own countenance. Accordingly the Connell postage stamp, which is now one of the rarest and most costly of all in the lists of collectors, was procured and was ready to be used, when Mr Connell's colleagues in the government discovered what was going on and took steps to prevent the new five cent stamp from being issued. The correspondence on the subject, which will be found in the journals of 1861, is curious and interesting, but it ended in the withdrawal of the objectionable stamps and in the resignation of Mr Connell, who complained that he had lost the confidence of his colleagues, and who in resigning, charged them with neglecting the affairs of the Province. Only a few of the Connell stamps got into circulation, the remainder of the issue being destroyed. If anyone could have foreseen the enormous value which they would attain at a future day a fortune might have been made by the lucky individual who succeeded in getting possession of them.

James Hannay, *The Life and Times of Sir Leonard Tilley*, 1897

MATTHEW BEGBIE

Matthew Begbie was a legendary judge who attempted to uphold law and order in the difficult conditions of a gold rush in central British Columbia during the 1860s.

In the days of the Cariboo gold rush sixty thousand miners, adventurers, and all the riff-raff that follow in the wake of a great mining excitement, filled the

Cariboo country. . . . Yet with all this rabble of people, rough characters and law-abiding men drawn from every quarter of the globe, Cariboo maintained as an orderly, safe district through the efforts of one man, Sir Matthew Begbie, who was judge and various officials all in one. He administered justice with a ready and iron hand, and put fear into the hearts of those of lawless tendencies. On one occasion he had convicted and fined a malefactor $200.

'That's dead easy,' flippantly said the culprit, 'I've got it right here in my hip pocket.'

'—and six months in jail. Have you got that in your hip pocket, too?', came the ready amendment to the sentence, thus vindicating the dignity of the court and proclaiming to all and sundry that a British court of justice, even though held under a pine tree, was not to be trifled with.

George Ham, *Reminiscences of a Raconteur*, 1921

SIR GEORGE-ÉTIENNE CARTIER

Co-premier of the United Province with Sir John A., 1857–8 and 1858–62, Sir George-Étienne Cartier served in Sir John A.'s cabinet between 1867 and 1873.

Separation of Executive and Legislature was too abstract and theoretical a reform, if reform it was, ever to attract public support. Representation by Population or 'Rep. by Pop.' as it was familiarly known, made a much more direct appeal, and appeared to be the readiest means of overcoming Lower Canada's alleged baneful domination. It was easy to make the Upper Canadian voter agree that 'three Frenchmen should not count the same as four Englishmen', and when in an unlucky moment Cartier, seeking to make the point that numbers were not all and that wealth should also be considered, declared that 'the codfish of Gaspé Bay ought to be represented as well as the 250,000 Grits of Upper Canada', it was only necessary to shout 'codfish' in Upper Canada, to make the welkin ring.

Oscar Douglas Skelton, *The Life and Times of Sir Alexander Tilloch Galt*, 1920

SIR LEONARD TILLEY

An early proponent of Confederation and a delegate to the Charlottetown and Quebec Conferences, Sir Leonard Tilley was defeated as Premier of New Brunswick in the election of 1865, but returned as Premier in 1866, and joined the Canadian cabinet of Sir John A. in 1867.

Another rallying cry of the anti-confederates throughout the Maritimes was that, under the proposed Confederation, the province would lose its current customs and excise tariffs, which would thenceforth be collected at the federal level. Under the proposal worked out at Quebec, 80 cents per head would be funneled back to the provinces to offset the loss of customs and excise revenue.

'Father, what country do we live in?' was the rhetorical question posed by A.B. Wetmore, the anti-confederate candidate opposing Tilley in St John.

'My dear son, you have no country, for Mr Tilley has sold us to the Canadians for eighty cents a head,' was the reply he'd give to his delighted audience.

Vincent Durant, *War Horse of Cumberland*, 1985

Tilley is often cited as the one who first urged the name 'Dominion' for Canada, but evidence for the claim is lacking.

It was intended that the name of the new state should be left to the selection of the Queen, and this was provided for in the first draft of the bill. But the proposal was soon dropped. It revived the memory of the regrettable incident of 1858 when the Queen had, by request, selected Ottawa as the Canadian capital and her decision had been condemned by a vote of the legislature. The press had discussed a suitable name long before the London delegates assembled. Some favoured New Britain, while others preferred Laurentia or Britannia. If the maritime union had been effected, the name of that division would probably have been Acadia, and this name was suggested for the larger union. Other ideas were merely fantastic, such as Cabotia, Columbia, Canadia, and Ursalia. The decision that Canada should give up its name to the new Confederation and that Upper and Lower Canada should find new names for themselves was undoubtedly a happy conclusion to the discussion. It was desired to call the Confederation the Kingdom of Canada, and thus fix the monarchical basis of the constitution. The French were especially attached to this idea. The word Kingdom appeared in an early draft of the bill as it came from the conference. But it was vetoed by the foreign secretary, Lord Stanley, who thought that the republican sensibilities of the United States would be wounded. This preposterous notion serves to indicate the inability of the controlling minds of the period to grasp the true nature of the change. Finally, the word 'Dominion' was decided upon. Why a term was selected which is so difficult to render in the French language (*La Puissance* is the translation employed) is not easy of comprehension. There is a story, probably invented, that when 'Dominion' was under consideration, a member of the conference, well versed in the Scriptures, found a verse which, as a piece of descriptive prophecy, at once clinched the matter: 'And his dominion shall be from sea even to sea, and from the river even to the ends of the earth.' [Zechariah, ix, 10].

A.H.U. Colquhoun, *The Fathers of Confederation*, 1916

GEORGE BROWN

The 'Galahad of Grittism', George Brown was owner-editor of the Toronto Globe *and a leading Reformer. While Maritime Union was being discussed in the eastern colonies, Brown proposed a coalition government for the Canadas in 1864 to achieve his wider dream of Confederation. His rival John A. Macdonald accepted, and announced the 'Great Coalition' in the House in June 1864.*

When Macdonald had finished, Brown rose, his great frame and powerful voice unsteady from emotion. In a conciliatory tone, he traced the federal plan from the Reform and Rouge Conventions held in Toronto and Montreal respectively in 1859. After the negotiations in the Maritimes and London, he said, it would be possible to tell whether the larger or smaller scheme was more likely to carry. Whatever happened, he would leave the Government as soon as the federal cause could no longer be advanced. As he sat down, the pent-up emotion burst all bounds. Members broke into cheers, clapped their hands, and rushed across the floor to congratulate one another. One elderly little French member, it was reported, tore over to George Brown, climbed up on his huge frame, flung his arms round his neck, and 'hung several seconds there suspended, to the visible consternation of Mr Brown and to the infinite joy of all beholders'. Hope was born again.

Dale C. Thomson, *Alexander Mackenzie: Clear Grit*, 1960

Brown's initiative had begun a month earlier.

The resolution had established a committee of twenty, with the member for South Oxford [Brown] as chairman. He had chosen nineteen prominent members of the House, men representing every opinion on the constitution: from proponents of the union as it stood, through advocates of rep by pop and 'joint authority', to those who argued for general federation—or even dissolution. Sixteen of the nineteen met more or less willingly with the chairman in a committee chamber of the parliament buildings on May 20. Galt, Chapais, and Hillyard Cameron were unavoidably absent; but those present included Cartier, John A. Macdonald and Sandfield Macdonald, Dorion, Cauchon and McGee, Holton, Mowat and McKellar. Brown began the meeting significantly and typically. He strode to the door, locked it, and pocketed the key. 'Now gentlemen,' he said emphatically, 'you must talk about this matter, as you cannot leave this room without coming to me.'

J.M.S. Careless, *Brown of the Globe*, vol. 2, 1963

In a letter to his wife on 28 August 1864, Brown makes clear that he and John A. did not always see eye-to-eye.

'Do you know you were very near being stripped yesterday of your honours of Presidentess of the Council? Would not that have been a sad affair? It was in this way. The council was summoned for twelve and shortly after that we were all assembled but John A. We waited for him till one—till half past one— till two—and then Galt sent off to his house specially for him. Answer—will be here immediately. Waited till half past two—no appearance, waited till three and shortly after, John A. entered bearing symptoms of having been on a spree. He was half drunk. Lunch is always on the side table and he soon applied himself to it—and before we had well entered on the important business before us he was quite drunk with potations of ale. After two hours and a half debate we closed the important discussions of three days on the constitutional changes and arranged finally all about our trip to Charlottetown and our course when there. John A. then declared he had an important matter to bring before us— the dispute with the Ottawa building contractors. You should know that the original *contract* for these buildings was $700,000—but when the Liberal party got into power they found that $1,200,000 had been spent—and $550,000 was claimed to be owing—but the works were not with all this half finished! The government in consequence stopped the buildings and appointed com- missioners to investigate the whole matter. They disclosed the most astounding folly and fraud in the business from beginning to end—and reported that instead of $550,000 being due to the contractors they were already over paid, and there the matter has stood ever since—nearly three years.'

Now that Macdonald was back in power, Brown said, his friends, the contractors, were making a new attempt to secure their claim. 'I was quite willing to send this thing to arbitration—but determined that men only of the highest character and position should be entrusted with it.' Macdonald pro- posed to appoint three men, two of them unknown to Brown.

'I asked that the matter should be delayed until I made inquiries—John A. would not hear of delay and insisted loudly, fiercely, that the thing should be settled then and there. His old friends in the Cabinet saw of course that he was quite wrong—but they feared to offend him and pressed for a settlement. Matters came to a point. He declared that if the thing was done then I would not sit in the council one moment longer. Mowat stood firmly by me and McDougall partly—moderately. Galt got alarmed and proposed a mode which in effect postponed the matter till Monday. I agreed to it and the council all but John A. adopted it. It was declared carried. Thereupon John A. burst out furiously declaring that his friends had deserted him and he would not hold office another day. The council adjourned in great confusion—John A's friends trying to appease him . . . I don't imagine for a moment that . . . [these appointments] will be pressed. It will be utterly ruinous to John A. if the whole affair goes before the public. He will not think of it when he gets sober. To say the truth, were our visit to the Lower Provinces and to England once over, I would not care how soon a rupture came. The constitutional question would then be beyond all chance of failure—and I would be quit of company that is far from agreeable.'

J.M.S.Careless, 'George Brown and the Mother of Confederation',
Canadian Historical Association Report, 1960

Brown found some pleasures in London during the 1866 Westminster Palace Hotel Conference on the British North America Act.

He passed some time usefully and happily in shopping for Oak Lodge, buying chandeliers, silverware, plate, and crystal; he did not accept an invitation to Oxford, in fact, because he was too busy with the chandeliers. The table silver would cost £250. The glassware was so expensive he was ashamed to tell Anne—'but we can afford it'. Then he and John A. Macdonald went to the opera together, saw *Lucretia Borgia*, and much enjoyed it. And finally, on May 31, there was Derby Day.

'Like the rest of the world,' said Brown, the Canadians journeyed to Epsom Downs, and went by carriage to see the fun of the road. It was a delightful day and a marvellous spectacle; he found that the reality of the Derby far surpassed its reputation. 'Such a scene and such fun—such good humour and such wonderful evidences of unbounded wealth!' There were half a million people swarming on the grounds. For the revels of the return journey he had a peashooter, and Macdonald furnished him with peas. As the throng of vehicles crawled in a tight, festive mass along the sixteen miles to London, Brown had a joyous time puffing away on the peashooter, through a counterfire of peas, bran bags and exploding bombs of flour.

J.M.S. Careless, *Brown of the Globe*, vol. 2, 1963

ANNE NELSON BROWN

Anne Nelson Brown is often referred to as 'The Mother of Confederation'. In 1862, at the age of 43, George Brown, a crusty and unbending man, met Anne Nelson in the summer and married her in November. By June of 1864 Brown had a wife and a baby daughter, and was 'hip-deep in love with both'. There is reason to believe that marriage mellowed him and altered his political stance.

Brown's about-face—his offer to form a coalition government in order to bring in Confederation—was so dramatic that some historians have suggested that the real originator of Confederation was not man but woman: Brown's new wife, Anne Nelson Brown.

Peter B. Waite, in *The Illustrated History of Canada*, ed., Craig Brown, 1987

Anne Brown had saved every letter her husband had ever written her. And since he wrote her as frequently as three times a day when he was away in Parliament, the correspondence was vast.

And it was informative. Of all the correspondence I know, a man's letters to his wife and *vice versa* will usually tell you more about him and his life than any other. Brown spared nothing. His whole energy, power, his delight in his marriage, his tremendous exuberance of spirit, were there in those letters, exclamation marks and all:

Quebec, Thursday, Oct. 27, 1864

My dearest Anne,

All right!!! Conference through at six o'clock this evening—Constitution adopted—a most creditable document—a complete reform of all the abuses & injustice we have complained of!! Is it not wonderful? French Canadianism entirely extinguished! I have only a moment to write you as I am just starting for Montreal [.] they are crying to me to hurry and my baggage is down. There they are again! You will say that our Constitution is dreadfully Tory—& so it is—but we have the power in our hands (if it passes) to change it as we like! Hurrah— . . .

By the time [J.M.S.] Careless had worked through these letters a new Brown emerged, warm, passionate, uxorious. [Alexander] Mackenzie had carefully left out all personal references when he had printed some of those letters in 1883. There were even Mackenzie's pencil marks on the letters to show the printer what should be included and what left out.

Peter B. Waite, 'A Historian's Adventures in Archivia and Beyond',
Papers of the Bibliographical Society of Canada, 1973, vol. 12

THE QUEBEC CONFERENCE

The Quebec Conference passed the Confederation resolutions in 1865.

The Confederation debate ended early on Saturday morning, March 11, with recalcitrant desk-rattling, whispering and bird singing from some members when the speaker was not to their taste. A lively account of the last hours of the debate was given by the Parliamentary correspondent of the *Stratford Beacon*:

. . . the House was in an unmistakeably seedy condition, having, as it was positively declared, eaten the saloon keeper clean out, drunk him entirely dry, and got all the fitful naps of sleep that the benches along the passages could be made to yield. For who cared at one, two, three, and four in the morning, to sit in the House, to hear the stale talk of Mr Ferguson, of South Simcoe, or to listen even to the polished and pointed sentences of Mr Huntingdon? Men with the strongest constitutions for Parliamentary twaddle were sick of the debate, and the great bulk of the members were scattered about the building, with an up-all-night, get-tight-in-the-morning air, impatient for the sound of the division bell. It rang at last, at quarter past four, and the jaded representatives of the people swarmed in to the discharge of the most important duty of all their lives.

At 4:30 A.M. the main motion was agreed to, 91–33. At this the House broke into ringing cheers, and as the Speaker was leaving the Chair the French Canadian members burst out with some old paddling song, the English Canadians following with 'The Queen', and the whole bawled forth with the same sorry energy characteristic of the fag end of a public dinner. And over by the St Charles River the convent bell was ringing five as the members trooped wearily home to their lodgings.

Peter B. Waite, *The Life and Times of Confederation 1864–1867*, 1962

Passage of the British North America Act through the Parliament at Westminster was brisk—perhaps even too brisk.

The mere mention of things colonial was usually sufficient to clear the House of Commons of all but the most obstinate parliamentarians; and the opening sentences of the colonial secretary were lost in the noise of members departing for the more intellectual atmosphere of the lobbies or neighbouring chop-houses. The few members who watched the British North America Act of 1867 in its speedy passage through parliament could scarcely conceal their excruciating boredom; and after the ordeal was over, they turned with lively zeal and manifest relief to the great national problem of the tax on dogs.

Donald Creighton, *Towards the Discovery of Canada*, 1972

DOMINION DAY

No book of this sort would be complete without at least one of the resounding paragraphs with which Donald G. Creighton concluded his volumes on Macdonald. This is his memorable description of the first Dominion Day, 1 July 1867.

By nine o'clock, the public buildings and many large houses were illuminated all across Canada. And in Toronto the Queen's Park and the grounds of the private houses surrounding it were transformed by hundreds of Chinese lanterns hung through the trees. When the true darkness had at last fallen, the firework displays began; and simultaneously throughout the four provinces, the night was assaulted by minute explosions of coloured light, as the roman candles popped away, and the rockets raced up into the sky. In the cities and large towns, the spectacle always concluded with elaborate set pieces. The Montrealers arranged an intricate design with emblems representing the three uniting provinces—a beaver for Canada, a mayflower for Nova Scotia, and a pine for New Brunswick. At Toronto the words 'God Save the Queen' were surrounded by a twined wreath of roses, thistles, shamrocks, and *fleur-de-lys*; and at Hamilton, while the last set pieces were blazing, four huge bonfires were kindled on the crest of the mountain. In Ottawa, long before this, Monck and Macdonald and the other ministers had quitted the Privy Council chamber; and Parliament Hill was crowded once again with people who had come to watch the last spectacle of the day. The parliament buildings were illuminated. They stood out boldly against the sky; and far behind them, hidden in darkness, were the ridges of the Laurentians, stretching away, mile after mile, towards the north-west.

Donald Creighton, *John A. Macdonald: The Young Politician*, vol. 1, 1956

THOMAS D'ARCY McGEE

Thomas D'Arcy McGee was a member of the Macdonald-Cartier cabinet in 1863 and of the 'Great Coalition', from 1864 to 1866.

A strong opponent of Fenianism, McGee had received numerous threatening messages, but they had not been taken seriously. Although a relative newcomer, he was popular and accepted as an important part of the Canadian political scene. Before his health had failed in recent months, and Sir John had married, the capers of the two men had become legendary. On one occasion when they were both in the Cabinet, so one story went, the inebriated Premier had leaned affectionately on his friend's shoulder and said, 'Look here McGee, two drunkards is too much for any government and one of us has to stop, so I suggest you quit.'

Dale C. Thomson, *Alexander Mackenzie: Clear Grit*, 1960

McGee, one of the finest orators in the cause of Confederation, was assassinated in 1868, a week before his forty-third birthday.

The debate drew to a close some time after one o'clock, and Macdonald drove home through the silent spring night to the 'Quadrilateral' on Daly Street. It was cooler than it had been. The sunny, chill, uncertain day had ended in a sharp return of frost. A bright full moon hung high in the sky; and, as he drove along Rideau Street, the thin brittle patches of ice in the rutted road were picked out clearly in the moonlight. It was nearly half past two when he reached the house. Agnes, who had waited up, flew down to open the door for him; and he had his late brief supper in her dressing-room, while the last remains of the fire glowed in the hearth, and the gas sang serenely overhead. He was in a relaxed and cheerful mood. . . . And, in his amused and amusing fashion, he told her something of the debate. The day had been long and full of exasperation; but it had ended at last in contentment. He lingered, savouring the peace of the silent house.

He was not yet in bed before the low rapid knocking began at the front door. In a minute he flung open the dressing-room window and looked outside.

'Is there anything the matter?' he called softly.

Then he saw the messenger, his lifted frightened face pale in the moonlight.

'McGee is murdered—lying in the street—shot through the head.'

Macdonald roused Hewitt Bernard. Together they drove back again, up Rideau and along Sparks Street toward McGee's lodging. Just beyond where Metcalfe Street crossed Sparks he saw the little group of still dark figures— McGee's landlady, the doctors, the police, and the printers from the Ottawa *Times*. He knelt beside the body, close to the pool of blood, to the half-smoked cigar, and the useless fallen new hat, and helped to lift his colleague and carry him into the house. He listened while the witnesses told their first excited stories. He went down to the *Times* office and telegraphed to the police of the neighbouring towns. It was five o'clock and the streets were grey with dawn, when he reached the 'Quadrilateral' again; but he was back again at his office in a few hours, setting in motion all available machinery for the capture of the murderer, whom everybody expected from the start to have been a Fenian. That afternoon, when the House met, there were several tributes, moving or laboured, to the dead man; but it was Macdonald who, in his practical fashion, proposed an annuity for McGee's widow, and a small settlement for each of the daughters. In the galleries his voice could scarcely be heard. His face was white with fatigue, and sleeplessness and shocked regret.

Donald Creighton, *John A. Macdonald: The Old Chieftain*, vol. 2, 1955

SIR JOHN A. MACDONALD (I)

Co-premier of the Province of Canada with E.P. Taché and with G.E. Cartier in the 1850s and early 1860s, Sir John A. Macdonald led the 'Great Coalition' after 1864, and was the Dominion's first prime minister, from 1867 to 1873.

Sir John Macdonald was a man with his feet on the earth and his head not so far above it. He seldom sought to climb to moral elevations where the footing might be insecure. For a time he drank freely but any whisper of censure only stimulated Conservatives to fiercer personal loyalty. He said himself that the country would rather have 'John A.' drunk than George Brown sober. . . . His drinking was exaggerated, as were his other faults and follies, by sleepless and insensate opponents. Very often the attack was so violent as to bring chivalrous souls to his side and actually react in his favour. Down to middle life and beyond Sir John Macdonald had periodical 'sprees' and nothing that he attempted was done badly. Sometimes he was disabled for public duty. The authorities seem to agree that not only may a 'spree' come unaware but that it is as uncertain in its going as in its coming. Begun in complete privacy it may develop various phases and attract more public notice than is desirable even though the performance may be original and artistic. Unlike any other pursuit every rehearsal is a performance and every presentation a surprise. The public seldom saw 'John A.' in liquor, but occasionally there were symptoms which even Conservatives could not mistake. Once he was to speak at a town on Lake Huron, but he was so long in sleeping off the consequences that the vessel on which he was a passenger dare not put into harbour. That was fifty years ago but not yet have local Conservatives discovered any humour in the incident or become reconciled to the graceless chaffing of their Liberal neighbours. A common story, resting upon no adequate authority, is that a shorthand writer once undertook to make a verbatim report of a speech which Sir John delivered at Kingston. When he had examined the manuscript he sent for the reporter, gravely intimated that he had read portions of it with pain and surprise, and with the mild austerity of a grieving father added, 'Young man, if you ever again undertake to report the speech of a public man be sure that you keep sober.'

There is an authenticated story of Macdonald in the early sixties. He was Attorney-General for Upper Canada, and lived in lodgings in Quebec. He had been absent from duty for a week; public business was delayed, and the Governor-General became impatient. He sent his aide-de-camp, young Lord Bury, to find the absent Minister. Pushing his way past the old housekeeper, Lord Bury penetrated to the bedroom where Macdonald was sitting in bed, reading a novel with a decanter of sherry on the table beside him. 'Mr Macdonald, the Governor-General told me to say to you that if you don't sober up and get back to business, he will not be answerable for the consequences.' Macdonald's countenance reflected the anger he felt at the intrusion: 'Are you here in your official capacity, or as a private individual?' 'What difference does that make?' asked Lord Bury. 'Just this,' snapped the statesman, 'if you are here in your official capacity, you can go back to Sir Edmund Head, give him my compliments, and tell him to go to h—; if you are simply a private individual, you can go yourself.' In after years Lord Bury often told the story but with more of affection than of censure for Sir John Macdonald.

Sir John Willison, Reminiscences Political and Personal, 1919

A characteristic remark . . . was repeated by Sir John in several forms. The first occasion was at the time of Confederation. Senator Dickey, of Amherst, though a delegate at the first conference, turned against the union on the ground that Nova Scotia did not get her due share of the subsidy then proposed. 'It turned out,' said Mr Dickey, 'that I was right; but people are never forgiven for being right against the opinions of others, and for a long time I was in disfavour. My name was mentioned in connection with the Lieutenant Governorship of Nova Scotia, but I said to those who brought the news, "set your minds at rest. I will not be chosen. What they want is not a man that is fit but a man that will suit." Sir John, not long afterwards, said to me, "Why did you kick up your heels so on the Confederation question? Have you gone over to the enemy? "No," I replied, "I am still a Conservative, and I shall support you whenever I think you are right." "That is no satisfaction," retorted Sir John, with a twinkle. "Anybody may support me when I am right. What I want is a man that will support me when I am wrong!" '

E.B. Biggar, Anecdotal Life of Sir John Macdonald, 1891

John A.'s legendary memory did not apply only to names and faces.

While living at Kingston, he went out into the country to a farm house near Adolphustown on business, and while waiting for the horses to be brought to the door, sat reading a book. When told the vehicle was ready, he dropped the book and came away. Nine years afterwards he visited the same house, and going to the book-case took down the same book and turning to a certain page, said: 'There's the very word I read last when I was here nine years ago.'

Ibid.

During one of the years of Lord Dufferin's administration, that talented Governor General delivered an address in Greek before the University of McGill College, Sir John Macdonald and Sir Hector Langevin being present with him. One of the reporters wrote in his report: 'His Lordship spoke in the purest ancient Greek without mispronouncing a word or making the slightest grammatical solecism.'

'Good Heavens,' said Sir Hector to Sir John, as they read the report. 'How did the reporter know that?'

'I told him,' replied Sir John.

'But you don't know Greek.'

'True,' answered Sir John, 'but I know a little about politics.'

Ibid.

One evening Lady Macdonald and Sir John were entertaining Sir Hugh Allan, when Lady Macdonald solicited from Sir Hugh a contribution in aid of some church work she had in hand. Sir Hugh hedged and pleaded inability to give what she asked, but she good-naturedly laughed off the plea, and told him he could not take all his money with him when he died. 'No,' remarked Sir John playfully, 'it would soon melt if he did.'

Ibid.

When the late David Thompson was sitting for Haldimand, in the days when the record of the riding was an unbroken series of Liberal victories, he was laid aside for nearly a whole session through illness. He got down to Parliament at last, and told the story of his reception as follows: 'The first man I met on coming back was Blake. He passed me with a simple nod. The next man I met was Cartwright, and his greeting was about as cold as that of Blake. Hardly had I passed these men when I met Sir John. He didn't pass me by, but grasped me by the hand, gave me a slap on the shoulder, and said, "Davy, old man, I'm glad to see you back. I hope you'll soon be yourself again and live many a day to vote against me—as you always have done!" Now,' continued Mr Thompson with genuine pathos, 'I never gave the old man a vote in my life, but hang me if it doesn't go against my grain to follow the men who haven't a word of kind greeting for me, and oppose a man with a heart like Sir John's.'

Ibid.

Once he went to speak against a Reform candidate in a North Ontario constituency. When he mounted the platform, after having taken too much strong drink and being shaken over a rough track on the train, he became sick and vomited on the platform while his opponent was speaking. Such a sight before a large audience disgusted even many of his friends, and the prospect for the Conservative cause that day was not bright. The opposing candidate, whom we will call Jones, ceased speaking, and John A. rose to reply. What could he say, or how could he act to redeem himself and gain respect or attention? 'Mr Chairman and gentlemen,' he began, 'I don't know how it is, but every time I hear Mr Jones speak it turns my stomach!' The conception was so grotesque and so unexpected, that the audience went off in fits of laughter, and disgust was instantly turned into general good humor and sympathy.

Ibid.

Mr Charlton (speaking on the question of maintaining order among the Indians in the North West)—'I would suggest the purchase of a few mountain howitzers, which in the case of emergency could be carried on the backs of mules. I recollect an instance of the effect of this in dispersing Indians in the United States. A small party of troops going through a mountain-pass were unexpectedly attacked by Indians. The emergency was great; they had not time to dismount the howitzers, but pointed them and fired from the backs of the mules, creating great consternation among the Indians.'

Sir John—'And among the mules.'

Ibid.

The revelations of scandal over payments to the Conservative party by the CPR rocked the House in the autumn of 1873, but for a time Macdonald delayed taking part in the debate.

It was November 3 before Sir John broke his silence. He had been visibly under the influence of alcohol all day, and in an encounter with Blake on a minor matter he had blundered badly. Three hours later he rose, pale, haggard, and looking as though a puff of wind would knock him down. He began slowly, uncertainly, and almost inaudibly, then gathered strength and confidence. The empty glass on his desk was removed frequently by the page boys and replaced with full ones, leaving the hushed members to guess if the colourless liquid was water or a stronger beverage. [Hon. Peter Mitchell, one of Macdonald's colleagues, recounted later that the Premier had arranged with three different persons to send in glasses of gin instead of the usual water.] Whatever the source of his energy and courage, it was a magnificent speech, well worthy of the veteran politician. Lady Dufferin and her friends were electrified with admiration and hope. When he sat down after five hours, there were smiles on the faces of the Government supporters again.

Dale C. Thomson, *Alexander Mackenzie: Clear Grit*, 1960

But within a few days, the government was defeated.

ALEXANDER MACKENZIE

Liberal Prime Minister of Canada from 1873 to 1878, Alexander Mackenzie took office when the government of Sir John A. fell. In the election of 1872 he campaigned vigorously and provided his own definition of Grittism.

During the spring thaw, wagon travel was impractical; he stuffed a few items of clothing and documents into saddlebags and galloped from place to place on horseback. Holding two meetings a day, he attacked the Macdonald clan in general and the 'miserable, pettifogging, peddling practices' of the Ontario Administration in particular. He denounced the Ontario Ministry as the 'mere creature of the Dominion Government', and claimed they, too, like their master in Ottawa, were only interested in remaining in office as long as possible. In a sense, it was an easy campaign. Completely on the offensive, and with no past record to encumber them, the Grits could carry the battle to the enemy. He stood for correct administration and parliamentary purity, Mackenzie told the electors; he and his fellow-campaigners were 'clear grit in every sense of the word'. What did it mean? called someone in Strathroy. 'Clear Grit,' he replied with an impatient flash of his steely, blue eyes, and an extra rasp of the Scottish brogue, 'is pure sand without a particle of dirt in it.'

Dale C. Thomson, *Alexander Mackenzie: Clear Grit*, 1960

A story from the election of 1864, when he ran against a Tory named Foley, suggests that Mackenzie was not to be trifled with.

One night during the contest, they found themselves at the same hotel as a group of Conservative campaigners. The latter were in a festive mood, and made merry until the wee hours of the morning. Despite the lack of sleep as a result of the revelry downstairs, Mackenzie rose as usual at 6 A.M. In the vacated main hall he found a large bundle of his opponents' propaganda. 'Facts for the Irish Electors', 'Black Record of the Grit Party', the headlines proclaimed. A freshly lit fire crackled in the big stove. The temptation was too great. 'I remembered that it was one of the undoubted rights of belligerents to capture and destroy any of the enemy's munitions of war which fell in their way,' he recounted to his partner later. 'I determined, therefore, to exercise our belligerent rights as to confiscation, which I immediately proceeded to carry out by opening the big stove door and thrusting the whole bundle into the roaring flames. Then I went for a long and peaceful walk through the quiet little village and out into the green fields and woods adjoining until the hour for breakfast slowly came 'round.' Foley lost the election.

Ibid.

A letter from the member for Brantford was interesting. One of his constituents, a Professor Bell, was promoting the use of a 'speaking telephone' invented by his son Alexander. To set off the publicity campaign, he wanted to install a line between Rideau Hall and the Premier's office. There was already an alphabet telegraph service between them, but the delicate machine was usually out of order. At twenty dollars per annum, Alexander Mackenzie decided that the Government could afford the new apparatus.

[Ottawa's first telephone book, listing 200 subscribers, appeared in 1882.]

Ibid.

Mackenzie . . . had a happy habit of writing letters to his family and friends while sitting at his desk in the Commons and not otherwise occupied. They are remarkably perceptive letters . . . and here is a sample, written on April 12, 1878, to George Brown, the editor of the Toronto *Globe*:

My Dear Brown,
. . . I gave John A. and his party two whole days for the Quebec business, but I insisted on a vote at 2 last night. This was resisted and speaking against time has been going on since. John A. got very drunk early last evening and early this morning they had to get him stowed away somewhere. McDougall of Three Rivers is also very drunk and kept the floor off and on for nearly two hours uttering utter nonsense and just able to stand.

Campbell of Cape Breton was in a shocking state. He got on the floor in front of the Speaker with his hat on and a stick in his hand which he flourished round his head daring the Gov't or any member to fight him yelling at the highest pitch of his voice. Plum Caron and others were also drunk but did not so seriously expose themselves. I suppose Dymond will write some description of the scene but I think the Globe should in plain language characterize this drunken brawl in the House of Commons. I am glad to say that not one person on our side tasted any liquor though there was the usual noises in putting down men like Plum who tried to force themselves on the House. I never saw such a scene with whiskey before.

Macdonald and his friends have been doing their very utmost to delay the business all through, and on several occasions drunken scenes occurred with him and others. About six this morning he drank a tumbler full of sherry and at eight Mills saw him drink a tumbler full of whiskey. The last dose laid him out and his friends hid him somewhere. . . .

Yours very truly

A. MACKENZIE.

. . . The *Globe*, as it happened, took Mackenzie's advice and printed a story about the duelling scene in the House, closely following Mackenzie's own words; several papers who quoted the *Globe*'s story were arraigned for libel, though nothing much came of it.

Norman Ward, *Her Majesty's Mice*, 1977

When the Mackenzie government's budget of 1878 did not increase the tariff, the Conservatives were startled.

Sir John Macdonald and the Honourable Charles Tupper did not disguise their surprise at the Government's action. The latter had to reply to the Finance Minister, but Sir John at a later stage admitted his own surprise. 'I came, I confess it, to hear his [Mr Cartwight's] speech, impressed with the idea that he was going to bring down an alteration of the Tariff.' According to current report, the Honourable Charles Tupper came to the House loaded up to denounce an increase of the Tariff, and to dilate—as he had done before—on the danger of permitting an entrance to the thin end of the Protectionist wedge!

Such an unexpected change in the situation would have appalled many another man. But in debate, nothing could appal Sir Charles. As usual he rose equal to the occasion. With surprising coolness he turned his guns, took up the opposite line of attack, and probably made a more forcible and effective criticism of the Government's course than if he had been able to use the mental ammunition which he had specially prepared for the occasion. . . .

When Dr Tupper concluded his speech about half-past ten o'clock, and shortly before the House adjourned, the Hon. Mr Mackenzie went across the Chamber to the front of the Doctor's desk, and the two doughty antagonists— the heroes of so many political battles—indulged in what seemed to the onlook-ers a very friendly and amusing conversation, which at times seemed to verge a little too near the hilarious for a legislative body with the Speaker still in the Chair. I watched the whole proceeding across the gangway, and was somewhat surprised when the Premier on returning came straight across the front of my own desk. Knowing that my opinion was that the Government had made a serious, if not fatal, blunder, in not dealing with the Tariff as originally intended, he went on to tell me his conversation with the member for Cumberland, which seemed to have amused him very much.

'What do you think Tupper has just told me?' he began.

'I have no idea,' I replied.

'Well,' continued Mr Mackenzie, 'I went over to banter him a little on his speech, which I jokingly alleged was a capital one considering he had been loaded up on the other side. He regarded this as a good joke,' Mr Mackenzie went on to say, 'and frankly admitted to me that he had entered the House under the belief that the Government intended to raise the Tariff and fully prepared to take up the opposite line of attack!'

Both of these political veterans were in the same box with regard to their action on this question, and the suddenness of their change of position on the eve of battle seemed to afford both of them not a little amusement as they bantered each other in a friendly manner. What the Liberal and Conservative parties did that night, however, was pregnant with importance. They were making history. Had Mr Mackenzie increased the Tariff, the Conservatives would probably have become—as already suggested—the Free Traders instead of the Protectionists of Canada, and our political history would have been quite different during the ensuing twenty years.

Hon. James Young, Public Men and Public Life in Canada, vol. 2, 1912

It is a pity we do not know more about the distaff side of society. There are a few tantalizing glimpses. The governor general's military secretary issued strict instructions for a presentation for the Princess Louise that was to take place in November 1878, in Montreal. The instructions about dress were, to say the least, unequivocal: 'Ladies are to wear low-necked dresses. . . . Ladies whose health will not admit of their wearing low-necked dresses may, on forwarding to the ADC-in-waiting, a medical certificate to that effect, wear square cut dresses. Dresses fastening up to the throat are not to be worn.' One of the funniest letters Alexander Mackenzie ever wrote was his description of a similar affair in Toronto in September 1879. His Grit egalitarianism was touched by the sheer amusement of the spectacle.

> Many of the number walked in evidently unable to see who the Princess was . . . and bowed to the wrong person or did not bow at all. Husbands in the hurry to get through trampled on wives dresses. . . . [A] stupendous woman a head taller than me and three times as thick went through with the preliminary movement to a curtsey. . . . Some one whispered, 'is that whole woman to be presented at once?' . . . One sedate judge was so flustered that he stepped on three or four feet of his wife's dress just as they passed me. She was about to commence bowing to the Marquis [of Lorne] when her husband's rear attack compelled her to bow backward. She managed, however, to cast a look backward which said as plainly as possible 'Wait till we get home.' A sudden move of one hand shewed that some tackling had given way, and she retired precipitately to repair damages. . . .
>
> P.B. Waite in Oliver Mowat's Ontario, ed. Donald Swainson, 1972

A journalist reveals glimpses of Mackenzie's last days in the House, in 1886.

One afternoon Mr Mackenzie started to leave the chamber. He got as far as the speaker's chair, and then his legs refused to function. There he stood. The member who had the floor paused. All eyes were focussed on the old warrior. Two of his friends went to his assistance. But he brusquely thrust them aside. Finally he motioned one of them to his side, and evidently told him to move one of the nerveless legs. This was done, and it had the effect of enabling Mr Mackenzie to slowly shuffle his way out of the House. It was a very pathetic spectacle.

To the last Mackenzie remained the stubborn, self-contained Scotsman he had always been. His disablement seemed to intensify his sensitiveness and independence. One afternoon I saw him in the corridor vainly struggling to get on his overcoat. His arms were above his head, and the sleeves kept them there. A member passing along went to his assistance and, after a good deal of trouble got the overcoat on him. Did the former Prime Minister thank him? He did not. Instead with a frown, he said:

'After this, will you please be good enough to mind your own business and give your help when it is asked for!'

That was his last session. Yet he passed out as he had lived, with his head held high.

Fred Cook, 'Giants and Jesters in Public Life', National Archives of Canada, n.d.

LORD DUFFERIN

Lord Dufferin was Governor-General of Canada from 1872 to 1878. His sometime secretary, the colourful writer Lord Frederic Hamilton, often evinced an errant memory and a jaunty disregard for the facts, even depriving Donald Smith of the honour of driving the last spike, but he did tell good yarns.

When British Columbia threw in its lot with the Dominion in 1871, one of the terms upon which the Pacific Province insisted was a guarantee that the Trans-Continental railway should be completed in ten years—that is, in 1881. Two rival Companies received in 1872 charters for building the railway; the result was continual political intrigue, and very little constructive work. British Columbia grew extremely restive under the continual delays, and threatened to retire from the Dominion. Lord Dufferin told me himself, when I was his Private Secretary in Petrograd, that on the occasion of his official visit to British Columbia (of course by sea), in either 1876 or 1877, as Governor-General, he was expected to drive under a triumphal arch which had been erected at Victoria, Vancouver Island. This arch was inscribed on both sides with the word 'Separation'. I remember perfectly Lord Dufferin's actual words in describing the incident: 'I sent for the Mayor of Victoria, and told him that I must have a small—a very small—alteration made in the inscription, before I could consent to drive under it; an alteration of one letter only. The initial "S" must be replaced with an "R", and then I would pledge my word that I would do my best to see that "Reparation" was made to the Province.' This is so eminently characteristic of Lord Dufferin's method that it is worth recording. The suggested alteration in the inscription was duly made, and Lord Dufferin drove under the arch. In spite of continued efforts the Governor-General was unable to expedite the construction of the railway under the Mackenzie Administration, and it needed all his consummate tact to quiet the ever-growing demand for separation from the Dominion on the part of British Columbia, owing to the non-fulfilment of the terms of union. It was not until 1881, under Sir John Macdonald's Premiership, that a contract was signed with a new Company to complete the Canadian Pacific within ten years, but so rapid was the progress made, that the last spike was actually driven on November 7, 1885, five years before the stipulated time. The names of three Scotsmen will always be associated with this gigantic undertaking: those of the late Donald Smith, afterwards Lord Strathcona; George Stephen, afterwards Lord Mountstephen; and Mr R.B. Angus of Montreal. The last spike, which was driven in at a place called Craigellachie, by Mrs Mackenzie, widow of the Premier under whom the CPR had been commenced, was of an unusual character, for it was of eighteen-carat gold. In the course of an hour it was replaced by a more serviceable spike of steel. I have often seen Mrs Mackenzie wearing the original gold spike, with 'Craigellachie' on it in diamonds.

Lord Frederic Hamilton, The Vanished World of Yesterday, 1950

Certain that the Canadian population must increase until its magnitude bore a close relationship to the physical size of the country, imperialists also supposed that the geographical situation of the nation must profoundly affect the character and outlook of her people. . . .

The adjective 'northern' came to symbolize energy, strength, self-reliance, health, and purity, and its opposite, 'southern', was equated with decay and effeminacy, even libertinism and disease. A lengthy catalogue of desirable national attributes resulting from the climate was compiled. No other weather was so conducive to maintaining health and stimulating robustness. 'A constitution nursed upon the oxygen of our bright winter atmosphere', exclaimed Governor-General Dufferin, 'makes its owner feel as though he could toss about the pine trees in his glee.'

Carl Berger, The Sense of Power, 1971

EDWARD BLAKE

Edward Blake sat in both (as was then customary) the Ontario legislature (1867–72) and the House of Commons (1867–91), as a Liberal. Declining the national party leadership, he held cabinet offices in the Mackenzie government from 1873 to

1878. He assumed leadership of the Liberals in 1880 and stepped down in 1887. A brilliant lawyer and powerful speaker, Blake was the only Liberal party leader who never became prime minister.

During my first years in the Press Gallery Sir John Thompson was the most powerful debater in the Conservative Parliamentary party, as Hon. Edward Blake was the most impressive and convincing speaker among the Liberals. Sir John Macdonald had greater authority than either, but his ascendency was the growth of years; the long result of a rare personality and a great prestige. Neither in Blake nor in Thompson was there any impelling spontaneity or magnetism. Blake was often heavy and sometimes monotonous. Thompson was always cold, sober, self-contained and distant. In his pilgrimages throughout the country Thompson was described by irreverent blasphemers as 'the ice-wagon'; Blake could be very lonely and remote. Once I saw the Liberal leader mooning in solemn abstraction over the exchanges in the reading-room when a colleague on the Liberal front benches, who had returned from dinner with 'a quart of wine visibly concealed about his person', if I may borrow language which Mr Alfred Boultbee applied to a clubmate, lurched against him, brought his hand down with tremendous force upon the bowed shoulders, and gurgled, 'Come—come 'long, you—you—old hulk, and have some fun.' The hulk put his hand affectionately across the back of his unsteady associate and shook with laughter. One could not know from the frosty exterior how intimate and companionable Blake could be in rare moments of self-revelation. But so often he was among the glaciers.

Sir John Willison, *Reminiscences Political and Personal*, 1919

Two members of the House, Hon. Edward Blake and Sir Richard Cartwright, were not 'good mixers'. It is said of the former that when a friend remonstrated with him for his chilliness towards his supporters and advised him to be more chummy with them, he asked what he was to do. 'Why, be more sociable and crack a joke or two with them.' 'How do you mean?' enquired Blake. 'Well, for instance, it's snowing out now, and if someone should pass a remark on the weather, you say "Oh, it's snow matter." ' And sure enough a few days later a good Grit follower overtaking the Honorable Edward on the broad walk remarked that it had been snowing hard. Mr Blake, suddenly remembering the pointer he had received about cracking a joke, but having forgotten the cue, promptly replied, 'Oh, it's quite immaterial.' Mr Blake was a great lawyer— a much greater lawyer than he was a politician.

George H. Ham, *Reminiscences of a Raconteur*, 1921

The journalist J.S. Willison recalled

the remark of a Hansard reporter when Mr Blake was making a speech of four or five hours' duration on the Canadian Pacific Railway. The colleague by whom he was relieved at the reporters' table, in order to be certain that the report would be complete and continuous, whispered, 'Where is he at?' The answer came with energy and emphasis, 'He is on the south branch of the Saskatchewan, running down grade and going like h——.'

Sir John Willison, Reminiscences Political and Personal, 1919

AMOR DE COSMOS

Born W.A. Smith, Amor de Cosmos was simultaneously Premier of British Columbia and a federal MP from 1872 to 1874.

William Alexander Smith became Amor De Cosmos on February 17, 1854, that being the date when the Bill changing his name was approved and signed by the Governor of California, John Bilger, after stormy and hilarious debate in the Senate and the Assembly. Change of name was a common practice in those days, the motives being often open to suspicion; but there is no doubt that many individuals chose thus to acquire distinction in the same way that a man wears a striking necktie or a woman dyes a lock of her hair. The case of De Cosmos caused great discussion because of his strange choice, and there was some doubt whether Legislative action was a proper method. The Legislature had the say until 1866, when power to change a name was given to the courts. . . .

De Cosmos' enemies declared that he changed his name to escape the vengeance of a group of Californian miners for some obscure action he is supposed to have taken as a member of the Vigilantes during the gold rush. How would a man named Smith believe that he could escape under the cloak of a name like Amor De Cosmos? He received nation-wide publicity over his petition to the Senate. He seemed to relish it. The name was unforgettable and a certainty for getting attention. . . .

In presenting the petition Senator Hall pronounced Amor with a broad 'A', so that it sounded like 'Armor', and another Senator, with typically senatorial humour, sprang to his feet with the suggestion that this was obviously a case for referral to the committee on military affairs. When the laughter had subsided, however, the bill passed three readings and was ready for submission to the Assembly. Not, however, without some difficulty being experienced by the newspapers. One journal reported the name to be 'Armor Debosmos', another had it as 'Amor De Casmos', another as 'Amos de Cosmos', and another as 'Amos de Bosmos'. Even the official journal could do no better than 'Amor De Cosmer'.

But poor Bill Smith, who wanted to be Amor De Cosmos, was in for much more trouble with his fancy new name. When the Bill went to the Assembly, there was a Mr Stow to jump up and propose that the 'de' be deleted as being 'too much of a furrin' title to be conferred by this Legislature'. Then there was a Mr McBrayne who tried to restore some good Anglo-Saxon flavour to the name. 'Why not delete the "de" and add "Muggins"?' he suggested. If Mr McBrayne had been taken seriously, one of the founders of British Columbia could have been Amor Muggins Cosmos.

Roland Wild, Amor De Cosmos, 1958

His early attempts at election were unsuccessful.

The next time De Cosmos ran for the Assembly he selected Esquimalt. A certain George Tomline Gordon was the incumbent, and the newspaper editor strengthened his campaign with some swinging blows that seemed certain to impress the twenty-six voters on the list in the little town. In reply to these assaults, the Gordon faction sought to smear De Cosmos by stating that they would not accept his nomination under the name of De Cosmos. They wanted it to read 'William Alexander Smith, commonly known as Amor De Cosmos.' This successfully brought out the fact that he had changed his name, and the untutored always ascribed an ulterior motive to this act.

The custom was for each voter to approach the returning officer and the roll clerks and announce his choice, for there could be no qualifications based on literacy. By three o'clock in the afternoon, ten citizens had announced in favour of Gordon, and ten had carefully given the names of Smith 'commonly known as De Cosmos'. There were only six more voters to be found, and it was thought that all of them had prudently hidden themselves away for the day rather than jeopardize any future plans they might have. Just then, however, a De Cosmos supporter named Young sought out and produced a 21st voter named Moore, who could be relied upon to do what he was told. A moment before the poll closed at four o'clock, he was escorted into the station and asked which man he favoured.

'Amor De Cosmos!' he cried obediently.

'Poll closed!' announced the Sheriff, as the Gordon supporters cheered. 'I find that there are ten votes for George Tomline Gordon, ten for William Alexander Smith known as Amor De Cosmos, and one vote for Amor De Cosmos. It is therefore a tie between two of the nominees. I must therefore cast the deciding vote. I vote for George Tomline Gordon.'

So De Cosmos lost his second election by having too many names.

Ibid.

PARLIAMENT

Parliament, a traditional and formal institution, also had its informal moments.

Some reference should be made to the great all-night debate, with which the session of the spring of 1878 closed, and which was in some sense the beginning of this celebrated campaign itself, resulting in the triumphant return of Sir John to power on the strength of the National Policy.

Mr Mackenzie had not that kind of suavity and conciliation in the House which Sir John possessed, and he often irritated his opponents by his bluntness in refusing requests of the Opposition on points of procedure. On this occasion he had refused to agree to an adjournment the night before, when many of the French members wished to speak. The Opposition determined to fight it out and tire out the ministry. The scene which followed had no parallel before or since the Government was established at Ottawa. While points of order were being argued, members hammered at desks, blew on tin trumpets, imitated the crowing of cocks, sent up toy-balloons, threw sand-crackers or torpedoes, and occasionally hurled blue-books across the House. Often the babel of sounds was such that neither the Speaker of the House nor the member who had the floor could be heard. Once in a while amid the din some member with a good voice would start up the 'Marseillaise', 'God save the Queen', 'A la claire fontaine', 'The Raftsman's chorus', or some plantation melody, and then the whole House would join in the song, with an effect that was quite moving. The feelings inspired by these songs would sway the House back into a quiet frame; but scarcely would the speaker who had the floor recover the thread of his discourse when such a pandemonium would be raised as made the listener think 'Chaos has come again'. When a speaker had at last made himself heard over the diminishing din of exhausted voices, and when he himself had exhausted his subject, he would keep the floor by quoting passages from law-books, books of poetry, philosophy and humor.

Mr Cimon, one of these speakers, filled up his time by reading the whole of the British North America Act in French, making humorous comments upon each clause. In some of these passages 'the grim features of Mr Blake', writes a chronicler of the scene, 'not merely relaxed into a smile, but broke into a laugh, that shook his big frame all over.'

As the night wore on, the spectators became tired, and the galleries were gradually cleared. Now and again a member strayed off, and would be found shortly afterwards stretched on a bench in the reading-room, or curled up in an alcove of the library fast asleep. But there were always enough members left in the House to keep up the fun. Even here, however, the exhausted figures of some members would be found reclining on their desks, quite unconscious of the paper missiles that were being pelted at them. In the afternoon Lady Dufferin had sat in the gallery, listening with amused bewilderment to the babel of sounds. As she rose to leave, a member struck up 'God save the Queen', and all the House rose and joined in the anthem with a patriotic fervor that was remarkable. Mr Mackenzie had just come in at that moment, and Mr Blake and he, after looking at each other in hesitation for a few moments, threw off their dignity and joined in. Just as the singing ceased, Sir John, who had been resting in his private room, appeared on the scene, and was greeted with a rousing cheer by the Opposition.

At one stage Mr De Veber rose to a point of order. The Speaker asked what it was, and De Veber said, 'The Minister of Marine and Fisheries is sitting at the clerk's table in irreverent proximity to the mace.'

'That's no point of order,' said the Speaker, and in the midst of the laughter which followed some one struck up 'Auld Lang Syne'.

A party of member organized an impromptu band, which was nick-named 'Gideon's Band', and began to play a species of music that was more discordant if possible than the voices and banging of desks which accompanied it. The *Citizen*, in its report, compared the voices of the members to the roaring of the beasts at Ephesus. The Speaker, after manfully battling against these insurmountable obstacles to order, at last gave up from a difficulty that was certainly 'constitutional',—his voice having entirely given out. Mr Cheval, a French member, had procured some new instruments described as 'squeaking machines', and these were added to the band. Some one wanted to put down Mr Cheval and his music, upon which he pathetically appealed to the Speaker. 'Mr Speaker, I wish to know which is more worse, de man dat trows blue books 'cross de House, or de man dat goes in for a small leedle music.' This entreaty was received with roars of laughter. The Speaker said both were unparliamentary, whereupon Mr Smith of Peel, whose role was leader of the orchestra, led off the House in another song, while Mr Cheval resumed operations on his squeaking machine. Mr Mackenzie sometimes exhibited a face 'as long as a family churn', and sometimes was beaming with goodwill, while Mr Blake kept himself amused and awake 'by performing some extraordinary finger-music on his desk'. Mr Smith of Peel got so hoarse from his orchestral performances that he simply croaked.

At one point in the proceedings Mr Campbell, horrified at this outrage upon decorum, came out near the clerk's table, and with the most violent gesticulations, swinging his arms and waving his hat, denounced the proceedings. Mr Mackenzie demanded that the Sergeant-at-arms should be called in to preserve order, but the Sergeant-at-arms, ensconced in a private nook of his own, was enjoying the fun too much to do anything of the kind. Once when Mr Plumb was speaking, Mr Macdonnell of Inverness, with mock gravity, called the attention of the Speaker to the fact that the member for Niagara was interrupting the music. 'An ominous silence ensued,' wrote the *Citizen* reporter, describing another stage of the proceedings, 'when Haggart, the powerful but merciful member for South Lanark, rises. He holds in his hands the memorial of Letellier de St Just to Lord Dufferin. In front of him in a solid phalanx the ministerial battalion is roaring, howling, hooting, singing, whistling, stamping, shouting and caterwauling. That frisky kitten Dymond is suspiciously toying with a waste-basket; while the genteel Cheval, who looks as if he had strayed into the House by mistake, is expanding a toy bag-pipe, for the purpose of dropping it into the inverted crown of Dr Brossé's slouch hat. At last Dymond lets fly his waste-basket among a group of ministerial friends. The toy bag-pipe appeared in Dr Brossé's hat again, and squealed to such a degree that he clutched it and threw it to another member, who stopped singing in order to blow it up again. But not understanding how to manipulate it, the noisy object set up such a wail as fairly brought down the House.' While this had been going on Lady Dufferin again came in, and when she left, the House once more gave

'God save the Queen', followed up with a cheer and such waving of handker-
chiefs as would have led a stranger to believe that Queen Victoria herself was
quitting the Chamber.

At last Mr Cheval burst his toy bag-pipe and retired with a broken heart,
amid the mock sympathy of his orchestra. A demand by Mr Dymond for a
speech from the Speaker was greeted with roars of laughter. At 4.15 A.M., that
patient functionary left Mr De Veber in his chair and went out to get something
to eat. In a few moments pages began to bring in coffee, which was greeted
with cheers from both sides. About six o'clock (at which hour, had it been
evening, the Speaker would have risen from the chair as a matter of course),
Mr Bowell rose and said he was willing to have six o'clock called, and go on
after getting something to eat.

'There is no six o'clock to-day,' added Mr Holton.

'Six o'clock was yesterday,' added Mr Mills.

'Oh, it's six of one and half a dozen of the other,' said Mr Blake.

'Then it's twelve,' reasoned Mr Bowell, amid laughter.

The House finally adjourned, after sitting for twenty-seven hours!

E.B. Biggar, Anecdotal Life of Sir John Macdonald, 1891

The old House of Commons, before the great fire of 3 February 1916, had a
different shape; the Speaker did not sit, as now, at the end of the long axis of
the House, but at the end of the short one. The old House of Commons was
spread deeply on either side of the Speaker, seven rows of desks, forty-four
feet on each side. The House had been originally designed for the 130 members
of the Legislative Assembly of the Province of Canada. Now, in 1885, it had
211 seats, upholstered in dark green leather and the walls to match. It was apt
to be hot and stuffy, for gas lighting tended to exhaust oxygen; members had
been complaining since 1867. Various remedies were tried; the introduction
of electric light after 1887 eased the problem without curing it.

There was, and was not, a House of Commons bar. It had been originally
closed in 1874, but it had been unofficially open since. MPs had to have a
restaurant; by custom the privilege was farmed to a restaurateur who would
not take it unless the profits of a bar were attached. When Laurier first entered
the House of Commons in 1874, it was not uncommon for half the MPs to
be under the weather when the House adjourned at midnight. In 1885 Parliament had not changed much. The Senate had a bar which had a reputation
for port; the specialty of the Commons bar was an amiable decoction of rum
which, as one newspaper correspondent observed, 'was very comforting to the
wounded heart'.

P.B. Waite, The Man from Halifax, 1985

GOLDWIN SMITH

An Oxford historian who became a journalist in Canada (1871), Goldwin Smith advocated annexation to the United States. He took a jaundiced view of Canadian politics and public life.

The standard complaint against the Canadian party system is reflected in Goldwin Smith's account of attending his first party picnic in Canada in the 1870s. After listening to the speakers harangue their opponents, Smith drew an old farmer aside and asked him what the real difference was between his party and the other. The farmer thought long before replying, 'We say the other fellows are corrupt.'

Abraham Rotstein, ed., in The Prospect of Change, 1965

Much of what is often called 'Victorian' morality was foreign to the age after which it was named. The full temperance experiment was still in the future; the Ross government of Ontario complained in 1897 of being between two fires, the temperance advocates on the one side and the liquor trade on the other. Drinking habits had changed in twenty-five years, but in this respect late Victorian Canada was still raw and lusty. James Edgar, from the depths of the Remedial Bill debate, wrote his wife that Moncrieff (of Imperial Oil) was speaking, but was drunk and getting drunker on gin and water. 'He has knocked his tumbler over once & sent for more.' Two weeks later Davin wound up an impromptu Blackfoot dance in the Commons smoking room, by springing up on the long table, laden with bottles and glasses, and jigging down the centre, kicking over everything in sight. But then Davin was notorious. Goldwin Smith . . . [in 1880] described for Sir John A. Macdonald a delicious incident on a Toronto horse-car:

> You know Alderman Baxter—he is a leading Conservative. He was sitting in the street car when a lady getting in dropped her handkerchief on his knees. He could not see it fall for his stomach. The lady was too shy to take it. The eyes of the passengers were fixed upon him. At last his attention was directed to the handkerchief. He took it for a part of his shirt, and opening his nether garments in a great hurry, tucked it in, to the delight of the crowded car. This from an *eyewitness*.

Peter B. Waite, Canada 1874–1896, 1971

LADY AGNES MACDONALD

Sir John A.'s Jamaican-born second wife, whom he married in February 1867, Lady Agnes Macdonald accompanied the Chief on his trip from Ottawa to Vancouver on the newly completed CPR during the summer of 1878. Sir John A. had regained the office of Prime Minister in 1878. When the Macdonalds reached the Rockies:

At Laggan Station, still some distance from the summit, they got out to examine the big 'mountain engine' which was necessary for both ascending and descending steep grades. It was then and there that Agnes had what seemed to her an even better idea of where to seat herself for the rest of the journey. '[F]rom the instant my eyes rested on the broad shining surface of [the engine's] buffer-bean and cowcatcher . . . I decided to travel there and nowhere else for the remaining 600 miles of the journey!'

The idea of the Prime Minister's wife riding the cowcatcher caused the crew no little consternation. What was she going to sit on, for example? This question she answered for them by choosing an empty candle-box, which she then placed on the buffer beam. The next thing to do was to have Agnes obtain John A.'s permission. When she approached him:

> The Chief, seated on a low chair on the rear platform of the car, with a rug over his knees and a magazine in his hand, looked very comfortable and content. Hearing my request . . . he pronounced the idea 'rather ridiculous', then remembered it was dangerous as well, and finally asked if I was sure I could hold on. Before the words were well out of his lips, and taking permission for granted by the question, I was again standing by the cowcatcher . . . and asking to be helped on.

At least some members of the Prime Minister's staff were as nonplussed as the crew by Agnes' unorthodox choice. Pope [Sir John's private secretary], for one, did not approve and wrote of Lady Macdonald's 'characteristic imprudence'. (As there was never any other mention of Agnes being imprudent, it seems more likely that he meant 'impulsive', for she was that.) One reason for their objections may have been that the younger gentlemen of the party—Fred White, George Johnson or Pope himself—had to take turns sitting with her in this exposed position, and at least Pope seemed to feel that she was asking a bit much.

On the last morning of the cowcatcher trip, Pope had reason to be upset. The danger that cattle might be on the track was ever-present, but on this particular day it was a number of young pigs that appeared just in front of the train. All except one managed to get out of harm's way, but that one was hit by the train and Pope declared that it passed between his body and the post he was holding. Had either of the passengers on the cowcatcher been hit by the animal, the impact could have been fatal. Pope rightly decided that this mode of transportation was not for him: 'I have not ridden on a cowcatcher since.' Agnes was aware of the possible danger of her exposed position but much less worried about it. On that morning, she wrote, she was admiring the scenery when 'There was a squeak, a flash of something near, and away we went. . . . The Secretary averred that the body had struck him in passing; but as I shut my eyes tightly as soon as the pigs appeared, I cannot bear testimony to the fact.'

The ride on the cowcatcher gave Agnes too much pleasure to leave room for fears. 'Enthroned on a candle-box with a soft felt hat well over the eyes, and a linen carriage-cover tucked around me from waist to foot . . .', she turned to the Superintendent who shared her 'peril' and decided that some word of comfort was necessary for him: 'This is *lovely, quite lovely*; I shall travel on this cowcatcher from summit to sea.' The poor Superintendent only surveys me with solemn and resigned surprise. "I suppose-you-will," he says slowly.'

Louise Reynolds, *Agnes: The Biography of Lady Macdonald*, 1979

SIR JOSEPH-ADOLPHE CHAPLEAU

Conservative Premier of Quebec from 1879 to 1882, Sir Joseph-Adolphe Chapleau became Secretary of State in Sir John A.'s cabinet in 1882 and held that office for ten years.

The custodian of the Great Seal in Canada is always the Secretary of State.

The Honorable J.A. Chapleau became a cabinet minister in July, 1882, and was allotted the portfolio of Secretary of State. He had long been designated for office in the government. Just before Christmas of that year Mr Chapleau's friends in the province of Quebec presented him with a magnificent sealskin coat which cost over one thousand dollars, to enable him to withstand the rigors of the Ottawa winter.

It has been the custom at every New Year's levee for the Prime Minister and his colleagues to make a formal call upon the Governor General, they being presented before the officials, the clergy, and the general public. On January 1, 1883, Sir John was there heading his colleagues of the cabinet, and on this particular occasion when presenting them to Lord Lorne, he could not refrain from having his little joke. Mr Chapleau was wearing his new sealskin coat, and when it came to his turn to be presented Sir John laid his hand lovingly on Mr Chapleau's shoulder and said, 'Your Excellency, and now I have the honor to present the Great Seal.' The Governor General caught the significance of the expression, and he and his ministers had a good laugh. Mr Chapleau enjoyed the joke as much as the others.

Fred Cook, *Fifty Years Ago and Since*, National Archives of Canada, n.d.

JOHN HENRY POPE

John Henry Pope represented the English-speaking minority of Quebec in Sir John A.'s cabinet after the Tories returned to power in 1878. Plain-spoken and of limited education, he was a great favourite in the House.

Sir John's most trusted lieutenant for years . . . 'John Henry', as he was familiarly called, had all the shrewdness and foresight of the statesman, and materially assisted in directing the policy of the party. He was not a polished or verbose speaker, but when he spoke the few words he uttered always meant something. Once when fiercely attacked by Sir Richard Cartwright in the

House, he made the shortest but most effective speech ever delivered in the Green Chamber. When Sir Richard had taken his seat amidst the loud applause of his followers, Mr Pope slowly rose and quaintly said: 'Mr Speaker, there ain't nothin' to it.'

The House cheered wildly, and Sir Richard warmly joined in the expressions of admiration. That ended the discussion.

George H. Ham, *Reminiscences of a Raconteur*, 1921

LOUIS RIEL

Métis leader of the Red River uprising in 1870, Louis Riel was elected as a Conservative to the House of Commons for Provencher in a by-election in 1873 and in the general election of 1874. He was expelled from the House on the motion of Orange leader Mackenzie Bowell.

The Clerk of the House, Alfred Patrick, had not known who Riel was until he was leaving his office. It had all happened quite casually. That afternoon Dr Jean-Baptiste Fiset, the newly re-elected representative of Rimouski, had come into his office and asked him if he would swear in a new member. Patrick replied that he would be pleased to do so. Dr Fiset then asked whether the roll might not be taken into another room. This, Patrick said, could not be done; the practice of signing the roll in his office would have to be followed.

Dr Fiset glanced about anxiously. He went to the door and looked out. It occurred to Patrick for a moment that he was acting somewhat strangely. Growing a little impatient, he asked Dr Fiset whether he really wished to be sworn in or not. Dr Fiset said that he did and that he had a friend with him.

He then brought in a stranger, who 'had a heavy whisker, not exactly black'. Patrick administered the oath to both of them. They both said solemnly: 'I do swear that I will be faithful and bear true allegiance to Her Majesty Queen Victoria.'

Having taken the oath, the two men signed the members' roll. 'I did not pay particular attention, as I was in a hurry,' Patrick later stated, 'and did not look at the roll until they were leaving the room. To my astonishment I saw the name "Louis Riel". I looked up suddenly, and saw them going out of the door. Riel was making a low bow to me, and I did not get a sight of his face. . . . Mr Fiset whispered to me, "Do not mention this, and do not say anything about it." After it was done, I went to the Premier at the Privy Council, and related to him the fact, at which he appeared to be astonished.'

Edgar Andrew Collard, *Canadian Yesterdays*, 1955

After Riel was tried and found guilty of treason following the second uprising in 1885, his execution was postponed pending inquiry into his sanity.

Three doctors were asked to see Riel, Dr Jukes of the Mounted Police, Dr Lavell of Kingston Penitentiary, and Dr F.X. Valade of Ottawa. All three seem clearly to have been impressed with Riel, both as a character and as a man. Lavell wrote privately to Macdonald, 'I confess I should be well pleased if justice and popular clamour could be satisfied without depriving this man of life.' Jukes and Lavell, operating within the narrow conventions of the McNaughten rule, found, publicly at least Riel did know right from wrong. But Valade believed him insane. A.E. Forget reported privately to Honoré Mercier that Valade 'l'a déclaré complètement aliéné et incapable de discerner entre le bien et le mal'. Dr Valade's report to the Government actually read:

> After having examined Riel in pte conversation with him & by testimony of persons who take care of him I have come to the conclusion that he is not an accountable being that he is unable to distinguish between wrong & right in political and religious subjects which I consider well marked typical forms of a kind of insanity under which he undoubtedly suffers but on other points I believe him to be quite sensible & can distinguish right from wrong.

The version published by the Government is heavily and misleadingly abbreviated:

> After having examined carefully Riel in private conversation with him and by testimony of persons who take care of him, I have come to the conclusion that he suffers under hallucinations on political and religious subjects, but on other points I believe him to be quite sensible and can distinguish right from wrong.

Macdonald does not seem to have been very comfortable about it all. November 15 he wrote Dewdney, 'I am anxious for tomorrow passing over.' The next day, at 8:30, on a bright cold morning, Riel was hanged in Regina jail. Almost his last words with Father André were,

> Sir John Macdonald is now committing me to death for the same reason I committed Scott [in 1870], because it is necessary for the country's good. . . . I was pardoned once for his death, but am now going to die for it.

The hangman was Jack Henderson, imprisoned by Riel in 1870. Dewdney telegraphed Macdonald in cipher, the words 'Hindrance carabine avenged dissipating. . . .' Hanged, buried as directed, is what it said.

Peter B. Waite, Canada 1874–1896, 1971

NICHOLAS FLOOD DAVIN

Known as the Voice of the North-West, Davin was the Conservative MP for Assiniboia West from 1887 to 1900. His first campaign, for the Ontario riding of Haldimand, was unsuccessful, but brought him to Sir John A.'s attention.

His campaign furnished many good stories which were current for years thereafter. One of the best related to me was with reference to his pursuit of the

Irish Catholic vote, which was at that time an important factor in Haldimand. Davin's own connection with religion was somewhat hazy, and he was not so hypocritical as to make any strong pretences of devotion. He had as one of his active workers a resourceful politician by name of Madigan (or something like that), who had procured a picture of the Mother Superior of an Irish convent, who may or may not have been related to Davin. In the course of a personal canvass among the Irish Catholic electors the following system was observed. The candidate and Madigan would drive up to a farmhouse and would of course receive a pleasant welcome from folk always glad to have the tedium of the day varied by the visit of a distinguished stranger. Davin would engage the man of the house in conversation about politics and tell a good story or two. Meanwhile, Madigan would discuss the candidate with the wife and casually produce the picture of the Mother Superior, with the remark that she was Mr Davin's sister. The woman would at once be interested and would broach the subject to the candidate, who would sigh and murmur a wish that he were as saintly as his dear sister. Though he failed of election he made inroads in unexpected quarters on the Reform candidate's support. . . .

Davin prized his reputation for ready retort and was even accused of preparing such retorts beforehand and placing apparently hostile agents in his audiences to ask seemingly embarrassing questions, which would be swiftly and amusingly answered. Next morning the report would read 'With ready wit, Mr Davin silenced his questioner, etc., etc.'. On one occasion he had arranged to address a meeting at a Grey County village in behalf of the late Thomas Masson, KC, of Owen Sound, who represented North Grey in the House of Commons. Before leaving Ottawa with Mr Masson, Davin took the precaution of leaving a copy of his speech (it being his habit to memorize his orations) with the Ottawa *Citizen*, then a Conservative organ. The copy had the phrase 'Cheers and applause' interlarded at appropriate intervals. It was also studded with questions to which the speaker had responded 'with ready wit'. Now it chanced that on the journey to Grey a blizzard arose and Messrs Masson and Davin were prevented from reaching their meeting. Davin took the precaution of wiring to the editor of the *Citizen* in these words, 'Let speech go.' He meant of course to withhold publication, but in newspaper parlance such a message is usually interpreted as a release or permission to print copy. The undelivered speech therefore appeared next morning with 'cheers and applause', 'ready retorts', and other ornaments in their proper place.

When Davin arrived back in Ottawa the first man he met said, quite innocently, 'That was a magnificent speech you delivered for Tom Masson'. 'My God,' said the orator, 'you don't mean to say it was printed after all!', and rushed for the *Citizen* office to find that his wire had been misunderstood. That was not the worst of it. On the Liberal side of the House sat one of the most caustic of Parliamentarians, Dr George Landerkin of Hanover, Ontario, who represented South Grey in the Commons and in later years became a Senator. Because of the proximity of his constituency to the scene of the alleged speech, Dr Landerkin was not long in learning the actual facts. One day, following the usual procedure, he rose before the orders of the day were called to 'draw attention of the House to the utterances of the member for West Assiniboia as reported in the Ottawa *Citizen*, etc., etc.,', and while poor Davin winced and frowned, read the speech in its entirety, giving diabolical emphasis to the 'cheers and applause' and the 'ready wit'. It is of great convenience to editors and important to public men that they should furnish newspapers with advance copies of their speeches, but it was a lesson to others not to interlard their masterpieces with extraneous ornaments.

Hector Charlesworth, More Candid Chronicles, 1928

HONORÉ MERCIER

Regarded as a father of Quebec nationalism, and founder of the Parti National, Honoré Mercier was Liberal Premier of Quebec from 1887 to 1891. Most Anglophone Liberals did not love him, and he was removed from office by the lieutenant-governor because of a scandal involving railroad financing.

There is a story, probably not authentic, that on the eve of polling in the Federal election of 1891 Mercier said to a friend, 'If I were leader of the Liberal party I would have a majority of twenty in Quebec tomorrow.' The friend asked why Laurier should not do as well since he had Mercier's most active and energetic support. 'The reason,' said Mercier, 'is that Monsieur Laurier is an honest man.'

Sir John Willison, Reminiscences Political and Personal, 1919

SIR JOHN A. MACDONALD (II)

Sir John A. Macdonald returned to office as Prime Minister in the election of 1878, largely on his 'National Policy' of tariff protection. He remained in office till 1891.

In the course of the debates by which he introduced the National Policy, Sir John remarked that those who cared to be protected at all, wanted all the protection they could get. They were like the squaw who said of whisky, that 'a little too much was just enough'.

E.B. Biggar, Anecdotal Life of Sir John Macdonald, 1891

While Protection was everywhere the rallying cry, other questions arose, among them the absurd charge of French domination. The Government's railway, North-West, and immigration policies were also under fire. A feature of the last-named came in for some adverse criticism. This was a system of assisting female immigration to this country with the object of providing wives for the prairie settlers, among whom there was a great shortage of women. This scheme, however excellent it might be in theory, did not work well in practice. A number of loose characters took advantage of its provisions to get out to Canada, and Sir John Macdonald, who as Minister of the Interior was specially responsible for the execution of this policy, decided to discontinue it. Amongst its warmest advocates was a certain MP, for many years a strong and consistent Protectionist, who after the National Policy had been placed on the statute book, feeling his occupation gone, took up this immigration scheme as an outlet for his surplus energy, and pressed it strongly upon the Government. One evening as the gentleman in question was waiting in my office for Council to break up, in order to learn the decision of the Government as to the continuation or abandonment of this policy of assisted immigration, Sir John walked into the room and seeing him, said, 'I'm sorry, Angus, but my colleagues and I have talked over the subject, and we have come to the conclusion not to go on with the assisted immigration, at any rate for this year.' Then, seeing the look of disappointment on his old friend's face, he put his hand kindly on his shoulder and added: 'You know, Angus, we must *protect* the Canadian w[hore]s.'   Maurice Pope, *Public Servant*, 1960

Once at an evening reception in London one lady leaned towards another and said in an earnest whisper: 'You say you have never seen Lord Beaconsfield [Disraeli]. There he is!' She pointed to a distinguished figure in the gathering. Yet the gentleman she had pointed out was not Lord Beaconsfield, the Prime Minister of England: he was Sir John A. Macdonald, the Prime Minister of Canada.

Nor did the mistake come about simply because this particular lady happened to be insufficiently acquainted with Lord Beaconsfield's appearance. Those who knew Lord Beaconsfield well could be similarly mistaken.

Perhaps the most dramatic of such mistakes occurred in 1881—the year of Lord Beaconsfield's death. Sir Charles Dilke, who had recently visited the dying Lord Beaconsfield, was taking a train at London's Euston Station. The clock had just struck midnight, when Sir Charles, looking at the door of the railway carriage, was astounded to see a figure, apparently that of Lord Beaconsfield, standing before him.

There Lord Beaconsfield seemed to stand, dressed in the same Privy Councillor's uniform that Dilke had often seen him wear on official occasions. Had it not been for the uniform, Sir Charles might more promptly have arrived at the conclusion that the figure he saw before him must be some person bearing an amazing resemblance to the former British Prime Minister. But the number of persons entitled to wear the uniform of a Privy Councillor was comparatively small and he was convinced that he knew them all by sight. The thought seems to have passed through his mind: could this be the ghost of Lord Beaconsfield appearing in Euston Station as the clock struck midnight?

Of his weird experience Sir Charles Dilke later wrote: '. . . it required, indeed, a severe exercise of presence of mind to remember that there had been a City banquet from which the apparition must be coming, and rapidly to arrive by a process of exhaustion at the knowledge that this twin brother of that Lord Beaconsfield whom shortly before I had seen in the sick room, which he was not to leave, must be the Prime Minister of Canada.'. . .

Certainly the members of the press gallery in the Parliament Buildings at Westminster, who saw Lord Beaconsfield day after day, were incredulous when Sir John A. Macdonald visited the House of Commons. The London correspondent of the Edinburgh *Daily News* made this remarkable resemblance the subject of a dispatch. 'Even with his hat on,' he wrote, 'it was sufficiently strong to deceive many people who must be familiar with the personal appearance of Lord Beaconsfield. When Sir John A. Macdonald sits or stands bareheaded the resemblance becomes almost embarrassing. Sir John is well aware of the freak of nature, and encourages it to the extent of closely imitating the singular coiffure of Lord Beaconsfield. He has the slight advantage of the British Prime Minister in quantity, but as to colour, and the little curl on the forehead, their hair is precisely the same. The resemblance is further carried out when Sir John talks. He has the same shrug of the shoulder, the same outspreading of the hands, and, in brief, all the little mannerisms so familiar in our own Benjamin.' . . .

Lord Beaconsfield and Sir John A. Macdonald met for the first time in the early autumn of 1879. Beaconsfield had heard about the striking resemblance that was said to exist between himself and the Prime Minister of Canada, and at this meeting he had an opportunity to form his own opinion.

On the day after Macdonald's visit he wrote to Lady Bradford: 'The Prime Minister of Canada arrived yesterday and departed by early train this morning. . . . He is gentlemanlike, agreeable, and very intelligent: a considerable man, with no Yankeeisms except a little sing-song occasionally at the end of a sentence. . . .

'By the bye, the Canadian chief is said to be very like your humble servant, tho' a much younger man. I think there is a resemblance.'

Edgar Andrew Collard, Canadian Yesterdays, 1955

When Sir John went to Washington [1887] in connection with the treaty with the United States, the Canadian party were treated to a boat ride on the Potomac. Sir John came early and alone, and while waiting for the others to come, a lady, the wife of a senator, fell into conversation with him, when the following dialogue ensued:

'I guess you are from Canada.'

'Yes, ma'am.'

'You've got a very smart man over there, the Honorable John A. Macdonald.'

'Yes, ma'am, he is.'

'But they say he's a regu'ar rascal.'

'Yes, ma'am, he is a perfect rascal.'

'But why do they keep such a man in power?'

'Well, you see, they cannot get along without him.'

'But how is that? They say he's a real skalawag, and—' Just then her husband, the Senator, stepped up and said:

'My dear, let me introduce the Honorable John A. Macdonald.'

The lady's feelings can be imagined. But Sir John put her at her ease, saying, 'Now, don't apologize. All you've said is perfectly true, and it is well known at home.'

E.B. Biggar, *Anecdotal Life of Sir John Macdonald*, 1891

On his visit to the Pacific Coast in 1886, Sir John stopped off a short while at Regina. As every one knows, that ambitious capital of three great territories lies in the midst of a dead level plain, extending in every direction farther than the eye can reach. While the Premier was standing at the railway station, he was approached by one of Regina's gushing sons, who asked him 'what he thought of the prospect?' swinging his arms around, so as to indicate the vast plain by which they were surrounded. With many a twinkle in his eye, and the quiet smile for which he was noted playing about his mouth, he said in slow and measured tones, 'If you had a lit-tle more wood, and a lit-tle more water, and here and there a hill, I think the prospect would be improved.' There was an awkward pause in the conversation till a new topic was propounded.

Ibid.

Another of the many of Sir John's devotees in humble life is Patrick Buckley, a cabman and proprietor of a livery stable in Ottawa, from whose vehicle, it is said, the assassin alighted who killed D'Arcy McGee. He had been Sir Allan McNab's coachman, and was about the only one of the household who could manage the gouty old man. In following his present avocation he kept to the seat of government in all its moves from city to city. For thirty-eight years he had driven Sir John, and from the time of Confederation the Premier seldom rode with anyone else. When Sir John was defeated and resumed his old profession at Toronto, Buckley went there too. When Sir John saw him driving along one day he hailed him, and went over to his cab to shake hands. During all the time Sir John was out of power this faithful old man insisted on driving him about, and refused to accept a cent for the service—a circumstance that could not be attributed to mere policy, as there seemed little likelihood that Sir John ever would be Premier again. It could not have been Buckley's good looks nor the pompous appearance of his vehicle that had won the favour of Sir John, for in former days his old sorrel horse and lumbering, faded, saggy-doored cab were the reverse of attractive, while the wizened, wrinkled face—over which a short sandy grizzly beard bristled out in all directions, and matched well with a pair of shaggy eyebrows, from beneath which a funny pair of big eyes twinkled—was more curious than handsome. A curious little cap he used to wear made his head look smaller than it really was. But Sir John in this odd figure read the one trait he required in a man for this service, and that was faithfulness. Under an exterior that seemed to cover only indolence and ignorance, no one hid more fidelity, discretion or punctuality. On whatever business Sir John required him, Buckley was always there, and on time, and no paltry consideration of an extra fare would induce him to risk the disappointment of Sir John. He might be in front of the Parliament Building knowing that he had a clear hour before Sir John would be likely to come out, but although his cab was a public one he would not move for any offers. One day Lady Macdonald came out of the Parliament Building and observed to Buckley that, as it would be twenty minutes before Sir John would be out, she would take a spin down to a place in Wellington street. 'No, my lady,' said Buckley, humbly but firmly. When he objected and she still pressed him, 'I can't leave this spot till I get the word from Sir John.' It was a kind of heroism like Mrs O'Dowd's at the Battle of Waterloo—and, by the way, expressed in the same words. Sir Frederic de Winton wanting urgently to communicate with the Governor General one day, made the same request with all the authority of his high office, but Buckley declined in a more blunt manner still, adding, as he jerked his thumb over his shoulder, 'There's plinty av cabs down there at the sthand.' Buckley used to think that no living man dressed with the same taste as Sir John, and what increased his affection for his chieftain was that the Premier would never allow the old man to carry his parcels from the cab. When he would insist on doing it, Sir John would say, 'No, no, Buckley, I am just as young a man as you are,' and would run up the steps with his own books. Buckley would often contrast this with the autocratic way with which some of the junior departmental clerks would order him to carry a parcel up to the office, while tripping up empty handed themselves; and then carrying the contrast on to every other member of Parliament, would sum up with, 'He's the most whundherful man in the worruld!' Once Buckley, after taking Sir John home, on an occasion when he was somewhat unsettled, drove up amongst a group of members in front of the Buildings, when he was stopped and one of the group said they wished to ask him a question, and as it was very important they hoped and believed he would tell them the truth. Buckley promised he would. 'Then,' said the questioner, 'was Sir John tight when you drove him down just now?' 'What do ye mane?' said Buckley, looking for some road of escape. 'Was he in liquor,—was he drunk?' 'Shure,' replied Buckley, 'I have driven him all these years, and I niver seen him *in betther health* in me life thin to-day.' The party had made a bet concerning Sir John, and were to decide it by Buckley. It was a clever cut for the old cabman between a collision with the chariot wheels of his conscience on the one side and the ditch of falsehood on the other; but it was agreed by all that Sir John himself could not have steered through more cleverly.

Ibid.

The expression used by Sir John in his last campaign, 'A British subject I was born; a British subject I will die,' which has become famous, was uttered many years before, as the following passage in his speech on Mr Blake's resolution, declaring the right of Canada to make her own commercial treaties, will show: 'Disguise it as you will, this means separation and independence. The hon. gentleman is moving by slow degrees to that point. This is a commercial movement, by and by we shall have something else, until at last we take a step for political independence. I have said to the House before that a British subject I was born, and a British subject I hope to die. The best interests of Canada are all involved in the connection between the mother country and her loving and loyal colony.'

Ibid.

In 'The Day of Sir John Macdonald,' by Sir Joseph Pope, there is this passage: 'About a month before Sir John Macdonald died Mr Laurier came to his office in the House of Commons to discuss some question of adjournment. When he had gone the Chief said to me, "Nice chap, that. If I were twenty years younger he'd be my colleague." "Perhaps he may be yet, sir," I remarked. "Too old," said he, "too old", and passed into the inner room.'

Sir John Willison, *Reminiscences Political and Personal*, 1919

SIR JOHN J. ABBOTT

Canada's third prime minister, Sir John J. Abbott took office in 1891 and died in 1893. A former mayor of Montreal, Abbott was government leader in the Senate from 1887 to 1891. Sir John A.'s secretary, Joseph Pope, describes the succession:

Following the death of Macdonald the party went through a series of short-lived administrations. John Thompson appeared the likely candidate to assume the post of Prime Minister, but he deferred in favour of Senator John Abbott, a man one could hardly call a political animal:

> I hate politics and what are considered their appropriate measures. I hate noto-riety, public meetings, public speeches, caucuses and everything that I know of which is apparently the necessary incident of politics—except doing public work to the best of my ability. Why should I go where the doing of public work will only make me hated . . . and where I can gain reputation and credit by practising arts which I detest to acquire popularity?

Similar to his above-quoted opinion on politics is Abbott's view of his stint as prime minister. 'I am here because I am not particularly obnoxious to anybody.'

Vincent Durant, *War Horse of Cumberland*, 1985

Because he sat in the Senate, and because of his high regard for Sir John S. Thompson, Prime Minister Abbott

offered Thompson Macdonald's old rooms just outside the Commons on the way to the Library. 'Sir John, take them,' said Abbott when Thompson demurred, 'and do not disturb yourself. They belong to the Premier.' Thompson refused as gracefully as he could. Eventually in the fall, pressed by Abbott again, he relented.

One condition Abbott made was that Thompson lead in the House of Commons when and if Langevin the senior minister, stepped down. This Thompson accepted; but another request of Abbott's, that Thompson occupy Macdonald's old seat, he refused. Thompson had for some years sat with Chapleau in the second row, behind Langevin and Macdonald. Thompson preferred to stay where he was and Macdonald's seat remained, for the time being, empty, a mute tribute to his death. Only in February 1892, at the beginning of that session of Parliament, was the change finally made.

P.B. Waite, *The Man from Halifax*, 1985

SIR JOHN S. THOMPSON

A judge and former Premier of Nova Scotia, Sir John S. Thompson moved to Ottawa in 1885 as Sir John A.'s Minister of Justice. He was Canada's fourth prime minister (1893–4).

Once, while Lord Aberdeen was governor-general, Sir John Thompson was dining at Government House on an evening in June when the mosquitoes were unusually troublesome. Lady Aberdeen suggested the shutting of the windows. 'Oh! thank you,' replied Sir John, 'pray don't trouble; I think they are all in now!'

Sir Joseph Pope, *The Day of Sir John Macdonald*, 1915

A civil service custom Thompson found peculiar was the habit of eating lunch at one's desk. Even the deputy minister ate a cold lunch that way. Old hands who liked to drink kept themselves well enough reinforced with alcohol during the day so that they did not get hungry. Narrow and severe in some ways, the civil service was generous with sick leave: if a man were away a year, he was still paid. Thompson kept breaking civil service customs. For example, when the deputy minister came to discuss business, usually an hour at a time, it was so awkward to see him standing that Thompson, several days running, told him to sit down. Burbidge never did, letting on he had not heard the request. Thompson only found out in mid-January that it was standard procedure for the deputy minister to stand, not so much from deference, but to distinguish him from other callers in the minister's office.

P.B. Waite, *The Man from Halifax*, 1985

By 1894 Thompson's health was failing.

Wednesday, 12 December was a bright day, characteristic of the lingering generosity of late autumn in England, the temperature a mild, equable 50 degrees or so; primulas still bloomed, and in sheltered gardens even a few roses. It was the day of Thompson's official swearing in as a member of Her Majesty's Privy Council. The only other Canadian admitted had been Sir John A. Macdonald, the result of his work for the Treaty of Washington in 1871. Thompson's had been for the Bering Sea arbitration. Thompson dressed with care; the invitation said 'plain morning dress'; that meant black knee-breeches and black silk stockings. That expensive Windsor uniform could wait for a while! A special train of the Great Western Railway would leave Paddington at twelve noon for Windsor. Paddington station was just north of Kensington Gardens; Thompson was there half an hour before train time, the first of the party to arrive. He seemed in good health; he told Mrs Sanford the previous morning that he felt better than he had for months. . . .

The train journey to Windsor took under an hour. The cermony of the Privy Council was set for 1:15 P.M., under the superintendence of the Lord Steward of Windsor, the Marquis of Breadalbane, six years younger than Thompson. . . . Despite later rumours to the contrary, it was not a long cere- mony, which was fortunate, for the Marquis of Ripon was sixty-six years old and Queen Victoria was not fond of allowing any of the company to sit down. The whole affair took not much more than twenty minutes. Notwithstanding, Thompson seemed rather crushed by the strain. It then appeared that he had not slept well the previous night but had made little mention of it. The company adjourned to the Octagon Room for lunch; after Thompson was seated, but before he had touched any food, he fainted. Lord Breadalbane and a servant helped him to a writing room nearby. There he sat down, his head in his hands, was given some water and the marquis sent for brandy. Thompson revived somewhat but was distressed at having made a scene, remarking to Lord Breadalbane, 'It seems too weak and foolish to faint like this.' Breadalbane replied sensibly, 'One does not faint on purpose. Pray don't distress your- self. . . .' Thompson wanted him to return to the Octagon Room, but Bread- albane waited until Thompson felt better then accompanied him back. Breadalbane offered his arm but Thompson walked in unaided, saying cheer- fully, 'I'm all right now, thank you.' It was about 1:45 P.M. In the meantime the queen's doctor, Dr Reid, had been sent for and arrived as Thompson again sat to lunch, and took a place beside him. Thompson mentioned that he had had pain in his chest. Suddenly, without a sound he collapsed, half against the doctor. The luncheon stopped abruptly; Dr Reid administered brandy and felt for Thompson's pulse. There was none. Thompson was dead.

Ibid.

SIR MACKENZIE BOWELL

Canada's fifth prime minister, from 1894 to 1896, Sir Mackenzie Bowell was a journalist from Belleville, Ontario, and a prominent Orangeman. He entered the House as a Conservative in 1867 and held several cabinet portfolios before being elevated to the Senate in 1892. Here is an early glimpse of him in the Commons in the mid-1880s.

When two quick-tempered men clash the sparks are apt to fly. Years ago, when M.C. Cameron, of Goderich, sat in Parliament, he was the champion heckler on the Liberal side. He could be real nasty, although I always thought he was moved wholly by the spirit of mischief. In private life he was one of the most amiable of men.

Late one night when the customs estimates were being considered Cameron didn't seem to like some of Hon. Mackenzie Bowell's answers to his questions. So he lost his patience, and, I think quite unintentionally, flatly contradicted something Bowell had presented as a fact. The latter, perhaps unduly sensitive as to his veracity, cried out:

'Does the honorable gentleman call me a liar?'

Cameron may not have caught the question, and answered in words that implied the affirmative. Bowell sprang into action at once. Seizing a glass filled with ice water, he started to hurl it across the floor at his tormentor, but a benign and opportune Providence saved him from this act of violence. Sitting right behind him his head resting on his outstretched arms, Henry N. Paint, of Cape Breton, was peacefully asleep. As Bowell swung the tumbler backward, its cold contents got down Paint's neck. With a yell, the sleeper sprang to his feet and proceeded to give a fantastic imitation of a man swimming for his life. Arrested by the yell, Bowell turned around, and when he saw the antics of the little old chap, he stayed his hand. A tragedy was averted. Bowell was a journalist, and the free masonry of the craft saw to it that not a syllable of this incident got into print.

Fred Cook, 'Giants and Jesters in Public Life', National Archives of Canada, n.d.

Col. J.B. Maclean, founder of Maclean's Magazine *and* Maclean Hunter Publications,

tried to persuade Sir Mackenzie Bowell, Prime Minister of Canada from December 1894 to April 1896, to reopen negotiations with Newfoundland for joining the Dominion. He came into the picture this way: Sir William White-way, Newfoundland's long-time Premier, and the man responsible for spanning the island with a railway, had come to Ottawa in 1895 to seek Bowell's support for a series of discussions concerning union. The Island government had been in a poverty-stricken condition for many years, and appeals to its sovereign authority, the British cabinet in London, met with only partial relief, grudgingly given. Most Canadians, especially public leaders, knew the situation and were concerned. Yet Bowell (a type who reserved his strength for the whim of the moment) curtly dismissed the visitor and his project, refusing even to submit the suggestions to cabinet.

Disappointed and frustrated, Whiteway was brought by a mutual friend— an advertiser in *Canadian Grocer*—to see Maclean in Montreal. If Canada would assume Newfoundland's debt of some $750,000, the Premier declared, the Island colony would readily agree to joining Canada. Maclean was impressed. Here was a deal of the greatest importance for the long future. Bowell, thought Maclean, could not have understood the significance of his decision; after all, he was a busy man with many problems, but as a former editor and still publisher-owner of the Belleville, Ontario, *Intelligencer*, as well as a long-service militiaman, surely he could be persuaded to give some consideration to round-ing out a nation.

So Maclean hurried to Ottawa and pleaded the case with the Prime Minister. The effort was totally wasted. Maclean never forgave Bowell and never forgot. When Newfoundland finally joined Canada as the tenth province in 1949, John Bayne Maclean was probably the only man alive who could explain exactly how and why it had *not* happened a half-century before.

Floyd S. Chalmers, A Gentleman of the Press, 1969

SIR CHARLES TUPPER

After dissatisfaction with Bowell forced a change, Sir Charles Tupper became Canada's sixth prime minister in May 1896, lasting a scant ten weeks. A doughty Nova Scotian, Tupper left provincial politics to become a Conservative MP in Ottawa in 1867, and held several cabinet posts in the governments of Sir John A.

Tupper's aggressiveness and lack of tact occasionally irked his leader. For close to two years the two men rarely spoke to each other; the result of a disagree-ment over Tupper's insistence that Macdonald send government business to a law firm set up by their sons in Winnipeg. When Tupper insisted, Macdonald had to become adamant, stating that he wouldn't have a gun placed at his head, even by one so close as Charles Tupper.

Vincent Durant, War Horse of Cumberland, 1985

In some Maritime provinces knights, Sir Frederick Borden, Sir Charles Tupper, the knighthoods seem to have had the effect of making them want to cover up the pressures, and the peccadilloes, that preceded and followed that precious 'Sir'. Tupper was known in the county across the celebrated Missaguash river, (the boundary between New Brunswick and Nova Scotia) as 'the ram of Cumberland County'. I have found only a little evidence to back up this sturdy sobriquet, and oral tradition in matters such as these is notoriously treacherous. My information is, however, that Tupper's adventures on the Intercolonial Railway between Amherst and Ottawa had become sufficiently well known in government circles that a porter was assigned to watch Sir Charles' compartment to see that he did not get himself or the government into trouble. On getting off the train in Montreal, Sir Charles turned to the porter, thanked him for his attention, and added, 'You were watching my compartment all right, but you forgot to watch the lady's.'

P.B. Waite, 'An Historian's Adventures in Archivia and Beyond', *Papers of the Bibliographical Society of Canada*, 1973, vol. 12, 1974

Secure in his position as one of the Fathers of Confederation, Tupper served as Canadian High Commissioner to the United Kingdom from 1884 to 1887, and again from 1888 until he was recalled in 1896, to rally the Tories, replace Bowell, and fight the losing electoral battle of that year against Laurier.

Mr Harris L. Adams has given, in the pages of the 'Farmers' Magazine', a graphic description of . . . when Sir Charles was High Commissioner for Canada in London. At that time Canadian cattle were freely admitted to Great Britain, and it appears that a consignment of them was condemned at the landing-wharves in Liverpool on the ground that some of the animals were affected with pleuro-pneumonia. The agent in Liverpool to whom the condemned cattle had been consigned, reported by cable to the shipper in Canada that the whole of the shipment would have to be slaughtered, because some of the steers were tainted with the dreaded disease. The shipper at once cabled to Sir Charles Tupper for advice.

Sir Charles was busy in his office shortly after the opening hours on the Thursday on which the cablegram was received. It was handed to him by his secretary, Mr Colmer. The usual course in such a case would have involved a certain amount of red tape and circumlocution. But Sir Charles disregarded precedents and procedure. He inquired from his secretary as to where were the nearest surgical instrument shops, and the nearest bookseller's who supplied medical books. He told him to reserve him a compartment on the first train to Liverpool. At the bookseller's Sir Charles got the latest works on the diseases of cattle, put them in his hansom cab, and was driven rapidly to the surgical instrument maker's. He emerged with a big case of instruments, and when he reached Euston station dashed along the platform with the books under one arm and the surgical instruments under the other. Colmer was in readiness for him, handed him his ticket, and saw him safe into his compartment. On the way down Sir Charles, so to speak, tore the heart out of the books so far as they related to the disease in question. By the time he reached Liverpool he was well up in the knowledge of pleuro-pneumonia.

Arrived there he drove immediately to the cattle yards and asked to see the condemned cattle that had recently arrived from Canada. Then he called for the inspectors who had condemned them. Sir Charles put each of them through a sharp examination. He made each one define his reasons for his action. Going again to the yards the inspectors were requested to point out an animal which they considered was affected. Each was asked to state what would be found, on dissection, to be the condition of the lungs and other organs of the body. Each man was pinned down to exact details. Then Sir Charles ordered that the condemned animal should be slaughtered. He then rolled up his sleeves and dissected the various parts—doing this with a thoroughness that left no opening for uncertainty. Another and yet another animal were brought in and subjected to the same operations. No symptom whatever of disease was found, and by the evening he had proved that the inspectors had been quite erroneous in their conjectures. Sir Charles left the cattle yard in triumph, and had the pleasure of writing to the Canadian shipper that his cattle were all right. 'As for the Liverpool inspectors,' says Mr Adams, 'they made no more condemnation of Canadian cattle lest, as they said, "that old devil from London should blow down here again".'

'Biographical Sketch', in Political Reminiscences of The Right Honourable
Sir Charles Tupper, Bart., ed. W.A. Harkin, 1914

It was a losing battle against Laurier in 1896, but none fought it harder than Tupper.

Hector Charlesworth, a noted Canadian journalist of the day, . . . gives an account of Tupper's involvement in the election in Ontario:

> He was reputed to be an egotist who used the first personal pronoun too abundantly in reviewing his notable past. So soon as he would open his mouth on the platform, a gang would start shouting, 'I, I, I' and keep it up all evening. In Orange centres also the populace was greatly inflamed against him for his willingness to impose separate schools in Manitoba, and heartily joined in the chorus.

One particularly bad scene occurred at Massey Hall, Toronto, where, as Charlesworth describes it: 'I shall never forget the sight of the grand old stalwart on the platform . . . for two hours declaming the speech he had set himself to deliver against a constant din of meaningless interruptions, for the Liberals had their "Cheer-leaders" to drown him out of every part of the hall. It was impossible to hear him, even at a distance of less than ten feet.'

That evening, June 19, Tupper had dined with John Beverley Robinson, an old friend who had been mayor of the city and Lieutenant-Governor of Ontario. Unknown to Tupper, his friend, who had accompanied him to the hall, died just before Tupper began to talk. So while upstairs Tupper fought the mob, in the basement his friend was laid out. As Charlesworth related it:

> Sir Charles knew nothing of this until after he sat down exhausted, when a friend whispered it to him. He braced himself, and left the scene giving no sign of emotion. The reporters knew of the incident, however; and it was horrible to

think of the unseemly riot going on above, while the body of one of Toronto's most distinguished sons lay stark below.

But if the old man of the Conservative party had to take abuse, he was also able to give it. Frustrated by the heckling, he turned on his attackers with: 'You men who are making these interruptions are the most block-headed set of cowards that I ever looked upon.' Coming from a man nearing his 75th birthday, this elicited a large uproar, and a cry of 'rub it in, old man'.

Vincent Durant, *War Horse of Cumberland*, 1985

SIR WILFRID LAURIER

Canada's seventh prime minister, from 1896 to 1911, Sir Wilfrid Laurier was elected to the House of Commons as Liberal MP for Arthabaska in 1874. In 1875 Laurier wrote to his friend James Young lamenting the opposition of the Ultramontanes to the Quebec Liberals. The Ultramontanes were extreme right-wing Catholics who demanded the supremacy of the Catholic Church over civil society and denounced liberalism in all its forms.

With . . . the Church more truculent than ever, . . . the search for new leadership among the *Rouges* of Quebec was desperate. There was little pleasure at the moment in the thought that it was centring on Arthabaska. 'As to myself,' Laurier wrote Young, 'I have the bones and sinew of the Liberal party. They push me ahead and would have me take a more active part in politics than I have done hitherto. I, however, feel very reluctant to do it. I am at present quiet and happy. The moment I accept office I will go into it actively and earnestly, and from that moment my quiet and happiness will be gone. It will be a war with the clergy, a war of every day, of every moment. . . . Political strifes are bitter enough in your province, but you have no idea of what it is with us . . . I will be denounced as Anti-Christ. You may laugh at that, but it is no laughing matter to us.'

Joseph Schull, *Laurier: The First Canadian*, 1965

Religion and politics have always been a volatile mixture, not least in Quebec.

One incident in the [1877] campaign it always gave Mr Laurier much pleasure to recall. A good supporter of his listened attentively one Sunday to a sermon in which his curé denounced Liberal Catholics. On the Monday he sought out the curé and asked whether it would be possible for a good Catholic to vote for a Liberal. 'No: impossible,' was the reply. Next Sunday, the curé, more discreet, exhorted his flock to vote according to their conscience. 'But', the query followed, 'my conscience tells me to vote for Mr Laurier; and yet you say if I vote for a Liberal it will be a sin. I think I must not vote at all.' The third Sunday brought a sermon denouncing political indifference, and insisting that it was the duty of good citizens to vote and not leave the suffrage to the uninformed and evil-minded. 'My curé,' responded the puzzled voter next morning, 'I cannot vote for Mr Laurier, for you tell me that if I vote for a Liberal I shall be damned; I cannot vote for Mr Bourbeau, for you tell me that if I do not follow my conscience I shall be damned; I cannot vote for neither, for you tell me that if I do not vote at all I shall be damned. Since I must be damned anyway, I'll be damned for doing what I like. I am going to vote for Mr Laurier.'

Oscar Douglas Skelton, Life and Letters of Sir Wilfrid Laurier, vol. 1, 1922

The influence of churches on voting, of course, could be a two-way street, as shown in this example from Ontario during the campaign of 1896.

One defeated Liberal candidate, himself a Protestant, reported a double-barrelled shot by a Methodist minister, who 'while declaiming in thundering tones against clerical influence in Quebec had the effrontery to declare that a ballot marked for me will stare the voter in the face at the Judgment Day, and condemn him to eternal perdition.'

G.P. deT. Glazebrook, A History of Canadian Political Thought, 1966

After succeeding Edward Blake as Liberal leader in 1887, Laurier toured Ontario during the summer of 1888 to reveal himself to the largest English-speaking wing of the party.

Mr Laurier's only serious addresses were delivered at Cannington and Guelph. Again and again during those summer days in Muskoka and throughout his leisurely journey across the Province, Laurier insisted that a French Canadian and a Roman Catholic could not hope to secure the common allegiance of Liberals in the English Provinces. Again and again he protested that his elevation to the leadership could be no more than a temporary expedient. In his speeches he declared that he was only a tenant of the office of leader until Mr Blake's restoration to health, and there can be no doubt that this was his hope and expectation. As a consequence he was not as aggressive nor as authoritative as could be desired. I did not think that he made a strong impression upon the meetings which he addressed. There was a lack of vigour and confidence. There was no energy in his deliverance. Nor was even the attraction of personality which was his great possession fully displayed. Only at Cannington did he reveal his actual quality. An Anglican clergyman with gross discourtesy arose in the meeting and shouted that they could not learn the true way from a Roman Catholic. Laurier retorted with passionate energy, 'You could—in politics,' and he proceeded in sentences of stern rebuke to flog the interrupter into humiliation and silence. The rest of the speech was animated and confident, in contrast to the tame and listless spirit in which most of it was spoken. I had the impudence to tell the leader that he should engage the belligerent divine to attend and interrupt at subsequent meetings.

Sir John Willison, *Reminiscences Political and Personal*, 1919

Laurier shared the obsession of Abraham Lincoln with national unity. He was an intense admirer of Honest Abe and his personal library contained many biographies of the US president. At Montreal in 1889, Laurier delivered a lecture in French on Lincoln, which included this translation of the Gettysburg Address.

'Voici maintenant quatre-vingt-sept ans, que nos pères fondèrent sur ce continent une nation, conçue dans la liberté et consacrée à l'idée que tous les hommes ont été créés égaux. Nous sommes maintenant engagés dans une guerre civile, dont l'issue doit décider si cette nation, ou toute nation ainsi conçue, ainsi consacrée peut durer longtemps. Nous nous rencontrons sur un des grands champs de bataille de cette guerre. Nous sommes venus pour consacrer une portion de ce champ de bataille, comme la dernière demeure de ceux qui ici ont donné leur vie, pour que cette nation vécût. Il est tout à fait convenable et juste que nous fassions ceci. Mais dans un sens plus large, nous ne pouvons ni consacrer, ni sanctifier ce sol. Les braves soldats, vivants et morts, qui ont combattu ici, l'ont impregné d'une consécration bien au-dessus de tout pouvoir d'y rien ajouter, ou d'en rien retrancher. Ce qui sera dit ici, le monde le remarquera peu et ne s'en souviendra pas longtemps, mais ce qu'ils ont fait ici le monde ne l'oubliera jamais. C'est plutôt pour nous, les vivants, d'être ici consacrés à l'oeuvre inachevée que ceux qui ont combattu ici, ont si noblement commencée. C'est plutôt à nous ici qu'il appartient d'être consacrés à la grande tâche qui reste devant nous, afin que de ces morts glorieux, nous prenions un nouveau dévouement à la cause pour laquelle ils ont donné la dernière et la plus complète mesure de dévouement; afin que nous prenions ici la solennelle résolution que ces morts ne seront pas morts en vain: que cette nation, par la volonté de Dieu, recevra un nouveau baptême de la liberté, et que le gouvernement du peuple par le peuple et pour le peuple ne périra pas de la terre.'

Alfred D. DeCelles, *Discours de Sir Wilfrid Laurier*, 1920

When Sir John A. Macdonald died in June 1891, Laurier pronounced a eulogy in the House with feeling, and concluded with this Lincolnesque prose.

It may indeed happen, Sir, when the Canadian people see the ranks thus gradually reduced and thinned of those upon whom they have been in the habit of relying for guidance, that a feeling of apprehension will creep into the heart lest, perhaps, the institutions of Canada be imperilled. Before the grave of him who, above all, was the Father of Confederation, let not grief be barren grief; but let grief be coupled with the resolution, the determination, that the work in which Liberals and Conservatives, in which Brown and Macdonald united, shall not perish, but that though United Canada may be deprived of the services of her greatest men, still Canada shall and will live.

House of Commons, *Debates*, 8 June 1891

Laurier's intellectual mistress was Emilie Lavergne, wife of his former law partner in Arthabasca. His friendship with Emilie was very close. Although Laurier had no children by his wife, Zoë, it was rumoured widely that Emilie's child, Armand, was Laurier's natural son, for he bore a strong physical resemblance to Sir Wilfrid.

Everything that was playful and affectionate in [Laurier] came out when he spoke of little Gabrielle, the Lavergnes' daughter. It was Armand, however, who intrigued and fascinated him and filled him with fatherly concern. 'That little man', he wrote, after the boy had visited him in Ottawa, 'is full of magnetism, winning and attractive, and at the same time so frank, so outspoken, so clever and also so ready-witted . . . in a few years, when grown up to manhood, with his naturally refined and reserved manners, with his expressiveness of countenance, and with . . . attention to his person which he now neglects but which will come with age, he will undoubtedly be a man not in a thousand, but in a million.'

Armand astonished his great friend by the lightness and ease with which he disposed of a considerable store of information. 'Quite naturally, quite unconsciously . . . he shoots off a remark here and a remark there which cause you to pause and wonder. What is more remarkable yet is the promptness and aptness of his repartees. This is his mother all over.'

The boy was lazy, and it worried Laurier. He refused to learn English and had learned to make a cause of it, describing himself to his mother as 'your son who will always be a patriot'. Laurier laughed at the sentiment. 'Happy age, is it not, when there can be so much enthusiasm for a cause so little deserving it.' On the practical side of the matter, however, he delivered a strong homily.

'Tell him that above everything else he must apply himself to learn English, that it is absolutely essential for such an intense French Canadian as he is; that it is the absolute condition which will enable him, some day, to defend the rights and privileges of his race. That ought to fetch him, I am sure . . . I would want him, when he is twenty, to be as familiar with one language as the other. You know and I know the great advantage it would be to him . . . at twenty, could he speak and write English as currently and fluently as French, his start in the world would be immeasurably advanced.'

Joseph Schull, *Laurier: The First Canadian*, 1965

Amaryllis, the Ottawa social columnist of Saturday Night *magazine, frequently commented on the activities of Lady Laurier and Emilie Lavergne, and was an important source for Sandra Gwyn's charming book* The Private Capital.

Since life doesn't unfold in straight lines, it is simplistic to suggest that Zoë's rising star pushed Emilie's into eclipse. . . .

Rather, although we cannot know for certain, what seems to have happened is that somewhere around the turn of the century, Emilie began to overplay her hand. Perhaps she presumed too much, offering Laurier advice he did not need and trying to intrude into the running of the government. It may even have been, as Amaryllis drops a fleeting hint, that the two disagreed sharply over Laurier's decision to send troops to South Africa during the Boer War. . . . But it is possible, indeed is probable, that Emilie was, in Amaryllis's words, 'the brilliant French Canadian lady who for love of notoriety pretends to entertain pro-Boer sentiments', who in December 1900 caused a fearful contretemps at a viceregal dinner party by haranguing the visiting young war hero, Winston Churchill. As corroborative evidence, Armand, in one of his '*Vive les Boers!*' letters to Emilie, dated June 18, 1901, tossed out the phrase, '*Comment est Kruger?*' which suggests that Emilie had named a pet dog or cat or canary after the South African prime minister.

In any event, sometime during this period, Laurier sent a messenger from his office to Emilie, with a package containing all the letters that she had written to him. It is also at this time that references to Emilie in the columns of Amaryllis begin to thin out noticeably. Befittingly, on the very last night of the old century, December 31, 1900, we find her shining in all her old glory, 'wearing a smart gown of black crêpe de Chine over cerise satin', chaperoning a gala debutante ball, along with five other prominent society ladies. We do not find her again until the following June 15, in an entry that, knowing what we know now, and as perhaps Amaryllis knew at the time, reads almost as an epitaph:

> Mr Justice [Joseph] Lavergne and his family are leaving next week to take up their residence permanently in Montreal. Mme Lavergne is one of the most charming women in Ottawa society, and everyone laments her departure.

Laurier, in what must have been a deliberate act of disentanglement, had transferred Joseph to the Montreal bench. The move was designed to look like a promotion and it increased Joseph's salary by $1000 annually. In the parting from Emilie, no lover could have been gentler. 'May you be happy in this new place which you now enter,' Laurier wrote to her on September 18, 1901. 'If it be in my power to help, never fail to come to me as a friend, an ever true, warm and sincere friend.' On November 29, in a letter occasioned by his sixtieth birthday, he sounded as if he regretted the new arrangement. 'Though there is now a long distance between us, my dear friend, I do not for one single moment forget you. . . . The friendship of the past has been too close to be followed by an absolute separation . . . I cannot help regretting the good old times.'   Sandra Gwyn, *The Private Capital*, 1984

Laurier's oratory in either language was eloquent, but not casual.

In the old House of Commons the seats rose from the floor at a more acute angle than in the present House, and there were about eight desks to every row. Sitting in the row behind Sir Wilfrid I had often noticed that, when one of the Ministers was putting through his supply, he would produce from underneath his desk a large volume which he seemed to peruse very carefully. I discovered one night on asking him that it was a book containing a splendid collection of idioms and phrases in English and French and that by his continuous reading of them he kept his mind stored with the apt words which he could use so gracefully and eloquently when he spoke, as he frequently did, purely extemporaneously.

E.M. MacDonald, *Recollections: Political and Personal*, 1938

His speaking tour of the West in 1910 brought Laurier into touch with some interesting people.

He came by Melville, Lanigan, Humboldt, and Prince Albert to Saskatoon, with the cheers of Germans, Frenchmen, Italians, Scandinavians, Poles, Armenians, Galicians, Doukhobors, and Russian Jews ringing in his ears. Saskatoon, the village of a hundred people five years before, was now a city of fourteen thousand, an Athens along the Saskatchewan, building its own university. Under a forest of bunting Laurier laid the cornerstone and told the crowd of a lad he had met that morning by the name of John Diefenbaker. 'You have some remarkable newsboys here. This one talked to me for half an hour at the railway station and then said, "Well, Mr Prime Minister, I can't waste any more time. I have to deliver my papers." '

Joseph Schull, *Laurier: The First Canadian*, 1965

Sir Wilfrid was a kindly, gentle soul, but he had also both moral and physical courage. His moral courage was demonstrated in the early days of his political life when he defied the Quebec hierarchy. After the burning of the Parliamentary buildings in February 1916, the session was resumed the next day in the Victoria Museum. It was at the height of the First Great War and naturally it was generally believed at the time that the buildings were set on fire by Germans. As a result there was a lot of senseless excitement. A proposal was advanced that the public should be excluded from the galleries of the temporary House of Commons. Sir Wilfrid was approached as to his views. He was adamant against such an idea. He said that the sessions of Parliament were the Grand Assizes of the Nation and the people had an immemorial right to attend these sessions and that right must not be interfered with. 'But,' pleaded the Speaker of the House, 'Sir Wilfrid, some criminal or crazy person may get in the gallery and throw a bomb down on our heads.'

Laurier drew himself up and replied: 'My dear sir, when you entered politics you took the risk of being hit by a bomb some day and that risk you will have to continue to run.' The galleries were not closed.

Arthur R. Ford, As the World Wags On, 1950

WILLIAM S. FIELDING

A Halifax journalist, William S. Fielding was Premier of Nova Scotia from 1884 to 1896, and Minister of Finance in Laurier's government from 1896 to 1911.

A hard worker himself, who often kept long hours, he was inconsiderate of his employees. A former secretary of Mr Fielding told me an extraordinary and almost unbelievable story in regard to him. He said that one evening at closing time Mr Fielding asked him if he could work that evening. The secretary said it was a little inconvenient as he had arranged to go to the theatre that evening. Mr Fielding urged him to cancel his engagement as it was important, which he did, 'phoning his wife and arranging for someone else to go with her in his place'. Mr Fielding, before parting, asked him the name of the show, which was starring a well-known actor.

The secretary returned to the office after dinner, but there was no Mr Fielding. He failed to turn up and the secretary delved into other work. To his amazement, after the show Mr Fielding walked into the office. 'Glad you reminded me of that show,' said Mr Fielding to the angered secretary, 'I enjoyed it immensely.'

Arthur R. Ford, As the World Wags On, 1950

In 1906, Finance Minister Fielding, with a perhaps subconscious but none the less discriminatory sense of fitness, altered the federal fiscal year. Up to then it had commenced on Dominion Day. Since then it has commenced on All-Fools' Day [April 1]. As a matter of fact, it was not long after this timely alteration that the financial trouble began and the public debt started on its upward flight towards the stratosphere.

Paul Bilkey, Persons, Papers and Things, 1940

JOSEPH HAYCOCK

A farmer-politician, Joseph Haycock led the Patrons of Industry group in the Ontario legislature from 1894 to 1902.

Haycock was a man of fine mentality, with a racy, original mode of speech, but a typical 'side-liner'. He was . . . entirely indifferent to convention and used to carry a large pair of wire cutters to tear off his chewing tobacco with. He explained that his teeth were getting too worn to bite it, and that one was always dropping and losing pen-knives; whereas with a pair of wire-cutters, the noise they made when they dropped was a safeguard against loss. At the time of which I speak, a quarter of a century or more ago, his teeth were incisive enough for all practical uses.

Hector Charlesworth, Candid Chronicles, 1925

SIR JAMES WHITNEY

Sir James Whitney was Conservative Premier of Ontario from 1905 to 1914.

One of the more ludicrous episodes in connection with the Speakership occurred under the Whitney regime, when a much respected but not very literate member held the post. He was drowsing in his Chair one night with his three-cornered hat awry, while Judge Duncan Ross of Elgin, a son of the former Premier and at that time member for West Middlesex in the Legislature, was speaking. Some Conservative banteringly shouted 'Order, Order!' The speaker suddenly woke up and said solemnly 'The Member for West Middlesex is out of order'. Ross at once asked, 'Mr Speaker in what respect am I out of order?' The gentleman on the dais was candid and remarked slowly 'I don't just know; but if you'll kindly repeat what you were saying I'll tell you.'

Hector Charlesworth, More Candid Chronicles, 1928

Although progressive in some areas, Whitney had firm negative opinions on giving the vote to women in 1906.

Whitney absolutely refused to countenance the grant of a provincial vote to some female Ontarians. John Smith, the member for Peel, attempted to get the legislature to contemplate, in a serious manner, giving the franchise to 'widows and spinsters qualified to vote in municipal elections'. Smith, in moving his motion, argued that 'women paid taxes, and that 90 per cent of the public school teachers looking after child tuition were women'. The premier, in turn, accused the unfortunate Smith of 'making a football of women's status in a way discreditable to himself . . . and a direct insult to women'. But he was less than clear in explaining the thinking that lay back of such remarks. Nevertheless, the Tory chief took the lead in giving the proposed measure short shrift, as his words to end the debate indicate: 'Now, if five members will stand up we can have a vote on it. Let us play the farce out.' In fact, nine stood for the measure, but sixty-six rose against it. Whitney, who thought women should not be exposed to 'the unlovely influence of party politics', could be satisfied.

Charles W. Humphries, 'Honest Enough To Be Bold': The Life and Times of
Sir James Pliny Whitney, 1985

On 25 January 1911, in response to federal leader Robert Borden's request for help in designing Conservative strategy against Laurier's policy of economic reciprocity with the United States, Whitney presented

embryonic arguments that could be developed and used against the reciprocity proposal, at least in Ontario: the disloyalty of the Grits; the threat to imperial unity; and the danger of annexation. Underneath Whitney's statements lay his constant concern for the future of the Empire and his ceaseless distrust of anything American. Superior British institutions in Canada were being threatened with ultimate replacement by inferior American counterparts. . . . Whitney commented that . . . 'There is no civilized country on the earth where morality of every description is at so low a level. Divorce, use of drugs, the revolver and the unwritten law are dominating forces there, and even the influences for good—and there are some—which come from there are generally tainted with some objectionable peculiarity. I hope the time will never come when our conditions "Must be nearer American conditions than Old World conditions".' John Strachan could not have said it better. In another instance, the premier's anti-Americanism led him to ridicule events south of the border: 'It is only a short time ago that one Legislature passed a resolution permitting the eating of pea-nuts during debates by the members, and another that the sheets of all hotel beds should be nine feet long. There are numbers of other instances which I could give you showing clearly the abnormal mental condition of the people.' It would be well worth a fight to avoid such a fate for Canada, or at least Ontario.

Ibid.

SIR CHARLES HIBBERT TUPPER

Son of Sir Charles Tupper, Sir Charles Hibbert Tupper sat as a Conservative MP from Nova Scotia and was Minister of Marine and Fisheries in Sir John A.'s cabinet from 1888 to 1891. In this story the word 'fixed' is a synonym for 'impregnated'.

'Once I was trying for election in Pictou (on Cape Breton). The election was hard fought but I won. However, I was subsequently unseated because some of my friends had been overenthusiastic in their support. Another strenuous election followed and again I was elected. After this I thought I ought to follow Sir John's example and call on all my supporters in the constituency and inquire about their families and so on. So I started. I went up to old John and I asked, 'How is your mare these days? Is the spavin all right?' and then to the next one to ask about his invalid wife and so on. Finally I called on one old man who was sitting on his porch. How's your sciatica? I asked him. Better he said. I inquired about his wife and then, 'How's your daughter Jane?' Immediately I saw I had made a mistake. His face fell and he looked very glum. I made as if to go away, but he said, 'My daughter Jane. She's been fixed!' I didn't know what to say, but he went on explosively, 'I wouldn't have minded so much if it hadn't of been a damned Grit that done it!'

Escott Reid papers, 'Canadian Politics: Notes and Interviews',
National Archives of Canada

JOHN ROBSON

John Robson was Liberal Premier of British Columbia from 1889 to 1892.

When 'Honest John' Robson was passing through Revelstoke on his election tour, he was met at the train by Pot Hole Kellie, then a candidate in the forthcoming election. 'Step off and meet some of my friends,' Kellie coaxed. And, when the unsuspecting premier obliged, Kellie said, 'Jump into one of these two comfortable rigs. While you ride around town you can talk over the mining laws with a few of our delegation. We are anxious to hear your point of view.'

They gave Honest John such a long ride around town that he missed his train. Then Kellie's vigilantes lodged the premier comfortably at a hotel and promised to put him on the next train west if he would co-operate. 'Now that we've heard your views privately, we'll arrange for you to hear ours publicly.'

They hired a hall and circulated handbills and posters urging all miners to attend a meeting to protest against Robson's 'injurious' legislation. Kellie and his friends whipped their capacity audience into a frenzy while the premier sat, unseen, at the sidelines. Then the chairman announced: 'Gentlemen, meet John Robson.'

The premier quickly captured the audience with his charming sincerity. 'I have been shown, beyond a doubt, that my party's legislation has been a blunder,' he said. Then, making a promise he was soon to keep, he said he would appoint two West Kootenay men to draft a new mining act. One of them was Pot Hole Kellie.

Kellie won a seat in the 1890 election, and was re-elected in the next general election. He died in Victoria in 1927. Today he is best remembered not as a kidnapper but as an honest man who helped to frame the B.C. Mining Act.

Ed Arrol, 'Canadianecdote', *Maclean's*, 1 July 1961

WILLIAM PATERSON

First elected as Liberal MP for Brant in 1872, William Paterson served as Minister of Customs in Laurier's government from 1897 to 1911.

As long as I can remember it has been an unwritten rule that a Minister of the Crown in Canada shall, once a year at least, extend some sort of hospitality to the party followers in Parliament. This usually takes the form of dinners or luncheons, large or small. Not always, however, were the guests confined to party supporters. Sir John Macdonald frequently invited some of his opponents to his dinners, and Sir Wilfrid Laurier, when he was Prime Minister, followed suit.

I first met the Hon. William Paterson, better known as 'Billy', when I came to Ottawa as junior for the Mail in 1883. We were both boarding at the Windsor Hotel, and it was there that I came to know him intimately. Mr Paterson was a stalwart of stalwarts of the Liberal party. He was blessed with a voice like a foghorn. It was said of him that when he 'got going' in the House against the Tories, his friends in Brantford had no difficulty in hearing him, although the telephone in those days was in the incipient stage of its development, and the radio was not born. . . .

The course of legislation travelled along quietly during the first few years of the Laurier regime. There were the customary party fights and there was the usual entertaining. But after three or four years it was observed that while the Hon. William attended all the social functions, he did not offer to act as host at one. This may have been due to ignorance of what was expected of him, or to his Scotch forbears. Anyway it devolved upon Jim Sutherland, the Chief Liberal Whip, to point out the path of social duty to 'Billy'. In justice to the Minister of Customs, be it said he was astounded at his remissness, once it was pointed out to him, and he immediately instructed the Chief Whip to repair his oversight. He gave authority to Mr Sutherland to arrange for the very best dinner that could be given, and to invite every member of the Senate and House of Commons in the Liberal ranks. As this meant one hundred and fifty or sixty guests and, as neither the restaurant of the Senate nor the House of Commons could accommodate more than eighty, it was decided to give two dinners instead of one. Mr Paterson stipulated that no intoxicating liquor must be served—only ginger ale, Radnor or 'Polly'. Jim Sutherland, being a busy man, invoked the assistance of two of the Junior Whips, both of whom came from the far West, to arrange the details.

The dinners were held in the Senate restaurant, and I had the good fortune to be invited to the first one. Sam Barnett was the restaurateur, and two days before the first function he was instructed to get fifty or sixty ginger ale bottles, have them carefully washed, and then half fill them with Seagram's whisky, topping off each bottle with ginger ale.

The eventful evening arrived. The 'strengthened' ginger ale was served to every guest except those at the head table, although I understand one was slipped to Sir Richard Cartwright, who was sitting on the right of the host and had been let into the secret. Within an hour the gathering had reached the acme of hilarity. Such a din had never been heard at a 'soft-drink' dinner. The Hon. 'Billy' beamed upon his guests, filled with delight at the success of his entertainment.

Presently he turned to Sir Richard and remarked:

'I have been a teetotaller all my life, as you know, Sir Richard, and I have always said that a man can get as jolly on ginger ale as on strong liquor.'

Sir Richard politely acquiesced, but had hard work in choking back his laughter. He repeated Mr Paterson's remark to two or three friends next day, and it was from one of these that I heard it.

Sam Barnett's bill for the dinner was not as large as one would have expected, although I was told that Mr Paterson expressed surprise at the large number of bottles of ginger ale that had been consumed. Mr Joseph Seagram was then Conservative member for North Waterloo and, although not an invited guest, as an evidence of good-will, he caused a couple of cases of V.O. to be forwarded to the Junior Whips for use at the banquet. And it was.

Fred Cook, Fifty Years Ago and Since, National Archives of Canada, n.d.

SIR CLIFFORD SIFTON

More than any other, Sir Clifford Sifton was the man associated with the immigration policies that filled the prairie west. He was Minister of the Interior in Laurier's cabinet from 1896 to 1905.

'In my judgement,' he told the House of Commons,' the immigration work has to be carried on in the same manner as the sale of any commodity; just as soon as you stop advertising and missionary work the movement is going to stop.'

D.J. Hall, Clifford Sifton, vol. 1, 1981

Indeed, the department was prepared to underwrite the production of 'editorial articles' for insertion in foreign newspapers. As Sifton put it, these would be articles

referring to Canada and incidentally giving information about Canada of such a nature as an English paper would be willing to publish and would consider to be interesting to its readers and also incidentally *not doing any injury* to the present administration.

Ibid.

With immigration were often associated discrimination and racism.

The Chinese had entered the province [British Columbia] because of the lack of an adequate supply of labour at a time when it was needed to build the railway and to develop the natural resources. Employers saw the Chinese as providing cheap and plentiful labour; the white labourer resented the Chinese who were willing to work cheaper. The political parties had to adopt an anti-Oriental stand or lose the labour vote, even though it meant that the wives of some politicians would have to forfeit the services of an Oriental scullery hand. Many members of the legislature were large employers and naturally wanted to block anti-Oriental legislation; others whose positions were less ambiguous were eager to take full advantage of the issue. Protests and petitions against the Chinese continued even after immigration fell to less than 700 persons a year after 1886 and after many left the province upon completion of the Canadian Pacific. And when the legislature in 1891 requested the federal government to raise the head tax to $200, it was also the occasion for the first protest against the entry of the Japanese, as an amendment to the motion asked that the Japanese also be taxed. From that year onwards, the Japanese were lumped together with the Chinese in the minds of most of the legislators who attempted to restrict in one way or another the entry of immigrants from Asia or their employment in the province.

Ken Adachi, *The Enemy That Never Was*, 1976

The Ukrainians were the prototype of 'Sifton's peasant in a sheepskin coat', which became the general image of the type of immigrant flooding into the Prairies in the early years of this century. Early colonization officers' reports were full of complaints about the difficulties encountered in settling 'The Galicians', 'The Bukovinans', 'The Ruthenians', . . . etc. Such complaints may have stemmed merely from the numerical preponderance of such people However, when it came to establishing and administering public school systems in the newly created Prairie Provinces, the Ukrainians certainly were perceived by the authorities as presenting a special problem. For a long time they resisted or sabotaged all attempts to establish local schools, refused non-Ukrainian teachers, and forced the establishment of special institutions to train 'Ruthenians' as school teachers, who then often turned round and taught classes in the Ukrainian language. Paul Yuzyk explains this early opposition by Ukrainians to English-language schools and teachers as stemming from their resistance to

> instruments of assimilation employed to wipe out their nationality, and culture. *Mistakenly* they considered the situation analogous to the one in Galicia where the ascendant Poles forced Polish schools on the Ukrainians and denied the Ukrainian people a separate existence.

We have italicized Yuzyk's use of the word 'mistakenly' because it would appear from government records that, on the contrary, in the early period the school system of the Prairies were seen as the one possible tool for producing some degree of homogeneity out of the wide variety of peoples. During these early years Ukrainians were the victims of a considerable amount of discrimination, being called 'Bohunks', 'Hunkies' and even 'white negroes'. In addition to the problems faced by individuals, Ukrainians as a group were denounced in the public press as an inferior and undesirable element and were the objects of scornful remarks by some Anglo-Saxon leaders.

These outside pressures, coupled with memories of persecutions suffered in the Western Ukraine, caused the Ukrainians in self-defence to take an increasingly active part in public affairs. Because of their patterns of settlement, they were provided with a strong weapon—namely the bloc vote. Ukrainians were not slow to learn about the political system and its advantages. Already in 1908 a Ukrainian was elected reeve of the municipality of Stuartburn, Manitoba. By 1912 there was a Ukrainian alderman in Winnipeg. In 1913 and 1915 Ukrainians were elected to the Alberta and Manitoba legislatures respectively and by 1926 they had a member in the House of Commons at Ottawa. . . .

Ukrainians continue to quote Lord Tweedsmuir's statement in an address to a Ukrainian group in 1936, 'You will be better Canadians for being Ukrainians.'

Elizabeth Wangenheim, 'The Ukrainians: A Case Study of the "Third Force" ',
Nationalism in Canada, ed. Peter Russell, 1967

HENRI BOURASSA

Grandson of L.J. Papineau and an important nationalist leader of French Canada, Henri Bourassa opposed Laurier over Canada's participation in World War I and championed the equality of the French and English, but opposed any idea of separation for Quebec. In 1910 he founded the influential Montreal newspaper Le Devoir, *and he remained its editor until 1932.*

Mr Bourassa was acutely conscious of the development of opinion in Quebec favourable to the Liberals, and he sought to retain his hold upon his following by the tactics which in the first place had given him his following—by going to extremes and outbidding Laurier. The chief article in the Nationalist creed was that Canada was everywhere a bilingual country, French being on an equality with English in all the provinces. This contention rested upon a conglomeration of arguments, assertions, assumptions, inferences, and it was backed by thinly disguised threats of political action. The opposing contention that bilingualism had a legal basis only in Quebec and in the Dominion parliament with its services and courts was interpreted as an insult. Mr [Armand] Lavergne, the chief lieutenant of Mr Bourassa, was wont to wax furiously indignant over the suggestion, as he put it, that he must 'stay on the reservation' if he was to enjoy the privileges that he held to be equally his in whatever part of Canada he might find himself. . . .

Bourassa included Laurier in the scope of his denunciations. Laurier's loyal support of the war and his candid admonitions to the young men of his own race made him the target for Bourassa's shafts. Something more than a difference of view was reflected in Bourassa's harangues; there was in them a distillation of venom, indicating deep personal feeling. 'Laurier', he once declared in a public meeting, 'is the most nefarious man in the whole of Canada.' Bourassa hated Laurier. Laurier had too magnanimous a mind to cherish hate;

but he feared Bourassa with a fear which in the end became an obsession. He feared him because, if he only retained his position in Quebec, Liberal victory in the coming Dominion elections would not be possible. Laurier feared him still more because if Bourassa increased his hold upon the people, which was the obvious purpose of the raging, tearing Nationalist propaganda, he would be displaced from his proud position as the first and greatest of French-Canadians. Far more than a temporary term of power was at stake. It was a struggle for a niche in the temple of fame. It was a battle not only for the affection of the living generation, but for place in the historic memories of the race. Laurier, putting aside the weight of seventy-five years and donning his armour for his last fight, had two definite purposes: to win back, if he could, the prime ministership of Canada; but in any event to establish his position forever as the unquestioned, unchallenged leader of his own people. In this campaign—which covered the two years from the moment he consented to one year's extension of the life of parliament until election day in 1917—he had repeatedly to make a choice between his two purposes; and he invariably preferred the second.

J.W. Dafoe, *Laurier: A Study in Canadian Politics*, 1978

DAVID A. LAFORTUNE

Lafortune was a Liberal MP from 1909 to 1922, for Montcalm and later for Jacques Cartier.

David Lafortune was a robust man with a deep, resounding voice. He spoke both languages fluently, was quick at retort, possessed a ready wit, and eventually gained the reputation of being the 'long distance' orator of the house. His record was seven hours continuously, equalled only by Sir Charles Hibbert Tupper, who took up the same length of time in a speech on alleged mal-administration in the Yukon, but after he had spoken four hours Sir Wilfrid Laurier kindly observed that as the member for Pictou appeared tired it might be well for him to adjourn the debate. 'Charlie' Tupper was glad to avail himself of the offer, and the next afternoon he was back at his desk, thoroughly recuperated, and able to continue his address for three hours more.

But there was no such lucky break for Mr Lafortune. When he made his lengthy speech he had to plod along without any suggestion from the Prime Minister to adjourn the debate. After he had concluded Sir Wilfrid went back to the spellbinder to compliment him. In the hearing of other members of Parliament the Prime Minister said, 'Well, David, I must felicitate you on your remarkable powers of endurance. I thought you would have continued longer; you seemed good for it, but I suppose your throat troubled you.' Lafortune smiled and remarked, 'Ah, Sir Wilfrid, it was not my throat that gave out, but another part of my anatomy.'

I have referred to Mr Lafortune's ready wit and aptness in retort, but one day he got more than he had bargained for. The Speaker at that time was the Hon. Edgar Rhodes, the late minister of finance. Often, if the Speaker becomes weary with the platitudes uttered in a set debate in the House, he retires to his chambers for a little relaxation. This particular day when David was giving his views on some question of interest to Quebec, Mr Speaker was called out of the chamber, and Mr Boivin, the Deputy Speaker, not being around, Mr Rhodes asked Mr W.A. Charlton, member for Norfolk, to take the chair.

Mr Charlton was then well advanced in years. Lafortune, who for a few moments had been looking behind him, did not observe the change in the presiding officer from Mr Rhodes to Mr Charlton, and when he swung round to Mr Speaker again he paused and then remarked in astonished tones, 'Ah, sir, when a few moments ago I addressed my remarks to you, personally, you were a man in the prime of life, indeed, I may say, both young and vigorous. But now what do I see? When my back was turned you suddenly became old and comparatively feeble. Your shoulders are bent and your hair, whatever there is left of it, has become very grey, almost white. How do you account for this sudden change?' To which Mr Charlton promptly replied, 'Any man would soon grow old being compelled to listen to you.' David joined in the roar of laughter against himself and later in the day, meeting Mr Charlton in the lobby, held out his hand and told him that he had got what he deserved.

Fred Cook, 'Giants and Jesters In Public Life', National Archives of Canada, n.d.

SIR JOHN S. WILLISON

Sir John S. Willison edited the Liberal Toronto Globe *from 1890 to 1902, and later, from 1903 to 1917, the Conservative* News. *His* Reminiscences, *published in 1919, contain many agreeable yarns.*

How many vagrant stories, gathered in a third of a century, lie at the back of one's memory. . . . I recall that when I was in the Press Gallery of the House of Commons a Liberal member who was reading his speech was called to order. Interrogated by the Speaker, the member confessed that he had 'copious notes'. He was, however, allowed to proceed. Not long afterwards a Conservative member was reading his speech, and Dr Landerkin stood up, and, addressing the Speaker, said, 'I rise to a point of order.' 'You mean', interrupted the Speaker, 'that the honourable gentleman is reading his speech?' 'No,' said Dr Landerkin, 'my objection is that he is reading it so badly.'

Sir John Willison, *Reminiscences Political and Personal*, 1919

It was said that [James] Conmee had a long and irreconcilable feud with a man at Port Arthur and that when he became a magistrate he had the object of his dislike confined in an out-house while he went through the Statutes to find if he had power to have him hanged. The story, of course, was exaggerated, but Mr Ewan told it in *The Globe* and Mr Conmee came down from Port Arthur to protest. His protest never got beyond the first few sentences. As Harry Lauder says, 'I couldna keep frae laughin', and Mr Conmee finally joined in the laughter. . . .

Ibid.

SIR RICHARD McBRIDE

Sir Richard McBride served as Conservative Premier of British Columbia from 1903 to 1915.

When the war broke out there was grave danger of an attack on Victoria and Vancouver by the German squadron in the Pacific commanded by Count Von Spee. Unknown to the people of Canada perhaps the most anxious day for the Cabinet was October 1, 1914, when word was received from the Admiralty that the German squadron after its defeat of Admiral Craddock's squadron off the island of Coronel near Santiago was believed to be heading north and that a bombardment of these two cities was a possibility.

Sir Richard McBride, the Premier of British Columbia, rushed to Ottawa to persuade Ottawa to buy two submarines which were at Seattle, having been built for the Chilean Government. They had not been paid for, and because of the war could not be delivered. They were offered to Sir Richard for the sum of $1,150,000 in gold. With the consent of the Dominion Government he agreed to buy them. It was against the neutrality laws to deliver them, but they slipped out of Seattle Harbour in the dark and arrived at Esquimalt safely. Sir Thomas White asked Sir Richard when he arrived in Ottawa if there were not Pacific coast defences. He reported: 'Yes, and they are good guns, too. Their only drawback is that the breech block of one has been lost and six inches have been broken off the muzzle of the other. But for these defects they are in excellent condition.'

Arthur R. Ford, As the World Wags On, 1950

SIR ROBERT BORDEN

Sir Robert Borden of Nova Scotia succeeded Tupper as leader of the Conservative opposition in 1901 and was Canada's eighth prime minister, from 1911 to 1920. His Memoirs *contain several droll stories, including this account of a train journey in the UK in 1893.*

From Durham we proceeded to Edinburgh. In those days there were no dining-cars and one had to rely on a luncheon basket. At Newcastle I purchased a basket with lunch for two, including a bottle of stout. The compartment was full and among its occupants was the wife of an army surgeon who gave us useful information respecting Edinburgh; immediately opposite to us were an elderly farmer and his daughter. At luncheon time my efforts to investigate the basket and to open the bottle of stout were crowned with disaster. The beverage, unexpectedly exhilarated by the motion of the train, impelled the cork with amazing violence and a cascade of highly emotional stout drenched everyone within range. With much foresight and fine presence of mind the farmer's lass had shielded herself in advance with a large newspaper. I attempted to stay the torrent with my hand but merely diverted the stream to some who had previously escaped. Two little children danced gaily and mirthfully under the cascade; their mother who was beautifully gowned gave me an appalling look at first, but quickly recovered her composure. 'Madam,' said I, 'the English language cannot do justice to the depths of my humiliation or to my desire to apologize,' and I attempted to mop the beverage from her gown. She was extremely kind and accepted my apologies. The old farmer had received the full impact of the first discharge. It had struck him between his eyes, the beverage had penetrated his nostrils and had thoroughly drenched him, including his new necktie of brilliant hue. In my confusion and pre-occupation I missed his philosophical monologue which my wife overheard. Sopping up the disastrous liquid with an immense red handkerchief, he soliloquized, 'Well, this is 'ard on a teetotaller.'

Robert Laird Borden: His Memoirs, vol. 1, ed. Henry Borden, 1938

Borden's Memoirs *tell of accusations relating to public expenditures while Sir Charles Tupper was Canada's High Commissioner in London (1888–96).*

It was the custom to read a list of articles provided for furnishing the High Commissioner's house. One Liberal campaigner, in reading the list, came across an item 'dinner-wagon'. Someone in the audience asked what a dinner-wagon was. The orator had not the slightest idea of its purpose but this did not deter him from the following vivid explanation:

'I am glad that question was asked. This man, Tupper, in London gives great dinner parties, paid for by your money and mine, to which he invites the swells of London. At these dinners every kind of wine is served, paid for by your money and mine. In great flowing goblets, it is passed around and the toffs whom Tupper invites to his dinners drink it until they can drink no more. Finally one of them slips off his chair and falls under the table. Then two of Tupper's flunkeys, paid for by your money and mine, haul the guest from under the table, place him on the dinner-wagon, take him to the front door, call a cab and send him home. Then another goes under the table and the flunkeys bring the dinner-wagon again and so on until all the guests are disposed of. That, ladies and gentlemen, is the purpose and use of this dinner-wagon, paid for by your money and mine.' The audience, marvellously enlightened, went home full of indignation at this scandalous and iniquitous misuse of public funds. *Ibid.*

Borden recounts an inquiry in 1899 over fraudulent ballots in a controverted election.

The Liberals then adopted the tactics of prolonging the investigation and did so with considerable success by aimless and protracted cross-examination of witnesses. We produced the Conservative electors who had marked their ballots at the poll in question. Among the Liberal obstructionists was Mr B.M. Britton who invariably asked each of them whether he could recognize his ballot. The reply was always negative until a rather lively tailor from Goderich, Ontario, replied confidently in the affirmative; evidently he had imbibed some stimulant that rendered him unusually self-assertive. He was directed to indicate his ballot among those placed before him. Finding his self-appointed task somewhat difficult: 'It's pretty hard,' he commenced, when Mr Britton interrupted him, 'Did you not swear you could recognize it?' The witness resumed his task of examining the ballots one by one. I was watching him narrowly when I saw his face lighten with a happy thought. He went over the remaining ballots very rapidly and confidently, then stood up and announced triumphantly, 'It is just as I expected, my ballot is not here, it is one of those that have been stolen.' The witness retired victorious and Mr Britton remained discomfited.*

*All our witnesses not under examination were excluded from the committee room. Mr Britton invariably asked each of them whether he had been discussing the case while he was not in attendance; the usual answer was in the negative but one witness answered in the affirmative. Mr Britton asked what had been said. The witness, apparently much confused, was unwilling to answer, but having been ordered by the chairman he replied, 'Well sir, we were just saying among ourselves what terrible foolish questions you gentlemen have been asking.' *Ibid.*

Partisanship always ran high, no less so after Borden became Prime Minister in 1911.

A Conservative paper covered the speeches of its leaders and more or less ignored the speeches of the Liberals and *vice versa*. Reports were biased and unfair. I recall an incident in 1913 which illustrates this point. The Naval Aid Bill debate was then at its height. I represented amongst other papers the Fredericton *Gleaner*, then owned and edited by the late James Crockett, an ardent Conservative and a great friend of Sir Douglas Hazen, a cabinet minister from New Brunswick. Sir Robert Borden had put forward his proposals and the whole country awaited the stand taken by Sir Wilfrid Laurier. A day came when Sir Wilfrid outlined his position, but preceding him Sir Douglas had also spoken, though with no particular bearing on the subject.

I wired the *Gleaner* to this effect: 'Sir Wilfrid Laurier has spoken on the naval question. How much do you want?' Then as an afterthought I added: 'Hazen spoke this afternoon. Do you want anything of his speech?'

Back came the wire: 'Ignore Laurier entirely. Send Hazen verbatim.'

Arthur R. Ford, *As the World Wags On*, 1950

Dr Eugene Forsey recounts one of Meighen's favourite stories about Borden. It had to do with the Manitoba Boundary Extension Bill of 1912 and the proposal to build the Hudson Bay Railroad.

There was a clause providing for a right-of-way five miles wide, and this got the Liberals very excited and in committee they went after the government very hard. Why on earth five miles? Where did that come from? Why not one mile? Or a hundred yards? The questioning was pressed by A.A. MacLean, Borden's colleague from Halifax, and finally Borden gave a reply that ended the matter abruptly, once and for all. Said Borden: 'The subject appears to exercise a special fascination in the fertile mind of the senior member for Halifax. He, with his special pertinacity, keeps asking why five miles. The answer, Mr Chairman, is that the matter was deliberated at length by Council, and five miles simply was deemed to be a convenient width. Deemed . . . to be . . . a con-ven-ient width.'

Then there was the one about the proposed grant of $250,000 to Sir Arthur Currie, the supposed hero of the First World War. Meighen admitted that the Tory cabinet had agreed to make the cash grant to Currie. But when they took it to caucus, it was met with opposition from every quarter. Not one good word was said about it. Finally, Borden said he had heard sufficient—it seemed evident that the government's proposal did not command the assent of caucus: 'I cannot see that any useful purpose would be served by prolonging the discussion. Indeed, had Sir Arthur himself been present and listened to what I've been listening to for the last half or three-quarters of an hour, I think he would tell us to take our $250,000 and stick it in our (long pause) . . . our . . . (pause) . . . EXCHEQUER!'

Charles Lynch, *A Funny Way to Run a Country*, 1986

In retirement Borden may have found new energy.

In the mid-thirties when George Black, MP for the Yukon, was speaker of the House of Commons, he and Mrs Black delighted in feeding the robins that gathered every year in the garden of their Ottawa home.

But one day they found that a big black cat was making a habit of having one robin for breakfast each morning. After several unsuccessful attempts to keep the cat away, George Black got a gun and shot it dead.

A few moments later, an angry woman banged on the Blacks' front door. When George Black opened the door, he got a severe tongue-lashing from one of the most prominent women in Canada—Lady Borden, wife of the former prime minister.

It was especially embarrassing because not only were the two families neighbors, but Black and Sir Robert Borden were old cronies. Twenty minutes after Lady Borden had left, George Black looked out the front window and remarked to his wife, 'Now, we're *really* in for it.' Sir Robert was coming up the front walk.

But when Black opened the door, Sir Robert was all smiles. With outstretched hand, he said: 'I want to thank the man who got rid of that damned cat. It's always had preference over every other living thing in our house. Even I used to come out second best.'

And the two men celebrated the occasion with a drink.

Diana McCandless, 'Canadianecdote', *Maclean's*, 6 May 1961

SIR SAM HUGHES

Journalist, Tory politician, bombastic and eccentric Minister of Militia after 1911, Sir Sam Hughes was fired from the cabinet by Borden in 1916. His send-off to a contingent of Canadian troops, in October 1914, was not an unqualified success.

Somehow, by 1 October, thirty loaded transports had dropped down the river to assemble at Gaspé. Another vessel, with a British battalion from Bermuda, joined the convoy before it sailed. The Newfoundland contingent, in another ship, would join the convoy at Cape Race. Indignant at the Royal Navy escort of venerable light cruisers, Hughes insisted on naval reinforcements. Then, as the convoy was about to sail, the minister sailed up and down the lines of waiting ships, delivering copies of his farewell message:

> Some may not return, and pray God they be few.—For such, not only will their memory ever be cherished by loved ones near and dear, and by a grateful country; but throughout the ages freemen of all lands will revere and honour the heroes who sacrificed themselves in preserving unimpaired the Priceless Gem of Liberty. But the soldier going down in the cause of freedom never dies—Immortality is his. What recks he whether his resting place be bedecked with the golden lilies of France or amid the vine-clad hills of the Rhine. The principles for which you strive are Eternal.

The soldiers lined the railings and pelted the minister's launch with copies of his immortal words.

Desmond Morton, *A Peculiar Kind of Politics*, 1982

The celebrated 'Ross rifle fiasco' was only one of several controversies that landed Hughes in trouble.

Hughes also became concerned that his cherished Ross rifle was in danger of joining other Canadian-designed equipment on the scrapheap. There could be no clearer challenge to Hughes's reputation as a military expert or to the minister's claim that he had given 'the boys' better equipment than the British. In fact, even on Salisbury Plain, men of the CEF had grumbled about the Ross; battle experience at Ypres had persuaded the men of the 1st Division to rearm themselves from dead British soldiers with the shorter, lighter, and far more robust Lee-Enfield. The most alarming problem with the Ross was its breech mechanism. Mud easily clogged the rifle and the heat of rapid firing soon made it impossible to extract expended cartridges. For soldiers facing a massed German attack that was a daunting problem. During the summer of 1915 an elaborate program to ream out the chamber of the Ross rifles was authorized by Hughes but, increasingly, loyalty to the Ross was the ultimate test of loyalty to Hughes. Garnet Hughes and Brigadier-General David Watson cheerfully passed the test; Arthur Currie, General Mercer, and a growing number of senior-officers in the Corps would not. Hughes insisted on a propaganda campaign to inform Canadian soldiers that the Lee-Enfield was inferior to the Ross. Despite rechambering and threats of harsh disciplinary measures, troops continued to switch the Ross for British rifles. Reports continued of jammed rifles, bayonets falling off, and soldiers' inability to use the Ross's complicated sights.

The political climax came when Gwatkin invited General Alderson to comment on a letter from an American citizen serving with the Canadian Ordnance Corps commenting on the relative merits of the Ross and Lee-Enfield. Alderson replied with passion and detail, spelling out ten reasons why 85 per cent of his men did not like Hughes's favourite rifle. He rejected the argument, beloved by Hughes and his allies, that the fault lay with the ammunition, protesting that he had done his utmost to speak well of the weapon but leaving no doubt why 'the men, who are good judges in these matters, should prefer the Lee-Enfield'. Hughes was furious. Nothing more was needed to convince him that Alderson was untrustworthy, biased, and incompetent. In a long, savage letter, he used his old weapon of innuendo to imply that General Alderson was utterly ignorant of rifles, had engaged in a long-standing conspiracy, and had been criminal in allowing bad ammunition to get into Canadian hands. Referring to Alderson's conclusion that he would not be fit for his duties if he ignored anything that endangered his men's lives, the minister concluded sarcastically: 'Your emphatic energy concerning what your intentions are, if you will pardon me, might be better directed to having your officers in every grade responsible in the premises make sure that none of the defective ammunition again finds its way into the Canadian ranks.' Next the minister commanded that copies of the letter would be sent to every CEF officer down to the rank of battalion commander, 281 in all.   Ibid.

THE FIRE IN THE PARLIAMENT BUILDINGS

The fire in the Parliament Buildings in 1916 as witnessed by a member of the Press Gallery:

It was a dull evening, with the estimates of the Fisheries Department under consideration. Sir Douglas Hazen was leading the House. I was writing my daily report and keeping one eye on W.S. Loggie, MP for Northumberland, who was drearily discussing the question of improved transportation for fish from the Maritimes. There was barely a quorum of members, and fortunately the spectators' galleries were almost deserted. Suddenly I noticed a commotion at the main door of the chamber facing the Speaker's chair. I saw two men rush in. One was C.R. Stewart, the chief door-keeper, and the other Frank Glass, MP for East Middlesex. One of them called out, 'There is a big fire in the reading room. Everybody get out quickly!'

Hon. E.N. Rhodes, who was deputy speaker, was in the chair at the time and at once, and without ceremony, adjourned the House. Everyone seemed dazed. The alarm was not taken seriously. I thought there was a fire in some part of the building, but did not imagine there was a disaster or that one was imminent. The two of us in the Gallery slowly picked up our papers, taking our time, and went down the winding stairs to the corridor. To our amazement we saw thick black smoke was pouring along the passage, although the passage south to the main lobby and the front doors was clear. I glanced into Room 16, the Conservative headquarters just back of the chamber, and saw that everyone had been warned and was gone.

By this time the black, almost oily smoke was rolling heavily. I ran to the main corridor and thence to the Press room on the west side of the building. I met Sir Robert Borden and his secretary without hats or overcoats, running towards the exit. Sir Robert shouted to me to get out. I dashed into the Press room, where only a dozen newspaper correspondents were working, and shouted 'Fire!' They thought I was crazy. John MacCormack, then representing the Montreal *Gazette* and today the New York *Times* correspondent in Vienna, went to the door and as he opened it the smoke poured in. There was a mad rush. We all got out safely, although Albert Carle, the correspondent of *Le Devoir*, had to crawl on his hands and knees to escape.

One of the first men I met when I reached the lobby was the late Hon. Martin Burrell. His face was badly burned, and he was rushed to the hospital. Mr Burrell's office was off the reading room, where the fire started, and he and his secretary, William Ide, had to rush through the flames to safety. Several members of the House took their time getting out of the chamber, and when the lights suddenly went out were nearly trapped. George Elliott, MP for North Middlesex, was given credit for presence of mind in saving all those in the chamber. He called to the members to join hands and he led them to safety. There were seven lives lost in the castastrophe, including B.B. Law, member for Yarmouth, who was in his room at the time on an upper floor. . . .

The newspapermen moved down to a little office the CPR provided, and there most of us worked all night and most of the next day until the fire was under control. The government took speedy action and moved into the Victoria Museum, where there was a fair-sized auditorium which was used as a House of Commons chamber. The House met here briefly on Wednesday and Thursday and adjourned until Monday. In the four days the Public Works Department showed that they could work fast and expertly if necessary. By Monday quarters had been arranged for the Cabinet Ministers, the members, the officials, and the staff. The dinosaurs, the pictures in the National Gallery, the Indian relics and the geological specimens were packed in the basement or moved to other buildings. Here until the new building was ready for opening the House of Commons met. It was the scene of many historic debates, including the one on conscription, which led to the formation of Union Government and the debate on the nationalization of the Canadian National Railway.

Arthur R. Ford, *As the World Wags On*, 1950

ERNEST C. DRURY

The rapid rise of the Progressive Movement brought a new United Farmers group to power in Ontario. E.C. Drury, UFO Premier from 1919 to 1923, was a friend of Col. J.B. Maclean, publisher of Maclean's *and* The Financial Post, *who was more than willing to provide help.*

When the United Farmers of Ontario swept into power with the election of 1919, they were totally surprised and quite unprepared, having not even settled on a party leader. Filling that gap was the first item on the new government's agenda; after being turned down by several hurriedly suggested choices— including the old Tory, Sir Adam Beck!—the UFO group conscripted Drury. Almost overnight, he faced the task of forming a cabinet from ranks innocent of experience in political life or governmental administration. 'A disaster for this province!' said the business-financial community. But the Colonel, always a free-standing individual with his own reasons, thought otherwise. He not only welcomed a government fortunate enough to have Drury at its head, but gladly lent Frank M. Chapman, editor of the company's farm paper, to help select cabinet members and assign departments. *The Financial Post*, in its first report concerning the regime, followed the Colonel's lead—and no one seemed to notice the highly pertinent—unintended—pun in the heading: 'Farmers Will Give Ontario Stable Government.'

Floyd S. Chalmers, *A Gentleman of the Press*, 1969

NELLIE McCLUNG

Suffragist, reformer, author of sixteen books, 'Our Nell' was one of the most important early feminists, and a Liberal member of the Alberta legislature from 1921 to 1926.

I wish you could see the proportion of my mail that tells me to go home and darn my husband's socks. I never would have believed one man's hosiery could excite the amount of interest those socks do—and yet, do you know, they are always darned! [1915]

Candace Savage, Our Nell, 1979

Nellie's Irish humor was always in conflict with her dour Methodism. A born mimic, goaded by [Premier] Roblin's taunt, she developed her natural histrionic gifts until she was hailed as one of North America's most dynamic speakers. Guest speaker at a men's club, 'Mrs Western Canada' once said: 'You men say "women are angels" and you plead that politics are corrupting . . . therefore you can't get women into public life too soon, since there is a shortage of angels in politics.'

Jean Bannerman, Leading Ladies, 1977

In 1914 Nellie McClung organized a theatrical presentation to dramatize her feminist views. From a newspaper report, 29 Jan. 1914:

How the Vote Was Not Won—Burlesqued in Women's Parliament

Smiles of anticipation, ripples of merriment, gales of laughter and storms of applause punctuated every point and paragraph of what is unanimously conceded to be the best burlesque ever staged in Winnipeg when the Political Equality League presented last night at the Walker Theater a suffrage playlet showing 'How the Vote Was Won', and a woman's parliament showing how the vote was not won.

The audience, which filled the house to the roof, were held up in the foyer and asked to sign a suffrage petition to the government, which many of them did. Men were actively engaged throughout the house in selling a pamphlet on 'The Legal Status of Women in Manitoba', by Dr Mary Crawford, in which they seemed to be very successful judging by the number of those seen in the hands of the audience as they left the theatre chattering or laughing uproariously over some choice bit of sarcasm which had particularly delighted them. . . .

Mrs Nellie McClung's appearance before the curtain was the signal for a burst of applause from the audience who instantly recognized the woman whom many of them had heard make such an eloquent speech on the floor of the Legislature last Tuesday morning. She explained that they would have to use their imagination as political conditions were reversed and women were in power. She couldn't see why women shouldn't sit in Parliament. It didn't seem to be such a hard job. She didn't want to—but you couldn't tell what your granddaughters might want to do. Her earnest statement that they had visited the Legislature and tried to get local colour, caused much mirth. In fact, had she been a star comedian her every sentence could not have brought forth more continuous applause.

The curtain rose revealing the women legislators, all with their evening gowns covered with black cloaks, seated at desks in readiness for the first session. . . .

Petitions were first received and read. The first was a protest against men's clothes, saying that men wearing scarlet ties, six inch collars, and squeaky shoes should not be allowed in public. A second petition asked for labour saving devices for men. A third prayed that alkali and all injurious substances be prohibited in the manufacture of laundry soap as it ruined the men's delicate hands. . . .

The pinnacle of absurdity was reached when a deputation of men, lead by Mr R.C. Skinner, arrived at the Legislature with a wheelbarrow full of petitions for votes for men. Mr Skinner said the women were afraid that if the men were given the vote that [they] would neglect their business to talk politics when they ought to be putting wildcat subdivisions on the market. In spite of his eloquent appeal he could not touch the heart of the premier.

The premier (Mrs McClung) then rose and launched her reply to the deputation, almost every sentence of which was interrupted by gales of laughter . . . [from] the audience which was quick to appreciate her mimicry. . . .

'I must congratulate the members of this delegation on their splendid appearance. Any civilization which can produce as splendid a type of manhood as my friend, Mr Skinner, should not be interfered with. . . . But I cannot do what you ask me to do—for the facts are all against you. . . .

'If all men were as intelligent and as good as Mr Skinner and his worthy though misguided followers we might consider this matter, but they are not. Seven-eighths of the police court offenders are men, and only one-third of the church membership. You ask me to enfranchise all these. . . .

'O no, man is made for something higher and better than voting. Men were made to support families. What is home without a bank account? The man who pays the grocer rules the world. In this agricultural province, the man's place is the farm. Shall I call man away from the useful plow and harrow to talk loud on street corners about things which do not concern him! Politics unsettle men, and unsettled men means unsettled bills—broken furniture, and broken vows—and divorce. . . . When you ask for the vote you are asking me to break up peaceful, happy homes—to wreck innocent lives. . . .

'It may be that I am old-fashioned. I may be wrong. After all, men may be human. Perhaps the time will come when men may vote with women—but in the meantime, be of good cheer. Advocate and educate. We will try to the best of our ability to conduct the affairs of the province and prove worthy standard-bearers of the good old flag of our grand old party which has often gone down to disgrace but never (Thank God) to defeat. . . .'

After the deafening applause and laughter of the audience had subsided . . . Mrs McClung was . . . presented with a gorgeous bouquet of . . . roses, which, it is rumored, was a token of appreciation of the woman premier's eloquence from two members of the Manitoba [Liberal] opposition who had . . . secreted themselves among the audience.

Candace Savage, Our Nell, 1979

AGNES MACPHAIL

Another early and impressive feminist, Agnes Macphail was elected to the House of Commons in 1921 and held her seat until 1940. Later she served as member of the Ontario legislature, from 1943 to 1945 and 1948 to 1951.

Obtaining a teaching certificate, she taught in rural Western schools. Her interest in co-operatives took her to the United States and Europe on a fact-finding visit. Returning to South-East Grey to teach, she became organizer for United Farmers of Ontario, thousands of whom affectionately called her 'Aggie'. Nominated as UFO candidate in 1921 she won the seat boasting: 'I never solicited a single vote nor kissed a single baby.'

'Women have to be twice as good to get half as far as men,' Agnes complained.

Her campaign clothes were simplicity itself—a blue serge suit, sailor hat, and spectacles. 'This outfit will take me either to the House of Commons or the House of Refuge!' she quipped. Later she added a cape which became almost her trademark.

Jean Bannerman, Leading Ladies, 1977

Heckler, during speech by Agnes Macphail, MP: 'Don't you wish you were a man?'

Miss Macphail: 'Yes. Don't you?'

Robert Thomas Allen, A Treasury of Canadian Humour, 1967

EMILY MURPHY AND THE 'PERSONS CASE'

Although there was a woman on the throne at the time, a Victorian judge in England (1876) ruled that 'Women are persons in matters of pain and penalties, but are not persons in matters of right and privileges.' This ruling was flung in the face of Emily Murphy, Alberta's (and the British Empire's) first woman magistrate.

All eyes in the hushed courtroom turned to the determined-looking woman on the magistrate's bench. Defense counsel Eardley Jackson, enraged by the stiff sentence meted out to a bootlegger, had just shouted at the British Empire's first [female] magistrate:

'You're not even a PERSON. You have no right to be holding court!'

In the stunned silence Magistrate Emily Murphy of Edmonton, flushed with rage, spoke quietly: 'Will defense counsel develop his argument?'

Jackson did. 'Under British common law, in a decision handed down in 1876, the status of women is this: "Women are persons in matters of pains and penalties, but are *not* persons in matters of rights and privileges.' Therefore, since the office of magistrate is a privilege, the present incumbent is here illegally. No decisions of her court can be binding.'

Jackson angrily stalked from the courtroom without even waiting to gather up his papers.

The date was Dominion Day, 1916. Afterwards Emily confessed to a close friend that this, her first day on the bench, was 'as pleasant an experience as running a rapids without a guide!'

Jean Bannerman, Leading Ladies, 1977

These then—Emily Murphy, Henrietta Edwards, Louise McKenney, Nellie McClung, and Irene Parlby—were the 'five interested persons' who fought the battle for the emancipation of their sex. All outstanding women, all devoted wives and good mothers, but not *persons* in the legal sense. Five intelligent feminists, they differed widely in background and upbringing, yet in outlook they thought as one. And when the battle raged they fought as one. They joined forces in the final skirmish of the battle which their leader, Mrs Murphy, fought for 13 years.

Every effort had been made by 1927 to convince the government that Canadian women had a just grievance. Ottawa turned a deaf ear to pleas and no official action was taken. In desperation Mrs Murphy called a meeting of the five at her home in Edmonton. They discussed the situation over a cup of tea on a sunny August afternoon. Though less famous an occasion than the Boston Tea Party, in its way it was as historic an occasion because of the far-reaching consequences it had for all Canadian women. Earnestly the five made their plans, drew up the petition and, hopefully, signed it.

The argument was heard in the Supreme Court of Canada on March 14, 1928, their lawyer being the distiguished Newton W. Rowell. Judgement was reserved. The verdict after an interminable wait for five weeks was a bitter disappointment. In the opinion of the Supreme Court, Canadian women along with children, criminals and idiots were not legally 'persons'. It was a crucial moment in the history of Canadian women. The five met again in a mood of sorrow mingled with anger. They agreed there was only one course left: appeal to the Privy Council in London, England—final court of appeal in the British Empire. It was their last hope.

After 19 anxious months had dragged by, Lord Sankey finally delivered the judicial opinion of His Majesty's Privy Council on October 18, 1929. Mrs

Murphy, wakened at 3 A.M. by a long distance phone call from London, danced excitedly up and down in a pink flannelette nightgown as she announced to her family: 'We've won! We've won!' The Canadian Supreme Court decision had been overruled. Throughout the British Empire newspaper headlines declared: 'Women are PERSONS!' Canadian women everywhere were proud of their acknowledged legal status, with the same rights and privileges as men. They could now share in every activity including the highest pinnacles of government.

Everyone expected that the next move would be the appointment of Emily Murphy as Canada's first woman senator, though each of the five had some advocates for this honour. Requests flooded in to Ottawa. However, when Prime Minister Mackenzie King made the appointment in February 1930 it was given to Mrs Cairine Wilson. . . . She was a Liberal who had done yeoman service for her party, but she was not a feminist. The only reward Emily Murphy ever coveted was to be Canada's first woman senator. When she heard the news Emily was bitterly disappointed. But all she said was: 'Cairine Wilson is a good woman.'

Ibid.

ARTHUR MEIGHEN

Canada's ninth prime minister (1920–1), Arthur Meighen succeeded Borden and held that office again for three months in 1926. He led the Conservative party from 1920 to 1926 and 1941 to 1942; from 1932 to 1941 he sat in the Senate.

As a member of Borden's cabinet he guided through the House the contentious bill to nationalize several private railroad companies, creating the CNR.

Shortly after Meighen became Prime Minister I wrote a piece for *Maclean's* magazine, in which I took the Conservative Party to task on a number of issues. I suggested the party was becoming divorced from its own supporters. I had been invited to attend a dinner celebrating Meighen's leadership at the Country Club in Ottawa. But after my article appeared I was cold-shouldered by so many Conservatives I felt it would be better, less embarrassing for Meighen, if I didn't show up at the dinner.

A day or two before, he called me and said he wanted to be sure I was going to the dinner. I said I wasn't and explained why. He insisted I show up, so to please him I agreed and took my place on the night in question at a table somewhere around the middle of the room in a not-too-conspicuous position. When Meighen arrived he spotted me, came down to my table, and brought me up with him to the head table, where he sat me at his right hand. That was the kind of man Arthur Meighen was.

Some of the big men in the party were jealous of him, among them R.B. Bennett. In comparison with Meighen, Bennett was all bluff and bounce. He was a powerful speaker, his speed of delivery in the House so rapid that he was known as Richard 'Bonfire' Bennett. . . .

This was Bennett: prickly, puffed up, and overbearing, he never bothered to hide his jealousy of Meighen, who surpassed him in so many of the things that touched Bennett's pride. At times, though, Bennett was capable of surprising and even endearing touches of frankness. 'I'd give anything', he told me one day, 'to have Meighen's mind.'

Grattan O'Leary: Recollections of People, Press, and Politics, 1977

He was essentially a very human person. I recall an occasion among many demonstrating this quality. He was to give an address in French. He couldn't find his text, or, curiously, his shirt or dinner jacket or black trousers. I came to his rescue, and the spectacle of Arthur Meighen's lank length perilously encased in my shirt, jacket, and pants was enough to make a saint laugh. Meighen went out with no change in expression, adding to the humour of it, and delivered his remarks in French without a single break. He'd memorized the entire text of some nine or ten pages.

The only time I ever saw him really taken aback was one night when a very witty Jewish Liberal, Sam Jacobs, made a strong protectionist speech, and when he sat down Meighen rose and invited the honourable gentleman to cross the floor and come to his spiritual home. Jacobs got up and said, 'Mr Speaker, one of my ancestors did that sort of thing two thousand years ago, and the world hasn't stopped talking about it yet.' Meighen raised his hand in salute.

Once, in a full flow of eloquence in the House, Meighen mentioned a policy he was particularly in favour of. 'That's in the platform of the Liberal party,' a voice cried from across the floor.

'Mr Speaker,' Meighen shot back, 'I am sorry to hear it. Had I a wish dearer to my heart than all others, the worst fate I could fear for it would be that some day it would get into a Liberal platform.'

Ibid.

After the election of 1925, Mackenzie King and the Liberals clung to power with only 101 seats plus the support of 25 Progressives, even though Meighen's Tories had 116 seats. In June 1926 King's minority government was rocked by a scandal in the Customs Department and faced a no-confidence vote in the House, which precipitated the celebrated King-Byng crisis.

For King it was a weekend of scurrying around, of consultations with the living and the dead, of lonely reflections and meditations, of trembling resolve. At last his mind was made up. He would not, could not, face defeat in the House.

On Monday morning the Governor General was confronted in his office by the chubby man with the round, pink face and outthrust, pugnacious jaw, demanding dissolution, a new election. Byng, perturbed, nonplussed, fixed King with his steely, no-nonsense eyes, the eyes that had gazed on Vimy Ridge: hadn't they made an agreement; wasn't it understood that, failing to control the House, King would hand over the reins to Meighen?

The pudgy little man wasn't having any. With an impatient movement (King could be autocratic in the grip of his convictions) he thrust all that aside, all talk of agreements, of handing over the government to his pale, sneering rival whom he detested. Wasn't that months ago? After all, he was Prime Minister of Canada. Was he expected to remember every little nuance, every gesture of a meeting more than seven months gone?

King's eyes almost filled with tears when he thought of all he had sustained in those months, the want-of-confidence motions, the jibes and taunts of Meighen and his crowd, the horrors of scandal; and now when he had survived all that, had operated his lame-duck government for six long months for the benefit of the country, this red-faced little Britisher was holding him to a casual undertaking, of whose details he could no longer even be certain! Byng was calmly telling him he was no longer prepared to serve his, Mackenzie King's, purpose. As far as Byng was concerned, the agreement covered the full term; and if King was unable to carry on at any time prior to the end of his term, then Meighen had to be given a chance. That was the undertaking.

Fortified by his consultations with the spirits, strong in the knowledge of his dead mother's approval, King wanted an election. When this was rejected, he simply tendered the Governor General his resignation. Not completely aware of the storm he was walking into, that doughty soldier did the only thing left for him to do. He summoned Meighen. When one division falls, throw another one in.

From then on King sat in the House, throwing up his hands, completely out of it, refusing to co-operate in any way. As far as he was concerned, the country was without a government; as in fact it was.

This left Meighen in a position where he could do one of two things, accept or refuse. If he refused, that meant, of course, an election, with no government in office; no one to run the country during the two months prior to the election. It also meant in a sense repudiating Byng, who had made an agreement. This Meighen could not do.

Borden was consulted; Borden said, 'You have no choice.' There were warning voices. Dr Beauchesne, the grand old Clerk of the House of Commons, a man of immense prestige, got word to Meighen through R.B. Hanson that politically he was putting himself in King's hands. Meighen was not deterred. . . .

The worst part of Meighen's defeat in the House was that it was purely accidental. A Progressive member called Bird was paired with an absent Conservative called Kennedy. Inadvertently he voted, and the motion was carried by one vote.

There was only one course open to Byng and that was to grant Meighen the dissolution he had refused King. King had his election issue: Byng should have granted him dissolution when he asked for it. He would argue that Byng had turned down the advice of the Monarch's duly constituted first adviser. Whitehall was attempting to dictate to Canada, reducing Canada from Dominion status to that of a Crown colony.

On that issue King fought the election, putting forward a carefully elaborated argument to the effect that Byng, with some kind of mystic connivance with the Tories (perhaps a communication through osmosis or extrasensory perception), had juggled the cards against him. Thus the man who had gone back on his word, the Prime Minister sworn to uphold the constitutional process, was using his own rejection of that process as a bludgeon to batter his way back into office, and in so doing was demeaning the Governor General.

Ibid.

In western Ontario, where memories of the old Scottish reformers lingered on, King fought as William Lyon Mackenzie's grandson, reviving the old fight against domination by Downing Street. We tried to tell Meighen that King was digging his (Meighen's) grave. I remember Arthur Ford, editor of the *London Free Press*, going repeatedly to Meighen, saying King was making tremendous headway in western Ontario on the constitutional issue. Stubborn, proud, unbending, Meighen sent back his answer, 'I am not getting down to that level.' He couldn't bring himself to believe the people of Canada were stupid enough to be taken in. Perhaps there is a moral in all this: never overestimate the intelligence of the electorate.

At last, realizing what was happening when it was too late, Meighen spoke in Guelph in a masterly performance, demolishing King's position, showing up the hollowness of it, the sham. In those days there were no radio and television networks to carry news instantly to the public; Meighen's speech was lost in the shuffle. It never got out to the people.

In 1926 King came back with 116 seats to Meighen's 91, picking up 11 seats in Ontario and the rest scattered through the Maritimes.

Ibid.

Mr Meighen is one of the greatest authorities on Shakespeare in Canada, although he would deny that he is a student of the poet—he is only a lover of his works. In any case, it is doubtful if there is any man in Canada with such an acquaintance of Shakespeare, or who can quote so extensively and so widely from his writings. He has an almost uncanny memory and 'thereby hangs a tale'.

Several years ago Mr Meighen visited Australia. On his return by boat the Vancouver Canadian Club decided that it would ask Mr Meighen to speak to the club, presuming he would talk on his impressions of Australia. A Marconigram was sent to him extending to him an invitation and asking for the title of his address. He replied, accepting the invitation and adding that his subject would be, 'The Greatest of all Englishmen'.

Naturally the club was surprised and a little disappointed at his subject. They wondered who was 'the greatest of all Englishmen'. The club was even more surprised when he appeared before them and spoke on the subject of Shakespeare. Without a note he gave an oration which held them spellbound and made extensive quotations from his plays and poetry.

It turned out afterwards that he did not even have a copy of Shakespeare with him on the boat, nor was there one in the ship's library. His numerous quotations were stored in his amazing memory.

Later he gave the same speech in Ottawa to the Canadian Club and again swept the members off their feet. The newspapermen were unable to report correctly his speech, and afterwards they approached him in his office for a copy. He did not have a copy, but he offered to dictate it to them, and sitting at his desk gave the speech again exactly as it was delivered to the Canadian Club. It has since been printed in book form, and will go down as one of the great Canadian orations. This is a side of Mr Meighen that few people know or realize.

Arthur R. Ford, As the World Wags On, 1950

One more Meighen story, this one involving Joe Clark's Uncle Hugh. Meighen and Clark were together listening to a paper on the life of William Lyon Mackenzie, Mackenzie King's revolutionary grandfather. The lecturer made the point that Mackenzie was long-winded, some of his speeches going on for hours, full of rambling disconnections.

Clark leaned over to Meighen and said: 'Arthur! He must have inherited that from his grandson!'

Charles Lynch, A Funny Way to Run a Country, 1986

STEPHEN LEACOCK

The famous humorist was a professor of economics and political science at McGill University from 1908 to 1936 and published a number of important textbooks. A Tory, Stephen Leacock opposed Laurier on Reciprocity with the US in 1911.

He was a campus landmark with his walking stick and ragged, bulky racoon coat. The regularity of his schedule was something of a local institution. He was always out of bed by five o'clock and at work by five thirty. He wrote for about four morning hours each day, seven days a week. His classes were arranged so that they occupied only three afternoons a week. He would arrive at the Arts Building after his customary stroll on the mountain, and after classes he invariably went to the University Club for a game of billiards with René du Roure. On the other hand, there were decidedly irregular aspects of his conduct as well. A young reporter who visited his Arts Building office was asked to wait while Leacock finished addressing a letter. She was shocked when he calmly drew together a small pile of the correspondence he had been finishing, walked to the window and threw it out on the lawn. He explained that it saved him a trip down to the mailbox: some passerby seeing a heap of addressed letters would post them.

Albert & Theresa Moritz, Leacock: A Biography, 1985

J.W. DAFOE

Liberal journalist J.W. Dafoe edited the Winnipeg Free Press *from 1901 until his death in 1944. Few political writers in Canada have enjoyed the nation-wide influence he did.*

The no less celebrated Tory journalist Grattan O'Leary tells of travelling to the 1921 Imperial Conference in Australia in company with Dafoe and others.

A.P. Herbert was there, representing *Punch*, Anthony Eden was there for the *Yorkshire Post*, and J.W. Dafoe for the *Manitoba Free Press*. The twenty-one-day voyage gave me an opportunity to compare political notes with Dafoe and I seized the occasion to ask him why he was such a dyed-in-the-wool Grit. 'Very simple,' he replied. 'I simply think of all the sons of bitches in the Tory Party, then I think of all the sons of bitches in the Liberal Party, and I can't help coming to the conclusion that there are more sons of bitches in the Tory Party.'

Grattan O'Leary: Recollections of People, Press, and Politics, 1977

Bruce Hutchison, another respected journalist, comments on what Dafoe and the Free Press *were aiming at.*

Whether the general public read it mattered little. Our target was the political establishment at Ottawa. The Page had no serious interest in circulation, only in argument. Had not Dafoe declared that a newspaper's readership, like a rose bush, needed frequent and drastic pruning? Yet somehow the circulation grew despite us.

Bruce Hutchison, The Far Side of the Street, 1976

BOB EDWARDS

A more witty and irreverent newspaper man was the creator of The Calgary Eye-Opener, *Robert Chambers (Bob) Edwards, who cocked snooks at politics and politicians from 1897 to 1921.*

In the recent [1911] election the Liberal government got canned because the people of Canada had a very shrewd suspicion that their own premier was trying to sell them out. They were willing to stand for a lot from Sir Wilfrid, but they couldn't stand for that!

That a proper amount of B.S. will raise a man above his fellows by causing them to think him wondrous wise, might be illustrated by the following yarn:

There were three pigs in a poke. The overcrowding was scandalous. Each accounted for the evil in a different manner.

The first pig said, 'This overcrowding is terrible; it is because we are in a poke.'

The second pig said, 'This overcrowding is disastrous; it is because we are pigs.'

The third pig spoke as follows, 'The overcrowding is undoubtedly appalling, but you are both mistaken as to the conditions that have caused it. It is not due to our being in a poke; neither is it due to our being pigs. The evil is the direct and inevitable outcome of certain spasmodic variations in the Law of Economic Utility.'

The other two pigs were much impressed, and without more ado elected the third pig leader among them. Still the overcrowding remained as bad as ever.

The Best of Bob Edwards, ed. Hugh A. Dempsey, 1975

Bob loved to take the mickey out of politicians.

'I beg pardon,' said a man to Clifford Sifton one day last session, 'but am I rightly informed that it costs you $50,000 a year to live?'

'You are.'

'Then why do you do it?'

Ibid.

A father, wishing to satisfy himself as to the future prospects of his son, decided to make the following test. 'Now,' he said, 'I will put here, where he will see them the first thing when he comes in, a Bible, some money, and a bottle of whiskey. If he takes the Bible he will be a preacher, if he takes the money he will be a business man, and if he takes the whiskey he will be no good.'

Having thus decided on the plan, he arranged the articles and concealed himself to await the son and watch results. Presently in came the boy, saw the money and put it in his pocket, took up the bottle of whiskey and drank it, put the Bible under his arm and walked out whistling.

'My gracious!' exclaimed the father, 'He will be a member of parliament!'

Ibid.

GRATTAN O'LEARY

A respected journalist who joined The Ottawa Journal *in 1911, Grattan O'Leary later edited that newspaper, and his autobiography is the source of many anecdotes. He was a Senator from 1962 until 1976, but the only time he stood for elected office was in 1925, when he contested a seat for the Tories in the Gaspé.*

Of course, I hadn't a chance from the beginning. My opponent, the Honourable Rodolphe Lemieux, a tower of strength in the Liberal Party, Speaker of the House of Commons, ran his campaign with a federal ship, the *Lady Grey*, up and down the coast. I was naive enough to denounce this blatant exercise of patronage until a very wise old Conservative, William Flynn (an uncle of Senator Jacques Flynn), pointed out to me that I was helping Lemieux to get re-elected.

'You're making him out a hell of a big man in Ottawa,' said Mr Flynn. I saw the logic and desisted. Well, of course, we had to have the classical encounter dear to Quebec hearts, the 'assemblée contradictoire', at which each candidate was allowed an hour to speak. It was an endurance contest, the place packed to the rafters, wreathed in smoke from hand-rolled 'Alouette' cigarettes, a situation in which the man with the loudest voice had all the advantage.

I didn't have the loudest voice, but I could make myself heard, and I was confident I could hold my own. Lemieux began with diabolical cleverness by paying high tribute to my career as a Press Gallery man in Ottawa, a young man of promise and brilliance, a credit to Gaspé.

Torn between being puffed up at these amazing and apparently sincere compliments and a suspicion that I was being had, I listened while he went on to express his distress at 'coming down here and finding my young friend O'Leary the candidate of the Protestants and Jews'. A rumble went round the room at this shot and I denied hotly that I was anyone's candidate except the voters'. The damage was done. I could feel the hostility creeping round me. I got through my remarks in stony silence from the crowd.

'That was a terrible thing to say,' I accused Lemieux afterward. 'I thought you were a gentleman.'

'Don't take it to heart, young man.' He laid a friendly hand on my shoulder. 'It doesn't matter what we say here. There are no reporters. Chalk it up to experience.' Whereupon he invited me to join a dinner party on the government ship. Of course, I refused. I went back to my hotel in a mood of disillusionment.

There was more to politics than simply putting up your case and your party's case in the most persuasive way possible. I was beginning to feel like a fly in a web.

Grattan O'Leary: Recollections of People, Press, and Politics, 1977

MACKENZIE KING (I)

Grandson of the 1837 rebel William Lyon Mackenzie, William L. Mackenzie King became Canada's tenth prime minister, holding that office (with interruptions in 1926 and 1930–5) most of the time from 1921 to 1948.

His voluminous Diaries *are the most extraordinary personal documents in our political history. He was much concerned about sin and nocturnal 'strolling' while a student at the University of Toronto in 1894.*

He found it difficult to concentrate on his notes of Professor George M. Wrong's history lectures:

> It was very hard for me to stay in. I felt I must go out & stroll round. Alas I have much to conquer as yet. Oh I wish I could overcome sin in some of its more terrible forms. Tonight has proven to me that I am very weak but I will pray to be made stronger. I wrote a little letter to Nurse Cooper & one to Nurse Rogers.

The following day he writes, 'I cried after coming home tonight. I feel very sorry for something I did last night. What sort of man am I to become? is the question that is bothering me at present.' On an evening about two months later, he says again that he 'felt very much unsettled and could not read', so he 'went out and strolled around for a while. I am ashamed to record all. I felt very sorry on coming home.'

The precise nature of his sins he does not tell us. But it can hardly be doubted that these 'strolls' were visits to prostitutes—the pattern of his life during the next few years strongly suggests this—or that he had learned how to find the prostitutes from fellow students who knew the way.

In the midst of these experiences, in February 1894, something new appears. The nineteen-year-old amateur libertine launches a one-boy program to *rehabilitate* prostitutes. (Did he know that that other Liberal, William Ewart Gladstone, had been engaged in the same pursuit, to the scandal of his friends, for most of his life? To King it would have been an inspiring example; but there seems to be no evidence that he had heard of it.) King's first subject was a member of a poverty-stricken family he already knew. We shall call her Millie Gordon, though that was not her name; names mean little in this context. She had had a small sister who had been a member of King's little congregation at the Children's Hospital and who had died at the beginning of the year. Calling to see Millie on 6 February at a respectable house where she had been staying,

King found that 'she was not there but in a house on King St'. He followed her there and begged her 'to stop her wicked life and turn to Christ'. On the 8th he found she was still there. 'We had a long and beautiful talk together':

> There was a young fellow there, a perfect scoundrel, I believe, who has wished to marry her, but she refused him and decided to come with me to Mrs—'s. . . . Miss Gordon and I left together. At Mrs—'s we had a long talk & a quiet talk together, a little hymn and a little prayer. . . .

Two days later King presented Millie with a 50-cent Bible, and wrote happily in his record, 'This has been a poor week for college work but a blessed week for the cause of Christ.'

His rejoicing was premature, for Millie proved to be a backslider. A few days later she went back 'to her place on King St'.

C.P. Stacey, *A Very Double Life*, 1976

He took his first drink in 1899.

The King household, one would gather, was strictly teetotal, as were many middle-class homes in Ontario, where, nevertheless, there was a great deal of hard drinking. Willie was definitely priggish about it, and about other things. In Cambridge early in 1899 he confides to his diary a description of a party with a group of 'classical students' who told 'filthy stories' and drank liquor. He writes, 'How vice seems to creep into the lives of men! A drop of whiskey has never passed my lips & never will so long as I possess health & strength & a will of my own. I am glad I find no enjoyment in such gatherings.' The first drink comes six months later in Toronto, but it is not whiskey. King is having dinner with two of his closest university friends, Professor and Mrs William Clark. Says King, 'I took a little claret at dinner, the first I have ever taken. I took it only because so often pressed by Mr and Mrs Clark, my reason against it being one of principle only, not fear.' One speculates that the Clarks were trying to ease their young friend out of a little of his priggery.

Many an Ontario youngster of that generation and the next, brought up to teetotalism, managed to overcome it. King overcame it, but very incompletely; its ghost haunted him all his life. He never became more than an abstemious drinker, but many references in the later diaries show that he worried enormously when he found himself moved even to small indulgences of this sort. It is evident that an aura of sin continued to hang about the brown bottle.* His experiences with bibulous politicians—including ministers—did not make him more tolerant. When Chubby Power, the Air Minister, missed a Cabinet meeting on 23 May 1944, King wrote, 'What a curse liquor is. The devil's principal agent, I believe.'

---

*At a Government House party at Christmas of 1930, King records, 'I took no wine or spirits of any kind, kept a glass of sherry in front of me, just to make clear to myself I could resist any temptation, refused a glass of champagne with His Ex. before coming away.'

Ibid.

King entered the Commons as a Liberal MP in 1908.

Through it all, sometimes in the background, sometimes in the foreground, was Mother. Four days after the election that made him a member of the House of Commons, Mackenzie King made to Sir Wilfrid Laurier a declaration such, surely, as few political leaders have listened to:

> I told him I was glad to be in prlmt. under his leadership and while my mother was spared to me. That my mother & he had been inspirations to me. I told him how mother had suffered poverty while a child because of her father's exile, and of inheriting through her a hatred of injustice and love for the poor, & a determination to vindicate the justice of the cause Grandfather contended for. Sir Wilfrid said he expected to [see] me go to the very front & rapidly. I told him he would find me faithful to him.

Mother, Grandfather, and Sir Wilfrid: these were, and would continue to be, his inspirations. Two of them were still with him when he spoke. When they died it would make surprisingly little difference.

Sir Wilfrid's private thoughts, unfortunately, are not on record.

Ibid.

King entered Laurier's cabinet as Minister of Labour in 1909. Although he was not re-elected in 1911 or 1917, King was chosen to lead the Liberal Party after Sir Wilfrid's death in 1919. The forces at work were described by Sir Allen Aylesworth (another of Laurier's ministers) in a letter to his brother.

There was a big time this week in Ottawa. You can judge of it from the newspapers.

The big thing of course was the question of the new Leader. Fielding would have got it almost without opposition if he had not supported the present [Union] Government last year and this. It was a big contract to undertake to beat him out. Every one of the 8 Provincial Premiers with most of the Provincial Ministers were on hand working for Fielding. Gouin was in it too—as strong as any of them because of the Big Interest influence. Gouin stands in with the wealthy capitalists of Montreal—and talks of blue ruin to the country if the tariff is seriously interfered with at all. Dewart and his friends from here were for Graham but, failing Graham, were in the same boat with the others. It was just a rich-man against poor-man fight for who should get their man for next Premier of Canada. I went down intending of course to do my utmost for Fisher—on the lines of Laurier and anti-Laurier. And that element continued in the struggle of course all through. But on those lines we should have won *easily*. So the Fielding and Graham crowd talked Socialism against King—and argued that Fisher was a rich man and an aristocrat—to beat *him*. We found that these lines of talk were getting lots of Laurier Liberals in the West and in the Maritime Provinces to agree to forgive and forget—and so to vote Fielding or Graham. Accordingly we had to consolidate the Fisher men and the King men—or lose. And that course being decided on Fisher and I turned in and nominated King. That did the business—though it was a tight squeeze in so big a Convention where hundreds of delegates were complete strangers to all of us Easterners. But the Frenchmen did the grand thing. They met in caucus—and actually turned Gouin down *cold*. They told him in plain English—that is to say in plain French—that he could run his own local Legislature, but that *they* would run themselves in Dominion matters—and they voted—practically solid—to stand by Fisher and me *because* we were English and had stood by Laurier and the French Canadian.

That is the inwardness of the whole business. Fielding got 25 or 30 votes from Quebec—all of them Englishmen—and not more than 30 all told—whatever the poor old fool Globe may say.

You never saw such friends as those Frenchmen are to stick to a man they like. Dozens of them *hugged* me. They'd have kissed me if I would have let them—and they voted—every man Jack of them—just to stand by the men who had stood by Laurier. That is the whole story in a nutshell—let the newspapers prattle all they like.

> Aylesworth, quoted in R. MacGregor Dawson, *William Lyon Mackenzie King 1874–1923*, 1958

One of the most amusing entries in the unexpurgated [King] diaries relates the appearance of Borden and Meighen in a vision, apologizing to King for the statement that he offered himself for Sir Robert Borden's Union Government in 1917 and was turned down. This story infuriated King all through his political life, and he went to great lengths to lay it by the heels, probably on account of its absolute truth. I had the story from Meighen himself and there is no doubt whatever that King offered his services to Borden in 1917. King, of course, had this wonderful advantage that whatever went wrong in the world around him he was able to put right in the spirit world, sanctioned by his mother's mystic applause and silent approval of the spheres. . . .

I see King, tears dimming his eyes, crying in the House over his poverty, his inability to entertain members. Once he gave a maid at Laurier House a dressing down for giving a cup of tea to the policeman on the beat. He wasn't buying tea for policemen. After his death his will was probated at a million dollars.

> Grattan O'Leary: *Recollections of People, Press, and Politics*, 1977

JAMES G. GARDINER

'Jimmy' Gardiner was a Saskatchewan Liberal MLA (1914–35) a cabinet minister (1922–6) and Premier of the province (1926–9 and 1934–5). He was federal Minister of Agriculture from 1935 to 1957.

By that time [1925] the federal election was over, Saskatchewan had returned to the Liberal fold, and King was seatless: that condition had been anticipated by Motherwell on the eve of polling day, when he asked Gardiner if Prince Albert could be opened for either King or G.P. Graham, one of King's opponents for the leadership in 1919, if it were needed. Gardiner had said it could, and since in the event both King and Graham were in need (the latter disgustedly beaten 'by a bootlegger and a jailbird') went east with the notion that so indispensable a man as himself might be in a position to strike for a federal portfolio.

Satisfied with his conversations in the east, he returned home to arrange for the resignation from Prince Albert of Charles McDonald, a freshman Liberal MP whose defeated opponent was a J.G. Diefenbaker, and who deserves a special footnote in history; in the House, (unlike Mr Diefenbaker) he spoke not once, and when in 1935 he was appointed to the Senate he died before being sworn in, thus completing an eccentric career as the only Canadian to be a member in both houses of the same parliament without uttering a word in either.

Contributed by Prof. Norman M. Ward, University of Saskatchewan

Immigration and settlement included educational policies, for apart from the use of territory for school lands the settlers had children to be taught, and well before Gardiner's time that had raised controversial questions about the languages in which they were to be instructed, and the admission or otherwise of religious observances and symbols into the schools. An appreciable proportion of the settlers . . . came from backgrounds where a more liberal view of the manufacture and sale of alcohol was taken than in Saskatchewan at the time, and they joined native Canadians in using the lands they had acquired as the sites for illicit stills; many in the southern parts of the province found running beer and liquor into the United States a profitable occupation which, if carried out with judicious care, was not necessarily illegal in Saskatchewan. (The chief trick was to refrain from exporting products made unlawfully in the province.) The domestic bootlegging, as Gardiner frankly conceded, was almost impossible to control from any centralized office such as the attorney general's office; given the scattered nature of the population, only local people could keep it down.

One citizen who fell out with the liquor laws was to cause Gardiner, still personally a prohibitionist, a great deal of difficulty: the federal Royal Commission on Customs and Excise, at work in the late twenties, recommended that legal action be taken against one Harry Bronfman on two sets of charges. It was the opinion of the Department of Justice, concurred in by Saskatchewan's Attorney General, that there was insufficient evidence on which to prosecute. Gardiner was accused of protecting bootleggers in return for campaign funds, and the opposition and its press made a considerable fuss over it. When the Conservatives attained power they promptly prosecuted Bronfman, and he was acquitted on all counts.   Ibid.

ERNEST LAPOINTE

A Liberal MP from 1904 until 1941, Ernest Lapointe held several cabinet portfolios between 1921 and 1941 and was Mackenzie King's principal lieutenant in Quebec. Lapointe began his close association with King at the 1919 leadership convention.

It was at the 1919 convention that Lapointe uttered his classic definitions of Liberalism and Toryism, definitions cherished in the Liberal Party to this day. 'A Liberal is a Liberal because he likes something or somebody; a Tory is a Tory because he hates somebody or something.' It was at this convention that Lapointe, with his large frame and powerful voice, established himself as a person of importance in the party and began that public allegiance to King which was to be the dominating characteristic of his political career.

Grattan O'Leary: Recollections of People, Press, and Politics, 1977

LOUIS-ALEXANDRE TASCHEREAU

The Liberal Premier of Quebec from 1920 to 1936, Louis-Alexandre Taschereau was no admirer of the 'welfare state', as this vignette of 1933 illustrates.

At a banquet honouring Archbishop Villeneuve on his elevation to the cardinalate, Taschereau insisted that Christian virtue and the duty of the church both lay in defending peace and social order. This they accomplished by teaching 'obedience to authority, respect for law and property, the sanctity of the home, the sovereignty of the father of the family in his little kingdom [and] the assurance that death is not an end but a beginning.' And while Taschereau never denied the state's obligation to provide emergency relief to the unemployed, he later bemoaned the psychological effect. Confusing the recipients of unemployment relief with rebellious middle-class youth who 'seem to feel that the state or their families owe them a living', Taschereau concluded that 'the dole . . . is the worst evil that ever afflicted Canada'.

Bernard L. Vigod, Quebec Before Duplessis, 1986

R.B. BENNETT

Eleventh prime minister of Canada (1930–5), Richard Bedford Bennett was a New Brunswick lawyer who moved to Calgary and prospered. He sat in the Alberta legislature from 1909 to 1911, and in the House of Commons from 1911 to 1917 and 1925 to 1935.

When Bennett was in the legislature of Alberta he was a maverick and a thorn in the flesh, not only to the local Alberta leader, who was Roly Michener's father, but also to Borden in Ottawa. Repercussions of what Bennett said in Alberta kept coming back and hitting Borden in the face. Then Bennett came to Ottawa as member for Calgary, in 1911, and some time in 1912 Meighen and Borden were walking up Elgin Street and they met Michener Senior. Michener said: 'Well, Borden, when R.B. was out with us, you used to complain that he caused you a great deal of trouble and you wanted to know why I couldn't exercise some degree of control over him. He's been here for a year now and I can't see you've exercised much control over him.'

Borden said: 'My God! Is it only a year? It seems like TEN!'

The Hon. Eugene Forsey, interview, Ottawa, 19 Feb. 1987.

After Meighen's defeat in the 1926 election, Bennett defeated Hugh Guthrie for the Conservative leadership at the 1927 party convention. Racism was casual and blatant. Bennett served as Prime Minister from 1930 to 1935.

It is doubtful whether Guthrie would have been elected in any case at Winnipeg against Bennett, but a slip of the tongue sealed his fate. In the opening remarks of his nomination speech he referred to 'this great Liberal convention'. He immediately corrected, 'Conservative', but it drew attention to the fact that he was a 1917 convert from Liberalism. 'Why do we have to pick a former Liberal as Conservative leader?' was the question many a delegate asked. . . .

There was an amusing incident during the interim when the first ballot was being counted. Naturally the tension was great. A negro delegate, who curiously came from the Peace River country, had slipped quietly on the platform to ask the chairman, Hon. E.N. Rhodes, some question. General A.D. McRae, who was the organizer of the convention and was sitting on the platform, grabbed the arm of the coloured delegate, brought him to the front, and announced: 'At last we have found our dark horse.' The convention went into almost hilarious laughter.

Arthur R. Ford, *As the World Wags On*, 1950

Bennett could not be called a 'team' player. It was often said that he ran a one-man government.

He was impatient with the red tape of government. He was not afraid to cut it, and if he wanted information he did not hesitate to call up the humblest civil servant. The story goes that one day, impatient to obtain some information and without waiting for his secretary, he telephoned some minor department for information. A girl answered.

'This is R.B. Bennett speaking,' came over the 'phone. The last thing in the world she expected would be the Prime Minister telephoning her. She thought it was some boy friend kidding her.

'Oh, yeah! This is Greta Garbo,' was the reply the astonished Minister heard over the telephone.

Ibid.

Bennett was said to be a dangerous man with the ladies, and this gave a sharp point to an exchange in the House concerning Doukhobor demonstrations in British Columbia.

Mr Esling: I was very particular to confine my request as to deportation, or as to some other means of controlling these people, to the radical fanatics. I made no reference at all to the community as a whole except to say that there was a very extensive community of industrious Doukhobors. My references were to the religious fanatics who today are offending the public by exhibitions of absolute nakedness. In order to bring this right home I would like to know what the Prime Minister would think if he went into his garden in the morning to pick pansies or violets and was confronted by six naked Doukhobors.

   Mr Mackenzie King: I would send for my honourable friend the Leader of the Opposition. . . .

   Mr Bennett: There would be a riot if you overlooked your own supporters.

Canada, House of Commons, *Debates*, 8 June 1928

In 1935, Bennett delivered on radio his promises for an economic 'New Deal'. H.H. Stevens was a long-time Conservative MP who formed the Reconstruction party in the same year.

With Herridge and Finlayson preparing the speeches, Bennett embarked on a series of radio talks inaugurating a program of social reconstruction to meet the shattering problems of the depression. Some of the speeches were so radical that even R.B. was struck by the incongruity. Coming out of Cabinet one day he slapped the venerable Sir George Perley on the back. 'How are you, comrade?' he quipped. Sir George was not amused. . . .

   Bennett had a dreadful fear of being tarred with Herbert Hoover's brush and being brought down in failure for lack of a program of popular appeal. He launched the Canadian Radio Broadcasting Commission (forerunner of the Canadian Broadcasting Corporation) in an attempt to 'Canadianize' the airwaves. Meanwhile Herridge supplied the philosophy, the ideological thrust, mostly directed against business and industry, and Rod Finlayson provided words and phrases.

   The differences between Bennett and Stevens were more than merely political. Bennett was a bit of a snob. He appeared everywhere in top hat and striped trousers and morning coat. Stevens had no time for that sort of nonsense. Bennett was a High Tory posturing as a Roosevelt Democrat. Stevens was a type to be met with on the Labour benches in England. He was quite a bit closer to Bill Herridge's type of thinking than he was to Bennett's. But then, Herridge could say things nobody else could; Stevens didn't happen to be married to Bennett's sister.

Grattan O'Leary: Recollections of People, Press, and Politics, 1977

In the federal election of 1935, Bennett went down to defeat, and Mackenzie King became Prime Minister again.

After Bennett's defeat the Conservative Party lost little time in throwing him from the battlements. This was one case in which a leader, who with a little encouragement might have stayed on, was sent packing, to go into exile in England with his melancholy memories and a peerage.

Here again, R.B. was in a sense hoist with his own petard. He was always threatening to resign. 'I'll go!' he'd say and wait for the objections to pour in. After the defeat in 1935 there were no objections. While Herridge exhorted the delegates at Lansdowne Park not to turn their backs on Bennett, R.B. sat by the telephone in his suite in the Château Laurier. The phone didn't ring. The party went about its business of electing R.J. Manion.

Ibid.

GRAHAM SPRY

A journalist, and chairman of the Canadian Radio League from 1930 to 1934, Graham Spry was an influential advocate of public broadcasting. He testified before a parliamentary committee that recommended the creation of the Canadian Broadcasting Commission (later the CBC), established by Bennett's Tory government in 1932.

Why are the American interests so interested in the Canadian situation? The reason is clear. In the first place, the American chains have regarded Canada as part of their field and consider Canada as in a state of radio tutelage, without talent, resources or capacity to establish a third chain on this continent. . . . In the second place, if such a Canadian non-commercial chain were contructed, it would seriously weaken the whole advertising basis of American broadcasting. The question before this Committee is whether Canada is to establish a chain that is owned and operated and controlled by Canadians, or whether it is to be owned and operated by commercial organizations, associated or controlled by American interests. *The question is, the State or the United States?*

Spry, quoted in Frank W. Peers, *The Politics of Canadian Broadcasting 1920–1951*, 1969 [Italics added]

J.S. WOODSWORTH

A Methodist minister and exponent of the 'social gospel', James Shaver Woodsworth led the Co-operative Commonwealth Federation (CCF) from 1933 to 1939.
From 1913 till 1917 he worked as secretary of the Canadian Welfare League and then of the Bureau of Social Research.

When the governments closed the Bureau because they wanted to be rid of its secretary, who had declared his opposition to the First World War, he and his family moved to Gibson's Landing on the West Coast. There this spindly, frail man, then in his middle forties, worked as a longshoreman, helped organize a union, and became active in the Federated Labour Party, at that time the name of the main socialist organization in British Columbia. He was on a speaking tour when he landed in Winnipeg at the height of the 1919 General Strike, edited the strikers' bulletin for a few days because its former editor was in jail, and was himself arrested and charged with sedition.

The charge against Woodsworth contained a bitter-sweet piece of unintended humour which is worth repeating because it is a revealing example of the thoughtless behaviour of law-enforcement agencies in situations involving critical questions of civil liberty. One of the counts in the charge was based on the publication in the strike bulletin of quotations from the prophet Isaiah:

> Woe unto them that decree unrighteous decrees, and that write grievousness which they have prescribed; to turn aside the needy from judgment, and to take away the right from the poor of my people, that widows may be their prey, and that they may rob the fatherless.
>
> And they shall build houses, and inhabit them; and they shall plant vineyards, and eat the fruit of them. They shall not build, and another inhabit; they shall not plant, and another eat; for as the days of a tree are the days of my people, and mine elect shall long enjoy the work of their hands.

No doubt the quotation sounded like subversive propaganda in the panicky atmosphere of the General Strike, but for the authorities to try to make its publication a criminal offence was idiotic and startling. Perhaps someone came to his senses because the charge against Woodsworth was never brought to trial. He often said that his arrest and the aftermath of the General Strike elected him to Parliament in 1921.

David Lewis, *The Good Fight*, 1981

Woodsworth sat as MP for Winnipeg North from 1921 to 1933, and was known as leader of the 'Ginger Group'.

Although the Progressive Party led by T.A. Crerar took the limelight in the federal election of 1921 by electing 65 members, the Independent Labour Party made an important beginning with the election of J.S. Woodsworth from Winnipeg. He was joined by William Irvine from Alberta who made the famous quip in the House of Commons: 'Mr Woodsworth is the leader and I'm the group.'

Lloyd Stinson, *Political Warriors*, 1975

With the outbreak of World War II, J.S. Woodsworth declared his pacifist opposition to the war and relinquished leadership of the CCF.

The parliamentary galleries were full on Friday, September 8, as the debate on Canada's role in the war began. Dr Manion, leader of the Conservative opposition, spoke earnestly but did not, in my memory, rise to the drama of the occasion. The prime minister did; he was at his convoluted best. It was not easy, while listening to him, to get a clear picture of his policies but he conveyed a sense of history and of his part in it. His speech was long; he proved once again the truth of Underhill's cutting remark that King had 'great difficulty compressing a ten-minute speech into half an hour'.

Coldwell spoke the next afternoon, on Saturday. He put the Council statement on the record and made a spirited defence of the policy and a strong plea for the defence of civil liberty and for steps to take the profits out of war. It was a good presentation, clear and persuasive.

But the hero of the debate was undoubtedly Woodsworth. As agreed at the Council meeting, he spoke before Coldwell, following King on Friday evening. His fellow MPs disagreed with him but they listened in respectful silence. He was interrupted only once, when an insensitive voice cried 'Shame' toward the end of the speech, but that merely added to the drama as angry eyes turned on the culprit. I sat immobile in the gallery, as did we all. Both intellectually and emotionally I disagreed with his argument. In the context of Hitler's *Mein Kampf* and his inhuman barbarism, Woodsworth's noble words seemed, and indeed were, irrelevant. But they were courageous and beautiful. They did not speak to the reality of the immediate crisis, but to the best of man's aspirations for brotherhood and peace.

David Lewis, *The Good Fight*, 1981

Tommy Douglas recalls the same incident.

Woodsworth's address, and the hushed response it received, has always been regarded as one of Parliament's great moments. The small, stooped man who had fought so many battles, now stood alone in an assembly that was obviously intent on going to war. And even now there was a greater drama, hidden from the eyes of most of those present. In speaking to Ralph Allen twenty-two years later, Douglas drew back the curtain, revealing further the courage of his falling leader. A few days before these events, Woodsworth had suffered a severe stroke. 'When he rose to speak he could scarcely see and one side was partly paralyzed. The night before Mrs Woodsworth had made a few notes at his dictation—a cue word here and there—and put them on cards in thick crayon letters at least an inch high. I slipped into the seat beside him and handed the cards up to him one by one while he made his moving but hopeless plea for peace. I knew that in a few minutes I would be voting against him, but I never admired him more than I did that day.'

Thomas H. McLeod and Ian McLeod, *Tommy Douglas: The Road to Jerusalem*, 1987

In the summer of 1942, when J.S. Woodsworth was desperately ill, he travelled west by train, and stopped in Winnipeg to confer with party members. Prostrate in his sleeping car, he told his followers, 'Winnipeg North Centre must be held, and of course the candidate must be chosen in an absolutely democratic way.' As they filed out he called after them, 'And it must be Stanley Knowles!'

Contributed by Janice Tyrwhitt, Roving Editor, *Reader's Digest*,
based on an interview with Dr Eugene Forsey

FRANK UNDERHILL

A professor of Canadian history at the University of Saskatchewan and later (1927– 55) at the University of Toronto, Frank Underhill was the first president of the League for Social Reconstruction (LSR), the 'brains trust' of the CCF, and drafted the Regina Manifesto of 1933.

The contribution to the CCF that brought Underhill more fame and recognition than possibly any other event in his life was drafting the Regina Manifesto. In later years he jokingly exaggerated its importance: 'I used to say in those days of youthful pride, that just as Thomas Jefferson had directed that there should be inscribed on his tombstone, not the fact that he had been twice president of the United States, but the fact that he had drafted the Declaration of Independence, so I intend to instruct my executors to put on my tomb the fact that I had drafted the Regina Manifesto. As time went on, however, I realized that the Regina Manifesto wasn't going to be quite as earth-shaking as the American Declaration of Independence, and so I have rescinded those instructions to my executor.' Woodsworth had asked him in the autumn of 1932 to head an LSR group which would draft a manifesto for the party in time for the CCF's January meeting of council. Underhill consented to do the initial draft himself, which would then be reviewed by other league members. January came and went without a completed draft. Again, in April, Woodsworth reminded him of his promise—the date for the CCF national convention in Regina was 14 July. Characteristically, Underhill waited to the very last minute—one weekend in mid-June, at his cottage in Muskoka—when, under pressure, he put together a typed draft. . . .

That last sentence in the Regina Manifesto, 'No CCF Government will rest content until it has eradicated capitalism and put into operation the full programme of socialized planning which will lead to the establishment in Canada of the Co-operative Commonwealth,' was not a part of either the LSR Manifesto or Underhill's original draft; it was added at the convention. Underhill denied in later life ever wanting such a sentence added, and implied that it was out of tone with the rest of the document.

R. Douglas Francis, *Frank H. Underhill: Intellectual Provocateur*, 1986

F.R. SCOTT

Poet, professor, constitutional expert, and civil libertarian, Frank Scott was (with F.H. Underhill) co-founder of the League for Social Reconstruction, which formulated early CCF policy. A Professor of Law at McGill University after 1928, and Dean of Law from 1961 to 1964, he was involved in the Royal Commission on Bilingualism and Biculturalism (1963–8). Many of his poems and stories reflect his concern with language issues.

BONNE ENTENTE

The advantages of living with two cultures
Strike one at every turn,
Especially when one finds a notice in an office building:
'This elevator will not run on Ascension Day';
Or reads in the *Montreal Star*:
'Tomorrow being the Feast of the Immaculate Conception,
There will be no collection of garbage in the city';
Or sees on the restaurant menu the bilingual dish:
DEEP APPLE PIE
TARTE AUX POMMES PROFONDES

The Blasted Pine, ed. F.R. Scott and A.J.M. Smith, 1960

A certain Canadian student enrolled in the Law Faculty of McGill in 1937. Coming straight from a Classical College, he had never met any Jews before, and sitting next to a fellow student one day, he said: 'There are too many Jews in this Faculty.' The man he spoke to was a Jew.

Later, when he realized what he had done, he explained to his new classmate. 'You know, it is only the lower-class French Canadians who hate the Jews. The upper class hate the English.'

F.R. Scott in *The Tamarack Review*, Winter 1982

There was a great gathering of the MacLean Clan in Montreal some years ago. Sir Charles Hector Fitzroy MacLean, 'The' MacLean, came all the way from Scotland to attend. During the evening reunion, when all the people called MacLean were celebrating, there entered three girls in kilts—MacLeans from the Lower St Lawrence, who could not speak a word of English.

They came forward and shook Sir Charles warmly by the hand, greeting him with the words: 'Monsieur MacLean, nous sommes aussi des MacLeans.'

He looked at them in embarrassment and said: 'I am sorry—I don't speak Gaelic.'

Ibid.

COLONEL J.B. MACLEAN

Founder of Maclean Hunter Publishing, 'the Colonel' often played a quiet role in politics, as in 1935.

Early in September—a few weeks before polling day—two young men of *Maclean's Magazine* advertising staff were deep in a plan to sell a double-page spread to Liberal headquarters for a rousing pre-election message. Speed was of the essence because of the early closing date of the October 15 issue. One of the salesmen, L.C. West, rushed back and forth to Vincent Massey, president of the National Liberal Federation, to learn first that a double spread was out of the question though a single page just might be considered, and to be told later that even this possibility must be vetoed owing to the depleted condition of party funds. 'Unless', added Massey, 'your Colonel Maclean, who has frequently supported Mr King, would care to donate the space.' Young West promptly reported the suggestion to the Colonel, only to have it just as swiftly turned down. But the latter, wise in the ways of publishing, had a second thought: 'Why don't you give them something concrete to consider? Draw up a rough layout for a double spread, having a strong message to show the public the danger of voting for these noisy new parties. Massey and his people might find the money then.'

West dashed back to his office and went into a huddle with his friend at the next desk, E.C. Calder.

'Sounds so easy,' West said, 'but where are we going to get that kind of copy on such short notice?'

'Write it ourselves! In the first place you need a heading that will tell the whole story,' and Calder reached for a sheet of paper and started to scribble, '—something like "It's King or". . .'

'King or Chaos!' West shouted happily.

Massey bought the ad. Within twenty-four hours he and his committee had abstracted the headline for use on billboards and other advertising-media which would reach the public several weeks before *Maclean's* was on the newsstands. But West and Calder didn't mind; they had sold their double page spread ad, complete with the original layout of Mackenzie King's picture on one side, a cartoon on the other showing the voter wisely taking the right road to prosperity and spurning the signposts marked, 'CCF', 'Social Credit', 'Reconstruction', 'Conservative'.

The Colonel was happy, too. He decided to help the Liberal campaign financially. In a private discussion with Mr Massey he stressed that this was to be considered his own personal contribution, with absolutely no involvement of his company which had never given money to any political party and never would. The amount of the donation happened to be $2100–exactly the cost of the advertisement in *Maclean's*.

Floyd S. Chalmers, A Gentleman of the Press, 1969

MAX AITKEN (LORD BEAVERBROOK)

Max Aitken (Lord Beaverbrook) of New Brunswick amassed a fortune before age thirty. He moved to England in 1910, owned several newspapers, and served as Minister of Aircraft Production in Churchill's wartime cabinet.

One evening he asked his landlady to mend a hole in the seat of his trousers. She replied: 'I can't mend your trousers till you pay me the fifty cents you owe me.' Max wandered into another room, looking for a needle and thread, and saw fifty cents on the landlady's bureau. He took the money to her with the words: 'here's your fifty cents', which was indeed true. The landlady mended his trousers. Max took them gratefully and remarked: 'Mrs Benson, it was your own fifty cents.' A satisfactory transaction.

A.J.P. Taylor, *Beaverbrook*, 1972

It seems a miracle to conjure millions out of nothing and, from that, it is easy to suggest that there was something crooked in the miracle. But Aitken was by no means alone in hitting the jackpot. His boyhood friend James Dunn made one fortune before the first world war, lost much of it owing to defalcation of a partner, and made another later. Dunn, too, started from nothing. He died in 1956, leaving $65 million. R.B. Bennett, Aitken's early patron, became Prime Minister of Canada and a peer of the United Kingdom. He left some 10 million, amassed mainly by Aitken's advice and increased by a fortunate legacy from a female admirer. The example of Isaak Walton Killam is even more striking. He was the first clerk in Aitken's investment company, Royal Securities Corporation, and a pretty feckless clerk at that. In 1919 Beaverbrook sold this corporation to him for some $6 million. In 1955 Killam died, leaving more than 150 million dollars. . . .

Aitken later became absorbed into politics and did not go on at the same rate. But he did enough to put him in the same class as Dunn and Killam. He gave most of his fortune away during his lifetime, and therefore it is difficult to say what he was 'worth'. At a rough guess, Aitken had nearly forty million dollars to his credit at one time or another.

Ibid.

Beaverbrook tried to entice the journalist Bruce Hutchison to write the biography of R.B. Bennett. Hutchison declined.

Unused to disobedience, the Beaver swept my objections aside. I could write exactly as I pleased, without interference from him or anyone. All Bennett's papers in the University of New Brunswick were at my disposal, all my expenses would be paid, and any fee that I cared to ask. Surely I could not refuse this splendid chance? Nevertheless, in what must have been my finest hour, I did refuse. Bennett's loyal friend was not to be put off so lightly. Would I think it over and meet him next day in his London flat? My momentary courage oozed out. I weakly agreed.

The Beaver was alone, except for a majestic butler, in something like an acre of apartment space when I called on him. His wee figure snuggled in a massive couch like a kitten, or perhaps a gargoyle on a Gothic façade. That man was irresistible in his homely charm, his innocent look, his language of sham modesty. But knowing that the Bennett biography would be his, not mine, I somehow resisted. The kitten no longer purred, the gargoyle ceased to grin as I left.

Still, he forgave me after a time, hired a girl reporter from Victoria on my bold recommendation, and sent me a letter of greeting with a curious postscript. For my information, Mackenzie King had been gravely ill on his last visit to London and, realizing he must soon die, had summoned Churchill to his bedside. As the two men were parting forever, King asked Churchill, his old comrade of war and peace, to kiss him. According to Beaverbrook, 'Churchill obliged'. I could print this historical footnote if I cared to.

It is printed here not because it has much importance to history but because it may show the combination of kindness, ferocity, and mischief which made Beaverbrook such a paradox. . . .

Bruce Hutchison, The Far Side of the Street, 1976

WILLIAM ABERHART

A radio evangelist and founder of the Bible Institute Baptist Church, 'Bible Bill' Aberhart created a grass-roots movement, the Alberta Social Credit League, between 1932 and 1935. In the election of 1935 he and Social Credit swept into power with fifty-six of sixty-three seats in the Alberta legislature. He remained Premier until his death in 1943.

'You don't have to know all about Social Credit before you vote for it; you don't have to understand electricity to use it . . . all you have to do is push the button and you get the light.'

William Aberhart, 1934, quoted in C.B. Macpherson,
Democracy in Alberta, 1962

The originator of Social Credit's ideas, the British engineer Major C. H. Douglas, visited Alberta in April 1934 and spoke in Calgary.

The Calgary Armouries were packed that night. A brass band played Old Country airs. The Calgary elite began to arrive, leaving their coats and hats in the Officers' Mess. Aberhart went up the steps to the platform to cries in unison, 'We Want Aberhart!' The band, as instructed, pulled out all the stops in an effort to drown the clamour. The President of the Canadian Club arose and approached the microphone (for, of course, the meeting was to be broadcast). He paid highest tribute to Douglas and hinted at future world shaking benefactions. The Mayor of Calgary then welcomed the speaker most warmly on behalf of the city and introduced him in most glowing and enthusiastic terms.

(Aberhart, hardly believing such high civic approbation of Social Credit, applauded with the rest.)

Douglas rose and waited for the applause to die down. He was a very bald and rather ponderous man of medium height, his white military moustache contrasting with his florid face. He started off badly with a series of allusions to the Alberta situation that served eminently to demonstrate a massive ignorance of the province. He went on in a somewhat monotonous matter-of-fact voice to say that the Social Credit movement would soon have new democratic leadership. His old friend C.A. Bowman, the eminent editor of the *Ottawa Citizen*, would shortly preside over an organizing convention of Canadian Social Crediters, probably in Winnipeg. He then proceeded, apparently unaware that his audience had any previous acquaintance with his theories, to outline some basic well-known concepts, and devoted his remaining time to discussions of rather abstract generalities.

He talked for nearly two hours. Some of his audience left, not unobtrusively. Others indulged in prolonged applause that did not have any relation to any particular point in his speech. Still others continued to demand, 'We Want Aberhart!' The speech ended without a single reference having been made to Aberhart. This provoked a large group to rush down from the bleacher seats and mill around the center of the hall, shouting 'We Want Aberhart!' A rather pompous alderman offered a vote of thanks, quite inaudible in the uproar. The chairman signalled for the alderman to stop and for the band to strike up. 'God Save the King' was played in fortissimo but was hardly to be heard above the din of riotous shouting.

On this note ended the only public meeting that Douglas ever addressed in Alberta. He had heard about the Wild West, now he knew.

The platform group were quickly escorted out of the tumult into the relative quiet of the Officers' Mess cloakroom. There, it is reported, an altercation broke out between Aberhart and Douglas. They had both borne unprecedented indignities relative to the meeting just concluded, and in a sense each had suffered at the hands of the other. Tempers were short, and shortly hot. Statements and counter-statements degenerated into a quarrel. Another report has it that shouting was between their aroused supporters, and that Douglas had the courtesy to compliment Aberhart on the strength of his very evident following. It was one of only three occasions that these men ever exchanged a word, face to face.

L.P.V. Johnson and Ola J. MacNutt, Aberhart of Alberta, 1970

'The Keg of Beer and the Ten-Cent Piece' story, invented by Aberhart, was widely used by the more secular Social Credit speakers. (Its alcoholic content and some of its fallacies dissuaded Aberhart from using it indiscriminately.) It went as follows:

Pat and Mike were rival saloon keepers in a dried-out prairie town now, in the depression, almost deserted. It was a hot day, and the two saloon keepers sat in their respective doorways waiting for customers that never came. Pat's stock-in-trade consisted of a keg of beer and a ten-cent piece. Mike's stock consisted of a keg of beer and a thirst.

Called Mike, 'Say Pat, I'd like a drink this fine day.'

'Why don't you help yourself?' replied Pat.

'It's my stock-in-trade and I can't afford to treat myself,' Mike argued.

Whereupon Pat thought of a way out. He crossed over to Mike's saloon, thrust his dime on the counter, and called out loudly for a glass of beer. Surprised, Mike filled the order.

Pat quaffed the glass, turned to Mike and remarked, 'Now you cross over to my saloon and buy yourself a drink, me boy.'

So for the rest of that day Pat and Mike crossed and recrossed the road, circulating the dime to buy a drink here and a drink there until both kegs were exhausted. The condition of Pat and Mike at the end of the day, being irrelevant, was not revealed.

Aberhart's original version had Pat and Mike in possession of a barrel with two spigots. At one meeting he was asked, 'Where does the beer come from?' 'From basement brewing,' he answered, 'we have no problems in production—only in distribution.'

Ibid.

He tried to humour the reporters with pertinent selections from his great fund of stories. One is worth particular mention: 'I feel in my present position like the girl in the labour room of the maternity hospital, who asked the nurse to relay the following message to her young man: "If marriage is like this, the engagement is off!" ' This was siezed upon as being immoral and filthy. . . .

Aberhart made no speech in the House nor did he participate in any debate. He introduced the first bill, and Act Respecting the Demise of the Crown (having to do with the death of George V and the ascension of Edward VIII), and moved adjournment of the House. That was all. His silence was attributed to one or another of three reasons. First, that after years as a schoolmaster, he would not be able to tolerate the interruptions of parliamentary debate; second, that he considered debate a waste of time, in a house that had no effective opposition; third, that he was following the Douglasian theory that the function of a member of the Legislature was to represent the mass desire of the people and make sure that the experts got desired results, leaving policy to the caucus and methods to the experts.

In any case, Aberhart left his speech making to the closed caucus in Edmonton and Institute broadcast from Calgary.

This silence in the House must not be taken as neglect of that institution. Other ministers slipped in and out of the chamber, but Aberhart kept his seat through 'every moment' of each Session.

A member of the seven-man opposition occasionally reproached the Premier for his silence, but his colleagues were content. They had ample guidance from him in caucus and were rather pleased than otherwise that they did not have to match his eloquence on the floor.

Ibid.

ERNEST MANNING

Ernest Manning succeeded Aberhart, and was Social Credit Premier of Alberta from 1943 to 1968.

According to legend, when spring arrived and the session dragged, now Senator Manning would order the gardeners to spread the best-of-all-possible fertilizers, good old-fashioned manure, on the flower beds in the Legislative Grounds.

Then he would make sure all the windows were open.

The breezes wafted through the House, the farmer MLAs sniffed, and the debate raced forward as they hurried to finish the session and get home to their fields.

Olive Elliott in the *Edmonton Journal*, 24 April 1976

A graduate student told me of the time he was campaigning for the NDP in rural Alberta, and he saw a farmer out in his field on a tractor. So he waited at the fence for him to come that way and when he did, went over to give him an election leaflet. The farmer took the leaflet, looked at it quizzically, and then said: 'Sonny—you see that road? Ernie Manning built that road.' And then he turned the switch on his tractor and drove away.

Contributed by Professor John Wilson, University of Waterloo

MITCHELL F. HEPBURN

The salty 'Mitch' Hepburn was Liberal Premier of Ontario from 1934 to 1942.

Mitch Hepburn laughed frequently and he made others laugh. His speeches (with the exception of the budget address) were never written out and were full of earthy humour. Preparing a speech, he first thought of a good joke and then built from that. Once at an impromptu meeting of farmers in the country, someone asked Mitch Hepburn to say a few words. He agreed and nimbly jumped on to the only rostrum available, a manure spreader. He looked down at the manure spreader and began with a wide grin: 'This is the first time in my life that I have spoken from a Tory platform.' As the farmers rocked with laughter, a voice from the back of the crowd roared: 'Throw her into high gear, Mitch, she's never had a bigger load on.' It was one of the few times on a platform that Mitch Hepburn did not have the last word.

Neil McKenty, Mitch Hepburn, 1967

Mel Jack was a Conservative activist. He worked at party headquarters in Diefen-baker's 1957 campaign and later was executive assistant to the Hon. George Hees. One of Jack's most vivid memories is of a by-election in the Ontario riding of East Hastings, when the Liberals under Mitchell Hepburn were in power.

'The issue was tax support for the separate schools,' Jack remembers, 'we were against it, and it was a Conservative sweep. Our big slogan had no words at all—people would meet one another and trace the sign of the cross in the dirt with the toe of their boot, then scratch it out. That meant you were against the separate school tax, and that's the way it was, and in parts of rural Ontario, still is.'

Charles Lynch, A Funny Way to Run a Country, 1986

The fact that Mitch Hepburn's health was somewhat uncertain made him more conscious of the health problems of others. Health legislation, Premier Hepburn always maintained, was his administration's outstanding contribution to the betterment of the province. The legislation of which he was most proud was occasioned by a chat the Premier had with the well-known Toronto pediatrician, Dr Alan Brown. The doctor told Mitch Hepburn of the incidence of disease and death among Ontario's children from impure milk. Although more than ninety per cent of the milk consumed in Ontario was pasteurized, the small percentage of raw milk produced in rural areas accounted for a disproportionate share of typhoid, undulant fever, and bovine tuberculosis. Because of the cost of installing purifying equipment (and, the mistaken belief that raw milk was the purest), a hard core of farmers was bitterly opposed to any compulsory pasteurization law. Dr Brown frankly told the Premier that he did not believe the politicians had the 'guts' to pass such a law because of the farm lobby.

Shaken by the information the doctor had given him on the rate of tuberculosis among children, Mitch Hepburn decided to see for himself. Together the Premier and the doctor visited one of the children's wards in the Toronto General Hospital. Down the ward they saw two long rows of cots. All were occupied by victims of bovine tuberculosis, the dread, milk-borne disease. There was no doubt about the horror of it or about the expression of compassion on Mitch Hepburn's face. Helplessly the Premier turned to the doctor. What could he do? The only solution, replied Dr Brown, was compulsory pasteurization of milk: 'Your Government has the power—if it wishes to use it—to empty hospital wards like these.' Mitch Hepburn was silent for a moment. Then he said simply: 'You have my word, doctor. It shall be done.'

With that decision, the Premier unleashed a storm of protest that threatened to split his Cabinet and to alienate his rural support. Letters and telegrams bombarded Queen's Park when the Premier announced that a law providing for compulsory pasteurization (to be applied in rural areas gradually) would be introduced in the 1938 session. On February 15, 1938, a delegation of the Ontario Agricultural Council (including neighbours of Mitch Hepburn's from Elgin) met the Premier at Queen's Park to oppose the proposed law. As he looked at his friends, the Premier was well aware that if he lost the farm vote his Government was finished. Many were predicting that Mitch Hepburn would back down, that the political risk was too great.

The Premier said nothing as the farmers' spokesmen presented the case against compulsory pasteurization: the machinery was too expensive; there was no evidence that untreated milk was the cause of disease. Mitch Hepburn's expression changed as he listened to the arguments. He was obviously impatient and annoyed. A thin unpleasant smile crossed his lips and his eyes turned a cold blue steel as he suddenly looked at one of the men in the delegation. From the Premier's amazing memory a name and a face had emerged. He turned on the farmer, and as the delegation sat stunned, Mitch Hepburn's voice snapped like a whip: 'I know you. How many children do you have?'

'I have five,' replied the man, startled.

'Didn't you have seven?'

'Yes. Two died.'

Tension crackled through the room. Mitch Hepburn, rigid and pale, his voice sharply pitched, barked: 'They died of bovine tuberculosis, didn't they? They drank milk from your cows and died?' There was a rasp of anger as the Premier continued: 'You came here today to protest against the pasteurization of milk. You have already lost two children to bovine tuberculosis, but that doesn't prevent you from coming here to ask this Government to withdraw its bill and leave your children and other children open to threat of death. What kind of man are you?' Then Mitch Hepburn turned to the other farmers and told them his decision on pasteurization was final: 'I know it may be strenuously opposed . . . but we are determined to go through with it.' Go through with it he did. In the session of 1938, a bill providing for the compulsory pasteurization of milk in progressive stages throughout all rural areas was passed by the Legislature.

Neil McKenty, *Mitch Hepburn*, 1967

JOHN BRACKEN

After R.J. Manion led the Conservative party nowhere from 1938 to 1941, the Tories chose John Bracken as leader in 1942. A former Premier of Manitoba (1922–42), it was Bracken who insisted that the party change its name to Progressive Conservative. He resigned the leadership in 1948.

The prize for the most ineffectual Conservative leader in my time would be a toss-up between Manion and Bracken. Bracken did reasonably well on farm questions, but once he strayed from the back forty he was lost. On one occasion, delivering a speech on the economy prepared for him by Rod Finlayson, he bitterly attacked the effects of a certain excise tax. The Minister of Finance, the urbane Douglas Abbott, rose in his seat and reminded Mr Bracken that the government had announced removal of the tax that morning. Bracken went right on with the speech as written, attacking the tax which no longer existed, incapable of changing gears once he was in motion.

Grattan O'Leary: Recollections of People, Press, and Politics, 1977

MACKENZIE KING (II)

Having defeated R.B. Bennett and the Conservatives in 1935, King resumed the office of Prime Minister and held it till he retired in 1948.

By the 1930s he was deeply committed to spiritualism; one means he used to communicate with the spirit world was table rapping.

This aspiration seems to have been realizable only on great occasions. On 12 May 1937, Coronation Day, in London, King went back to his hotel when all the ceremonial was over and—evidently alone—'tried the little table'. He recorded, 'What I got was Mackenzie—also Mother—Love from all here.'

The reader is at liberty to believe, if he wishes, that King's messages actually came from the spirit world. My own opinion, I regret to say, is that they came subconsciously out of King's own head. (How the rapping was produced I do not pretend to explain; doubtless there was some form of 'unconscious pressure'.) My opinion is strengthened by the manner in which the 'spirits' told King what he most wanted to hear. One striking example may be mentioned. At the end of the year 1933 King casts his usual annual balance and reflects that he is entering on a new phase of 'the old old battle'—'plutocracy vs. the people & their rights': 'I go into it with my life consecrated as never before to the cause, and with the knowledge that I am not alone but have great forces fighting with me. . . . I do not want power unless it is given me to use it for the good of my fellow men. I pray God that my life may be worthily devoted to their service, and that I may be able, under divine guidance, & through the power of the spirit to help better conditions in this country & the world—to make thy kingdom come Thy will be done on earth as it is in heaven.' With King's mind working along these lines, no one need be surprised that less than a month later King's spiritual guide 'Meyers' revealed to him that he, King, had received a special favour from God:

> What he told me . . . was . . . wonderful . . .—a consecration to God's service in the service of Humanity—God['s] grace having saved me from my sins and His love chosen me to help to work out his will 'on earth as it is in Heaven'— The supreme prayer of my life heard, and answered with the assurance of God's strength & vision being vouchsafed in time of need. There have been forecastings of this all along the way, but nothing so direct & immediate and now that it has come, I can hardly believe it. The time chosen is that which above all others I would have,—just before the important speech on the address which opens the real work of the session.

Once again we see King as the chosen of God. The combination of simple-mindedness and egotism required to produce this result leaves one slightly breathless.

C.P. Stacey, *A Very Double Life*, 1976

In 1937 King travelled to Germany to meet Hitler.

His belief that through intervention he could avert war had a national as well as a personal component. He sought to make Canada's voice heard in 'a situation which threatens to engulf her in a world war and which, by being heard, might prevent such an appalling possibility'. His confidence was derived from a simplistic view of both the European crisis and Hitler: a situation viewed in terms of juvenile personal associations and a projection onto the German leader of his own hopes and desires. His decision is best considered in his own words:

> I had been born in Berlin [now Kitchener, Ont.] in Canada, in a county which had several communities of German names, and had represented that county in Parliament. Had also lived one winter in Berlin and felt I knew the best sides of the German people . . . if I were talking to Hitler I could reassure him what was costing him friends was the fear which he was creating against other countries. That there was not so far as Canada, for example, and other parts of the Empire were concerned, any thought of continued enmity toward Germany but a desire to have friendly relations all around. . . .

The structure of the interview only reinforced this predisposition. A great deal of the diary record of the encounter focuses on the physical surroundings and appearance of Goering and Hitler, and the whole entry reflects King's personal satisfaction in the formal courtesy and laudatory tones of such diplomatic occasions. He did not hesitate to read personal approval into the slightest gestures, observing that 'Hitler nodded his head as much as to say that he understood', and 'he would turn and look at me sideways and would smile in a knowing way as much as to say you understand what I mean.' There was none of the lack of courtesy, the personal invective, the criticism of the opponent that King associated with the enemy.

To a man obsessed with signs and divine guidance there were many auguries of God's purpose. His Bible reading the day of the meeting was by chance just that chapter that he had read to his mother prior to her death. His day was filled with meetings and symbols associated with 'witnesses' and parallels. He could believe that 'it would seem to be the day for which I was born—Berlin 1874'. Nor did King have any difficulty with the German leader, and noted: 'while he was talking . . . I confess I felt he was using exactly the same argument as I had used in the Canadian Parliament last session.'

In his summary King stressed Hitler's mysticism, his deeply religious nature, his humble origins, and the fact that he was a 'teetotaller, and also a vegetarian, unmarried, abstemious in all his habits and ways'. These were characteristics of the virtuous not of the enemy, as was the need for 'quiet and nature to help him think out the problems of his country'. A man who had so much in common with Mackenzie King, who could look 'most direct at me in our talks together', who 'never once became the least bit restless during the talk', could not be other than 'eminently wise'.

King saw and heard only those things that he needed to see: 'a genuine patriot', a 'simple peasant', a man 'with whom it should be possible to work with a good deal of trust and confidence', and was completely duped. Once he returned to Canada he did not find it difficult to find further evidence to reinforce his original misperception:

> I felt I wanted to read to Joan something re Hitler, to talk of his life. I had cut out recently articles concerning him. I am convinced he is a spiritualist—that he has a vision to which he is being true—His going to his parents' grave at the time of his great victory—or rather achievement—the annexation of Austria was most significant—I read aloud from Gunther's Inside Europe, concerning his early life—his devotion to his mother—that Mother's spirit is I am certain his guide and no one who does not understand this relationship—the worship of the highest purity in a mother can understand the power to be derived there from—or the guidance. I believe the world will yet come to see a very great man—mystic in Hitler. His simple origin & being true to it in his life—not caring for pomp—or titles, etc., clothes—but reality—His dictatorship is a means to an end—needed perhaps to make the Germans conscious of themselves—much I cannot abide in Nazism—the regimentation—cruelty—oppression of Jews—attitude towards religion etc., but Hitler . . . the peasant—will rank some day with Joan of Arc among the deliverers of his people, & if he is only careful may yet be the deliverer of Europe. It is no mere chance that I have met him & von Ribbentrop & Goering & the others I did—it is part of a mission I believe . . . 'Divine Commission Fulfilled' says Hitler etc. The world scoffs at these. They are given in ridicule—but they are I believe true—He is a pilgrim—his love of music—of Wagner Opera—his habits abstinence, purity, vegetarian, etc., all evidence of the mystic who is conscious of his mission & lives to it. Strange this bringing together of Hitler & Bunyan, both I believe are meant to guide me at this time to the purpose of my life—which I believe to be to help men to know

the secret of the path to peace, in industrial & international relationships—If I can only live to that they will know I have been with Him that end will be achieved. I pray God I may so live that men see that I have been with Him.

Joy E. Esberey, *Knight of the Holy Spirit*, 1980

On 9 November 1938 a violent pogrom was carried out on Hitler's orders.

Kristallnacht—called crystal night because of the broken glass from Jewish homes and businesses littering the streets in every city, town, and village in Germany and Austria—was organized by the Nazis to terrorize the Jews. Countless synagogues, Jewish stores, and homes were plundered and razed; men, women, and children were wrenched from their homes, beaten, and shot or dragged off to concentration camps; in all, scores were killed, hundreds injured, thousands arrested.

The tragic events of *Kristallnacht* finally moved the Canadian prime minister. 'The sorrows which the Jews have to bear at this time,' he wrote in his diary, 'are almost beyond comprehension.' 'Something', he added, 'will have to be done by our country.' Coincidentally, on the following day King personally shared in Jewish grief as he attended the funeral of Mrs Heaps, wife of the Jewish member of Parliament, and he was again overwhelmed by the breadth of the tragedy about to envelop the Jews in Europe. Writing in his diary that night, he noted that it would be 'difficult politically' and his cabinet might oppose him, but he was going to fight for the admission of some Jewish refugees because it was 'right and just, and Christian'. . . .

It was, then, a desperate group of Jews ushered into King's office on November 23. It included both Jewish MPs and the leaders of all the important community organizations, including the Congress, the Jewish Immigrant Aid Society and the Zionist Organization of Canada. They pleaded with King and his immigration minister, Thomas Crerar, to open up Canada's doors a crack and admit ten thousand refugees whom the community would guarantee would not become public charges. But they were politely rebuffed; King pointed out that unemployment in Canada was still high and that his first duty was 'the avoidance of strife, . . . maintaining the unity of the country', and fighting 'the forces of separatism'. He said that he sympathized with the refugees, but had 'to consider the constituencies and the views of those supporting the Government'. Making virtue out of vice, King explained to an aghast Jewish delegation that *Kristallnacht* might turn out to be a blessing, that, rather then aggravating the Jewish situation in Europe, it might improve it: these tragic events had generated such revulsion worldwide that 'the solution of the problem of immigration may have been facilitated'. Germany, King explained, would be cowed by the international reaction to *Kristallnacht* and desist from further actions against the Jews.

How hard it must have been for the Jewish delegates to ignore the irony in King's claim that Hitler and his cabinet would be moved by the outcry over *Kristallnacht* when King and *his* cabinet had not been. Oscar Cohen, representing the Congress at the meeting, recalled that 'it was a sweet minuet which was being danced, at the end of which everyone bowed to everyone else and left the room empty.'

Irving Abella and Harold Troper, None is Too Many, 1982

In 1938 journalist Bruce Hutchison was granted an interview with King in the PM's private study.

Even when we were lifted to the third floor in an elevator recently donated by one of King's rich friends, the monologue continued. His hide-out, and Canada's real hub of government, was unknown to the contemporary public and had yet to become a national shrine. To me it was fascinating in its contrived and costly ugliness, the litter of tinsel bric-a-brac, the array of royal photographs and other trophies of the chase, the illuminated portrait of King's mother beside the fireplace, the cougar skin on the floor, and next to the big desk a small table which, its owner explained, had once belonged to the English poet George Meredith. (Every man should have such a table, King remarked, to hold a cup of tea and some biscuits for sustenance in long working hours.). . .

The prospects [for peace], he believed, were favourable, despite all the current rumours of European war. After talking to Adolf Hitler a few days previously, he pronounced a verdict which was confidential then but has since become notorious. The German dictator, he had found, was 'a simple sort of peasant' and not very bright, who wished only to possess the Sudetenland of Czechoslovakia. That insignificant prize would satisfy him and the theft of foreign property did not seem to disturb King. No, he said, Hitler did not intend to risk war. And to those peaceful motives King undoubtedly felt that he had made his own valuable contribution.

At midnight, having finished his chore, the Prime Minister accompanied me to the door and saw me safely into his limousine with the best wishes for my future. I was exhausted from listening, he apparently refreshed from talking without pause since six o'clock. If I had seen something of a secretive little man in a hermitage forbidden to the public, it was not much after all. He would die before the nation discovered the real motivation of his life. Leaving him that night, I had no hint of the truth. The practising spiritualist and amateur mystic in communication with the dead of another world still seemed to me only a political genius in this one. Like everybody else, save a very few lip-sealed confidants, I was always to misunderstand the living King.

Bruce Hutchison, The Far Side of the Street, 1976

A year and a half later [December 1941] the Japanese air force bombed Pearl Harbor, and a wave of pent-up racial hatred poured across the continent. The Canadian government declared all of British Columbia west of the Cascades a 'protected area'. The Japanese-Canadian community on the Pacific coast was ripped apart. Government clerks separated husbands from wives and children.

While the victims waited to be shipped off to work gangs or to camps in the interior, the authorities penned them up in livestock pavilions at the Vancouver exhibition grounds. The government seized the land and boats of the Japanese, and put them up for auction. The fact that more than half the 22,000 people affected were either Canadian-born or naturalized Canadian citizens mattered not at all. As Ken Adachi has written, 'Not one effective voice of protest had been raised by white Canadians; even the CCF Party, for some years an uncompromising champion of citizenship rights for the Japanese, expressed itself in favor of the evacuation "for reasons of defence".'

Thomas H. McLeod and Ian McLeod, Tommy Douglas: The Road to Jerusalem, 1987

The army 'plot' that soaked Mackenzie King:

During the early part of World War II some of the Royal Canadian Engineers stationed in England were assigned to build a section of road outside Croydon airport. Using heavy roadmaking equipment, they poured the concrete and finished the job in record time.

Since Prime Minister Mackenzie King was in England at the time to inspect Canadian troops serving overseas, he was asked to cut a ribbon and declare the road officially open. (For many years my daughter cherished a snip of this ribbon.)

At that time, many of the troops were angry and bitter over Mackenzie King's reluctance to conscript men for overseas duty. Furthermore, men who had left good positions in Canada to join up found that the army was not then well equipped and some uniforms were hand-me-downs from World War I. Throughout the prime minister's visit, army authorities enforced strict discipline to prevent the soldiers from demonstrating against him.

It rained continuously on the day of the ribbon-cutting ceremony. My husband was an officer in the RCE and one of his sergeants was assigned to hold an umbrella over the prime minister's head as he made his speech, cut the ribbon, and declared the road open. King later remarked that the big black umbrella had failed to keep him dry; and though he never knew why he got soaked, the incident aroused many loud guffaws in the barracks. The sergeant had cut a triangular hole in the umbrella and directed a steady stream of water down the prime minister's neck.

King returned to Canada none the worse for his travels. And the boyish prank may even have helped the war effort, by allowing some of the troops to give vent to their pent-up feelings.

Ella Blatchford Marcus, 'Canadianecdote' Maclean's, 23 Sept. 1961

Diplomat Arnold Heeney reports on Mackenzie King at the 1946 Paris Peace Conference.

Apart from a few ceremonial occasions, and these were few, the Prime Minister attended few of the conference sessions. He occupied himself in Paris, visiting friends, paying homage at the shrine of one of his heroes, Pasteur, and alternately basking in the historic quality of the occasion and worrying about what was happening in Ottawa. Our delegation was staying in the dated splendour of the Hôtel Crillon on the Place de la Concorde where King had managed to obtain the suite Woodrow Wilson had occupied in 1919. From time to time he would meet the members of the delegation and, when he was not taken up by grand occasions, Norman Robertson and I would often take meals with him in the hotel restaurant. At such times King would usually manage to have one of us sign the bill, not so much to take advantage of us but in order that his own expense account should be kept to the minimum against the possibility of criticism in Parliament. As a result of such harmless stratagems the Prime Minister's expenditures invariably appeared to be among the lowest of the Canadian delegates, on one occasion actually below those of his valet, the loyal and invaluable Nichol. In the same way he was consistently suspicious of what the rest of us were doing with the public purse. On one occasion when Brooke Claxton had organized a modest delegation vin d'honneur in his honour to celebrate one of the many anniversaries in the Prime Minister's year, King said to me as we left: 'I hope Claxton hasn't put the cost of that champagne on his expense account.'

Arnold Heeney, The Things That Are Caesar's, 1972

The graceful diarist Charles Ritchie shares a similar recollection.

August 24, 1946
Fête of the Liberation of Paris.
The Prime Minister's forthcoming departure for Canada will be no loss to the Canadian Delegation and certainly not to the Conference or to the peace-making process. He has produced no ideas and no leadership. He just goes through the motions. He seems principally concerned with petty fiddle-faddle about his personal arrangements. However, if any member of the delegation leaves the hotel for a ten-minute stroll or to keep an official appointment, the Prime Minister senses his absence by some uncanny instinct and, on his return, subjects the absentee to a sad stream of reproach. 'At one time it would have been thought a privilege to serve the Prime Minister of Canada. Now it seems that young people think only of their own pleasure.' He insists for the record on keeping his personal expenses recorded at a derisory figure. I sat next to him in the Crillon dining-room the other night when he was consuming with avidity a lobster thermidor which must have cost twice as much as his whole daily expense account.

Charles Ritchie, Diplomatic Passport, 1981

One apparently rational aspect of King's concern about retirement relates to finance. It is not unnatural for an ageing man with no close family to be concerned about his future and his capacity to provide for his needs until the end. For a man who two years later was to leave an estate of three-quarters of a million dollars, however, the reaction must be characterized as excessive. King was still concerned with depleting his capital and sought alternatives whereby he could continue to provide for his needs out of income. He considered the possibility of staying on as president of the privy council after retiring from the leadership, because it 'would enable me to have still an additional income which I will need'. His letters to his friend Violet Markham painted a harrowing picture:

> As I give up my salary as Prime Minister, my indemnity as a member of Parliament, the government allowance for a car, free transportation on the railways of the country, the use of the frank etc., I shall be giving up a great deal, indeed *all* that has left me without concern for the where-with-all of existence . . . and I shall be without pension or remuneration of any kind. This will mean of course that I shall have to live on my capital, supplementing it with such income as I might find it possible to make, through writing, or by other means.

He also talked of possible earnings from speaking engagements or special missions. King had cried poverty for so long that even as intimate a friend as Miss Markham was deceived. 'There has never been any mystery that you are a poor man without private means,' she wrote. 'I know how indifferent you have been all your life to money.' As she had in 1909 Miss Markham prepared to come to the assistance of her old friend. She may even have interpreted the statement 'I feel that if, meanwhile, [financial] embarrassment should become apparent, the wherewithal will come from somewhere to enable me to finish out my days without experiencing the ills of penury' as a hint. In October 1948 she made arrangements to send money to him despite currency restrictions in England. The significant thing is that King did nothing to deter her. Further, when she faced the bigger problem of trying to obtain dollars for her trip to Canada to visit him, King offered no help at all.

Joy E. Esberey, Knight of the Holy Spirit, 1980

When Professor R. McGregor Dawson left the University of Toronto for Laurier House in 1951 to write the official biography of Mackenzie King, he intended the work to comprise two volumes (although the number grew after his death). Encountering his friend D.G. Creighton, Dawson raised the question of what titles he should choose. 'You called your biography, *Macdonald, The Young Politician*, and *Macdonald, The Old Chieftan*. Do you have a suggestion?' 'Well, McGregor,' snorted Creighton, 'I suppose you could call them, *King, The Young Son-of-a-Bitch*, and *King, The Old Son-of-a-Bitch*.'

Contributed by Professor John Wilson, University of Waterloo

THE ANGLICAN BISHOP

The 'telegraphing' of votes, or impersonating of voters, has not been unknown in any province of Canada at some time, and reflects a jaunty aspect of our 'underground' political lore.

This may be apocryphal, but it is so widely believed in anglophone Montreal that something of the sort must have happened. It seems that in about 1930 or 1935 the Liberals 'telegraphed' many votes, including that of the Anglican Bishop, John Farthing, who was well known as a high Tory. As the story goes, a little Jewish man presented himself at the poll and when asked for his enumeration slip pulled out one marked with Farthing's name. When asked his name he rather hesitantly said that it was John Farthing. The DRO, possibly somewhat suspicious, asked him his occupation, whereupon the voter glanced at his enumeration slip, read it with obvious consternation and stammered out that he was a bishop! The Liberal scrutineer then insisted he could vouch for the man, and since there was no Tory scrutineer present, he was allowed to vote. Half an hour later the real bishop arrived in full regalia and asked for his ballot, but was told that there must be some mistake as he had voted already. At this point the Liberal scrutineer jumped up and threatened to have Farthing arrested for attempting to impersonate a voter.

> This story was offered by several kind correspondents, in different forms, citing different dates. The version here was contributed by Professor Garth Stevenson, Brock University.

C.G. (CHUBBY) POWER

Chubby Power was Liberal MP for Quebec South (his father's former seat) from 1917 to 1955. Despite Mackenzie King's reservations about his temperance, he held cabinet portfolios after 1935 until he resigned over the conscription issue in 1944. He sat in the Senate from 1955 to 1968.

Two incidents stand out in my mind with respect to the 1921 election. The first was the great political meeting held by Meighen at the drill hall in Quebec City during the campaign. At that meeting I would say that 90 per cent of the audience—and it was an immense audience, even for Quebec—were French Canadians, and probably not more than 75 per cent understood English. Practically the entire audience was not only bitterly opposed to Meighen, but eager to have revenge on the party that had imposed conscription. Meighen's followers and entourage were not particularly impressive. James Scott, who was the candidate against me and a popular man in Quebec, succeeded in introducing Meighen commendably and without any great trouble, but immediately on Meighen's attempting to speak there were interruptions from all sides.

Anyone at the meeting would after five minutes of his speech have been sure that it would have been impossible for the orator to carry on for more than a few more minutes. But he gradually took command of the crowd and overawed all his interrupters. His answers were sharp, incisive, cutting, and unsparing of anyone's feelings. The extraordinary factor is that few of the audience, and practically none of the interrupters, even understood the phrases that he addressed to them, but his manner, his air of conviction, and his readiness in reply were such that they were driven into silence.

It would be difficult to imagine anyone placed in a similarly difficult position being able to overcome the obstacles Meighen overcame that evening. I can only account for it by the thought that he appeared to be alive, resourceful, sure of himself, unafraid. Before long it was seen that Meighen would not only be able to finish his speech but would receive the plaudits of the crowd. I have been at many of our most turbulent *assemblées contradictoires*, but never has it been my privilege to witness such a demonstration of the sheer strength of a fighting personality. He made no attempt to please; he simply crushed opposition.

The other incident occurred while I was driving down to one of the country parishes below Quebec with Ernest Lapointe. Lapointe was a man without any great prejudices, a kindly, good-hearted chap in every respect. It was a beautiful Sunday morning and I was watching the scenery as we proceeded. Turning to Lapointe, who I suppose had been preparing his speech for the day's perform- ance, I said to him, 'This is indeed a beautiful country and the scenery mag- nificent.' Ernest, waking up from the consideration of his speech, turned to me and said, 'Yes, too damn good a country to let Arthur Meighen run it.'

A Party Politician: The Memoirs of Chubby Power, ed. Norman Ward, 1966

In the mid-Twenties Chubby Power used to spend his weekends touring the taverns of the poor sections of Quebec City, drinking five-cent glasses of beer and listening to people's beefs. When King once objected that cabinet ministers shouldn't be seen in taverns, Power replied, 'Listen, if you want my resignation, I'll write it. But I won't give up the taverns and I bet I'll win my seat in the next election and you won't win yours.' Which was exactly what happened.

Peter C. Newman, *Home Country*, 1973

My own strongest effort was put forth in endeavouring to make something of the part of my resolution that asked for an inquiry into the interlocking of directorates as between banks, trust companies, insurance companies, and important industrial concerns, and the effect of such interlocking directorates on the general financial and economic condition of the country. I tried to show that it was contrary to the best interests of the country to have almost the entire money power and credit power concentrated in the hands of a very few people. The difficulties I encountered were due partly to my own lack of knowledge of the subject, and partly to the fact that I had no witness other than the bankers themselves, from whom I hoped to elicit evidence contrary to their own strongly held views. Sir Charles Gordon—unlike most of the other bank presidents, who were quite courteous in their replies—made no secret of his impatience at being interrogated by mere amateurs in the business of banking. According to Sir Charles (and he said so emphatically) there could be no higher certificate of honesty, integrity, and zeal for the public good, than appointment to the board of directors of the Bank of Montreal. He admitted with some pride that these appointments were made largely on his own rec-ommendation, though sometimes in consultation with other directors. The ordinary shareholder had little or nothing to say in the matter. It followed, of course, that notwithstanding the financial interests of these directors in large corporations they were men of such lofty moral character that no influence would be exercised by them to receive favours or to combine their financial interests otherwise than for the greater advantage of Canada.

A motion requiring that a clause be inserted in the Bank Act prohibiting the practice of interlocking directorates between banks, insurance companies, and trust companies, received the support of five members but was defeated. The sequel to this was that when the Bank Act came up for revision ten years afterwards, in 1944, I was then a member of the cabinet; I found, much to my dismay, that my colleague in the Finance portfolio, Mr Ilsley, rejected all suggestions that directorates of this kind should be interfered with. Ilsley, indeed, in a speech in the House strongly supported the view that these interlocking directorates were in the general interest of Canada. I wrote an indignant letter to Ralston, who at the moment was Acting Prime Minister. It made a bit of a row, sufficient to merit a letter of kindly admonition from Ralston, and to attract from Ilsley a great deal of disapproval, which I continued to receive during the remainder of our careers in the government.

A Party Politician: The Memoirs of Chubby Power, ed. Norman Ward, 1966

SIR WILLIAM MULOCK

Postmaster General in the Laurier cabinet (1896–1905), Sir William Mulock was Chief Justice of Ontario from 1923 to 1936, and was still twinkling when he died in 1944 at the age of ninety-nine years.

There was a time (thirty or forty years ago) when judges sat on the bench until they died or became total vegetables. The Prime Minister of the time, Mack-enzie King, was worried about old boys on the Ontario Court of Appeal. Not the least of the Prime Minister's problems was Chief Justice Mulock who was then in his nineties. The Prime Minister sent his Minister of Justice to Toronto to talk to Mulock CJO with a gentle hint that it was time to stand aside. The Minister of Justice was admitted to the chambers of the Chief Justice and he hedged but he finally suggested with great diplomacy, that the Prime Minister felt it was time for some of the judges (including the Chief Justice, of course) to retire. Chief Justice Mulock said: 'I entirely agree. I have been telling them for ages that they are just too long in the tooth, but they won't listen.'

Contributed by Professor Graham Parker, Osgoode Hall, York University

VINCENT MASSEY

Briefly a member of Mackenzie King's cabinet in 1925, Vincent Massey failed to win a seat in Parliament. He served as Canadian High Commissioner to Britain from 1935 to 1946, and was Governor General from 1952 to 1959.

The one aspect of Massey's personality which I could never come to terms with was his snobbishness and his extraordinary admiration of the British upper classes. Having myself attended an English public school and reacted against its intolerance, its élitism, its basic assumption that the British were born to be empire builders, I could neither understand nor condone Massey's belief that Britain's aristocracy personified the most admirable features of western civilization. I remember accompanying him to Newcastle-on-Tyne for the launching of one of the Tribal class destroyers. Massey was invited to lunch by Sir Eustace Percy, the vice-chancellor of the university, and when I was introduced to Sir Eustace he asked whether I was by any chance related to Count Paul Ignatieff. I said 'Yes, he is my father,' upon which Sir Eustace said he had been minister of education in Lloyd George's cabinet when father came to England, that he was a great admirer of the educational reforms father introduced in Russia, and that I simply had to stay for lunch along with Vincent.

I could see this did not suit Mr Massey at all, but there wasn't much either of us could do about it. During lunch Massey started holding forth on his favourite subject—the virtues of the British and how they were the only people in the world who knew how to rule others justly and effectively. Sir Eustace looked at him quizzically. 'And in what respect, Vincent,' he said, 'do you consider that ideology different from the one we are fighting?' Mr Massey was clearly taken aback, though I am sure his faith in Britain's God-given talent to excel above all other nations remained unshaken.

George Ignatieff with Sonja Sinclair, *The Making of a Peacemonger*, 1987

GENERAL GEORGES VANIER

During World War II, General Georges Vanier was military adviser to the Prime Minister. Later he served as Canada's Governor-General, from 1959 to 1967.
He accompanied Mackenzie King to Britain in 1941.

The visit did not start off on a propitious note. As the high commissioner's private secretary I had made arrangements for an honour guard to be at the

Prestwick airport and had promised the commanding officer that I would signal the approach of the prime minister so that his men could present arms. What I did not realize was that Mr King would emerge not from a door but from the bomb-bay of the converted Liberator in which he had crossed the Atlantic. Not a rifle moved as the prime minister carefully lowered himself to the ground and retreated from the aircraft, presenting his backside to the honour guard.

Next to disembark was General Georges Vanier, at the time Mackenzie King's military adviser. He had lost a leg in World War I, and though he managed remarkably well with an artificial leg, he always carried a spare in case of trouble. 'Would you mind finding my spare leg?' he said to me as he left the plane. He was followed by Norman Robertson, the under-secretary of state for external affairs. When I asked Norman where I might find the general's leg, he replied that I was shouting into his deaf ear and he couldn't tell what I was saying. Jack Pickersgill, the prime minister's executive assistant and the fourth member of the official party, turned out to be deaf in the other ear and couldn't hear me either. It occurred to me that this strange delegation was not likely to add anything other than confusion to an already confused war effort.

George Ignatieff with Sonja Sinclair, *The Making of a Peacemonger*, 1987

Near the end of his eight years as Governor General, Vanier still personified an old soldier's gallantry.

An old man sick unto death, sat in a Montreal public stand in his own province on St Jean Baptiste Day as louts hurled refuse and bottles at his prime minister and himself. He didn't shout 'Stop it you fools.' He didn't cower and flee. Instead, he kicked his wooden leg into position and simply stood up to face the barrage. It was a gesture. But then, the old man was a governor general of Canada and people cared about him and his office.

John Fraser, *Telling Tales*, 1986

SIR WINSTON CHURCHILL

In December 1900 the young Churchill made a lecture tour of North America, including Toronto and Montreal, speaking on his experiences in the Boer War.

At several points in the speech he introduced lantern slides of photographs showing 'your gallant Canadians' on the march across the veldt or hoisting the Union Jack over a hard-won objective. When a member of the audience, Dr Francis J. Shepherd, McGill's Professor of Anatomy, rose to ask why all the Colonial troops pictured seemed to be Canadian, the lecturer was ready with a breezy comeback: 'Oh, those troops will all be Australian when I get to Australia.'

Floyd S. Chalmers, *A Gentleman of the Press*, 1969

Journalists pursued Churchill to Niagara Falls after the Quebec Conference in 1943.

We saw Churchill only twice, and he was out of sorts both times, though the cheers of the crowd when he appeared at the Quebec City Hall seemed to brighten him up. Roosevelt was much the sunnier of the two and managed to be congenial towards the host, Prime Minister Mackenzie King, something Churchill never bothered to do.

After the conference, Churchill went trout fishing in the wilds of Quebec and then proceeded to Niagara Falls with his daughter Mary. A few of us went there to lie in wait, and when he finally arrived we were told that we could approach him as he stood on the brink of the falls and that three questions would be permitted.

Harold Fair, known as Fanny, was selected for the first question, since he represented Canadian Press and hence had priority. As it turned out, his one question was all that got asked.

'Mr Churchill,' he said, 'have the falls changed much since you were last here in 1904?'

The great man looked at Fanny Fair with an expression that said this was a peculiar question to put to a man who held the destiny of the world in his hands. Then, glowering, he took a long puff on his newly lighted cigar, turned ponderously toward the raging waters, gave the entire panorama a slow scan, and then returned his gaze to the questioner.

'The main principle,' he intoned, 'remains the same.'

Charles Lynch, *You Can't Print That!*, 1983

JAMES L. ILSLEY

A Liberal MP from Nova Scotia from 1926 until 1948, James Ilsley was Minister of Finance between 1940 and 1946. In 1948 he was spoken of as a successor to Mackenzie King.

'I suppose many people would consider you a natural successor to Mr King,' I remarked. He shook his head: 'I haven't got what it takes to be prime minister,' he replied. I protested that he was widely respected as a man of outstanding intelligence and integrity, and that his record as wartime minister of finance was admirable by any standard. What other qualifications did a prime minister need?

'Well,' said Ilsley, 'I'll tell you a story which illustrates the difference between me and Mr King.' Early in the war, it seems, a delegation of prominent Montreal citizens came to see the prime minister and demanded that he put a stop to the proliferation of pornographic literature. After listening attentively to their presentation, King assured them that never since he entered public life had he heard a delegation plead a worthier cause. He wanted to thank each and every one of them for bringing this vital issue to his attention; and as he did so, he shook their hands and ushered them out of the door. Ilsley and Ernest Lapointe, both of whom were present at the meeting, asked King what he proposed to do about pornographic literature. 'Go back to work,' was the reply. 'That's something I just couldn't do,' Ilsley concluded. Without actually spelling it out, he was telling me that, if prime ministers had to be hypocrites who knew how to manipulate people, the job was not for him.

George Ignatieff with Sonja Sinclair, The Making of a Peacemonger, 1987

IAN A. MACKENZIE

Between 1935 and 1948 Ian MacKenzie, a jovial British Columbian, held various portfolios in King's cabinets.

Wheat policy was the crucial concern of the three prairie provinces, whose federal members serenaded the House of Commons with endless speeches on the tribulations of the wheat farmer and his importance to the country. Because most of the prairie members in the 1945 Parliament were also members of the opposition (CCFers, Social Crediters or Conservatives), they had a tendency to dwell on the inadequacies of the government's wheat policy in debates that took on the quality of an endless tribal rite. Ian Mackenzie, while still the government's [Liberal] House Leader, summed up the stupefying wheat debate in verse:

> To the mating bird, the dearest word
>   is tweet, tweet, tweet;
> To the orphan lamb the saddest word
>   is bleat, bleat, bleat;
> To the maid in love, the dearest word
>   is sweet, sweet, sweet;
> But the blank-damnedest word I yet have heard
>   is wheat, wheat, wheat.

Robert Bothwell and William Kilbourn, C.D. Howe: A Biography, 1979

CAMILLIEN HOUDE

'Mr Montreal', Camillien Houde was mayor for most of the years (with interruptions) between 1928 and 1954. He was not an Anglophile.

At a Montreal civic banquet for the King on 18 May 1939, George VI noted that Houde was not wearing his chain of office. 'Tell me, Mr Mayor, when do you wear your chain?' Houde replied, 'Only when I have important visitors.'

Contributed by Prof. John Wilson, University of Waterloo

It has been said that Mayor Houde spoke English better than he cared to admit.

At the opening of a Montreal Alouettes' football season [1949?] Mayor Houde was invited to take part in the ceremonial kick-off, and said: 'Ladies and gentlemen, I am 'appy to be here to kick off your ball. In the future I 'ope to be here to kick all your balls off.'

Contributed by K.D. Doolittle, Toronto

MAURICE DUPLESSIS

Founder of the Union Nationale in 1935 from the ranks of the provincial Conservatives, Maurice Duplessis was Premier of Quebec from 1936 to 1939 and 1944 to 1959.
Duplessis had broken with Camillien Houde, Mayor of Montreal, but the two were reconciled in 1948 to their mutual advantage.

As Houde was leaving Duplessis's house in Trois-Rivières, their long-lost friendship was sealed with one of Duplessis's jokes that expressed the bond of vindictiveness that united them. He described the travelling salesman who arrived in a Montmagny hotel and was offered a bed in which Sir Wilfrid Laurier had slept, for a slightly increased price. He accepted but spent a sleepless night made miserable by bedbugs. On emerging the next morning he told the proprietor, 'You said I would be sleeping in Sir Wilfrid Laurier's bed; you did not tell me that I would be sleeping with the whole Liberal Party.' Duplessis and Houde laughed uproariously on the doorstep of Duplessis's home and were powerful allies for the rest of their lives.

Conrad Black, *Duplessis*, 1977

In 1938 Premier Duplessis received the members of the Rowell-Sirois Royal Commission on Dominion-Provincial Financial Relations. He opposed the Commission and its recommendations, but treated them differently in private.

The aloofness of the Union Nationale leader in public was in marked contrast to his attitude behind closed doors. At a luncheon reception given by Lieutenant-Governor Patenaude, he met the commissioners and their staff, and, after a few drinks, decided to invite them to his office at the end of the day. Anxious to oblige, and hoping he was having a change of heart, they hastened to accept. Duplessis was in high spirits when they arrived, and received them with boisterous good humour and large quantities of champagne. Although Dafoe was a teetotaller and Sirois and St Laurent very moderate drinkers, they went along with the spirit of the occasion. Eventually the premier

declared in a loud voice to a member of the commission staff that he thought
they were a fine bunch of fellows, and that he was inviting them all to dinner
in the Château Frontenac. Once again, the group submitted to his will. As
they had been bidden, they assembled in the hotel lobby promptly at eight
o'clock to meet their host, and to be taken to a private dining-room. The
minutes passed, and then the quarter-hours, but Maurice Duplessis did not
appear. About 8:45 P.M., as they were debating whether to try to find a meal
somewhere else, he burst through the revolving doors, followed by a string of
acolytes. Flushed and unsteady, he glowered at them, and snorted that he
wished people from Ottawa would learn to keep appointments on time when
they came to a provincial capital. Then, having delivered the reprimand, he
laughed uproariously at his own humour, and led the way to the elevator. At
table, he continued to enjoy himself at their expense, proposing frequent toasts
and insisting that those he drank with call him by his first name. He took
particular delight in poking fun at the more sober members of the group. Dafoe
was his favourite target, and the great newspaperman was subjected to such
rudeness that both Sirois and St Laurent were embarrassed as residents of
Quebec at the treatment accorded him, but all three managed to maintain their
composure. As soon as the meal was over, and it was obvious that the really
serious drinking was about to begin, they withdrew with a tremendous sense
of relief. The party continued for several hours, champagne being brought in
by the case; when one brand was found to be of inferior quality, it was tossed
through the fire-escape door. As the drunkenness increased, the bawdy good
humour turned to rowdiness, and glasses, dishes, and other movable objects
soared through the room. An ardent baseball fan, Duplessis proved expert in
knocking out electric light bulbs with champagne glasses. One man was hit by
flying glass, and had to be escorted down the fire escape and through the front
door of the hotel to give the impression that he had been hurt in a street
accident. Some time in the early hours of the morning, the secretary of the
commission, Alexander Skelton, was huddled behind a chair, peering through
the bars, determined to witness the end of the spectacle. He was the last of the
visitors to have direct contact with the Quebec government before the commission moved on to the Maritimes.

Dale C. Thomson, *Louis St Laurent: Canadian*, 1967

Few could match him on a fast ad-lib. When, during an election campaign, a
heckler shouted: 'What about St Laurent?' (then Prime Minister of Canada),
M. Duplessis cried: 'Never yet has the St Laurent overflowed the St
Maurice.'...

For almost a quarter-century (with a hiatus of just one war-time defeat) he
bestrode his province like a Colossus. His grip on the party was so strong that
many of his followers lived in downright fear of LE CHEF. Once, during the
1948 provincial election, I asked a precinct organizer what I regarded as an
innocuous question: was it true that followers of the UNION NATIONALE contributed 25 cents a month to the party coffers?

The subordinate blanched perceptibly, and looked away in embarrassment. 'You will have to ask the Chief,' he replied.

Duplessis's election tactics were blunt and forceful. From the platform, he cried to his audience:

'Do you want a new hospital? Do you want a new bridge? Electric lights? A new School? Then vote UNION NATIONALE. I would hate to force gifts on you that wouldn't be appreciated.'

Stuart Keate, 'Introduction' to Pierre Laporte, *The True Face of Duplessis*, 1960

Duplessis had another way of picking up information. He had a well organized police. It is said that he had secret files on every leading political, civic or church authority in the province. Their conduct, favours received from the Government, their speeches, and legal violations were all listed. Two incidents will prove that Duplessis was informed well and quickly on the comings and goings of persons he kept an eye on.

The Mayor of Three Rivers—it was J.A. Mongrain at the time—was stopping over at Quebec. He had telephoned me at the press gallery: 'I would like to talk things over. I'd like to consult some newspapermen on some problems.' Mongrain at the time was one of Duplessis' bitterest opponents.

I went to his room at the Château Frontenac accompanied by another journalist.

We had left the Legislature without talking to anyone. We had gone directly to the Mayor's room. We had been alone in the elevator. In the corridor we had met no one. A single other person had come into the room: a bell-boy who had brought us a bucket of ice. An hour later, we had left as discreetly as we had come. Not, of course, that we had any reason or wish to hide; it just so happened there were few people around at the time in the corridors of the lobby of the Château Frontenac.

Back at the Legislature at six P.M., just as the sitting adjourned for dinner, I met Duplessis who said, as I stood amazed: 'Mr Mongrain was well?'

Pierre Laporte, *The True Face of Duplessis*, 1960

Duplessis would use the session not only to measure himself against his adversaries, but to reassert control over his followers. Except for Sauvé, all of them were subject to his constant interventions and meticulous domination. He would 'whisper' to them as they spoke, interrupt them if they made a mistake or in any way displeased him, tell them to sit down if he thought they had gone on too long, or tell them to resume speaking even after they had sat down if he wanted them to add something, usually some new paean of praise directed to him personally or at least to the government. He would make interim comments on their remarks: 'Very good, Daniel, continue,' he would say to Johnson. He would distribute as signs of favour the honour of speaking in debates, and would summon his orators to his side for final coaching on what to say. Perhaps the ultimate in unabashed subservience was achieved by the once refractory Laurent Barré, who abruptly sat down in the middle of his

remarks and explained afterwards to the press that he had done so because the
battery had fallen out of his hearing aid and he could no longer hear Duplessis's
instructions to him.

Conrad Black, Duplessis, 1977

Were Duplessis's political stories authentic? No one will ever know. One thing
sure, he knew how to give them the appearance of truth.

One day in Ottawa, Duplessis chatted with Joseph (Joey) Smallwood, Premier
of Newfoundland and a Liberal. He was telling him, in the presence of a group
of newspapermen, that Sir Wilfrid Laurier had once made a statement that
was to serve as the basis of all Liberal party principles.

Smallwood leaped to the lure. He asked what it was Sir Wilfrid had said.
Duplessis, smiling as he did only on such occasions, described at length the
scene where Sir Wilfrid had made the statement, enumerated those who were
present, and reviewed the impression the stateman's remarks had left.

Mr Smallwood: 'Yes, but what did Laurier say?'

Mr Duplessis: 'He said the Liberal party has but one principle . . . and that
was to have none!'

Everyone burst out laughing . . . and some wiseacres claim that Mr Smallwood exclaimed:

'That's fine! But why the devil did he go and say it in public!'

Pierre Laporte, The True Face of Duplessis, 1960

The worst defeat anyone can remember Duplessis sustaining in Assembly
repartee occurred in his first term as Premier. The amiable Joe Cohen was
speaking to an unattentive House when Duplessis, apparently somewhat in his
cups, loudly interjected that the legislature need not bother listening to the
only Jew in the room. Cohen shot back, pointing to the crucifix that Duplessis
had placed above the Speaker's chair: 'No, there are two of us.' Jean Martineau
witnessed this and says that he never knew Duplessis to suffer such a put-down,
bef·re or after.

Conrad Black, Duplessis, 1977

ANDRÉ LAURENDEAU

Respected journalist and editor of Le Devoir *from 1958 to 1968, André Laurendeau
was co-chairman (with A. Davidson Dunton) of the Bilingualism and Biculturalism
Commission (1963–8).*

*On 4 July 1958 he attacked Duplessis in a notable editorial, and developed the
concept of 'le roi nègre'.*

A few days previously, Mr Duplessis, having decided in the course of a press
conference that he could no longer tolerate the presence of *Devoir* reporter

Guy Lamarche, had at first told him to leave, and, this failing, had then had him ejected by the police. While *Le Devoir* had of course protested as vigorously as it could, and had been backed up staunchly by the other major French-language newspapers of the province, the English-language press had said little or nothing about the matter. As a result we have the theory of the 'Negro King', the essential features of which we must now examine.

'Usually,' Mr Laurendeau writes, 'the English are more sensitive than we are to infringements of all forms of liberty. This is why Mr Duplessis has a bad press outside of Quebec.'

In this, prejudice plays some part but 'We would be wrong to explain everything by ethnic prejudices. The British conquered their political liberties a little at a time. They know their price that much better, and they are usually more alert to threats against them.'

If Ottawa tries to muzzle free discussion, all the English papers complain that liberty has been violated. Witness the pipeline affair. Yet, 'In the Legislative Assembly of Quebec, incidents of that type occur every day. Our English papers take them with hardly a murmur. Why?'

Mr Laurendeau then affirms that neither the *Montreal Star* nor the *Gazette* really protested the Lamarche incident. He goes on:

'Quebec's Anglophones behave like the British in one of their African colonies.

'The British are too wise, politically; they rarely destroy the political institutions of a conquered country. They surround the Negro King, but they let him behave as he pleases. Occasionally he will be permitted to cut off heads if it's customary. It would never occur to them to demand of a Negro King that he conform to the high moral and political standards of the British.

'The Negro King must collaborate and protect the interests of the British. With this taken care of, the rest counts for little. Does the little king violate the rules of democracy? Well, what could one expect from such a primitive creature?

'I don't attribute these attitudes to the English minority of Quebec. But things happen as though some of its leaders believed in the theory and practice of the Negro King. They pardon in Mr Duplessis, chief of Quebec's natives, what they wouldn't stand for in one of their own.

'One sees it daily in the Legislative Assembly. It was evident in the last municipal election. It has just been verified at Quebec.

'As a result, democracy and parliamentary practice regress, and arbitrary rule goes uncontested. There is constant collusion between Anglo-Quebec finance and everything that is the most rotten in the politics of this province.'

Hugh Bingham Myers, *The Quebec Revolution*, 1963

GEORGE A. DREW

Leader of Ontario's Conservative party after 1938, George Drew was Premier from 1943 to 1948.
   One of his enemies was J.E. Atkinson, owner of the Toronto Star.

Atkinson encountered Attorney General Price in a hotel lobby. 'I do not like that leader of yours,' he said, pressing a bony finger against Price's chest. 'He called me an evil old man. I resent being called old.' Then unsmilingly he went on about his business.

'I don't hate George Drew,' he told a reporter to whom he was giving instructions. 'But he is an exceedingly dangerous man because of the things he stands for, and he must be eliminated.'

By early 1948 Bracken was on the way out, and Drew was in the running for leadership of the federal Conservative party, to be decided at a convention in October. Mr Atkinson thoroughly approved of his ambition. He thought there was no better way of rendering Drew harmless than to make him leader of the federal Conservatives.

Ross Harkness, *J.E. Atkinson of the Star*, 1963

Drew was leader of the federal Conservatives from 1948 to 1957. Journalist Charles Lynch remembers

the unfortunate Drew, who looked and sounded so much like Mr Ontario that Uncle Louis St Laurent wiped the floor with him. In those days, the prime minister's office, along with his entire entourage and the Department of External Affairs, was in the East Block of Parliament, and one night, following a Press Gallery Dinner, Drew paused on his way home and relieved himself against a corner of the East Block, saying that since he'd never get inside the place he might as well anoint the outside of it.

Charles Lynch, *You Can't Print That!*, 1983

BROOKE CLAXTON

Brooke Claxton, who served as defence minister from 1946 to 1954, had been a sergeant-major in the First World War.

Claxton . . . loved to discuss world military strategy with his executive assistant, Paul Marshall, before a huge wall map, both men waving enormous drinks as pointers to soft underbellies and critical fluid fronts. On Claxton's military transport plane, the bar opened before the wheels came up, the steward rushing headlong down the canted aisle with the first for the minister. Claxton loved a party, and was always the last songster still upright at the piano, still fending off his wife Helen, who kept trying (vainly) to steer him home or, if they were out of town, to their barracks or hotel room.

Claxton insisted on seeing nearly all files. He could not delegate work, important or trivial. The files grew floor-to-ceiling in his office in the ramshackle old wooden defence headquarters on Elgin Street (in the days before pay and accommodation of civil servants became more important than policies). The files and the detail finally did him in because he couldn't keep up, with or without booze. A minor scandal of detail which he hadn't had time to deal with (it was too far down in the pile) became public and set the country giggling: horses on the payroll of the Army works service at Camp Petawawa, Ontario. Claxton furiously maintained that there were no horses on the payroll. But they were there all right, as entries of teams which turned out to be non-existent but whose teamsters, pocketing the money, were real enough. And there was the matter of the missing railway spur line at the camp, pulled up surreptitiously and sold for scrap. Prime Minister St Laurent handled the affair easily and lightly in the 1953 election campaign: 'Boys will be boys,' he said, and everybody smiled and the Liberals breezed to another re-election.

Dave McIntosh, *Ottawa Unbuttoned*, 1987

ROY THOMSON

Founder of the Thomson chain of newspapers, Roy Thomson was made Baron Thomson of Fleet in 1963.

[He] arranged for a Federal Minister to open the new building and plant he had provided for the Guelph *Mercury*, and, using the bluntest means at his disposal, persuaded Canada's Progressive Conservative Party to consider him as its candidate for the newly created Toronto Riding of York Centre.

Thus Cabinet Minister Paul Martin formally opened the Guelph *Mercury*'s new building, and, in his speech, remarked that whenever he entered a strange town he always bought a paper—at which Thomson, grinning broadly, interjected: 'Me too—and its plant!'

Russell Braddon, *Roy Thomson of Fleet Street*, 1965

LOUIS ST LAURENT

Minister of Justice from 1941 to 1946, and Minister of External Affairs from 1946 to 1948, Louis St Laurent was Canada's twelfth prime minister (1948–57).

Late one night King called St Laurent to his office and told him bluntly there was danger of a military takeover unless the troops could be reinforced through conscription. When St Laurent told me the story sitting in his apartment in the Roxborough over three years later he still couldn't be sure whether King meant what he said.

'What could I do?' Expressive Gallic shrug. 'I had to pretend I believed him. I even had to pretend that I believed that he himself believed what he was saying. Is that too complicated? In any event, it made no real difference. I had already made up my mind that conscription must come. There was no other way. It was just a question of when and how.'

King had been categorical in his affirmation of the coming revolt of the military. 'I have information from the most reliable source,' he told St Laurent. 'The Army may rise up against the Government if steps are not taken to fill up the battalions overseas.' St Laurent looked at me with his tight little smile. 'You know the top brass in the Army, O'Leary, and so do I. Do you think it is likely they were ready to revolt?'

I said I hadn't heard anything about it; nevertheless, everyone knew the situation in 1944 was pretty ticklish. King's reliable source must have been McNaughton, I suggested. St Laurent nodded. 'Obviously, some kind of ultimatum was conveyed to King. He seemed sincerely afraid that we were on the borderline of anarchy.'

'He should have been afraid,' I said. 'After all, his refusal to deal with the issue created the situation in the first place.'

King said he had authentic information the Chiefs of Staff were no longer in control. There was a definite possibility of civil war. All across Canada the military were demanding action. It was conscription or else. Sitting there in St Laurent's apartment, having a drink with him, the story seemed to me a wild chimera out of the distant past.

'He was deadly serious,' St Laurent said. 'I assured him of my full support because I had already decided on my course.' Obviously King didn't want the kind of dilemma that smashed the Liberals under Laurier in 1917. It wasn't the state of public order King was worrying about but the state of the Liberal Party in Quebec.

'I gave him the impression that I believed the situation was as he described it,' St Laurent said. 'I was really quite sceptical. King appeared satisfied with my reaction and within a few days we brought in conscription.'

Grattan O'Leary: Recollections of People, Press, and Politics, 1977

During the 1949 election campaign St Laurent became known as 'Uncle Louis'.

Rolling through the sparsely settled hinterland of Alberta *en route* to Vancouver, the train stopped briefly at the small town of Edson. The station platform was crowded with children who had been brought down from the local school by their teacher—incidentally a militant member of the CCF Party—to see their Prime Minister at first hand. Touched by their presence, St Laurent chatted to them about their country, explaining the significance of Newfoundland's entry into Confederation, and telling them in simple terms the meaning and promise of being young Canadians. Thanking them for coming to meet him, he remarked that if it was in his power he would give them a holiday from school for the rest of the day. Immediately there was a huddle of members of the local school board who were present, and, as soon as the Prime Minister had finished speaking, it was announced that the holiday had been granted. A scream of delight welcomed the statement, and the children waved enthusiast-ically as the train moved out of the station; St Laurent stood on the rear platform of the last car and waved back happily until they were out of sight. At the next few stops, he made a point of speaking to the children present, and again received an enthusiastic response, both from them and from their proud parents. Deep in the Rocky Mountains later in the day, one reporter from a Conservative newspaper remarked ruefully to another: 'Uncle Louis is going to be hard to beat.' The nickname stuck, and St Laurent had found his feet as a politician.

Dale C. Thomson, *Louis St Laurent: Canadian*, 1967

Last night was Mr Nehru's dinner in honour of the Prime Minister—white tie and decorations (if any). At the hour of dinner I had a call to go to the Prime Minister's bedroom. I found him standing in the middle of the room, white tie, white waistcoat, tailcoat, long woollen underwear, no trousers. He said, 'Here now, I suppose my trousers have been left on the plane.' That was precisely what had happened. Everyone else in his entourage had his trousers, but the Prime Minister was trouserless. Like Sir Walter Raleigh throwing down his cloak for Queen Elizabeth to walk upon, I said, 'Take mine, Prime Minister', but a second look at his girth and mine showed that this was a physical impossibility. I called one of the innumerable servants to inquire after a pair of spare trousers, but apparently there are none in this vast palace. We sent him running to the nearest bazaar in New Delhi to purchase a pair. The moments ticked by. The Prime Minister was already eleven minutes late for dinner. Finally the servant returned bearing with him an extremely greasy pair of second- or third-hand trousers of such circumference that they had to be fastened round the Prime Minister's waist with safety-pins. During the whole of this agonizing ordeal Mr St Laurent remained perfectly unperturbed and patient, with never a word of complaint. My mind boggled at the thought of what Mackenzie King would have said in these circumstances.

Charles Ritchie, *Diplomatic Passport*, 1981

One of the most bitter parliamentary confrontations occurred in May 1956, when the St Laurent government imposed closure to speed the passage of the Trans-Canada Pipeline bill. The bill was introduced by C.D. Howe.

[CCF critic] Stanley Knowles recalled the last time closure had been applied (by Premier Bennett's government in 1932) and he quoted Opposition Leader

Mackenzie King, who denounced its use as 'autocratic power to the nth degree'. Then, looking across at the government front bench, Knowles said: 'If there is anything in spirits walking this earth after a man like Mackenzie King has passed on, I am sure his ghost must be haunting every cabinet minister every night . . . of this debate.' By exercising closure for the sake of their pledge to Trans-Canada, they had allowed the demands of a private company to override the rights of 'this free and independent Parliament of a sovereign nation'.

Since Louis St Laurent had not participated in the debate, George Drew told the House he hoped that Howe had not imposed closure on the Prime Minister too. Drew called Howe the real head of government now, and Fleming conjured up the spectacle of a weak prime minister hiding behind a reckless minister 'unrepentent over his own lust for power, the same man who said "if we wanted to get away with it who would stop us?"' St Laurent was nicknamed 'Louis the Silent', Canada was called 'the Dominion of Howe', and Trans-Canada PipeLines the government's 'Colombo Plan for Texas tycoons'. George Hees conjured up a scene in which its greedy directors plotted to 'get good old C.D.' to hand over Canada's resources. 'You can just see the boys sitting around the room cutting up the melon in advance.'

'Through all this hubbub,' Grant Dexter of the *Winnipeg Free Press* reported to his readers, 'the most arresting figure on the government side of the House was Prime Minister St Laurent. He sat impassive, expressionless, chin in hand, an open book on his desk, silent. His aloofness is almost unbelievable.' St Laurent had hoped he would not have to speak in the debate, but as each day passed it became clearer that he must.

When he finally did, the signs of depression and weary old age vanished. He reviewed with great dignity, clarity, and firmness the whole history of the pipeline project and its crucial importance to the nation, without a single reference to the insults heaped upon him. He only referred to closure briefly and euphemistically as 'the distasteful responsibility of having to resort to the standing rules of the House', adding that the majority had its rights and duties as well as the minority.

Robert Bothwell and William Kilbourn, *C.D. Howe: A Biography*, 1979

C. D. HOWE

In the cabinets of Mackenzie King and St Laurent, C.D. Howe held many portfolios. As Minister of Munitions and Supply he directed Canada's wartime production, and as Minister of Trade and Commerce in 1956 he sponsored the bill for the Trans-Canada pipeline. Howe was one of Diefenbaker's favourite targets.

Diefenbaker's tactics were calculated to show Howe in a bad light by getting him hopping mad in the House of Commons, staging the spectacle of an angry, elderly man performing a series of tantrums. The tantrums were remembered by politicians and the press, who forgot the provocation. Diefenbaker's master-stroke was to pin on Howe the phrase everlastingly associated with him: 'What's a million?'

The exchange arose from a 1945 debate on Howe's war estimates. The estimates debates had a tendency to drag along while the opposition probed for some politically useful weakness in the government's case. The estimates under discussion totalled $1,365 million. When replying to a question about that sum, Howe exclaimed to the House, 'I dare say my honourable friend could cut a million dollars . . . but a million dollars from the War Appropriations Bill would not be a very important matter.'

Diefenbaker spoke the next day. His version of Howe's remarks was different: 'We may save a million dollars, but what of it?' Howe jumped to his feet. He had said no such thing; Diefenbaker was 'a past master of distortion'. Diefenbaker was incensed at the slur on his reputation. Howe was guilty of bad manners and must withdraw his remarks. Eventually, after much bellowing back and forth across the floor of the House, Howe retracted his epithet, which was promptly forgotten. But Diefenbaker's was refined and sharpened, until it finally emerged as 'What's a million?'—the epitome of Liberal arrogance and condescension toward Parliament. Even those who knew that Howe had not said it argued that he might have. Some Liberals agreed.

Robert Bothwell and William Kilbourn, *C.D. Howe: A Biography*, 1979

Howe's face was grey from exhaustion. The winter of 1945–46 was punctuated by colds, flu and bad temper. Another vacation, this time in Cuba, did little good. It was a sour Christmas.

What Howe heard on New Year's Day made it even sourer. In 1945 there were five living Canadian 'Right Honourables', members of the British Privy Council. The title was awarded only for great political distinction, conferring prestige and status in a country that had done away with other titles. King was the only serving politician to be 'Right Honourable', but in the past other ministers had, from time to time, acquired the honour. In 1945 the British government asked King if he had any nominations. 'Undoubtedly,' King replied, he would suggest Ilsley, Minister of Finance, and St Laurent, Minister of Justice. Malcolm MacDonald agreed with King, and passed on the advice. The good news was announced on New Year's Day, 1946. When Howe returned, tired and irritable from Cuba, his friends commiserated with him on his absence from the list.

He immediately requested an interview with the Prime Minister; it took place on January 15. It was not, King recorded in his diary, a happy occasion. Howe felt slighted, he told his leader, that his war service was not appreciated; he, and not St Laurent or Ilsley, had 'carried the heaviest load in the war effort'. St Laurent had only entered the cabinet in 1941. It was obviously time to go, Howe said; he was very tired 'and the work of the office irritated him'. That was true enough, as King could see. The immediate solution was obvious.

Instead of resigning, Howe should go off on another vacation. After all, King later observed, 'His loss would be a real one to the Ministry.'

Howe always found it difficult to resist King's blandishments. Instead of resigning, he went back to his office to brood. It was there that Jack Pickersgill, King's principal assistant, found him. Pickersgill had been sent to make peace, and to present King's elaborate excuses. The British Privy Councillorship was none of King's doing; it was all British Prime Minister Attlee's idea; King was blameless. Howe glared at Pickersgill. 'Jack,' he said finally, 'that's a God-damn lie.' That ended the matter, but only so far as Howe personally was concerned. 'I admit,' Howe incautiously told one of his friends, 'I really would have liked that degree!'

                                                                                    Ibid.

Although Howe had a certain admiration for St Laurent, the relationship was very different from that with Mackenzie King. 'King never interfered,' C.D. told me. 'He let me have my head. He didn't know a damn thing about business or industry. Didn't really give a damn. But St Laurent, with his experience as a corporation lawyer, is always one jump ahead. He knows exactly what's going on. You never have to spell things out. This is good in some ways. But'—C.D. paused to address his ball, sighting down the long, green fairway at St Andrews—'you can't put anything over on the bugger.'

                        Grattan O'Leary: Recollections of People, Press, and Politics, 1977

M. J. COLDWELL

M.J. Coldwell was an activist school teacher and Labour alderman in Regina before he became leader of the Saskatchewan Farmer–Labour Party in 1932. A CCF MP from 1935 until 1958, he succeeded J.S. Woodsworth as national leader of the CCF (1942–60).

In January, 1922, a sophomore alderman, he took up his defense of the unemployed in Regina, opposing the city policy of black-listing those recipients of relief who refused the employment the city offered them. 'If we want to add fuel to the flames of Bolshevism', he said, 'the best thing we can do is to send these men into the street. I am not a radical or anything of the kind, but I will not take the responsibility of putting a fellow creature on the streets.'

One of his first acts as alderman was to investigate the administration of relief in the city. Disguising himself as a tramp, he applied for a relief voucher and went to the designated restaurant to discover whether the men's complaints about the inadequacy of the food supplied were accurate. They were, and Coldwell was successful in having that particular restaurant dropped from the list. His investigation outraged the city official in charge of the relief programme and the feud between the two continued until 1924 when Coldwell's further investigation of the administration of the system resulted in the official's resignation.

Walter Young, 'M.J. Coldwell', *Journal of Canadian Studies*, vol. 9, 1974

In the spring of 1932, the young T.C. Douglas wrote to Woodsworth seeking advice. Woodsworth urged him to contact Coldwell.

Almost as soon as Douglas wrote to Coldwell, the schoolmaster showed up on the preacher's front step in Weyburn. His manner of arrival delighted [Douglas's wife] Irma and provided Douglas with a tale he often told through the years. Irma answered the door when Coldwell knocked, and he asked, 'Is your father home?' The meeting initiated a bond between M.J. and Irma which lasted throughout Coldwell's life. In his final years, when M.J. was alone, Irma guided him on his weekly shopping expeditions.

Thomas H. McLeod and Ian McLeod, *Tommy Douglas: The Road to Jerusalem*, 1987

As leader of the CCF during the pipeline debate of 1956, Coldwell lost his temper— almost.

The house met at 2:30 P.M.

MR COLDWELL—REFERENCE TO ARTICLE IN OTTAWA 'CITIZEN' OF JUNE 2
Mr M.J. Coldwell (Rosetown-Biggar): Mr Speaker, I rise on a question of privilege. On page 1 of the Ottawa *Citizen* of Saturday, June 2, the following sentences appear:

> Then, white-faced, but determined, the Speaker moved the next vote. The opposition could restrain itself no longer. Coldwell, shaking his fist, advanced on the Speaker. 'You bloody fool,' he shouted above the bedlam.

Mr Speaker, I wish to say that never in my life anywhere, at any time, in any place, have I used those words to anyone. Earlier above the din I had sought to be heard on privilege. I advanced toward the table and I said: 'You are a dictator, Mr Speaker,' and I repeated 'dictator' several times. Again, let me say that I never in my life used the foul language attributed to me.

Canada, House of Commons, *Debates*, Monday 4 June 1956

JOHN W. PICKERSGILL

'Clear it with Jack' was the insider's familiar word during the governments of King and St Laurent. Jack Pickersgill rose quickly from the Department of External Affairs to the prime minister's office, and from 1953 to 1957 was in the cabinet as Secretary of State. Between 1963 and 1967 he was a member of the Pearson cabinet.

Most Canadians first heard of Pickersgill in June 1952, when St Laurent appointed him to succeed Norman Robertson as secretary to the cabinet and Clerk of the Privy Council. This was a nonpolitical job, but Pickersgill had become a political creature and St Laurent soon saw that it might be more useful to have Pickersgill in the cabinet. That meant not only promoting him over the heads of 160 Liberal backbenchers but also finding a constituency he could win.

This problem was solved by Joey Smallwood, the Premier of Newfoundland, who had become friendly with Pickersgill during the negotiations leading up to confederation. At one critical moment it was Pickersgill's quick thinking that had saved the whole project. Mackenzie King had felt that Newfoundland should join Canada only if a substantial majority of her people voted for confederation. The first plebiscite ended in a stalemate. When Pickersgill heard on the morning news that a bare 52 per cent had supported union in the second vote, he dug up the percentages of the popular vote received by the Liberals in every election under King. At ten o'clock that morning King placed his first daily phone call to Pickersgill. 'Well, did you hear the Newfoundland result?' he asked coolly, implying that the vote wasn't high enough to warrant confederation. 'Yes. Isn't it wonderful!' Pickersgill shot back gleefully. 'Do you realize, sir, that the Newfoundlanders want union with Canada by a considerably higher percentage than Canadians voted for you in any election except 1940?' King, obviously surprised, replied with a snort, but the plebiscite figures suddenly became acceptable.

Peter C. Newman, *The Distemper of Our Times*, 1968

I loved to watch Jack Pickersgill in the House. Sometimes he got Pearson into trouble because he could be devilish as hell. Pickersgill's way of dressing added to his reputation as a crafty figure. He wore a sort of a coat that hung loose—it looked something like a cape—and this wide-brimmed black hat. He reminded me of Black Bart, a bandit in silent movies I saw as a kid. In the House they used to say he wore only one blue serge suit that got shiny with use. He probably had three or four the same, but it seemed like he had only one.

He always wore suspenders and he'd hook his thumbs under them and stretch them out so far we were sure they'd break. In the House, when he made a real good hit against Mr Diefenbaker, or when he asked a zinger question, he'd snap his braces and slide down under his desk until he'd pretty near disappear under the table he'd get laughing so much—all you could see was his head. You'd wonder if he was going to disappear completely. He was laughing at the Tories and laughing at himself, too. I liked him very much. I also thought he was a hell of a good minister.

Eugene Whelan with Rick Archbold, Whelan: The Man in the Green Stetson, 1986

JOSEPH SMALLWOOD

Liberal Premier of Newfoundland from 1949 to 1972, Joey Smallwood brought Canada's tenth province into Confederation in 1949.
   He acquired his familiar nickname in 1946.

Conscious of the political value of an easily remembered diminutive, he set out to create one. During one outport rally, where the children, as always, were clustered close round the foot of the dais, he stopped in mid-speech and declared, with an air of irritation: 'Ladies and gentlemen, I am going to have to stop. I cannot continue. I cannot go on. That boy down there, in front of me, has just called me Joe Smallwood. My name is not Joe Smallwood.' The audience listened in horror to his apparent *lèse-majesté* and suffered for the poor boy who in fact felt no pain since he did not exist. 'I will not be called Joe Smallwood. I will not allow it. My name is not Joe Smallwood. It is not Mr Smallwood.' He kept the crowd in suspense a second longer. 'My name is *Joey* Smallwood.' There was an instant of incomprehension, and then cheers and laughter. Joey Smallwood repeated this performance at meeting after meeting until he no longer needed to: The legend was feeding off itself.

Richard Gwyn, Smallwood: The Unlikely Revolutionary, rev. ed., 1972

In 1946 the British government announced that Newfoundland, which had been ruled by an appointed Commission, could elect representatives to a convention to advise on the political future. Joey worked hard for Confederation.

One of the Convention's first acts had been to set up a steering committee of ten or twelve members. Bradley and I were members of it, as were Cashin, Hollett, Fudge, Job, and Ashbourne. It was a sort of Cabinet that was supposed to regulate the order of business of the public sessions, but about the only thing I remember clearly about it was the wrestling match between Peter Cashin and myself. John McEvoy, as chairman of the Convention in succession to Bradley, was presiding on this occasion. I sat on his right, Cashin on his left, with the other members ranged around the large table between us. I forget the precise topic that was under discussion, but the first thing I remember happening was that Cashin got into a rage, rushed behind the chairman to me, and struck out with his fist at me. I caught his wrist and so warded the blow off, but Cashin, losing his balance, fell to the floor. I, holding both his wrists, was dragged to the floor with him, and there we both were, now I on top of him, then he on top of me. I continued to hold him by the two wrists and thus prevented him from taking a poke at me.

It all happened so quickly, and so unexpectedly, that the others were taken by surprise; and it was a few minutes before several of them rushed over and hauled us apart. We stood facing each other then. I lit a cigarette and, with both of us still held apart, I said, 'Cashin, I'll show you how scared I am of you,' and with that blew a mouthful of cigarette smoke into his face. He struggled to get at me, but his friends held him, as mine held me. Malcolm Hollett (or was it Pierce Fudge?) was hit in the face by Cashin's elbow, and became a little weak and was led to a sofa. Tom Ashbourne kept repeating, 'How disgraceful, how disgraceful.' As he was a loyal friend of mine in the Confederate cause, I assumed that he was condemning Cashin.'

Joey Smallwood, *I Chose Canada*, 1973

During World War II, Smallwood had run a piggery, supplying meat to the air base at Gander.

On receiving an honorary degree at Waterloo Lutheran University in Ontario, I remarked that it was my presence in Gander, as boss of the piggery, that had started the ball rolling for Confederation. I went on to lay down two indispensable qualifications for premiers of Newfoundland: that they should have served an apprenticeship at cleaning out after pigs—for a knowledge of pigs, two-legged as well as four, was very valuable; and that they should have spent many hours out on our Newfoundland barrens and marshes, picking berries. Frankly, I said, I couldn't see how a man could be fit for the office without those qualifications.

Ibid.

I remember a Parish Priest meeting me one day. He was very excited and aggressive and said, 'Do you know how much money is coming into my Parish now from Ottawa?'

I said, 'No', and he gave me some figures that he knew of. He was naturally delighted about it and I am sure his parishioners were equally delighted at receiving this new money. Very few would consider that 'this will come no matter what Government is elected'; most thanked Joey for having brought it about. I remember seeing a letter in the kitchen of a home of one of my constituents in a Placentia Bay settlement, addressed by Joey Smallwood to her, in which he said:

'Dear Friend, I promise that you will receive for the rest of your life the sum of at least $30.00 a month. I am sure that you will greatly benefit by this payment.'

Then, the letter went on to say:

> 'If your husband (or your spouse) is over seventy years of age, he (or she) will receive the same amount. Your sincere friend, Joey Smallwood.'

One can imagine the tremendous effect that such a letter would have, seeing that it was sent to nearly all persons over seventy years of age in Newfoundland.

William J. Browne, Eighty-four Years A Newfoundlander, 1980

When Newfoundland entered Confederation and became part of Canada, Joey, as first premier, moved into what had been Canada House, the home of the recalled Canadian commissioner. Nobody in Ottawa had the nerve to ask him to leave and he stayed on for years, using the Canadian china, silver, and crystal, the stuff with the emblem. When he finally was persuaded to find other quarters, nobody ever found the dishes or the cutlery.

Frank Moores once told me that his biggest surprise when he took over from Joey wasn't anything he found in the files, because there were no files. It was a switchboard in the premier's office that enabled him to cut in on telephone calls of any of his cabinet ministers, without their knowing. Moores had it taken out, but only after pondering its usefulness. Joey was a great eavesdropper—it was reported that, at the farm, he had the entire lane leading away from the house lined with hidden microphones, so he could hear what guests were saying about him after they departed.

Charles Lynch, A Funny Way to Run a Country, 1986

A diminutive figure crouched over the wheel of a vast, custom-built Cadillac or Chrysler Imperial, Smallwood can commonly be sighted hurtling through fog at seventy miles an hour, two wheels across the centre line, or smartly overtaking round a corner. According to St John's legend, he was once spotted doing this by an RCMP control car, which gave chase and finally overtook him. As the officer approached, notebook in hand, a familiar face peered out the window. 'My God,' the officer said. 'Yes,' replied the Premier, 'and don't you forget it.'

Richard Gwyn, Smallwood: The Unlikely Revolutionary, 1968

Once I accompanied Stanfield to a Maritime Premiers Conference in Newfoundland. That was before the posh new Government building was built. But whereas in Halifax we always met in the Red Room, with an attendant guarding the outside door and a convenient telephone booth to enable us to make calls (although incoming calls were discouraged. We simply did not answer the phone) the Government of Newfoundland had a very special Cabinet Meeting place and there we held our Conference.

The door was locked. The telephone was in a disappearing box at Mr Smallwood's right hand. No one else could make a call or take one. There was an enormous window covered with an even more enormous drape. This could be opened or closed electrically and Mr Smallwood had the switch at his right hand. He demonstrated for us how the thing worked. The huge drapes gave an impression of deep secrecy. Not even light was admitted unless the Premier said so.

I recall one amusing interlude at this meeting. During an interruption, Premier Smallwood who was Chairman went out of the room and during his absence we had a recess. Stanfield's attention was caught by the wastepaper basket, and he juggled it. About ordinary size, but it was very heavy.

'Is this gold?' Stanfield asked jokingly, not dreaming that it was. But it was! Stanfield never fully recovered from the shock.

E.D. Haliburton, *My Years With Stanfield*, 1972

I recall being in Newfoundland for one of Joey's landslide elections, and just as the polls were closing I crossed the lobby of the Newfoundland Hotel to go to the returning office to watch the results. Don Jamieson was on the television, doing the election anchor job, and he was giving a resumé of the election and its issues, without a note, and so I paused to watch the virtuoso in action, having once heard him refer to a local church dignitary as 'His Arse, the Gracebishop'. Jamieson's only rival as a TV free-wheeler was René Lévesque, and he gave us a ten-minute riding-by-riding summary of the campaign that was masterful. Just as he was winding up, there were noises off-camera and into view came Smallwood, pulling up a chair beside Jamieson. Now remember, not a single return had yet been reported.

Jamieson welcomed the premier and asked what he could do for him.

'I came,' said Joey, 'to tell you how I won this election.'

'Pray proceed,' said Jamieson, or words to that effect.

Joey was just getting into stride with his victory statement when the first return of the evening was shoved across Jamieson's desk. It showed Joey's candidate trailing his Tory rival by twenty votes to two. Joey didn't blink. He recognized the poll, which was in St John's, and he named the streets and some of the Tory voters, and said he had spent time there that very morning driving people to the polls, but without much hope because he'd always had trouble there. He resumed his victory statement when a second result came in, from a poll in another part of the city. Again the Liberal trailed by a margin of ten to one, and Joey went into his description of that neighbourhood and its people, which was not flattering. He predicted the good news would be coming in shortly, which it did, and Joey wiped the floor with the Tories, as he did in every election but his last. Where else but in Newfoundland, I reflected, would a premier come on TV to explain his victory before a single vote was counted?

Charles Lynch, *A Funny Way to Run a Country*, 1986

Lester Pearson recalls a TV interview with Joey.

Joey was a spellbinder and he knew it. So I let him do the talking, not that I could do anything about it anyway. His introduction was usually longer than my speech as he explained what a great man I was and what clowns or villains the opposition were. Above all, how wonderful it was to be a Newfoundlander living in the best place in the world, now better than ever, thanks to Confederation, Liberalism, and Mr Pearson's Liberal government. This kind of introduction always had the desired result of ensuring that I got a good reception for my own brief remarks. I remember especially a television interview in St John's during one campaign. The Premier decided that he would take the place of the interviewer. Joey was certainly qualified to do so, for he was an experienced and skilled radio and television performer. It was the easiest half-hour I ever had before the camera, and may have been my most successful. Mr Smallwood introduced me in a few flattering sentences and then asked the first question. This took ten minutes or so, more statement than question, at the end of which came the query, 'Do you agree with me on my assessment?' My reply had to be 'Yes, indeed,' for it had been a paean of praise for our party, its record, and its leader. Two more statement-questions and my hearty agreement, and the broadcast was over, with a 'Thank you' and 'Benediction'.

Mike: The Memoirs of the Right Honourable Lester B. Pearson, Vol. 2, 1948–1957, ed. John A. Munro and Alex I. Inglis, 1973

Pearson recounts a tale of campaigning with Joey.

Mr Smallwood was not the kind of politician to concede that the Opposition had or deserved any chance of winning. Everybody was, naturally, on the side of progress, happiness, and Liberalism. Our crowds, therefore, were always the biggest, our meetings the most enthusiastic, our victory certain. He refused to concede anything to the Tories. Once in our procession from the airport he called my attention to the masses of people lining the street and to the cheers I was getting. The evidence on both counts was, I thought, far from conclusive, but it was a good welcome. Then our cavalcade had to halt momentarily. 'Look at them,' Joey exulted, 'they're all on your side. Everyone in St John's is. Everyone.' I called his attention to the scowling hostile face of a man on the curb, who seemed to be shaking his fist at us. 'Not everybody,' I demurred, 'look at that chap.' He did, but was not abashed. 'Well, we'll put him down as doubtful.' That was as far as he would go.

Ibid.

When the mantle of political leadership had at last passed from Smallwood to Frank Moores, a rich fish merchant, the joke-telling took to the air. On his plane he suggested throwing 10 one-dollar bills overboard to make 10 people happy; another raised it to 20, to make double that number happy. Whereupon a Smallwood stowaway countered, for Moores's benefit, 'Why don't you throw yourself overboard and make everybody happy?'

Herbert Lench Pottle, *Fun On The Rock*, 1983

SIR ROBERT BOND

Here is a snippet about a predecessor of Smallwood. (In Newfoundland, time is always half an hour—different.) Sir Robert Bond was Liberal Premier from 1900 to 1908.

His estate, 'The Grange', was situated at Whitbourne, a settlement in Trinity Bay, about 40 miles north of St John's, as the crow flies. In the same community there resided also the Rev. John Reay, retired. Once, when Mr Reay wished to have the loan of a certain book from Sir Robert's library, he sent a messenger to fetch it. Sir Robert's word was: 'If Mr Reay wants a book from my library, he will have to come here to read it.'

It also happened that a few months later Sir Robert wished to have the use of Mr Reay's lawn mower, and sent a house-servant to borrow it. Whereupon Mr Reay gave him this message: 'If Sir Robert wants to borrow my lawn mower, he will have to come here to use it.'

A star like Bond rarely lit up the Newfoundland firmament. From time to time other political lights, mostly of much lesser magnitude, darted across the canopy but were soon lost forever from view in the enveloping haze. The haze, when not outright fog, became the standard political climate, under cover of which the extremities of patronage and self-interest were pushed to the limit. Over the generations the extremes of the Newfoundland political weather had the effect of widening the gap between the masters and the masses—recently humoured politically as 'the toiling masses'. The more extreme the prevailing political climate, the more it has always favoured those who hold the purse strings—a political outcome which is forecast as follows:

> The rain descendeth from above
> Upon the just and unjust fellow;
> But mostly on the just,
> Because the unjust
> Has the just's umbrella.

Herbert Lench Pottle, *Fun On The Rock*, 1983

T. C. DOUGLAS

Tommy Douglas was CCF Premier of Saskatchewan from 1944 to 1961, and national leader of the New Democratic Party from 1961 to 1971. A Baptist preacher and an exponent of the Social Gospel, he became politically active in 1931, and held a federal seat (Weyburn) from 1935 to 1944.

Despite his increasing political activity, Douglas still found time for a wide range of pastoral and community duties. In the little study in his church on the corner, a couple of blocks from downtown, he wrote his sermons, his papers for McMaster, and his speeches on farmer-labour co-operation. The church itself was a distress centre and relief depot as well as a political head-quarters. It was a place where ideas took root, and the results swept through the community. The study also became a counselling centre from which Doug-las worked with delinquent boys sent to him by a local judge, trying to find homes and work for them.

His job as a social worker caused him some headaches, but it did provide him with another story for future occasions. One day, in a fit of overzealousness, he agreed to take delivery of eleven delinquents who had appeared in court. In addition to scrubbing them clean in his own bathtub and re-clothing them from the church basement stocks, he undertook to develop an athletic program that would help fill their spare hours and teach them the virtues of fair play. He also hoped to keep them out of trouble with the law. Inevitably, in their boyish yearning for the good things of life, they slipped their leash and com-mitted another break and enter. Once discovered, the plunder of cigarettes and chocolate bars that remained was handed over to the aggrieved shopkeeper, and the boys trooped back to the pastor's study. In Douglas's words, 'I pro-ceeded to give them my very best lecture. . . . Pretty soon they began to cry and the tears flowed. . . . It was a fine reconciliation.' It was a time to apologize and repent—and the repentance included returning to the pastor his watch, his knife, his pen, and some other odds and ends they had lifted off of his desk while he delivered his sermon on the wages of sin.

Thomas H. McLeod and Ian McLeod, Tommy Douglas: The Road to Jerusalem, 1987

Early campaigning was often strenuous.

[T.H. 'Tommy'] McLeod had many duties including driving Douglas to out-of-town meetings. McLeod recalls one occasion when the two Tommys were driving down an unpaved country road with loose gravel on both sides. The car in front was sticking to the middle of the road, not allowing anybody to pass. Douglas was, as usual, running late, and only after vigorous horn honking was the motorist persuaded to yield enough to allow Tommy McLeod to try the hazardous operation of passing while navigating the loose gravel. McLeod was giving his full attention to the road when he saw Douglas with the car door open leaning out and addressing a few well chosen words to the stubborn motorist. McLeod recalls doing his best to keep the car on the road with one hand while reaching over, grasping Douglas's collar and hauling him back into

the car with the other. Douglas was a scrapper, sometimes more pugnacious
than prudent.

Allan Blakeney, 'The Early Years', NeWest Review, May 1987

Tommy resigned his federal seat in 1944 to lead the CCF to power in Saskatchewan.

Douglas's platform performances highlighted the 1944 campaign across the
province: the lively, boyish appearance; the captivating cadence of the rhetoric;
the head thrown back; the light glinting off the rimless spectacles; one hand
on the hip while the other cut the air with a measured stroke; the almost
cough-like laugh that signalled impending rapier thrust; above all, the integrity
of the man.

Important as the speech might be in winning a following, however, the
meeting really began when the speeches were over. For as long as time would
allow, Douglas would remain near the stage, surrounded by people anxious to
shake his hand and give their advice or tell him their troubles. It was now that
he established the bond between himself and his followers. He had a remarkable
ability to concentrate his attention on whoever stood before him. As long as
the conversation lasted, that person was the only person in the world. He had
a great memory for names and for family ties and family affairs, and this
knowledge came readily into play on a second meeting. Anyone meeting
Douglas for the first time thought they had made a friend; on meeting him for
the second time they were sure of it. As an opposition politician commented,
'Douglas doesn't need to kiss babies, babies kiss him.'

Thomas H. McLeod and Ian McLeod, Tommy Douglas: The Road to Jerusalem, 1987

Well in advance of the 1948 election Douglas and Tucker tangled in debate,
the most widely publicized occasion being a huge afternoon rally at Crystal
Lake when each man spoke for an hour from the canvas-covered back of a
truck to a throng of 1,500 people. Here the charge of CCF 'communism' was
not well received, according to *Leader-Post* reporter Ken Liddell: 'Brightest
interest the crowd took in the proceedings came during Mr Tucker's rebuttal
when, in answering an allegation by Douglas that he was the servant of big
interests, Mr Tucker said that Premier Douglas's group was receiving the
support of the Communist party. The crowd booed this no end.'

The writer described the pair as a 'frisky young colt' and a 'plodding work
horse', and the difference in size—Tucker was a very large, heavy-set man—
led to one of the most frequently quoted exchanges between the two men. As
Liddell heard it: 'Mr Tucker had said the Liberals had introduced mothers'
allowances when Premier Douglas "was just a little fellow" and the premier
countered with the remark that "I am still a little fellow. Tucker is big enough

to swallow me, but if he did he would be the strangest man in the world because he would have more brains in his stomach than he has in his head." '

Doris French Shackleton, Tommy Douglas, 1975

As Premier after 1944, Douglas also held the portfolio of Minister of Health. His government was the first to establish a public hospital insurance plan in 1946, and in 1960 announced that it would introduce public medical insurance.

The Premier gave up the health portfolio in 1949, but he never gave up his plan of establishing a comprehensive health insurance scheme in the province. For him, attainment of this objective was not simply a matter of political expediency but a deeply held personal commitment based on the teaching of the social gospel that we are, indeed, 'our brother's keepers'. It was also rooted in his experience as a youth, when he had suffered from osteomyelitis in one leg, and was put in a public ward as a charity patient. The house doctor said that the leg would have to be cut off. Fortunately, an orthopedic surgeon took an interest in the case and offered to provide treatment for nothing in return for agreement that young Tommy could be used as a patient for demonstration purposes for medical students. The treatment was successful, and he was saved from spending his life as a cripple. Speaking of that event during the 1960 election campaign he said:

'Had I been a rich man's son the services of the finest surgeons would have been available. As an iron moulder's boy, I almost had my leg amputated before chance intervened and a specialist cured me without thought of a fee.

'All my adult life I have dreamed of the day when an experience like mine would be impossible and we would have in Canada a program of complete medical care without price tag. And that is what we aim to achieve in Saskatchewan by 1961—the finest health service available to everyone in the province, regardless of ability to pay. This is our goal of a compulsory prepaid medical care insurance.'

E.A. Tollefson, 'The Battle for Medicare', NeWest Review, May 1987

Mr Justice Emmett Hall, whom Diefenbaker appointed chairman of the Royal Commission on Health Services in 1964, had a high regard for Tommy.

Mrs John Diefenbaker, that's Edna Diefenbaker, was ill. John had gone to Australia on some mission. While he was there Edna took a very serious turn. She was in St Paul's Hospital in Saskatoon.

As soon as the premier heard of this (because going back to 1950 you didn't fly from Australia in a few hours) he phoned me, as I happened to be chairman of the board, to tell me and her doctor, Dr David Baltzan, that whatever had to be done, wherever we had to find the help that might be needed, or whatever it would cost, it was to be done. It would be at the cost to the province.

It was an indication of the caring that he had for others, whether in his own political field or not.

E. M. Hall, 'A Tribute to Tommy', Regina Memorial Service Booklet, April 1986.

Allan Blakeney, NDP Premier of Saskatchewan from 1971 to 1982, remembers Tommy losing the Regina seat in the election of 1962. (Another seat was opened for Douglas in BC, which he held until he retired in 1979.)

The election of 1960 had the fierce opposition to public medicare and the campaign of fear mounted by its opponents. At the height of the following crisis in the federal election of June of 1962, Tommy was the candidate for the new party, the NDP, here in Regina.

I remember riding in a car caravan—that's how we conducted elections in those days, great long car caravans starting at the airport and going down through the city. I rode in that caravan with Tommy. Thousands of people were lining the route, most of them staring coldly at the man who worked so hard for them.

And on election night when Tommy went down to a crushing defeat, I remember the message of hope he gave to his tired and grieving workers. No words of reproach or recrimination, just the words of the old Scottish poem:

> *Fight on, my men, said Sir Andrew Barton.*
> *I am hurt, but I am not slain.*
> *I will lay me down and bleed awhile,*
> *And then I'll rise and fight again.*

Allan Blakeney, 'A Tribute to Tommy', Regina Memorial Service Booklet, April 1986.

Elmer Diefenbaker wrote to his brother John:

[Appended to a letter dated December 2, 1962]

Did you hear about Tom Douglas during the by-election in British Columbia calling Regina on long distance?

On completion of the call, Tom asked the operator the price of the call. When she told him Tom answered: 'In Saskatchewan I could 'phone to hell and back for that.'

Replied the operator: 'Why, sir, in Saskatchewan that is a local call.'

Personal Letters of a Public Man, ed. Thad McIlroy, 1985

If [David] Lewis was uncomfortable with the Douglas style of political presentation, Douglas was no less uncomfortable with the big new style of the party he led. Characteristically, however, Douglas expressed his discomfort mildly and with humour. At one of the first 'new-style' NDP fund-raising affairs, a $50-a-plate dinner in Toronto, Douglas began his obligatory speech-with: 'It's always a pleasure to speak to a group of the underprivileged proletariat.'

On another occasion, again in Toronto, party organizers and publicity men were brain-storming about how to get attention and give the NDP a 'with-it image'. It was the 1960s and Toronto had opened up, with Yonge Street featuring strippers and topless go-go. One of the publicity types, only half in jest, suggested that an NDP rally should be led by a naked lady riding a horse down Yonge Street. Douglas considered this proposal carefully and finally said: 'I think that would be a very good idea, it must have been years since the people of Toronto have seen a horse.'

Michael Bradley, Crisis of Clarity, 1985

T.C. Douglas and his wife Irma think they'll steer clear of Jamaica on their next vacation after a Christmas holiday that included robberies, a punchout, an attempted break-in and a reprimand from the Jamaican police.

Mr Douglas, MP for Nanaimo-Cowichan-The Islands, went to Jamaica looking for sun and relaxation, but all he found was trouble.

A member of Mr Douglas's Ottawa staff said in a telephone interview yesterday that the former national leader of the New Democratic Party and his wife were strolling along a beach on the second day of their vacation when two young men approached.

The men grabbed Mrs Douglas and held a knife at her husband's throat. Mr Douglas, one time Manitoba amateur bantam-weight boxing champion, let fly with a punch and hit one of their assailants in the face. Both men fled. Later, the 68-year old MP was given a stern lecture by Jamaican police for being so pugnacious.

The Globe and Mail, 5 Jan. 1973

ROSS THATCHER

A former CCF MP for Moose Jaw (1945–55), Ross Thatcher was Liberal Premier of Saskatchewan from 1964 to 1971.

Thatcher's rise within the Liberal Party came partly because of a Douglas miscalculation. After his defection from the CCF, Thatcher gained prominence as a critic of Saskatchewan's crown corporations and the premier challenged him to a debate on the subject. In the spring of 1957, when Thatcher was contesting the Assiniboia federal seat for the Liberals, the two men squared

off in the town of Mossbank, southwest of Moose Jaw. Nearly 1000 people crowded into the hall where the event took place, while many more sat
in their cars outside in a heavy downpour and listened to the debate on the
radio. . . .

Bob Moon, a *Leader-Post* columnist, observed the next day, 'There was no
clear winner officially, and it may be doubted if a single vote was changed.'
However, Thatcher had emerged as 'a new factor in Saskatchewan politics,'
said the Calgary *Herald*, 'not because he won but because he did not lose.'

Thomas H. McLeod and Ian McLeod, Tommy Douglas: The Road to Jerusalem, 1987

Ross told me he chose Mossbank as the site of the debate with Douglas because
it was a strongly Liberal area. He expected a large collection would be taken,
and that Tommy might not insist on half of the money for the CCF. But when
Ross approached Tommy to ask about sharing, Thatcher was brought up short.
'The little S.O.B. outsmarted me. He'd already told the press that the entire
collection would go to the Red Cross.'

Contributed by Jim Coutts, Toronto.

STANLEY H. KNOWLES

*CCF/NDP MP from Winnipeg North Centre (1942–58 and 1962–84), Stanley
Knowles was a master of House procedure. In 1984, following a serious stroke, he
was named an Honourary Officer of the House, a most extraordinary retirement gift
and mark of respect. Both he and T.C. Douglas were students at Brandon College, a
Baptist institution.*

The theologs, being for the most part older and more mature than their fellows,
played a leading role in student life. Some of them went on to distinguished
careers in the ministry; and although the Baptist church was already turning
to the right in the 1920s, several, like Douglas, would later join the socialist
party and even stood for election. One of these was Stanley Knowles, a fellow
member of the Typographical Union. The decorous behaviour of the Knowles
of later years, the dean of the House of Commons, is difficult to reconcile with
that of Knowles the college cheer-leader, leading his troops in a resounding
rendition of the yell 'Hippy Skippy'.

Thomas H. McLeod and Ian McLeod, Tommy Douglas: The Road to Jerusalem, 1987

For 38 years, he lived in a room rented from his Ottawa friends Walter and
Marjorie Mann, but spent virtually all his time on the Hill, in his office by 8

A.M., still there at 11 P.M. When Alistair Fraser was Clerk of the House, he dropped in one Christmas Eve on a brief errand and found the Centre Block deserted—by everyone but Knowles. Knowles ordinarily ate his sparse dinner in the Parliamentary restaurant. Once Marjorie Mann persuaded him to come home for dinner; he infuriated her by reading Hansard at the table. The Manns once introduced him to bridge, without success. 'He would have been a superb player,' says Mrs Mann, 'but the spirit of the game was alien to him. He thought a finesse was cheating.'

Contributed by Janice Tyrwhitt, Roving Editor, Reader's Digest, Toronto.

Diefenbaker once offered Knowles the Speakership; Knowles turned it down because he wanted to go on fighting for his causes and his constituents. Coldwell speculated that Diefenbaker wanted to get Knowles off the firing line; Diefenbaker was convinced Knowles had said this, and for years they detested one another. When Knowles was proposed as a delegate to the 10th UNESCO conference in Paris in 1959, Diefenbaker growled, 'I wouldn't nominate Stanley Knowles for dogcatcher.' Knowles retaliated by gently teasing; he discovered that he and Olive Diefenbaker, both descended from the Pilgrim Fathers, were distantly related, and he always greeted her as 'Cousin' while her husband glowered. But, when Olive died, Diefenbaker summoned Knowles back to the house after the funeral, and spent two hours pouring out his grief to someone he now saw as an old friend.

Ibid.

For all his austere appearance and habits, he [Knowles] had an apt but wholly political sense of humour. On a Speaker's Tour of Russia he introduced Conservative Gerald Baldwin, adding with a twinkle, 'In Canada he's known as a Red Tory.' Baldwin, who had been relegated to lowly positions at official dinners, promptly found himself moved to head table by his Communist hosts.

Ibid.

HUGH JOHN FLEMMING

The Conservative Premier of New Brunswick from 1952 to 1960, Hugh John Flemming may not have been directly involved in this patronage case, but he might deserve credit for this delightful story.

Once upon a time there were two great breweries in New Brunswick; one was called Moosehead and the other Red Ball. Being good Maritime breweries they made campaign contributions to the government of the day, in this case to the Conservative government of New Brunswick, that of Hugh John Flemming.

As to the beer, I always preferred Moosehead, myself, as the better of the two. Apparently the people of New Brunswick felt so; only 15 per cent of beer sales were Red Ball. The Moosehead brewery thought so also, for they decided that their campaign contribution to the New Brunswick government need only be a fraction of that of Red Ball Brewery. The New Brunswick government thought this kind of discrimination not only unfair, but also unwise. They knew how to retaliate. The edict went forth from Caesar, in this case the Liquor Commission of New Brunswick, that local beer in New Brunswick would be sold in the exact proportion of one Red Ball to two Moosehead. These proportions were to be applied monthly. There was not much doubt that the New Brunswick inhabitants broadly preferred Moosehead. The result was that for the last 10 days in each mortal month it was virtually impossible to buy any other local beer but Red Ball in the far-flung empire of the New Brunswick Liquor Commission.

P. B. Waite, 'An Historian's Adventures in Archivia and Beyond', Papers of the Bibliographical Society of Canada, vol. 12, 1974

W. A. C. BENNETT

A Conservative MLA in British Columbia from 1941, W. A. C. Bennett left the Coalition government's ranks to sit as an independent in 1951, organized a Social Credit party, and in 1952 began his twenty-year term as Premier.
His new party started slowly, but soon gained momentum.

Before the age of the Coalition had ended, Bennett had already decided that the Legislature was a barren vineyard. The fruits of his labours were ready to be plucked outside—and the time was now. His evenings and weekends were devoted to meetings, preparing for the expected election.

Frank Calder, the Indian MLA, warned the House March 13: 'He has already started rallies, and is so far ahead of us it isn't even funny.' But some of the meetings were funny. With Chant and Donald Smith, Bennett staged a major rally at Nanaimo, the busy city seventy miles north of Victoria.

When Smith went to check the hall, he found three people and some reporters. He went backstage to Bennett and said it was too bad, but the meeting must be called off. Bennett told him if only one man showed up, he was entitled to the full message, the same way as a crowd of 1,000.

The three played musical chairs, each chairing the meeting while another spoke. By the end of the meeting, half a dozen were present. So a Social Credit group was formed, complete with president, vice-president, and secretary.

Paddy Sherman, Bennett, 1966

During the 1952 election W.A.C. Bennett got help from the Social Credit Premier of Alberta.

Social Credit was showing a surprising capacity to chuckle at itself. Three church ministers were running as candidates for the movement. When the Reverend Hansell [an Alberta Social Credit MP] was to speak at Kamloops for the Reverend Phillip A. Gaglardi, a line at the end of campaign advertisements read: 'Checking facilities for halos available.'

On June 5, Premier (the Reverend) E.C. Manning of Alberta apologized to a crowd of 5,000 in Vancouver for not wearing a halo. Before he began to speak, they chanted their party ditty, to the tune of 'John Brown's Body':

> BC Social Crediters will never, never stop,
> Till BC's Social Credit from the bottom to the top.
> No more CCF-ers, no more Liberal lollipop,
> And the Tories are all gone.
> CHORUS:
> You have seen the light, so shed it,
> You have learned the truth so spread it.
> Raise your voice for Social Credit,
> And BC shall march on.

Ibid.

Bennett was sworn in as Premier of BC on 1 August 1952.

Following a brief reception and skirmish with news hounds, the new government retreated to Bennett's hotel for refreshments. The waiter took orders for martinis and scotch and sodas, but when it was Bennett's turn, he said, 'Anybody can drink what they like tonight—as long as it's tea, coffee or Ovaltine.' They all complied, becoming the first government ever to be sworn in on Ovaltine.

David J. Mitchell, *W.A.C. Bennett and the Rise of British Columbia,* 1983

After a campaign promise to make the province debt-free, [Bennett] called in about $200 million worth of long-outstanding bonds, on which as little as 3 per cent interest was being paid. Ceremoniously he had them piled onto a floating raft, and, with press photographers present, fired a flaming arrow into the bundle. Then, to finance new projects, he blandly borrowed new money at 5.5 per cent interest.

Gerald Clark, *Canada: The Uneasy Neighbors,* 1965

One year he [Bennett] reacted violently against the aspirations of Quebec, unleashed a tirade against two tongues, unfair accommodation of the French, and 'hand-outs' from Ottawa to the Québécois. Another year he lent \$100 million to the Quebec Provincial Government, with the fine political axiom: 'Where your treasury is, there your heart is also.' Perhaps he meant it, too. He was privately aghast to find once that a reporter had lent some money for a day to one of the premier's friends—without charging him interest on it.

Few premiers, including those of Quebec, have put such a strain on the bonds of confederation while all the time insisting he would still be a Canadian when the rest of the country had moved south.

After one flurry of secessionist noises—and he did little to quell them, pointing out that B.C. was the only part of Canada that would dare, or could afford, to go it alone—he enthusiastically urged that Canada's future governors-general should live part of the year in British Columbia to encourage unity.

Paddy Sherman, Bennett, 1966

TILLY ROLSTON

Canada's first woman provincial cabinet minister, Mrs Rolston became Minister of Education in W.A.C. Bennett's BC government in 1952.

Reporters . . . heard excited ministers asking each other who they were, and what portfolios they held. They began asking questions of the ministers, to find what kind of crew now held the keys to power.

Mrs Rolston they knew. At sixty-five, when she became Canada's first full woman Cabinet minister, she was grandmother to nine, a gay, party-loving type, fond of foreign travel; her main qualification for her new portfolio was that she taught for two fleeting years before her marriage. Her primary claim to political fame was her successful battle to get coloured margarine made legal in the province. She was quick of tongue, and only once could anyone recall her being crushed. An MLA had asked her in the Legislature: 'Do you think you are as good as a man?' She answered: 'Yes.' Came the scintillating reply: 'Well, that's too damn bad. You ain't.' Now she had proved her point.

Paddy Sherman, Bennett, 1966

AGNES KRIPPS

Mrs Kripps was a Social Credit MLA in British Columbia during the 1950s.

The [BC] chamber produced, not so long ago, the ineffable Agnes Kripps, a Social Credit bottle blonde who wakened the slumbering MLAs one day with her proposal that all the sniggering about sex education in the classrooms could be removed if the word sex was eliminated and replaced by a new program that she would call Biology of Living Today—or BOLT.

Dozing cabinet ministers snapped to attention. Newspapers covering the faces of sleeping backbenchers were blown aloft. 'I'm bolt upright just listening to you,' shouted an opposition member as Agnes, sensing deep trouble, floundered on. 'It's okay for the bolts,' shouted Herb Capozzi, a millionaire Socred wit, 'but what about the nuts?' With the House in clear chaos, MLAs falling off their chairs in glee, a near-tearful Mrs Kripps appealed to their sense of fair play and cried in despair: 'Mr Speaker! Mr Speaker! Will you please bang that thing of yours on the table!'

Allan Fotheringham, Maclean's, 25 Jan., 1988

CHARLOTTE WHITTON

The first woman mayor in Canada, Charlotte Whitton held municipal office in Ottawa from 1951 to 1964.

'Whatever women do they must do twice as well as men to be thought half so good . . . luckily, it's not difficult.'

Columbo's Canadian Quotations, 1974

JEAN DRAPEAU

A master of political longevity, Jean Drapeau was Mayor of Montreal from 1954 to 1957, and 1960 to 1986. He first came to prominence as a nationalist Bloc Populaire *candidate in a 1942 federal by-election and in the 1944 provincial elections, opposing conscription.*

The [1942] campaign in Cartier was fierce and dirty. 'The Liberals had a machine that has not been equalled since,' says David Lewis, the future leader of the New Democratic Party who ran for its forerunner, the CCF, in Cartier. 'And if it was possible, the Communists had an even bigger machine behind their candidate, Fred Rose.' The four candidates facing the Bloc were all Jews and *Le Devoir* reported that the Bloc candidate 'commented with humour' that 'there isn't very much Canadian about those guys. They sound more like Jerusalem Canadians.'

Lewis remembers the rough-and-tumble voting day—brass-knuckle fights in polling booths between rival gangs of telegraphers wheeling from poll to poll to vote in other people's names and arriving simultaneously; others voting from long lists of fictitious people registered at fictitious addresses. 'Sometimes even dogs and cats were enumerated.'

Brian McKenna and Susan Purcell, Drapeau, 1981

Drapeau's biographers make much of his membership in the Order of Jacques Cartier, a secret society allied with the Union Nationale.

Many conservative French Canadians who played a leading role in the nationalist movements of the thirties and forties were inducted into a secret brotherhood called the Order of Jacques Cartier. Its enemies called the organization the 'Ku Klux Klan' of French Canada. The large Montreal branch was known to insiders as La Patente—'the thing'—in the same manner that members of the Honoured Society of Calabria called their mafia 'Cosa Nostra'.

While the order bore passing similarities to both the Klan and the Mafia—which was originally conceived of as a protective organization for rock-poor Italians—the order never resorted to the murderous tactics of either.

The organization had a benign beginning, started in 1926 by a group of Ottawa civil servants who had been denied good jobs in the Ottawa hierarchy because of English-Canadian bigotry. With the blessing of the church and its bishops in French Canada, the order became a counterbalance to Protestant groups in Canada such as the Freemasons and the Loyal Order of the Orange Lodge, the extremist Ulster-based brotherhood so redolent with hatred for anything Catholic and French.

In an extremism bred by the Great Depression, the order flowered underground, incorporating the worst aspects of right-wing nationalism, a rigid authoritarianism and anti-semitism. In the 1940s much of the leadership worked toward an independent, French-Catholic state patterned after Mussolini's Italy or Franco's Spain.

Drapeau has denied membership in the order, but friends from the period and a former commander of the order unequivocally confirm that he had been fully initiated and sworn in.

The ritual of initiation was called VAPDA—*le Voyage au Pays des Ancêtres*, the Voyage to the Land of Our Ancestors—a harkening back to the roots of Quebec. . . .

[At the ceremony] the brothers lined up according to their rank in the order, arms upraised at an angle, and cried out emphatically: 'Secrecy! Secrecy! Secrecy!' Members were forbidden to reveal their membership even to their wives.

The order had a rigid military structure. Commands were passed down from a supreme council, its 25 members secretly chosen from across French Canada. The names of the supreme 25 were revealed only on need-to-know basis. Attached to the supreme council was a permanent secretariat which handled administration, fund-raising, publication of bulletins and the official magazine of the order, *L'Emérillon*. Below the secretariat was a series of regional councils and secretariats.

The order was made up of hundreds of individual cells organized in institutions such as credit unions, but mostly the cells were based on the geography of Catholic parishes. The order was determined to have eyes and ears in every sphere of French Canadian life, particularly in politics, both on the provincial and the local level. The Union Nationale became virtually the political wing of the order. The order had members in youth organizations, municipal councils, the civil service and police forces, as well as in schools and on school boards, in parent-teachers' organizations, on executives of teachers' associations and teachers' colleges, to influence the curriculum and ensure that a conservative and narrowly Catholic atmosphere prevailed. The order ensured as much as possible that vacancies were filled by a member of the order or someone who would be sympathetic. In 1959, when Paul Desrochers was elected director general of the Catholic school commissions, he was taken aside and asked to become a member of the order, which he did. The order had a deep influence on the editorial boards and staffs of the newspapers *Le Devoir* and *Le Droit* in Ottawa, *L'Evangeline* in New Brunswick, the magazine *Relations* and *L'Action National*. The clergy had a powerful voice in the order and were official members. The local parish priest would be the chaplain of the local cell. He would answer to the regional chaplain who would in turn be under the authority of the chaplain-general, named by an assembly of French-language bishops. Montreal archbishops, including the liberal Charbonneau and his successor, Paul-Emile Cardinal Léger, were significant fo ces in the order.

Ibid.

One key area for the new police chief [Lucien Saulnier] would be organized crime, which was flourishing in Montreal in 1970. Its power and profits were growing dramatically. Despite the best efforts of the crack RCMP drug squad, Montreal had remained as a major port of entry for the multi-million-dollar heroin industry. With ties to the Sicilian and Calabrian mafia dating back to the days when Cuba was the transfer point for heroin from Marseilles, the Montreal family headed by Vincenzo Cotroni was making a killing. Illegal gambling was on the rise and Montreal crime families were netting millions.

Former justice minister Claude Wagner had charged that the mafia had penetrated Expo 67: 'Fleur de Lys Linen Supply Inc. is a front for chief Montreal bookie Joe Frankel.' Obie's Meat Market, operated by William Obront, the banker of the Montreal crime family, a man connected with international mafia figures like Myer Lansky, had controlled all meat concessions at Expo. A subsequent inquiry into mob-run meat rackets revealed that tons of beef sold at Expo came from carrion—animals that died of a whole series of diseases.

Organized crime controlled almost all of Montreal's 5,000 pizzerias, forcing them to pay outrageous prices for pepperoni—also made from carrion—sold by a mafia-owned meat company, and to buy cheese at inflated prices from a cheese company linked to the Montreal family.

It was also later revealed that as much as $100 million a year was being made by the Montreal underworld on loansharking, with interest rates up to 1000 per cent. Collections were made with baseball bats but physical violence was seldom necessary.

Ibid.

Controversy surrounded the financing of construction for the 1976 Olympic Games in Montreal.

There is something about giant stadiums that conjures up the roar of a lion killing in the Colosseum, the terrible cry of a crowd in heat. Certainly the athletic complex Taillibert had begun to sketch for Montreal was a panoramic movie set whose potential might bring tears to the eyes of a Leni Riefenstahl.

'As French Canadians,' says the mayor, 'the only way we're going to survive is to make our mark not only in this country, but on the entire continent. We must never be poor copies of others. This is why I chose Roger Taillibert to build these Olympics. He is one of the five greatest architects in the world—and I don't know the other four, if they exist.' . . .

While representatives of anti-poverty groups demonstrated outside, the mayor described the magnificence of the complex in grandiloquent terms, while shunning all discussion of cost—except to reassure Montrealers that it would not cost them one cent. 'The Olympics can no more have a deficit,' Drapeau would say later, 'than a man can have a baby.' . . .

While the Trudeau government adopted a hard line, the Bourassa government essentially left the mayor with the impression of an open-ended agreement. Bourassa had spent time as a young civil servant in Ottawa and had come to reject the careful competence of treasury board officials. Learning about the projected $172 million deficit, Bourassa weighed a series of factors before deciding not to challenge Drapeau's omnipotence. He calculated that the Olympics would generate massive tourist revenue, would bring prestige to Quebec and would divert people's attention from separatism: 'If they're talking about the Olympics,' Bourassa remembers thinking, 'then they're not talking about separatism.'

Ibid.

JOHN DIEFENBAKER

Canada's thirteenth prime minister (1957–63), 'the man from Prince Albert', John Diefenbaker held a special place in many hearts.
His early defeats in the 1920s and 1930s would have crushed a lesser man, but he became an MP in 1940 and leader of the Conservative party in 1956.

Each defeat suffered by John Diefenbaker became a step forward. Early in 1940 he was defending an arson case, then in its preliminary hearing, at Humboldt, in Eastern Saskatchewan. William B. Kelly, president of the Lake Centre Conservatives, sent him an invitation to appear at the Party's nominating convention to be held at Imperial, Saskatchewan, where he would express his thanks to voters who had supported him two years before in the provincial riding of Arm River, which was territorially part of Lake Centre.

John Diefenbaker requested the permission of the magistrate to leave the case to his partner in Prince Albert, J.M. Cuelenaere. The magistrate agreed, but the partner was involved in a case and, at first, could not go to Humboldt. Fortunately, the Prince Albert case ended suddenly, and Mr Cuelenaere was able to take over the Humboldt case while Mr Diefenbaker proceeded to Imperial, ninety miles away. He spoke at the convention. He was nominated. But he withdrew. In the midst of the convention, a fire broke out in the town, and the delegates all left the hall to view it and give assistance. When they returned to the political business of the convention, they decided to award the nomination to Mr Kelly. Just as John Diefenbaker was ready to return to Humboldt, with the engine of his motor car running, a farmer stopped him to ask advice about a cattle deal. The convention was still arguing about a candidate, and a friend, Ed Topping of Prince Albert, came out and proposed that John Diefenbaker should return to the hall. When he did so, Mr Kelly announced he would withdraw if Diefenbaker would stand. They talked the situation over with the executive of the party, and they proposed to meet again early in February. Such a meeting was never held, since Prime Minister Mackenzie King dissolved Parliament on January 28, 1940, and the motion that John Diefenbaker should be the Conservative candidate in Lake Centre stood. He won the seat on March 26, 1940, by a majority of 280 votes. Meanwhile, he had left the nominating convention at Imperial, and had driven back to Humboldt, where he won his court case.

B.T. Richardson, *Canada and Mr Diefenbaker*, 1962

The year 1948 . . . saw the first attempt by the Liberals to get rid of Diefenbaker by gerrymander. In the 1945 election he had increased his margin in the Lake Centre riding from the narrow 280 ballots of 1940 to a more comfortable 1,009. But the redistribution of constituency boundaries carried on by the Liberal-dominated parliamentary committee in 1948 cut the south end, where he had heavy support, off his riding and added to its eastern tip some sections that had gone CCF in past elections. The Liberal manoeuvre backfired. His constituents, angered at the obvious attempt to muzzle their MP, gave Diefenbaker a 3,432 margin in the 1949 general election, the largest vote he ever got as a private member. His victory contrasted sharply with the national picture. George Drew, the former Ontario premier, had waged a vigorous campaign, but became so desperate for issues that he concentrated on such trivia as the 'noisy engines' in the North Star aircraft purchased by Trans-Canada Air Lines. He won only forty-one seats, the second-lowest total in Conservative history.

The Liberals tried an even more vicious trick in the 1952 redistribution, when they wiped out Diefenbaker's Lake Centre seat altogether. A part of the Moose Jaw riding, where the CCF's Ross Thatcher was strongly entrenched, was added to the Lake Centre constituency, which became Moose Jaw–Lake Centre. Diefenbaker had been the lone Saskatchewan Conservative elected in the 1949 campaign, and there seemed no other seat in the province worth contesting. (When they weren't trying to get rid of him through redistribution, the Liberals found other methods of harassing Diefenbaker. At one point the federal government rented an empty house next to his home at Prince Albert and converted it into a foster residence for unwed Indian mothers.)

Peter C. Newman, Renegade in Power, 1963

Any politician counts himself lucky to have a good marriage. Diefenbaker had *two*. His first wife, Edna, was a joyous, witty woman who won the hearts of newsmen and voters. In 1949, Diefenbaker campaigned on personal popularity; westerners reviled his leader, George Drew, as a bastion of Bay Street. Later Edna Diefenbaker declared, 'Mr Coldwell (the CCF leader) was very nice to us. He didn't say a word against John, except once, but then he said something very nasty.' Coldwell, the soul of courtesy, was shocked. 'I don't remember saying anything nasty about John,' he protested. 'Oh, you did!' cried Edna, all innocence. 'You said that a vote for Diefenbaker is a vote for Drew!'

Janice Tyrwhitt, 'Remembering the "Chief"', Reader's Digest, August 1980

Passions were stirred by the pipeline debate, 1956.

Frequently, the Chair refused to recognize Opposition members on points of order or questions of privilege, although parliamentary rules clearly provide for such objections. Precedents presented by Davie Fulton and Stanley Knowles, some of them established by C.D. Howe himself and clearly applicable to the debate, were ruled irrelevant. 'I am wondering,' M.J. Coldwell, the usually imperturbable leader of the CCF, exclaimed at one point, 'whether we are in the old German Reichstag or the Canadian Parliament.' At 3:17 A.M. on May 22 second reading passed, again under closure. After a day of wild verbal crossfire—with the Opposition quoting everything from the Bible to the BNA Act against the Liberals, Howe remarked to a colleague, 'I was never so bored in all my life.' . . .

Parliament became a bedlam. Rulings, points of order, questions of privilege, and appeals from rulings piled on each other, and on May 25, when Donald Fleming refused to sit down, because the committee chairman wouldn't 'see' him, he was 'named' by the Speaker. 'This isn't the way to run a peanut stand, let alone Parliament!' Fleming shouted in deep indignation as Walter Harris, the Liberal House Leader, introduced a motion to suspend Fleming 'from the service of the House for the remainder of the day's sitting'. Just after the motion to suspend him had been passed by the Liberal majority, and Fleming was walking stiffly down the green-carpeted centre aisle of the Commons, John Diefenbaker exclaimed: 'Farewell, John Hampden!', in reference to the seventeenth-century British statesman who led the revolt of parliamentarians against Charles I. . . .

Early in the afternoon of May 31, Louis St Laurent moved closure to get the bill out of committee. After two divisions on procedural points, Colin Cameron rose on a question of privilege to read two letters which had appeared in the May 30 edition of the Ottawa *Journal*. One of the letters was from Dr Eugene Forsey, the eminent Canadian expert on parliamentary practices. 'The Speaker's words seem to imply', Forsey wrote, 'that if the rules get seriously in the way of doing something the Government very much wants done, no reasonable person can expect the Government to follow them or the Speaker to enforce them.' Cameron suggested that this constituted an attack on the dignity of Parliament. The Speaker agreed and guided the member on the correct procedure in bringing the matter before the House. This was the situation when the House went home on the night of May 31. The pipeline bill seemed finally to have been derailed. The Speaker had already ruled that Cameron's motion was debatable. This meant the Opposition could speak on it until Howe's deadline had passed.

That night, four cars, including that of a Liberal cabinet minister, were seen outside the Speaker's home. When the House met at 11:00 A.M. the next day, which was labelled 'Black Friday' in Tory propaganda, George Drew rose to continue the debate on the Cameron motion. He got as far as 'Mr Speaker . . .' when he was cut off. 'I have read carefully the articles complained of,' the Speaker said, 'and I have come to the conclusion that because of the unprecedented circumstances surrounding the pipeline debate . . . it was and is impossible, if we are to consider freedom of the press as we should, to take these two articles as breaches of our privileges . . . therefore I rule the motion made by the honourable member for Nanaimo out of order.' Having ruled the motion which he himself had helped to draft out of order, the Speaker then moved that the House should return to the time before the motion was put— in other words, that the proceedings after 5:15 P.M. of the previous day simply did not exist. This was not a ruling but a motion by the Speaker, and therefore not a matter that could be debated or voted on.

Opposition members swarmed out in fury into the green-carpeted aisle of the chamber, shaking their fists at the Speaker while the Liberal backbenchers resumed their cynical sing-song:

> I've been working on the pipeline
> all the day through,
> I've been working on the pipeline
> just to make the Tories blue.
> Can't you hear the Tories moanin',
> getting up so early in the morn'
> Hear the CCF'ers groanin', for
> the pipeline's gettin' warm.

The Canadian House of Commons had, in effect, been shorn of its rights and rules which the Speaker is sworn to uphold. No fewer than fourteen Standing Orders were clearly violated by the Speaker that day. . . .

John Diefenbaker remained behind his Commons desk that day, one of the

most subdued of the Opposition members. At the moment when his colleagues
rushed out to threaten the Speaker, he turned to George Pearkes, and said:
'I've never felt like this in my life. I'm choking. But I'm going to stay in my
place.' That night he told a friend: 'At last I understand the meaning of
revolution.'

Peter C. Newman, *Renegade in Power*, 1963

'They never thought that I would be Prime Minister,' John Diefenbaker used
to say. 'Only one man ever predicted that someday my fellow Canadians would
elect me to the highest office in the land. He was a fellow called Davidson, a
Conservative organizer in Saskatchewan, back in the '40s when western Tories
were almost as scarce as Grits in heaven. It was election night, and all our
candidates had lost their deposits.

'That terrible night in his committee room, a shabby little second-floor room
with an old desk and a few kitchen chairs, Davidson sat with a bottle of rye
in one hand and a tumbler in the other, contemplating the devastation, every
one of his candidates wiped out. And he sighed, and he filled his glass, and he
swirled his whiskey round, and he said, "They never sent that money from
Toronto for my campaign, the way they promised." And he sighed again, and
he sipped his whiskey, and it was right then that he predicted that I would
become Prime Minister. Right there in that little room he looked at me and
he said, "Diefenbaker, if I only had that money, I could make you or any other
damn fool Prime Minister of Canada."'

Janice Tyrwhitt, 'Remembering "The Chief"', *Reader's Digest*, August 1980

One summer evening in 1950, after a dinner party at his house in Prince Albert,
he was entertaining friends with a wicked imitation of Mackenzie King when
a local radio station called: King had just died. Sir John A. Macdonald was
Diefenbaker's official hero, but King was the politician he envied. Though he
joked about King's mysticism, he devoured *Hansard* searching for the secret
of the wily old Liberal's success. Instantly solemn, Diefenbaker turned to his
guest of honour, David Walker, and whispered, 'Dave, my future now has just
begun.'

Ibid.

*The election of 1957 was an upset, putting Diefenbaker at the head of a minority
government.*

His time had been so long coming that only he was sure it would come. Even
after he won the Conservative leadership in 1956 few expected him to win the
country. An editorial in *Maclean's*, written ahead of publication, reflected
Gallup Poll indications and Press Gallery expectations of Liberal victory: 'For

better or for worse, we Canadians have once more elected one of the most powerful governments ever created by the free will of a free electorate.' When it appeared the morning after the 1957 election, Diefenbaker had it framed to hang over his bed. At his first news conference as Prime Minster he greeted *Maclean's* Ottawa editor, Blair Fraser, 'Good morning . . . Prophet.'

Ibid.

Working for the Chief was no sinecure. His staff had to be companions, advisors, trouble-shooters and dogsbodies. Jim Nelson's first assignment as press secretary was guarding the Prime Minister's briefcase on a flight to Toronto; on landing he peeked inside and discovered it held one clean shirt.

His aides soon learned that anything mechanical was alien to him. John Fisher, his special assistant in the early '60s, persuaded him to buy an automatic signature machine for signing letters; he detested and discarded it. Appalled to find there was no lock on the door of the Prime Minister's office to protect him from cranks and assassins, Fisher installed an electronic lock, controlled from the desk. When a visitor arrived Fisher would buzz the Chief to release the lock, but the sound always confused Diefenbaker who would then grab a telephone, sometimes a hotline to Washington, while Fisher gave up and banged on the door.

Ibid.

His letter writers were humble people, ordinary men and women in every walk of life, including the poor, the ill, the handicapped and the aged; among them were women whose husbands were in prison; young boys who had gone wrong; people who could not help him in any way but wished to assure him of their support. They felt they knew him personally because he had been a feature of the political landscape for as long as many could remember. To the Chief, his correspondents were more than mere signatures. Some amused him; others annoyed him immensely. Nothing annoyed him more than to have a clergyman adopt a high moral tone. He had a short way with correspondents who displeased him.

Dear Sir:

This is to inform you that some crackpot is using your name and has recently written to me over your signature putting forward views so eccentric in nature and so much at variance with your usual logical style that the letter could not possibly be from you. I felt I owed it to you to bring this to your attention.

That usually ended the discussion.

Thomas Van Dusen, The Chief, 1968

When John F. Kennedy came to Ottawa, in May 1961, the Prime Minister met him at the airport, where Kennedy joked about Mr Diefenbaker's French.

Later Kennedy addressed both Houses of Parliament. I had heard Churchill speak in the Canadian Parliament during the war, and a number of leaders since then, but only Kennedy conveyed the same sense of greatness. Canada had negotiated an enormous wheat sale to China, representing a shot in the arm to the economy and a large political boost in Western Canada. The Americans, however, for reasons of foreign policy, were not willing to make grain loaders available. Mr Diefenbaker, in discussing the matter with President Kennedy, pointed out bluntly to him that unless Canada got the loaders, he as Prime Minister would appear on national television and tell the story to the people. Finally the loaders were made available, and the wheat went to China as contracted.

The Chief, however, did not soon get over his annoyance at what he considered unwarranted American intransigence. Nor was he prepared to accept what amounted to, in his estimation, an American veto over Canada's foreign relations.

This disagreement marked the beginning of the strained relations between Prime Minister Diefenbaker and President Kennedy. Mr Diefenbaker often quoted the president as having said, 'When I ask Canada to do something, I expect Canada to do it.'

Any statement along these lines was, of course, calculated to raise the hackles of the Canadian Prime Minister. The rupture became serious when Gilbert Champagne picked up off the floor of the Prime Minister's office a crumpled ball of paper, bearing in the margin a scribbled reference to 'that S.O.B.', apparently referring to Mr Diefenbaker. This, to put it mildly, was not well received. The Prime Minister did not for a moment subscribe to the explanation set out in Theodore Sorenson's book, *Kennedy*, that the initials were 'O.A.S.' President Kennedy did not assist the relationship between himself and the Prime Minister, while on his Ottawa visit, by professing to doubt that the 150-pound marlin caught by Diefenbaker off Jamaica had actually been brought in by the Chief.

Ibid.

A master storyteller, the Chief enjoyed listening to anecdotes as well as telling them. He appreciated stories which cast a light on the foibles of human nature. Bilingual jokes, common in Quebec, were among his favourites. Chief purveyor was J. Eugene Granger, CNR conductor between Quebec and Chicoutimi. . . .

Granger was a frequent visitor in the Chief's House of Commons office. When Eugene arrived, he was immediately ushered in. Presently those waiting by appointment in the reception room were puzzled at the hoots of laughter emanating from within the Chief's office.

A Granger story to the Chief's liking concerned a Toronto man convicted of murder in Quebec. Asked at the foot of the scaffold whether he had a last request, he replied, 'I'd like to learn French.' At this point, the Chief's hooting would be accompanied by Granger's deep bellow.

Ibid.

William Grogan, a well-known Winnipeg radio personality, later was an adviser to Robert Stanfield.

Grogan . . . recalled the day Diefenbaker dedicated the [Ukrainian poet Taras] Shevchenko statue, which coincided with the advent of portable tape machines at Radio Station CKY, where Grogan was one of the top on-air personalities of the time. The new Ampex tape machine was sent off to the dedication ceremony, and when the tape came back to the station it was Grogan's job to slice out a brief clip for the evening newscast. He listened to the speech with growing unease, as Diefenbaker quoted at length from the translated works of Shevchenko, without saying anything that would contain a wallop in ten seconds.

Then Grogan heard it. Diefenbaker worked himself up into a fever pitch about the brotherhood of man, as proclaimed by the poet, and he proclaimed, in his most stentorian tones, that 'Our souls are tied together!' Long pause, for effect. Then: 'ALL our souls are tied together!'

So, says Grogan, 'I put it on a little piece of tape and made it part of the newscast package, with an intro setting the scene. Well, we ran this clip on the noon news, a couple of times in the afternoon, on the major news package at supper time, and later in the evening. And it got some more play the next day, which was Sunday, by which time it was ready for the waste bin, except that the phones began to ring after the first newscast without the clip on it.

'A typical call would ask where was the story about Dief and the arsoles— there were still people who hadn't heard it, and they were gathering around their sets. So we had to take it back out of the ash can and run it more times, and the requests went on and on. Play arsoles. It got more requests than the top ten songs. Monday, we ran it five times, and we were running promos on the air saying that the excerpt from Mr Diefenbaker's speech would be heard on the next newscast, for those who had phoned in to demand it. It went on through Tuesday and, finally, other news was piling up and the program director, Jack Stewart, said get that damn thing off the air, he never wanted to hear it again. So we took it off, but I still have the tape to this day.'

Charles Lynch, A Funny Way to Run a Country, 1986

By 1962 Diefenbaker's press relations had reached their breaking-point. That winter the Prime Minister confided to an associate that he felt the really effective opposition to his regime was coming not from the Liberal Party but from the reporters on Parliament Hill. In January 5, 1962, at the annual meeting of the Progressive Conservative Association of Toronto, he attacked 'the servile press which day in and day out preaches the doctrine that we in Canada are economically not making the advancement we should'. By election eve the feelings between the country's political press and the Prime Minister had deteriorated to such a degree that some Ottawa correspondents were convinced Diefenbaker was trying deliberately to goad reporters into intemperate criticism so that he could appeal to the elector's sympathy as the victim of a spiteful press that deliberately distorted all the good he had tried to do.

Ill feeling between the Prime Minister and the press developed almost as soon as the 1962 election campaign began, when the surge of affection he had expected to feel from the crowds was not forthcoming, and the reporters accompanying him reported this fact. . . .

Instead of attacking the Liberals and praising his own accomplishments, Diefenbaker turned his speech in Edmonton that night into a tirade against . . . unnamed forces which, he claimed, had been in clandestine opposition to him over the years. 'Strong interests are against us,' he warned his audience in grave and mysterious tones, 'but whatever the strong interests may be, I prefer to have the people with me.'

When Charles King, a correspondent for Southam News Services, reported of the Edmonton meeting: 'In the same city where the Conservative campaign caught fire in 1958, the Diefenbaker bubble burst Friday night,' Diefenbaker refused to answer any further question put by him. The next evening at Trail, British Columbia, the Prime Minister shouted at King: 'I have nothing to say to you at all. Anybody can ask me questions but not you . . . I mean that, too. That's final with you.' He continued to berate King, rudely and bitterly, . . . 'I thought you were through with that kind of thing . . . it's another diabolical concoction'. . . .

Diefenbaker eventually strained his relations with accompanying reporters so badly that as he climbed on the Prime Minister's aircraft on another leg of the campaign, Val Sears of the Toronto *Star* summed up the feelings of most correspondents at that stage when he sarcastically remarked: 'To work, gentlemen. We have a government to overthrow.'

Peter C. Newman, Renegade in Power, 1963

Diefenbaker was noted for his peculiar use of language.

The man who invented this slippery speech form actually explained it once during the 1963 campaign to the Toronto *Star*'s Val Sears. . . . 'You know,' Dief told Sears, 'sometimes I think of a clever phrase during a speech and I start to say it and then I stop and think "that's taking me down a road I don't want to go" and change direction, or I don't finish the sentence. That way, they can't pin me down. They say: "Diefenbaker said so-and-so", and they go and look it up and there's a turn somewhere. They can't catch me out.'

Dief's mangled attempts at franglais, of course, were legendary. His finest hour came when, in a speech in Quebec that was carried province-wide on radio, he manfully attempted his mandatory few sentences in French. What his speech writers had given him was, 'J'espère que mes voeux seront appréciés.' (I hope my good wishes will be well received.)

How it came out, in the famed Prince Albert pronunciation, was: 'J'espère que mes veaux sauront après shiés.' (I hope my calves will know how to shit afterwards.) Radios fell off the tables all over Quebec.

Allan Fotheringham, Look Ma . . . No Hands, 1983

Office of the Prime Minister
Ottawa
April 17, 1963

Dear Elmer,

I went by car today from 24 Sussex Street to Rideau Hall and at 12:05 noon I resigned as Prime Minister, effective Monday next at noon. On that date I will have served five years and nine months. . . .

Olive is working hard getting the residence ready for the change-over. It is going to be difficult in the Leader of the Opposition's home as we will have to get a new staff, but after a week or so things will become fairly routine. . .

With all good wishes,
Your brother,
John

P.S. I should tell you a story I told the Governor General this morning when I called on him. Mr Meighen used to tell a story that when he first went to Portage to open his law office in 1916 there was a bookstore next door. He went in and received little attention from a clerk who did not appear one bit interested. While he was there a lady came in and she said to the clerk:

'Have you a "Life of St Paul"?' to which he replied:

'I haven't the life of a dog and am getting the hell out of here Monday next.'

When I told General Vanier this he told me the best example of humour he had ever heard was Howard Green's answer to the press men who asked for the reason for his defeat and his reply was:

'I have given the matter the fullest consideration and having examined the problem from all its angles reached the conclusion that it was because I didn't get enough votes!'

Personal Letters of a Public Man, ed. Thad McIlroy, 1985

When Peter Newman wrote *Renegade in Power: The Diefenbaker Years* he took a copy of the book to Diefenbaker's office. An aide took it in to the prime minister. Diefenbaker made his usual comment that he never read fiction and tossed the book into a tray. When the aide returned later, without knocking, Diefenbaker was reading the book voraciously (he was a speed reader), holding it between his knees under the desk.

Dave McIntosh, *Ottawa Unbuttoned*, 1987

Dief could come up with a story to meet any occasion, even a casual telephone call.

Everybody knew that the Rt Hon. John G. Diefenbaker was a great admirer of Sir John A. Macdonald. Year after year people who found letters from Macdonald in cupboards or attics sent them to him. He, in turn, kindly gave the Public Archives an opportunity to copy them. One day when he telephoned to say that he had several letters which we could borrow I thanked him, said I would send a messenger to pick them up and added, 'By the way, Mr Diefenbaker, what is your office number?' There was a pause, then a chuckle, and I heard him calling to his secretary in the outer office, 'What is the number of the room I am in?' She told him, he repeated it and then said, 'You know, Dr Smith, that reminds me of something that happened once to the Bishop of Rupert's Land when he was travelling by train in Saskatchewan. The conductor came along to punch tickets but the Bishop couldn't find his. 'That's all right, Bish,' said the conductor, 'You take your time looking and I'll stop on the way back.' Eventually the conductor returned but the Bishop was obliged to confess that he had been unable to find his ticket. The conductor said, 'Well, I guess it's all right. I'm sure you wouldn't be travelling without a ticket.' 'It may be all right for you, young man', retorted the Bishop indignantly, 'but what about me? How do I know where I am going?'

Contributed by Dr Wilfrid I. Smith, Public Archives of Canada, Ottawa

The Rivard case provided one of the great political lines of this century. Rivard had escaped jail in Montreal by scaling the prison wall on a garden hose in 45°F weather after telling his guards he was going out to water the rink. During the 1965 election campaign, when crammed meeting halls became hot and sweaty, Diefenbaker would say, 'It was on a night like this that Lucien Rivard went out to water the rink.' Diefenbaker brought the house down every time with this, no matter how often he used it. Sometimes, when he didn't use the line, people in the crowd would shout, 'Tell us about the rink, Dief.' It was generally believed that Tom Van Dusen, Diefenbaker's press-and-every-other-kind-of aide, gave The Chief the line, but Van Dusen insists to this day that Diefenbaker himself was the originator.

Dave McIntosh, *Ottawa Unbuttoned*, 1987

When the Chief was in full flight it was fatal to interrupt. His expression would turn to horrified astonishment, the pointing finger would flick like a rapier, and the member, pinked with a phrase, would fall back gasping. Interrupted by Paul Martin, he quoted Scripture: 'Paul, Paul, thou art beside thyself.' He loved interruptions and interjections and had a number of 'spontaneous' ripostes ready for such occasion. He counted as lost any Hansard report of one of his speeches not plentifully sprinkled with interruptions. 'Shows I was getting to them', he would say with satisfaction. When a brilliant young Newfoundland member thought he would try foils with the Chief, the Chief shot out without breaking stride, 'When a hunter is after big game, he does not stop for rabbit tracks.' The member subsided rather breathlessly.

There is no question that Government members, having put their heads into the lion's mouth, became more wary. To all appearances, they went so far as to frame a mutual agreement to refrain from interrupting the Chief. When he began, the Government benches watched tensely, giving the impression of sitting on their hands by arrangement. As the Chief went on, his remarks progressively more pointed, some member ticked on the raw would forget the agreement and spring to his feet, demanding a retraction or the right to ask a question. The result was the same, a flick of the rapier or the whistle of the broadsword, and another member stretched hors de combat.

Thomas Van Dusen, *The Chief*, 1968

Tempers ran high at the Conservatives' annual convention in 1966, at which Diefenbaker's leadership was challenged. His press aide Tom Van Dusen recalls:

There were people who would step up to the Chief when he was walking along the hall, young males, young warriors, and shout some uncouth challenge. I saw a Cape Breton member of Parliament [Bob Muir] who was walking along beside Diefenbaker. Without breaking his stride, without turning his head, without changing his expression, he lifted his left fist about four and a half inches and connected with the chin of the individual who was yelling at Diefenbaker. That person spread himself out on the floor and didn't get up. The MP kept on walking and kept on chatting away to the Chief as though nothing had happened.

Diefenbaker: Leadership Lost, ed. Peter Stursberg, 1976

At the following party convention in Toronto, in September 1967, Diefenbaker was replaced as leader by Robert Stanfield. Adviser Greg Guthrie remembers The Chief's withdrawal after the third ballot.

After these hours of waiting, knowing he was going down to defeat and . . . humiliation, he decided to go back to the hotel to eat. We went out, and we got in the car, and Jim Johnston came out and said, 'It's necessary to give a note to the chairman that you've officially withdrawn.' So he scribbled this out and the car was in the middle of the street—I remember this policeman holding up traffic on each end—and Jim Johnston took the paper and scurried back into the Maple Leaf Gardens and we took off down the street.

The Chief was completely relaxed. He was a new man. It's just as if a great burden had been lifted off him. We were rather depressed and hot and tired, and all of a sudden this strange, reedy tenor split the silence. It was the Chief, singing 'When You Come to the End of a Perfect Day'. It was a very appropriate piece but it was a very poor rendition.

Ibid.

Diefenbaker held his Prince Albert seat until his death in 1979. Peter C. Newman
describes his 1972 nomination meeting, when The Chief was seventy-seven.

This campaign, his fifteenth, began as always with a nominating convention
at the Orpheum Theatre, the converted vaudeville house in downtown Prince
Albert. Summer had one more week to run and half a dozen Indians dozed
on the benches near the Hudson's Bay Company fur depot on River Street.
The combines were still out harvesting and Diefenbaker's people worried about
packing the eight-hundred-seat theatre.

But the Orpheum filled quickly that night as a seven-piece band called The
Cottonpickers (MUSIC ANY WAY YOU LIKE IT) struck up a kind of Hawaiian
gavotte, then went on to play polkas and country rock. J.J. Cennon, a local
disc jockey, came on stage to warm up the audience: 'Did you hear about
Trudeau's accident? He was taking his morning walk when he was hit by a
motorboat.'

Here, in this draughty little theatre, Diefenbaker had first conjured up those
grand visions that later claimed the emotional conquest of a decade. And now
the man who refused to sip Napolean brandy with Winston Churchill, who
had called General Eisenhower 'Ike' to his face, and who had saved the Commonwealth by standing up against South African apartheid was reduced to this
praetorian guard of hometown loyalists. Still this was *his* army, and there was
a rush of sheer happiness (that made you realize how rare joy is in crowds)
when the barbaric evocation of the bagpipes heralded the Chief's arrival.

But after eight nominating speeches, itemizing the Great Man's glories, there
was a bad ten minutes as Bob Fair, a Saskatoon businessman, nominated his
brother, Bill, as an anti-Diefenbaker Conservative candidate. 'The PC party
has gone from a majority two hundred and eight members in 1958 to a minority
of seventy-two members at the present time,' he began. 'What happened? Who
was to blame? The party? Or *the leader*?' It was a chilling moment. Every eye
in the house turned on John Diefenbaker and suddenly people were remembering all the tragedies, small and large, that had cost their man his power,
understanding a little of why he was being challenged here on his home ground
by a spoiler, a young man impatient with the old man and his dreams.

Diefenbaker's speech, the only major address of his campaign, was one of
those impressionistic spectaculars in which, like most self-made men, he sets
out to worship his creator. He is old, so old now, but the mercurial touches
are still there. The half-smile, the devastating scorn for his opponents. By
alternating clipped participles with long open vowel sounds he achieves a
Biblical cadence, the glancing immediacy of his language enforced by gesture.
The right hand swooping down in accusing chops as the whole man sways to
the melody of his words. 'Why do I continue in public life?' he demanded,
then answered his own question. 'I still have work to do for Canada. So much
to do. So little time to do it.' . . .

The actual campaign began next morning. Word was out that they were
going to get Dief this time. (*They* were always going to get Dief but nobody

ever did because you cannot defeat a man who assesses himself at his own valuation.) Bill Berezowsky of the NDP, a stocky, energetic socialist with a good, windblown face, put on the best campaign any candidate had ever run against the former PM. His initial slogan aimed at Diefenbaker's age was GIVE YOUTH A CHANCE. Bill Berezowsky is 68. . . .

Later [Diefenbaker] made fun of Pierre Trudeau's contention that Otto Lang was Canada's greatest wheat salesman. ('If Otto Lang had to cross a field with four cowpies in it, he'd manage to step in all of them before he'd make it to the other side.')

Peter C. Newman, *Home Country*, 1973

Diefenbaker was fond of saying that he would be the last prime minister raised on a homestead because there was no more homestead land. He recalled how his father, William Thomas Diefenbaker, paid $250 for 121 tillable acres in 1904 by sitting on a milking stool in a queue in Prince Albert from Friday night to Monday morning when the land office opened. Young Diefenbaker had taken tea and buns to his father so that he could keep his place in the queue. 'When my father got rich later on,' Diefenbaker would say, 'we moved into a sod hut.' When the Diefenbaker home was moved to Regina as a museum, the curators tried to put a door in the north side to speed up visitor traffic. Diefenbaker had to over-rule them: 'In those days nobody ever put a door on the north side of a house.'

Dave McIntosh, *Ottawa Unbuttoned*, 1987

As his years on Parliament Hill drew to a close, Dief became increasingly demanding and testy and eternally obsessed by trivia. Only with Keith [Martin]'s help and the collaboration of the rest of the office staff could the appearance of normalcy be maintained. They had to do it. He was, after all, a national treasure. But he was like an aging actor whose one famous role had been usurped; his former glory had dwindled to fewer fans, some faded clippings and the endless replaying in his mind of past scripts and praiseworthy scenarios.

In the stuff of our friendship there is also some sadness; for although John George Diefenbaker was a man touched by greatness, he was not all he could have been. If he wasn't the best prime minister Canada has ever seen, he was arguably the best opposition leader in our history. He was devoted to his country and gave us great oratory, something that is sadly lacking today. He could rouse crowds and rally public opinion. He could also evoke feelings of great frustration and anger in those of us who wanted him to be superb always. His pettiness and egocentricity were upsetting, and his vindictiveness sometimes frightened even me. Those characteristics of his dark side drove good people away from him.

When Lester Pearson died in 1972, I paid my respects in the Hall of Honour, and visited Dief in his office. We chatted about Pearson and Dief said: 'You've seen my funeral plans and you know that it'll be different for me—my casket will be open.'

'Well, you know, sir,' I offered, 'why Pearson's had to be closed?'

'No,' exclaimed Dief, showing a sudden and dramatic interest as he leaned forward at his desk to await every word of the explanation.

'Well, in addition to the cancer which killed him, Mr Pearson developed jaundice at the end and this causes a lot of discoloration.'

'Well, this is it!' said Dief triumphantly. 'You see, I knew there had to be something. Well, what in the world.' And with that, Dief pounced upon his phone and dialled a number with which I was very familiar. 'Olive,' he shouted into the mouthpiece. 'He was as green as a beet.'

I could hear Olive's incredulous response even from where I was sitting. 'Who?'

'Pearson. He's as green as a beet!' Now, I never knew jaundice to turn someone green, nor had I ever seen a green beet. Perhaps he meant to say green as a bean. In any event, he kept saying it as he redialled the phone to call all his cronies across the country with these most strange tidings.

Sean O'Sullivan with Rod McQueen, *Both My Houses*, 1986

Sean O'Sullivan, himself an MP from 1972 to 1977, was executive assistant to Diefenbaker from 1970 to 1972.

As keen an observer of Canadian affairs as Dief was, he most liked it when all eyes were on him. He regarded himself as something akin to a national shrine. And if you cared anything about him at all, he expected your homage always, but particularly on two days: his birthday, September 18, and the anniversary of his election to Parliament, March 26. In Ottawa, where national days, independence celebrations, and feast times were part of everyday life, for Dief and all who loved him these two occasions were especially to be honoured. Each year, both days would begin with him pretending they were nothing special. When the prime minister rose in his place in Parliament to pay tribute, Dief would feign surprise at achieving yet another milestone of age or gaining more lustre as the dean of the House of Commons. The ritual would continue later in his crowded office as he received personal greetings from MPs, staff and all sorts of people connected with the Hill. He paid close attention to who showed up and who stayed away. For days after, he'd pester staff and friends, saying: 'Where was Mr X? Why didn't Y show up?'

Knowing the command-performance level that each of these days had reached, I was fully aware I would be counted among the missing and presumed dead in March of 1977 when I was travelling with a parliamentary delegation in the Middle East. In order to stay in Dief's good graces, Claude Wagner, his wife, Gisèle, and I sent a joint telegram from Tel Aviv saying: 'CONGRATULATIONS UPON ANNIVERSARY OF YOUR FIRST ELECTION.' Feeling I had covered myself appropriately, I thought nothing more about it until I returned to Ottawa.

Whenever one of his loyalists had been away, Dief expected to be first on the agenda upon your return, so I showed up at his office feeling jaunty and ready to flatter him with reports of how highly the Israelis thought of him. Before I opened my mouth he lit into me.

'Were you drunk?' he snarled.

'Sir?'

'Were you drunk? That is the only possible explanation.'

I had no idea what he was going on about and could only repeat another dumbfounded, 'Sir?'

'Don't play cutesy with me. This is the most damnable thing I've ever seen. And from you, of all people, I never . . .'

Finally, I was able to say: 'I don't know what you're talking about.'

'This is what I'm talking about.' And he flung my telegram across his desk toward me. I picked it up and read the message: 'CONGRATULATIONS UPON ANNIVERSARY OF YOUR FIRST ERECTION.' I never was able to convince him that the mistake was unintentional.

Sean O'Sullivan with Rod McQueen, Both My Houses, 1986

Dief did not . . . like what Trudeau was doing to the country. He thought Trudeau was a leftist and had a questionable background. In private, Dief would ask why Trudeau had been denied entry into the United States. What was he doing in the canoe on the way to see Fidel? While Dief would never come right out and say it, his views would lead any jury of listeners to believe that Trudeau was a communist, if not now, then certainly in his youth. 'They call him PET', Dief would splutter at visitors to his office as he drew attention to Trudeau's initials. 'Did you ever look up "*pet*" in the Larousse dictionary?' His eyes would dance with delight as the visitor leafed through the book he handed them. Before they'd even found the reference he'd say: '"*pet*" in French means "fart". It's the pejorative for *fart*.'

Whenever Dief wanted to tell an off-colour joke, he blamed it on George Hees. Dief would hear a good story, but in keeping with his own particular self-righteous image of himself, he'd be reluctant to retell it. So, he'd put it in the mouth of Hees, a man to whom Dief regularly ascribed all kinds of improprieties. One of his favourites went like this: 'Have you heard the one Hees is telling? It's the most awful thing. He's going around asking people: "What's the difference between a cactus and the Conservative caucus? On a cactus, the pricks are all on the outside."' As he finished, Dief would laugh along with the rest and feel he was home free because he'd blamed the whole thing on Hees.

Ibid.

ELLEN FAIRCLOUGH

The first woman appointed to a federal cabinet, Ellen Fairclough was Secretary of State and later Minister of Citizenship and Immigration in the Diefenbaker cabinet from 1957 to 1962.

Canadian cabinet ministers tend to be tightwads, and no matter how often their pay and expense allowances go up, they can't be persuaded to pick up a tab and they hardly ever reciprocate all the diplomatic hospitality that comes their way in the Ottawa whirl. As for giving parties, they are poopers. The result is that whatever entertaining is done for diplomats or visiting dignitaries falls to the Governor General or to the Speaker of the House of Commons, and the cabinet ministers get off scot free.

A notable exception to this pattern was Canada's first woman federal cabinet minister, Ellen Fairclough, who loved going to parties and loved giving them, even if she had to cough up some of the cost out of her own ample purse. Ellen was Diefenbaker's secretary of state, a job that gave her a special responsibility for visiting dignitaries, and she was on deck when Patrice Lumumba came flying into Ottawa.

Lumumba was prime minister of the Congo, and a strutter, and a stud. His memory is revered in revolutionary circles in various parts of the world, and there is a vast university in Moscow that bears his name, where foreign students are indoctrinated into the gospel according to Marx. He brought an entourage of thirty to Ottawa, and no sooner were they ensconced in suites in the Château Laurier than they sent a message to Howard Green, the austere secretary of state for external affairs, asking, 'Where are the women?'

Green, a prim and proper man with a minimal knowledge of the world outside Canada and no knowledge at all of Africa, sent back word that the Canadian government did not deal in such matters. One of Green's aides, in delivering the reply, let slip on the sly that maybe the distinguished guests could try the By Ward Market, the hangout for hookers, just two blocks down the street. Upon receipt of these tidings, Lumumba went into a snit, and when it came time for the welcoming reception in the hotel that evening, with Howard Green as the host, he refused to show up. Finally, he was persuaded to come, but the party had all the makings of a major fizzle, with Congolese and Canadian men standing around in surly silence and Howard Green frowning into his perpetual glass of orange juice, of which he consumed hundreds of barrels during his years at the diplomatic trough.

Enter Ellen Fairclough. With one twitch of her finely sculptured nose, she detected that the party was dead on its feet. 'Whoop-de-doo!' she shouted, 'let's get this thing on the road!' And she sashayed up to the prime minister of the Congo and told him to cheer up and enjoy himself.

Ellen did everything but chuck Lumumba under the chin. She led the assemblage in song and flounced up and down the room, and she got Lumumba laughing, and the rest of the Congolese loosened up too. The liquor flowed more copiously than Howard Green would have liked it to, either in the interest of temperance or the government's purse strings, it being well known that John Diefenbaker frowned on drinking at the public's expense. But Ellen's silver hair was flying and her arms were waving like wings, and the evening was a great success, and the Lumumba visit was off to a flying start.

After the party was over, Ellen returned to her suite upstairs in the hotel, exhausted but happy, having done her duty for Queen, country, and Howard Green. She changed into her nightdress and was about to flop into bed when there came a hammering on her door. She threw the security chain into place and opened the door a crack, revealing two of Lumumba's burly henchmen standing in the hall.

'Yes?' quavered Canada's first woman federal cabinet minister.

'The prime minister thanks you for the lovely party,' said the larger of the two envoys. 'He wishes you to know that he finds you charming and that he will receive you now in his quarters.'

'The hell he will!' said the proud Ellen, and she moved to slam the door, but one of the callers blocked it with his booted foot.

There ensued a scene in which the two men tried to unhook the chain, and when that proved impossible they tried to break it, but fortunately for Ellen's honour, and Canada's, the Château Laurier has strong doors and everything held against the Congolese onslaughts. The men went away, and Canada's first woman federal cabinet minister rested in peace.

Charles Lynch, *You Can't Print That!*, 1983

ALVIN HAMILTON

Known as an idea man in Diefenbaker's cabinet, Alvin Hamilton was Minister of Northern Affairs from 1957 to 1960, and of Agriculture from 1960 to 1963.

In modern society, so busy and so harassed and so denuded of leisure, there is little opportunity for the average man—if he exists—to acquire the complex factual data essential to judgments of national affairs; yet his judgment is demanded, his verdict is sought. He lacks the time to some extent, but even more he lacks the privacy and the social stimulus for thinking his way to a rational conclusion.

Back home in Vanguard, Saskatchewan, Bill Henderson—one of the three Henderson boys who built the first brick store (and brick outhouse to go with it) back in 1912—used to get the *New York Times* Sunday edition and spend the week going through it carefully up on the second floor of his store. He was also a faithful listener to CBC news broadcasts; the combination of background and spot news produced an informed voter. How he voted I never inquired. By the same token, my brother Dick spends many of his evenings on the porch in a sea of papers and magazines, and is regularly inquired for by Senator Connally on his way through, although this, God knows, has had no effect on the local voting pattern, which is still activated by the slogan 'Alvin sold them Chinks the wheat'.

This illustrates as well as anything else the reality that for the most part the assembly and assessment of data is not done personally, and cannot generally be. Alvin Hamilton sold the first massive shipments of wheat to China; his successors continued to exploit the market thus opened. He and they both acted in face of adverse pressure from Washington which had embargoed its own trade with China; payments were made on complex credit arrangements. The whole complicated transaction was fairly (though anachronistically) summed up in the slogan 'Alvin sold the wheat'.

James M. Minifie, *Who's Your Fat Friend?*, 1967

Hamilton's opinion of TV in the House and its effect on Question Period:

It's just like a bunch of baboons out there, everyone getting up and showing their red behinds. And the baboon with the reddest behind—he gets to be the top baboon of the day on TV.

The Globe and Mail, 8 Jan. 1983

GEORGE C. NOWLAN

Minister of National Revenue (1957–62) and Finance (1962–3) in Diefenbaker's cabinet, George Nowlan of Nova Scotia was an unusually popular and respected MP.

One of the highlights of the Diefenbaker years was the Canadian tour under-taken by Her Royal Highness Princess Margaret, and it is remembered in legend chiefly for the fact that in Victoria she danced all night with young John Turner, an event that put Turner on the political glamour road. There has been much speculation over what might have happened had Margaret and Turner wed, in terms of her subsequent career, and his. The fairy tale might have come true had the press not seized on the brief affair and exposed it to so much light that it faded.

Margaret was the glamour item in the Royal Family at the time and people still referred to her as Margaret Rose. But she was showing signs of having a mind of her own and not wanting to be led around with a ring in her nose while on tour. Her thoughts about the Turner business have never been revealed—about the only thing about the workings of her mind and body that hasn't. Nor have we ever heard from Turner himself on the subject. But it's a fact that she became more and more cranky as the tour progressed, and by the time she reached Nova Scotia she was fed to the royal teeth with the whole business.

Her host for the Nova Scotia segment of the tour was George Nowlan, in his role as the senior federal cabinet minister from the province. Nowlan was a tall, ambling figure of a man who had been a country lawyer all his life and had an easy way with people, not to mention an even easier way with the bottle. He was one of those unusual people on whom strong drink had a beneficial effect, heightening his good nature and sharpening his wits. At the time of the cabinet rebellion that toppled Diefenbaker in 1963, Nowlan was the nominee of the rebels to succeed Diefenbaker as party leader and prime minister. It didn't happen, but it very nearly did, and many of us have wondered longingly what it would have been like to have Nowlan as PM, since he had so many of the racier characteristics of Sir John A. Macdonald.

Despite his lifestyle, Nowlan was able to keep the support of his bible-belt constituents in the Annapolis Valley where, it was said, vices counted for nothing as long as they were concealed, and appearances were what mattered. Nowlan was a man of magnificent appearance.

When Princess Margaret boarded the Royal Train at Digby, Nova Scotia, for the trip through the Annapolis Valley on the way to Halifax, Nowlan greeted her warmly and joined her in acknowledging the cheers of the Digby multitude. Then the train set off through Nowlan's riding, slowing down at each level crossing so that the people assembled could get a look at the Royal Person. It was drizzling rain and it was cold, and after three level crossings Princess Margaret informed Nowlan that she was too tired to go out on the observation platform any more and that she proposed to lie down and rest.

'But Ma'am,' said Nowlan, as he himself recounted the story later, 'these people have been waiting for hours in the rain to see you.'

'I don't care. I'm not going out.'

'But you owe it to them.'

'I do not.'

'Well then, consider that these are my people and you owe it to me.'

'I'm not going.'

Short pause while Nowlan took a deep breath.

'Well then, Ma'am,' he said, 'in that case, it is my painful duty to inform you that if you don't go out and wave at the people I am going to take you over my knee and whale the bejesus out of you.'

Shocked silence.

'You wouldn't dare!'

'Wouldn't I,' said Nowlan, flexing his big hands. 'Here's another crossing, and if you don't go out you're going to get it!'

She went, and the crowd cheered, as did all the crowds, all the way to Halifax.

Charles Lynch, *You Can't Print That!*, 1983

DALTON CAMP

National President of the Conservative Party from 1964 to 1969, Dalton Camp helped to hasten the departure of Diefenbaker and the arrival of Stanfield.

Diefenbaker was due to address the Quebec Progressive Conservative [1966] annual meeting at the Motel des Laurentides in the Quebec City suburb of Beauport on October 1, and it was part of [national organizer James] Johnston's assignment to make certain that the Chief be shown appropriate homage upon arrival at Ancienne Lorette airport. To swell the airport crowd, Johnston decided to take with him most of Diefenbaker's French-Canadian supporters. Just before climbing into the airport limousine, Johnston took aside some of the party's Young Turks who seemed to be running the session and told them patronizingly that they should keep the meeting discussing non-controversial matters until he returned with the Chief. Unfortunately for Johnston, the three young Tories he chose—Michael Meighen (grandson of the former Conservative prime minister), Brian Mulroney (the young Montreal lawyer who had served as executive assistant to Alvin Hamilton in Agriculture) and Peter White (an executive assistant to Daniel Johnston)—were young in years but not in political experience. White had previously arranged for Diefenbaker to be driven from the airport to the provincial legislature for a courtesy call on the Quebec premier. This—plus the fact that most of Diefenbaker's supporters were at the airport—gave the young Tories and their friends enough time to rush back into the meeting and ram through a series of resolutions calling for the federal leadership to be reviewed every four years, starting in the fall of 1967.

A not insubstantial quantity of political power changed hands that day but in retrospect it provided one of the great comic scenes of Canadian politics. There was the trio of young Quebec Tories—all English-speaking and all in their twenties—using a set of pre-arranged manoeuvres to swing the meeting against Diefenbaker. Meanwhile, the Chief and his retinue of flacks, ensconced in rented black limousines, were being escorted by six motorcyclists of the Quebec Provincial Police, their sirens screaming, along a circuitous route to the premier's office. Johnston somehow managed to fill forty-five minutes exchanging pleasantries with Diefenbaker. By the time the Diefenbaker entourage finally arrived at the motel where the party meeting was being held, they found the province's delegates (274 strong) had been firmly pledged to support Camp's reassessment motion.

But even as political support was being removed from under him, Diefenbaker's personality had lost little of its power. That night, Camp and Diefenbaker confronted each other for the first time in a year.

'Hello, Mr President, how's your pilgrimage going?' Diefenbaker asked.

The normally poised Camp was rattled enough to reply: 'Good evening, Prime Minister.'

'Now, that's what I like to hear. You just keep that up.'

'I always think of you as Prime Minister.'

Peter C. Newman, *The Distemper Of Our Times*, 1968

There was a telling little incident when the convention ended Saturday night, September 1, 1967. Camp waited in a corridor in Maple Leaf Gardens to see Stanfield. But Stanfield did not come. Camp waited half an hour, then left. Yesterday's hero, he was already the party's pariah.

Dave McIntosh, Ottawa Unbuttoned, 1987

ROBERT THOMPSON

An Alberta MP, Robert Thompson led the national Social Credit Party from 1961 to 1967.

He advocated many things that few responsible Canadian politicians would oppose, but most of his declarations somehow came out as convoluted clichés, flavoured by a wistful candour that made it impossible to dislike the man. Certainly his most memorable contribution to Canadian politics was the statement that 'the Americans are our best friends, whether we like it or not'. . . . During a debate on February 1, 1965, while trying to explain why Social Credit could not take the same position as it had with the Diefenbaker minority administration in 1963, he declared: 'We've had not one but two elections since then, and two rights do not make a wrong.'

Peter C. Newman, Home Country, 1973

RÉAL CAOUETTE

A Social Credit MP from Quebec, Réal Caouette led the Ralliement des Créditistes from 1963 to 1976.

I covered the Canadian electoral campaign of 1962 which saw the rise to national prominence of Réal Caouette. He was not easy to cover. He habitually used the heavily accented French of the backwoods, and lapsed into even broader dialect for colloquial anecdotes which kept the audience in ecstasies of laughter; they also carried a shrewd political point.

One of these anecdotes was about the farmer who married a city girl; she was very pretty and tender-hearted, but she didn't know a thing about farming. The farmer had a setting hen, and just before her eggs were due to hatch he went away to the provincial fair. Before he left he told his pretty little wife to take special care of the chicks when they hatched, as if they were her own.

When he got back the first thing he asked about was the chicks. His pretty little wife burst into tears.

'They're all dead,' she sobbed.

'*Bon Dieu*! What happened?'

'Why,' she said, 'I wrung their necks!'

'Wrung their necks . . . .'

'Yes, to save them from dying of starvation. That hen was no good. I felt all over her and she didn't have a nipple to give the chicks.'

This used to bring down the house. Stout and amply endowed ladies rocked and rolled in their seats, tears of mirth streaming down their cheeks. Caouette moved in for the kill: 'And that's just like the Grits'—or the Tories'—farm policy, that is to say, conducted by people who had no notion of what it was about.'

James M. Minifie, Who's Your Fat Friend?, 1967

LOUIS JOSEPH ROBICHAUD

The first Acadian premier of New Brunswick, Louis Joseph Robichaud held office for the Liberals from 1958 to 1970.

In September 1964 the Canadian premiers and the prime minister, Lester Pearson, met in Charlottetown to commemorate the meeting of the Fathers of Confederation one hundred years earlier. Robichaud took this opportunity to make the unexpected suggestion that the time had come for the four Atlantic provinces to form a union. Understandably the other premiers were cautious, as well as unprepared. Walter Shaw was the least enthusiastic. Robert Stanfield agreed with the principle and felt it deserved consideration and Joey Smallwood made light of the matter pointing out that the major stumbling block would be who would be premier. Pearson commented that the province's name would be 'The Islands of Nova Brunsland'.

Della M.M. Stanley, Louis Robichaud, 1984

ALLAN E. BLAKENEY

NDP Premier of Saskatchewan from 1971 to 1982, Allan Blakeney was a member of Premier Woodrow Lloyd's cabinet during the 1962 doctors' strike over Medicare. A year after the strike, Blakeney addressed the sensitive issue of freedom of the press:

How was this freedom interpreted by many Saskatchewan editors?

Speaking before the 1963 Canadian Managing Editors' Conference, this question was answered by A.E. Blakeney, then Minister of Public Health and a former Rhodes scholar. Mr Blakeney opened his remarks by saying, 'No government, no politician has anything to gain by quarrelling with the press.'

In this address he was not seeking such a quarrel but rather attempting to measure the performance of the press against generally accepted standards of good journalism.

Mr Blakeney acknowledged the 'undisputed privilege of editors to express their opinions on the editorial page'. But at a time of high public tension he challenged their right to sell space for advertisements that added to the frenzy of the people. As an example he cited a full-page ad that had appeared in the weekly Indian Head *News*. Under the refrain 'You are going to lose your doctors', the text read: 'It will be too late when the pain comes in the middle of the night. When the baby suddenly starts choking, when the good farm worker is mangled in the power-takeoff, when the car plunges off the road and scatters dusty bodies in the ditch, when that heart attack comes . . . if this sounds emotional, or even hysterical—good.'

The press of the province had distorted the news, Mr Blakeney asserted, by giving an unbalanced emphasis to items that were published. The selection of newspaper items is 'a matter of delicate editorial judgment', Mr Blakeney suggested. He said the province's newspapers had deliberately suppressed relevant news. . . .

Another example was cited by Mr Blakeney:

> In some cases suppression of material information was direct, outright and substantiated. Three days before the federal election last June signs saying 'doctors get out' and 'vote CCF' were painted in prominent public places in Regina. The *Leader-Post* used a three-column picture to focus attention on the incident. Almost immediately two men were arrested for painting the signs. In view of the circumstances and the timing it seemed important to inform the public that the two men arrested and later convicted were not, as might be supposed, adherents of the CCF party. Both men were members of the Liberal party and one was in fact a director of the Regina Liberal Association at the time. Four unsuccessful attempts were made to persuade the *Leader-Post* to make this information public.

> Robin F. Badgley and Samuel Wolfe, *Doctors' Strike, Medical Care and Conflict in Saskatchewan*, 1967

LESTER PEARSON

Canada's fourteenth prime minister (1963–8), Lester Pearson taught history at the University of Toronto after World War I, then joined the Department of External Affairs, becoming Deputy Minister in 1946. In 1948 'Mike' entered politics as Minister of External Affairs in the St Laurent cabinet, and in 1957 he won a Nobel Peace Prize. He describes an early encounter with Diefenbaker:

My first exposure to Mr Diefenbaker on the hustings had come during the 1953 election campaign, when his path and mine continually crossed. By

accident, I found myself at least once a week speaking in some place either just
before or just after him. I remember in Moncton we both made speeches on
the same night as the circus. The next morning the Moncton *Transcript* published the score board: Circus first, Diefenbaker second, Pearson third. As I
was nearby so often, he began to attack me in his speeches as a nondescript,
unimportant person, trying to make a great name for himself through diplomacy at the United Nations and by spending the poor taxpayers' money on
striped pants and white tie parties. He had two wonderful examples to show
how I was wasting money on these faintly immoral diplomatic extravagances.
He talked about a dinner I gave in Rome for the NATO Council when I was its
chairman in 1952. It was a great dinner, catered by the best hotel in Rome and
served in a beautiful mediaeval palace. Dief had heard about this and he played
on it to his audiences: 'Can you imagine how much this must have cost you
poor fishermen?' and so on. In response I wired to Ottawa for the exact figures
which were on record. The dinner came to just over $10.00 a head for
everything, which was about half as much as it would have cost at Ottawa's
Château Laurier. So I read the costs at my next meeting and thought, 'Well,
we'll hear no more about this.' It did not work that way. We kept on hearing
about that dinner and also how I was trying to curry favour with the Liberal
back-benchers to secure the next leadership of the party by sending a delegation
of them to Paris each year to attend a NATO meeting. Mr Diefenbaker did not
point out these were all-party delegations and that he himself had been on
them. I had great fun making play with Mr Diefenbaker's exaggerations, but
I might as well have saved my breath. These were his two pet stories about
me for the rest of the campaign. Nevertheless, he could be, and was, discounted.
He was thought then, as still in 1956, to be merely a talker. The PM and C.D.
[Howe] were the doers. We did not realize that the time for talking, for swaying
public opinion against the government, was then beginning. The full lesson of
the pipeline debate was not understood.

Mike: The Memoirs of the Right Honourable Lester B. Pearson, vol. 3, ed.
John A. Munro and Alex I. Inglis, 1975

*Pearson defeated Paul Martin to become the leader of the Liberal party in early 1958.
On 28 January of that year he introduced to the House a motion calling for the
Conservative minority government to resign and hand over power to the Grits without
an election.*

When I took my seat, I knew immediately that my first attack on the government had been a failure, indeed a fiasco. There was some applause from our
side for my speech, not for the resolution, but only hoots and jeers from the
government side of the House. When Donald Fleming, a student of mine at
the University of Toronto years before and always a good friend, groaned:
'Mike, it is sad to see you come to this,' he was trying to be kind. I had made
a spectacle of myself by coolly inviting the government to turn over their seals

of office to those of us who had, a few months before, been rejected by the electorate. One of our back-benchers came up to me afterwards, as I was sitting alone in a state of some depression, and said: 'That was a magnificent speech, Mr Pearson. It's too bad you didn't stop before you ended it.'

Ibid.

In the following election the Liberals were reduced to only 48 seats.

When the results of the election came in on the night of 31 March 1958 there was hardly a party left to keep liberal.

On that night my wife and I watched the results as they came in at our national headquarters in Ottawa. Within a couple of hours it was all over but for the shouting, or rather, with our company, the groaning. There was a large electoral map on the wall and, as a result came in, a blue or red star was stuck on the relevant constituency. After the initial and encouraging returns from Newfoundland and some later from Quebec, the blue stars began to dominate the scene in a thoroughly dismaying manner. It was my first big setback since Hamilton Collegiate Institute where I had been defeated by three votes for the presidency of the Literary Society by a red-haired chap named McClellan who was very good-looking and got the girls' votes. We were reduced to forty-eight seats. My own constituency, Algoma East, was, for some reason, one of the last to report. My wife, who until that time had stood up bravely to the evidence of a great defeat, finally broke down. 'We've lost everything,' she moaned, 'we've even won our own constituency!' No devotee of political life, for a moment she thought there might be an honourable if not flattering exit through an adverse decision by the voters in Algoma East. That exit was closed.

Ibid.

Domestic politics seemed to him grubbier than he had thought and he longed for the world of international diplomacy. He had never been interested in politicking—though he had done the necessary chores dutifully—and the hatred felt by Maryon Pearson, his wife, for the process was a party legend. She was given to wearing sunglasses on platforms, to glaring at voters when she could be persuaded to remove her 'shades', as the new-guard Grits called them behind her back, and to insulting MPs, their wives, and their workers with a lethal wit—though she could be charming to people she liked. Once, when Pearson was still in opposition, Gordon Edick was riding into Toronto from the airport, sitting with the driver in the front seat of the Pearsons' hired limousine. As the car sped along the highway, he started yelling over his shoulder in the leader's general direction the kind of numerical rundown of party prospects all good sportsmen-politicians love. Mrs Pearson turned to her husband and said in a queenly manner, 'Who *is* this man?' 'This man' was one of the party's most faithful workers and he had gone out to the airport in the first place out of kindness as a one-man welcoming committee.

Christina McCall-Newman, *Grits*, 1982

Pearson was born on St George's day and he has found himself a dragon to slay—John Diefenbaker. Pearson's dislike for the prime minister is seldom mentioned off the Ottawa gossip circuits. In part it stems from the complacent tolerance of one with a secure reputation behind him for a rival to whom final victory has come too late in life. In part it is Pearson's strong belief that the prime minister is not sincere. He once told a fellow MP in the Commons lobby, 'John was at his ingratiating best today—like a cobra.' During the '58 campaign, he told what he thought was a closed audience in Calgary that the Bill of Rights 'shows Diefenbaker to be the fake he is'. When this burst into the newspapers, Pearson hastily claimed he had been misquoted. But he said it and meant it.

Richard Gwyn, 'Pearson', Saturday Night, Sept. 1960

The election of 1963 gave Pearson and the Liberals a minority victory.

Once I took part in an election rally at Newtonbrook where I was born, a village then but now a suburb of Toronto. The fact that I left Newtonbrook with my parents at the age of six weeks did not prevent my friends from proudly displaying a banner, 'Welcome, Lester Pearson, Home Town Boy'. A cynical member of my staff once observed that my mother must have been a truly miraculous person to have given birth to me in so many different places! If I was greeted somewhat excessively by the banner in Newtonbrook, the balance was restored a few days later when I arrived at a Holiday Inn in another town where I was to spend the night. It was edifying to read the message in glittering lights on a sign at the entrance: 'Welcome Liberace and our Prime Minister.'

Second billing was also my lot when I was campaigning with a local celebrity on a platform or on main street. This was invariably true if my companion was a sports hero. I once spent an afternoon during the 1963 election with Red Kelly, a great hockey star, who was seeking election, at my urging, in York West. While motoring from one meeting to another, we noticed some youngsters playing ball in a vacant lot. We both thought it would be fun, and might interest our press entourage, if we stopped for a few minutes to watch. We also stopped the game because Red was soon recognized, and was surrounded by excited youngsters clamouring for his autograph. He was somewhat embarrassed that no one took any notice of me, and asked one small boy, happily contemplating Red's signature, 'Don't you want Mr Pearson's too?' The reply put me in my place: 'Mr Pearson, who's he?' Even as Prime Minister, I had to accept that in the autograph market it would take five 'L.B. Pearsons' to get one 'Red Kelly'. My sporting experience helped me to accept this evaluation.

Mike: The Memoirs of the Right Honourable Lester B. Pearson, vol. 2,
ed. John A. Munro and Alex I. Inglis, 1973

Electoral lists could be elastic in Newfoundland, as Pearson discovered.

Smallwood was totally committed to politics, and knew everything about political tactics—especially, his envious opponents would say, the trickier kind. He used to smile at these accusations and put them down to jealousy. Never did I campaign in Newfoundland without a motorcade from the airport at St John's to the hotel with, naturally, many more cars than there were in the welcome for the Tory leader the week before. Then there would be a drive through the streets in an open car. On one occasion the weather was so atrocious, with cold and sleeting rain pelting down, that I assumed the drive would be called off. My mistake. We started at the appointed time with the leaders in the lead in an open car. Joey insisted that I sit up with him at the back so that everybody could look at me. So far as I could see 'everybody' was 'nobody' because the streets were empty. He assured me, however, that faces were pressed against every pane of glass and that I should wave and smile enthusiastically for their benefit. I felt foolish, and was miserably soaked and cold. At one point our road went through a cemetery and I thought that here, at least, I would be able to get down and crouch from the elements for a few moments. 'No, no,' said Joey, 'stay up there and wave. Some of your most faithful voters are in there.'

Ibid.

My favourite Pearson story was the one he told about the morning in 1963 when he awoke to the realization that, the night before, he had been sworn in as prime minister of Canada. He rose and did his ablutions, and while he was looking in the mirror adjusting his polka-dot bow tie, wondering what the first challenge of high office would be, the telephone rang. It was a message from Governor General Vanier from his sick bed in Government House. Would Pearson come to Vanier's bedside with all speed to attend to an urgent matter of state?

Ah, thought Pearson with relish, this was it. The summit. The first big problem and the first big decision. He hastened to Rideau Hall and was ushered into the bedroom of his old friend.

'Thank God, Mike, you are here. We have this awful problem to settle.'

'Ready, sir!' said the eager Pearson. 'What is it?'

'It's Vincent.'

'Vincent?'

'Vincent Massey, he's been driving me crazy!' Vanier indicated a pile of correspondence on a bedside table. 'He's been flooding me with letters for months, and I've been passing copies to that man, but he won't do anything.'

'That man?'

'Diefenbaker. He hates Vincent, you know.'

'Yes, I know,' said the crestfallen Pearson. 'But what's the problem?'

Vanier sighed. 'Vincent is building Massey College at the University of Toronto and he wants his coat of arms over the archway.'

'So?'

'So the Massey coat of arms contains nothing to indicate that Vincent was Governor General. It's all ploughs and pitchforks and threshing machines. He wants the coat of arms amended.'

'So?'

'So the application can't go forward without the government's endorsation, and Diefenbaker wouldn't give it, and Vincent is enraged.'

'Is that all?' asked Pearson, deflated.

'All!' fumed Vanier. 'Nothing has caused me more trouble.'

'Well,' said Pearson, 'it need trouble you no more. I agree to whatever it is Vincent wants.'

'It's not that simple,' said Vanier. 'It needs the approval of your secretary of state.'

'Who is my secretary of state?'

'I believe it's Jack Pickersgill, Prime Minister.'

'Well then, Pickersgill agrees.'

'No,' said Vanier, 'it's not that simple. It has to be stamped with the Great Seal of Canada.'

'Where is the wretched thing, then?'

'It is in the custody of Pickersgill.'

Pearson picked up the phone and demanded to be put in touch with Pickersgill, and when contact was made, he instructed his secretary of state to round up the Great Seal with all speed and get it over to Government House in his own hands. Pickersgill got busy and arrived with the Great Seal, and the documents were processed on the spot and dispatched to London, and the Massey coat of arms was properly amended before being inserted into the wall of Massey College. Pearson said that, after that episode, he never did take affairs of state too seriously, using the Massey incident as his measuring stick.

Charles Lynch, *You Can't Print That!*, 1983

Pearson would usually eat lunch (oysters or clam chowder, poached eggs and apple pie) in his office and leave at six with at least three hours of work in his briefcase. He could master complicated briefs and memos very quickly, signing most of his comments with the initials PM (for Prime Minister) instead of a plain LBP. He could be tough in dealing with the advice proffered in some memos, dismissing it with the marginal comment 'This won't do', but more often he left the memo writer puzzled about his intentions. One senior adviser recalled ending his memorandum on an important political problem by suggesting alternative courses of action. Pearson sent it back, with a notation beside the two suggested options that merely read: 'I agree.'

Peter C. Newman, *The Distemper Of Our Times*, 1968

Pearson always followed the World Series with fascination no matter what crisis might be claiming his attention. He could name the starting line-ups and batting averages of most American teams. On May 10, 1963, during his first official call on President John F. Kennedy at Hyannis Port, his knowledge was put to the test by Dave Powers, the resident White House baseball expert. While Kennedy listened, the two men traded managers' names, World Series statistics and other diamond lore. It was Powers, not Pearson, who tripped up on some southpaw's 1926 earned-run average. 'He'll do', Kennedy remarked, and the two leaders proceeded to equip Canada with nuclear warheads.

Ibid.

Pearson's amiable and irreverent lack of pretension was noticeable even in the trivia of his office arrangements. John Diefenbaker had always kept in full view as a symbol of his power the red NORAD emergency telephone that connects the Prime Minister of Canada directly to the President of the United States. 'I can get Ike any time,' he would boast to visitors. Pearson not only removed the instrument from his desk, but hid it so carelessly that one morning during the winter of 1964 when it rang, he couldn't find it. Paul Martin, the External Affairs Secretary, was in the PM's office at the time. The two men heard the NORAD phone buzzing, couldn't locate it and began to chase each other around the room like a pair of Keystone Kops.

'My God, Mike,' said Martin, 'do you realize this could mean war?'

'No,' Pearson puffed, 'they can't start a war if we don't answer that phone.'

The instrument was finally located behind a curtain and the caller—who wanted to know if 'Charlie' was there—turned out, by incredible coincidence, to have both the wrong number and accidental access to one of the world's most private hot-lines.*

*Pearson used the hot-line only once. On April 21, 1967, while he was being driven to his summer residence at Harrington Lake, his car struck a rock and broke its transmission. The hot-line was the only telephone available, so Pearson called Washington to arrange for a tow truck to be sent out from downtown Ottawa.

Ibid.

The best example of the American reaction to the Canadian mouse came when Lester Pearson, as prime minister, made a celebrated speech at Temple University in Philadelphia, advocating that the United States pause in the bombing of North Vietnam. Pearson had been invited to lunch with Lyndon Johnson the next day at Camp David, and was whisked there by helicopter. No mention was made of the speech during lunch until, over coffee, Pearson asked the president, 'What did you think of my speech?'

There followed one of the more remarkable of LBJ's many remarkable performances. Muttering 'Awful', the host took his guest by the arm and led

him to the terrace before launching into his tirade. Johnson strode the terrace
in a rage, sawed the air with his arms, and made full use of his famous
vocabulary. Canadian Ambassador Charles Ritchie and White House aide
McGeorge Bundy, watching from the lunch table, finally grew embarrassed
and went for a long walk through the woods. When they returned, almost an
hour later, Johnson was still at it. In near-apoplexy, he rode over every attempt
Pearson made to reply. Finally he grabbed the prime minister by the lapels and
shouted, 'You pissed on my rug!'. . .

American presidents can never be bothered to remember the names of
Canadian prime ministers. When Lyndon Johnson invited Lester Pearson to
his Texas ranch in 1965, he greeted the Nobel Prize-winner before the television
cameras, and said how much he was looking forward to hosting 'Mr Wilson'.

After dinner and many drinks, the voracious Johnson insisted on turning on
the evening news—and the report of his own welcoming speech. When he saw
himself greeting his 'old friend . . . Mr Wilson', he was at first completely
bewildered and then apologized expansively. Said Pearson, 'Think nothing of
it, Senator Goldwater.'

Allan Fotheringham, Capitol Offences, 1986

This is my favourite and the only one I have direct from Pearson himself. He
told it to four or five of us over lunch in the early 1970s.

Pearson was at Lyndon Johnson's ranch to sign the Auto Pact. The time
came for the official signing, with photographers and various officials present.
Johnson said, 'Well, you Canadians have fucked us again—you always do. I
might as well face up to it. Gimme the goddamn pen. All right, I'll sign the
fuckin' thing, but I want you to know that *I* know you've taken us on this
one.' He signed.

Pearson went on:

'Of course, LBJ didn't understand *anything* about what the Auto Pact said
or meant.'

Pause, of Jack-Benny duration. Then:

'And neither did I.'

Contributed by Robert Fulford, Toronto

Winning politics depends not so much on how smart you are as on how dumb
your opponent is. Lucky Pierre Trudeau had Robert Stanfield and Joe Clark
for antagonists.

There was Stanfield in the catbird seat in 1968. He was a new leader for the
Conservatives after the ousting of John Diefenbaker. The Liberals were in wild
disarray as they fought internally and savagely over the party's leadership
pending the imminent retirement of Lester Pearson.

And then the Liberals were defeated in the House of Commons on a vote
of confidence, mainly because so many of them were away advancing their

individual aspirations or, like Mitchell Sharp, waiting for a likely candidate to back to ensure himself a posh cabinet portfolio. Incredibly, Stanfield blew it, mostly because he never understood the difference between politics and government: politics is gaining power, government is keeping it. Poor Bob, or Boob, as Diefenbaker called him.

Pierre Elliott Trudeau announced his candidacy for the Liberal leadership February 14, 1968, but his campaign and those of the other half-dozen serious candidates were quickly eclipsed five days later when, late in the evening, the Liberals lost a Commons vote, 84 to 82, on tax legislation. The relaxed Bob Winters, acting prime minister, went to the telephone in his temporary office on the third floor of the Commons to call Pearson, on holiday in Jamaica. We reporters hung around the door until Winters came out.

'What did Pearson say?' we demanded.

'He said, "O God",' Winters replied delightedly.

Pearson flew back from Jamaica right away to salvage the situation by persuading Stanfield to agree to a day's adjournment of the Commons while he devised a motion saying the vote on a tax measure, always considered a vote of confidence, was not really a vote of confidence and could be overtaken by a new vote. One of the persuaders Pearson used was Louis Rasminsky, governor of the Bank of Canada and already a proven political toady. . . . Speaking of 1968, Stanfield said: 'The government lost a vote of confidence in the House. If the Opposition had prolonged that debate, with continued uncertainty as to the life of the government, the Canadian dollar would have gone down out of sight. . . . I say that no Canadian government has been in more serious financial difficulties than . . . in 1968, and I know what I am talking about.'

Stanfield after all that time (more than two years) apparently did not see that he had been had by Pearson and Rasminsky. It was true that the government had had to borrow nearly $ 1 billion on international markets to cover a currency exchange crisis. But did the prospect of a Stanfield government make it a likelihood that the bottom would fall out of our dollar? Hardly, but Stanfield was jigged like a squid.

Dave McIntosh, Ottawa Unbuttoned, 1987

ALLAN MACEACHEN

An adroit Parliamentary tactician from Cape Breton, Allan MacEachen held various portfolios in the governments of Pearson and Trudeau, including Finance and External Affairs. It was during one of his two stints as government House leader that he extricated the Pearson administration from a troublesome spot in 1968.

The Liberals' concentration on the leadership campaign took its almost inevitable toll on the evening of February 19. The House of Commons was half empty when Mitchell Sharp's important budget resolution imposing a 5 per cent surcharge on taxes was called for a third and final reading. Altogether forty-eight Liberals were absent from the House, mostly hustling delegates on the campaign trail. They included three leadership candidates, Paul Martin, Joe Green, and John Turner, although Turner, unlike the other two, had arranged to be paired with a Conservative member so that his absence had no effect on the result. Prime Minister Pearson was holidaying in Jamaica. In these embarrassing circumstances the money bill was defeated by a vote of 84 to 82, a situation that would normally force a government to resign and call an election. The country was plunged into a major political crisis.

Pearson returned hurriedly to Ottawa the next day to try to salvage what he could from the wreckage of his government, stuttering and stammering his indignation. He immediately telephoned Opposition Leader Robert Stanfield and arranged for a twenty-four-hour adjournment of the House. And he met with a few selected cabinet ministers, including John Turner, in Allan Mac-Eachen's West Block office to try to find a way out of the disastrous situation. Eventually the wily Maritimer MacEachen came up with a solution—to move a motion declaring that 'this House does not regard its vote on February 19 in connection with the third reading of Bill C-193, which it carried in all previous stages, as a vote of non-confidence in the government.'

This carefully worded motion offered the splinter Créditiste Party, which was desperately afraid it would be decimated in an election, a chance to reverse itself and vote with the government. Thus, on February 28 the period of acute political uncertainty was ended by a vote of 138 to 119 and the Pearson government survived.

But the political bill had been paid. In the heat of the argument on the validity of the government motion, New Democratic Party Leader Tommy Douglas summed up: 'This government is like a ship without a compass, without a chart and without a rudder. And last Monday night it was without a skipper. As a matter of fact while the skipper was off the bridge the crew was shooting craps over who was going to wear the captain's hat.'

Jack Cahill, *John Turner: The Long Run*, 1984

PAUL MARTIN

Elected a Liberal MP in 1935, Paul Martin served in the cabinets of Mackenzie King (1945–8), of St Laurent (1948–57), and of Pearson (1963–8), after which he was Liberal leader in the Senate and High Commissioner to the UK.

Shortly after our wedding, Mackenzie King invited Nell and me to a dinner he was hosting for three recently married Liberal members. It was the first time I had visited Laurier House as a guest of the prime minister, and I was a little nervous. Coaching Nell a bit beforehand, I explained that this man was my boss and that much of my career would depend on him. Nell told me not to worry. When we arrived at the door, the prime minister laid on all his charm for her. 'How do you do, Mr Prime Minister?' began Nell. 'My husband thinks you're a very great man.' 'And what do you think, Mrs Martin?' 'Well,' said she, 'I'm going to need some convincing.' I just about dropped from embarrassment and fidgeted for the rest of the meal. King seemed to take it in good form, though. At about four o'clock the next afternoon, there was a knock at the door of our little flat on Delaware Avenue. I was in the back of the apartment and heard Nell say, 'Hello, Mr King'. It was the prime minister, who had been so taken with Nell that he had come to invite her out for an afternoon stroll. I did not dare make an appearance. When Nell returned, she quipped, 'Well, Paul, you're made now!' This was her sweet revenge for my fretting.

Paul Martin, A Very Public Life, vol. 1, 1983

One day at the United Nations [Pearson] and I went to a baseball game together, as we often did, and during that game—it wasn't one of the most exciting ones, although he found every game exciting—I suggested to him that, important as our foreign policy was, the really big question in Canada was the problem between the French and the English, and how to resolve this. And I found him surprisingly interested.

His foreign policy, the foreign policy that he recommended as Undersecretary or that he practised as Secretary of State for External Affairs, was not predicated in any way on the 'French Fact', as it later became known. So I was very surprised this day to find that he was intensely interested in the French-English problem and that he recognized that the unity of the country depended on these two groups getting along well together. He said, 'We really have to do something about this.'

'Well,' I said, 'this surprises me because you don't show that in your friendships; you don't show that in what you say at the United Nations and elsewhere.'

'I know,' he said. 'But we're not going to hold Canada together unless we do find some way of accommodation. Do you know what I think we should do?' he went on. 'We should bring home to the people of Canada generally the facts of this problem, an understanding of this problem. They don't all realize the extent to which Quebec and English-speaking Canada must get along together if we're going to hold the unity of the country. They don't understand that. I think we ought to really have a royal commission on this. I think we ought to have a public exposure of the facts.'

Paul Martin, quoted in Peter Stursberg, Lester Pearson and the Dream of Unity, 1978

Because of the minority government situation [1963–5], Keith Davey was maintaining the party apparatus in a state of electoral readiness with the aid of

Richard O'Hagan, who was now serving as Pearson's press secretary, and Jim Coutts, who had become his appointments secretary. The three men were kept busy stroking the egos of the Liberals out there in the hinterland, mindful of how much their aid would be needed when the party had to go to the country again. They passed on inside stories about the cabinet's vagaries and exploits, telling funny tales about the old-guard party regulars, Jack Pickersgill, Lionel Chevrier, and Paul Martin. Coutts was a superb mimic and he developed an imitation of Martin that always caused his audiences to howl with laughter, depicting the minister touring his riding and doing his famous trick of inquiring after the relatives of his constituents as though they were all dear friends. 'And how is that fine woman, your mother?' Martin was supposed to have asked a young farmer at an evening meeting, only to have him drawl in reply, 'Same as she was when you asked me that in town this morning, Mr Martin. Dead.'

Christina McCall-Newman, *Grits*, 1982

For the most part, my conciliation succeeded and I believe that the parliamentary discussion of foreign policy was one of the high points of the Pearson years. Of course, it gave me a reputation for meandering sentences and prolixity, but by and large the opposition respected my efforts to provide balanced explanations in debate. Naturally, there was a certain amount of joshing. When I protested one day that I did not wish to play politics with foreign policy, John Diefenbaker honked with laughter and reminded members of days when the shoe had been on the other foot. On 4 November, Gordon Churchill rose to complain that, with only five minutes left of the day's sitting, he was not sure that the minister of external affairs would have time to answer all the questions that were before the House. Stanley Knowles said that five minutes would give me 'time for only one sentence'. As I took to my feet, I bowed mock-heroically to the opposition benches. Murdo Martin, the NDP member for Timmins, sent over some deflating verses he had penned:

> The acme of pomposity, with voluminous verbosity
> And a neverending flood of words to say;
> For futility infernal, watch our Minister External,
> As he struts his stuff on Orders of the Day.
>
> He has the rare ability, or vocabular agility,
> With verbiage to drown each point at hand.
> And he seems to fear relations, that we have with other nations
> Will be endangered if we EVER take a stand.

Paul Martin, *A Very Public Life*, vol. 2, 1985

Martin contested the Liberal leadership in 1958 and again in 1968.

Paul Martin wanted my support—he expected it, because we'd known each other so long, we were old friends, and our ridings were next to one another.

I'll say one thing for Paul: he didn't try to bribe me with a Cabinet post or some other plum. But I'd made up my mind I was going to support Trudeau, and when I told Paul to his face he was none too happy.

I delayed going to see him about it because I knew it would be unpleasant. But he called me four or five times and finally I said I'd come over and see him. When I got to his office I didn't beat around the bush. I said, 'You know who I'm going to support, anyway. I'm supporting Trudeau and I've made up my mind.' So he asked me why and I said, 'Because Pierre Trudeau can lead us to a majority government and I don't think you can. I don't think you have enough support from Quebec.' Just like that. That remark about Quebec would have hurt him, too, because he was bilingual and from a French Canadian family and he claimed during his campaign that if he won we could still say that we'd kept the principle of alternation going—that an English leader should be followed by a French leader. Many people believed that Pearson was unofficially supporting Trudeau for that reason. They brought back the same nonsense about alternation when Jean Chrétien ran against Turner in 1984— and it probably cost him the leadership. In 1968, it certainly helped Trudeau's chances.

As you can imagine, old Paul wasn't too happy when I said these things to him. And he tried to argue with me. He said, 'Gene, out of the caucus I've got thirty-two members supporting me and a number of those are from Quebec.' He was wrong and I told him so: 'Paul you don't have any thirty-two. You've got five.' I even told him who they were; I gave him the names, but he didn't believe me. Then I said, 'Does this mean you were lying those times when you told me I was the wisest politician in the caucus?' 'No,' he said, 'I meant what I said then and I mean what I say to you now. I want your support.' Then I said, 'You don't have a hope in hell of winning and I'm going to throw my support where it will do some good. I'm going to support Trudeau and I'm going to make a public announcement.' Then he kind of begged me. He reminded me that we were both from Windsor and of how it would look if his own neighbour didn't support him. He cried at the end. It was a hard meeting.

Eugene Whelan with Rick Archbold, Whelan: The Man in the Green Stetson,
1986

GERDA MUNSINGER

Rumours circulated in Ottawa during Diefenbaker's administration concerning the relations of at least one cabinet minister with a woman who might be a security risk. Accusations were made in the House in 1966 that created a rather breezy sex scandal.

The result was another judicial inquiry, this time by Mr Justice Wishart Spence of the Supreme Court of Canada. The newspapers had a field day, especially when Gerda Munsinger, who was said to have died some time before, was discovered by Robert Reguly of *The Toronto Star* in Munich very much alive and kicking. . . .

While Mr Justice Spence censured Diefenbaker in his report, no more damage was done to him in the eyes of the public than was done to the Liberal Party for resurrecting an incident that had occurred several years before. It was looked upon as dirty politics and was not appreciated by the public even though they seemed to enjoy all the salacious details of what had happened.

It was rumoured, for example, that another ex-cabinet minister had also got to know the lady rather well, but it turned out he had only taken her to lunch on two occasions. Gene Whelan, the Liberal Member of Essex South, came back to Ottawa one Monday after spending the weekend at his home in Amherstburg to report he had been talking about this to two die-hard Tory farmers. They said they had always favoured the ex-cabinet minister in question as the successor to Mr Diefenbaker. 'But not no more. Any man who would spend money giving lunch to that kind of woman, and couldn't get no farther, don't deserve to be Prime Minister of Canada!'

Walter L. Gordon, *A Political Memoir*, 1977

In the newspapers the affair was blown up into an intrigue of glamour and passion. It was rumoured that the RCMP had taken pictures of Gerda and her lovers in action through a special light fixture in the ceiling of her bedroom, that the police had a tape-recording of a wooden leg going bump in the night, that DOT planes had been used for secret rendezvous and so on. To astonished Canadians it sounded as though the Diefenbaker Years had been one long champagne bash. Gil Purcell, general manager of the Canadian Press, won a limerick contest sponsored by *Maclean's* with the verse:

> There was a young lady from Munich
> Whose bosom distended her tunic.
> Her main undertaking
> Was cabinet making
> In fashions bilingue and unique.

Peter C. Newman, *The Distemper Of Our Times*, 1968

WALTER GORDON

A partner in the accounting firm of Clarkson, Gordon and Co. after 1935, Walter Gordon served on several royal commissions and was Minister of Finance (1963–5), and President of the Privy Council (1967–8), in the Pearson cabinet. An ardent economic nationalist, he was co-founder (with Peter C. Newman and Abraham Rotstein) of the Committee for an Independent Canada.

I had my first taste of this other kind of work—other than regular auditing, that is—shortly after enrolling as a student. The firm was retained by the Royal Commission on Customs and Excise to examine the books and records of a wide variety of enterprises which the commission proposed to investigate. Newton W. Rowell, KC, was chief counsel to the commission. He was a distinguished and successful lawyer who had previously enjoyed a remarkable political career, first as leader of the Liberal Party in Ontario and then as President of the Privy Council and acknowledged second-in-command in Sir Robert Borden's wartime government. Mr Rowell, who was a confirmed teetotaller, dominated the commission and used it to launch a crusade against the bootleggers and other elements of the liquor trade. Like the United States, most of Canada at that time was suffering under Prohibition, a form of masochism much favoured by Mr Rowell and like-minded Calvinists in English-speaking Canada.

It was my good fortune to be attached to this commission throughout its tour of Western Canada as a sort of glorified office boy. My duties were to assist Colonel A.E. Nash, the partner in charge of all the investigations being done by our firm for the commission. My job was to see that copies of reports were available on time for the commission's sittings, and to do odd jobs for all and sundry. The importance of my rather ill-defined responsibilities was brought home to me as the commission was approaching Winnipeg. I was called into private consultation by one of the commissioners, a judge of the Supreme Court of Ontario, who had impressed me at several of the hearings. He was a large man who had the ability to sleep soundly through much of the day but, at critical moments, without appearing to wake up, to ask extremely pertinent questions of the witnesses. This technique must have required much practice.

The commissioner informed me that I appeared to him to be a perspicacious young man who should go far in the profession. He then asked if I would perform a small service for him. I was much flattered by his compliments and promised to do anything I possibly could to help him. This settled, he asked that, on arrival at each city where the commission was to sit, I should seek out the most reliable bootlegger and purchase two bottles of the best available Scotch whisky. He suggested that, if I had any trouble in finding a good bootlegger, I should consult the senior officer of the RCMP in the area. He added that, if I could manage to deliver to him the required necessaries of life without the knowledge of Mr Rowell, it would spare everybody's feelings. My recollection is that I was able to carry out this mission satisfactorily.

Walter L. Gordon, A Political Memoir, 1977

That summer [1940] had its lighter moments. I remember working very late at the Bank one Friday or Saturday evening when a worried-looking official came to my office and urged me to go and talk to Donald Gordon, the Deputy Governor of the Bank, as quickly as possible. I presumed I was appealed to as the only other person of any seniority in the building at the time, even if in my case it was quite undefined. It happened that [Governor Graham] Towers was away that weekend and Donald Gordon was in charge of things. Donald, who later made a tremendous reputation as Chairman of the Wartime Prices and Trade Board and after the war as President of the Canadian National Railways, had immense energy and a vast capacity for work. There were times, however, when he became a bit carried away and this was one of them. He told me that a French battleship with forty million dollars in gold bullion aboard was in Halifax harbour. Gordon said the Foreign Exchange Control Board was most anxious to get its clutches on the gold but that he had just received a telephone call from Halifax advising that the French warship was getting up steam preparatory to sailing off to Martinique. The gold was still on board. Gordon claimed that, as Deputy Chairman of the Board, he was authorized to prevent this from happening, and that it was his duty so to do. He said he was going to order the commander of the shore batteries at Halifax harbour to stop the French battleship from leaving. He hoped a shot across the bows would be sufficient, but if not it would be necessary to sink the ship.

I had a nasty feeling that a new role for the Bank of Canada might be in the making. As Donald was not in a mood to listen to any doubts as to his authority to order Canada's armed forces into action, another approach was called for. Accordingly, I telephoned a friendly admiral who had been very helpful to me in connection with the shipping situation. Fortunately he was at home and not yet asleep. Without disclosing what was going on at the Bank, I ascertained particulars of the relative firepower of the Halifax shore batteries and of the French battleship. I was able to report to Donald Gordon that, if the shore batteries managed a direct hit on the warship, the effect would be not dissimilar to a shot from a peashooter on the retreating back of a policeman, but that a return broadside from an irritated battleship would make the explosion in Halifax harbour in 1917 seem like a small display of fireworks. In other words, Halifax would be completely levelled and practically all its population killed. In the circumstances, I suggested the forty million dollars in gold was hardly worth it, especially as we would not get it anyway. Donald agreed to my pleading and Halifax was saved.

                                                                        Ibid.

I suggested [in 1940] that the federal government should announce the taxes that it intended to impose, including the excess profits tax which already had been advocated. At the same time, the government should offer to enter into an agreement with any province that would give up its rights to levy taxes for the duration of the war. Provinces that agreed to do this would be paid a fixed amount each year based roughly on the amounts of their present tax revenues augmented somewhat in the case of the poorer provinces.

The federal government should make it clear that no province was being forced to enter an agreement. They were all free to go on levying their own taxes, but in that case they would not qualify for the fixed amounts to be paid by Ottawa. Moreover, the taxpayers in any province that failed to enter an agreement would be required to pay a total level of taxation that would not be bearable; that full tax rates to be levied by the federal government, plus the taxes imposed by a province that was unwilling to enter an agreement, would exceed one hundred per cent of taxable income in many cases. But I argued that would be the responsibility of the provincial government in question, not of Ottawa. It was my submission that a scheme along these lines would work and that every province would have to accept it if the federal government was firm enough. The situation would become chaotic, however, if the federal government were to get cold feet and start making special deals with individual provinces.

[Deputy Finance Minister W.C.] Clark, as was his custom, peppered me with questions, but I could see from his excitement that he thought this might be the answer to our problem. He asked Bill Mackintosh to join us and we went through the proposal with him again. Then we called on Mr Ilsley, and after much discussion he agreed to lay the plan before the cabinet. A small cabinet committee was set up to go into it in detail, one of whose members was the Honourable P.J.A. Cardin of Sorel, an intelligent man of considerable toughness. I remember him saying when the proposal was explained to him, 'Young man, I like your plan. It would be like playing poker with the provinces, but this time the federal government would have all the aces. I think a plan like this would work. But we in Ottawa must not waver. It will work but only if we remember that the strength is on our side.'

That was the essence of the wartime tax agreements. The emphasis, all of it, was on the agreement angle. No mention was ever made of what might happen to any provincial government that did not go along; in other words, the alternative would in effect mean double taxation. It became my job to work out the details, and it took a year before all the provinces signed up. The last to do so was Ontario. Finally, [Ontario Premier] Mitch Hepburn arrived in Ottawa to discuss the proposal, accompanied by half a dozen of his cabinet ministers and a dozen or so officials. Mr Ilsley opened the meeting with me beside him. It took us half an hour or so to explain the proposal, laying great emphasis on the agreement angle. Mitch Hepburn, who was quick and intelligent and accustomed to use rather pungent language when he wished to shock people, listened carefully. He then walked around to me and whispered loud enough for Ilsley to overhear, in language designed to upset him, 'Walter, does this mean you've got us by the——?' I replied, also in a whisper, 'Yes, Mitch, and we intend to keep on squeezing until you sign.' Hepburn seemed to think this was funny. He laughed and said he would go back to the hotel as it would take his colleagues several days before the truth dawned upon them. This is more or less what happened but finally Ontario, after a good deal of expostulation, signed the agreement which was to last for the duration of the war.

Ibid.

In 1961 the Liberals held a policy conference in Kingston.

A very heated debate took place over foreign policy, and specifically about the recognition of Red China. Delegates at the closing plenary session late on the last afternoon were not willing to approve the resolution presented to them and demanded another session of the sub-committee on foreign policy. This was agreed to, and it was decided that I should act as chairman during the discussion. About four hundred delegates attended, half of whom violently advocated the recognition of Red China without reservations and the other half as violently opposed doing anything of the kind.

It was a difficult meeting. Delegates were tired after three long days of discussion and debate. Strong language was used and tempers flared. During the course of this, my secretary came to the platform to inform me in a whisper that there was an urgent telephone call for me from Toronto. I replied that I could not possibly leave the meeting and gave her a message to relay to my caller.

After an hour or so, the debate quieted down to a point where I was able to suggest a compromise resolution, which Pearson had helpfully drafted for me in advance, to use in case of emergencies. Nobody liked the suggestion very much, but after some further argument it was approved reluctantly. I did not want four hundred delegates to go home depressed or angry, so I said there was something I wished to tell them in the strictest confidence before the meeting was adjourned.

I referred to my secretary's appearance and the urgent telephone call which I said happened to be from the head of a Red Chinese delegation in Canada to negotiate with the Department of Agriculture. These people had been in touch with me a week or two before, presumably because I had visited Peking in 1959 and they knew of me. (I had referred them to Ottawa and naturally had informed the authorities there about this.) I told the delegates that I had asked my secretary to give the Chinese representatives the following message: 'Mr Gordon cannot speak on the telephone just now as he is closeted with a select group of fellow conspirators plotting the overthrow of the Canadian government.' This story—it happened to be true—relieved the tension, and the meeting broke up with everyone in better humour.

Ibid.

Before Pearson himself began to campaign [in 1965], Keith Davey and I started to give a daily press briefing at Liberal headquarters on Cooper Street, Ottawa. The main purpose was to let Liberals across the country know we were in business and also to keep the press happy by giving them something to write about no matter how unimportant. At one of these meetings, a reporter asked me to comment on a speech by Senator Wallace McCutcheon the night before in which he had criticized Liberal policies in general and me in particular in no uncertain terms. I answered that, if Wally McCutcheon really had such strong feelings, he should give up his Senate seat and run against me in Davenport. I challenged him to do so. The next day, McCutcheon replied: 'If all the people who disagree with Walter Gordon were to run against him in Davenport, there would be more candidates than voters.' There is no doubt he scored on the exchange.   Ibid.

We had planned to stage a major rally at the Yorkdale Plaza in Toronto during the last few days of the [1965] campaign. Gordon Edick and David Greenspan, our two experts in this field, were in charge of the arrangements and a crowd of twenty-five thousand turned up. Gordon had checked everything just before the meeting, but when Pearson appeared to speak, it was discovered that the public-address system had gone dead. After considerable confusion, Pearson tried to address the crowd through a loud hailer, but this was not successful. It was simply impossible for him to make his speech. Understandably, this was upsetting to the Prime Minister, but the crowd was enthusiastic and good-natured and did not seem to mind. I was moving around quite a bit, and at one point at the back of the hall, I overheard the conversation between two middle-aged ladies:

First lady: 'This is the most exciting political meeting I have ever been to. Such a tremendous crowd and we have seen everybody so well and so clearly.'

Second lady: 'Yes, and we have not had to listen to any political speeches!'
                                                                                                     Ibid.

The question of cabinet secrecy or the lack of it was a matter of considerable concern to many of us especially when it became evident that one or more ministers were deliberately leaking stories to the press. The matter was raised one day by Joe Greene, who had succeeded Harry Hayes as Minister of Agriculture and was one of the most popular members of the House of Commons. . . .

At the funeral service for Georges Vanier, the distinguished and much-beloved Governor General, members of the cabinet were expected to wear formal clothes. This meant quite a run on the local outfitter whose stock was limited. Joe turned up in a morning coat of decidedly old-fashioned cut and a stove-pipe hat that must have been at least one hundred years old. He was Abe Lincoln to a tee. Larry Pennell whispered to me that *The Man from Illinois* was playing at the Renfrew Theatre which was advertising there would be a personal appearance that evening. Joe had discovered that for an extra two dollars he could keep his clothes until the following morning.

But Joe is shrewd as well as entertaining and on occasion can go right to the heart of things. When the Prime Minister was complaining about the leaks from cabinet, Joe interrupted to say it would be a very simple matter to stop them. Looking directly at a certain minister, he said, 'We all know where the leaks come from. If one of our colleagues were to receive a sentence of five years in the penitentiary, I expect the whole problem would be resolved.' After a rather pregnant silence, we proceeded to discuss another subject.

On another occasion, I raised the question of cabinet leaks but in a lighter vein. One morning before cabinet began, several ministers commented on an article by Peter Newman which had appeared in *The Toronto Star* and other newspapers the previous day. Newman, an extremely talented writer as well as an able and industrious reporter, had quoted with remarkable accuracy what was said by a number of ministers at a recent cabinet meeting. This was still the topic of conversation when the Prime Minister arrived. I asked him if it would not be a kindness to give Newman a chair on the grounds that it was most uncomfortable for him to have to crouch for several hours under the table while cabinet meetings were in session. I was delighted to notice two ministers looking surreptitiously under the table to see if Peter was really there.

Ibid.

I had not seen Mike Pearson in the more than four years since I left Ottawa in March 1968, except casually at two or three large receptions, and once on a plane trip. But in November 1972, I began to hear stories that he had cancer and did not have long to live. . . . [A]fter checking with Patsy Hannah, Mike's daughter, I went to Ottawa on November 28, 1972. My note about this reads as follows:

> I found him in better shape than I had been led to believe. Clear in his head, witty, and quite reconciled to whatever may be in store. He said he was due for another set of chemical treatments in the hope the cancer may be contained. He did not appear to have much hope of success, however.
>
> I congratulated him on the first volume of his memoirs. He said someone else would have to complete the remaining two volumes. He is trying to complete his recollections of certain events and individuals but stated he would not have time to do the necessary checking.
>
> Mike quite obviously was pleased to see me. He said he was troubled by two things that happened when he was PM. The first was about Favreau. Pearson came very close to acknowledging he had been in the wrong in not stating Favreau had spoken to him about Rouleau-Rivard, etc.
>
> The second matter as he put it was the way he and I had 'drifted apart'.
>
> I stayed with him for 30–40 minutes. He kept on pressing me not to leave— but I had been warned that he gets tired very easily.
>
> If it helped him to see me again—and our conversation was very easy; no strain—I am glad I went.   Ibid.

JUDY LAMARSH

Judy LaMarsh held the portfolios of Health and Welfare (1963–5) and Secretary of State (1965–8) in Pearson's cabinet. She established the Royal Commission on the Status of Women.

Although Judy LaMarsh was not the first woman in a Canadian Cabinet— Ellen Fairclough was the first and had been a Minister in the Diefenbaker

Government for almost six years—there were really no facilities for women in the Parliament Buildings. If she wanted to go to the lavatory, she had to leave the Cabinet room, walk the length of a long corridor, down a flight of stairs to the secretaries' can, as she put it, on the next floor. Once, when she was caught short, she went to the men's room while one of the Ministers stood guard, and was astonished at all the marble fittings. The House of Commons was a private men's club, and there was no changing it.

Peter Stursberg, Lester Pearson and the Dream of Unity, 1978

Judy LaMarsh was better at telling stories on other people than on herself, but one she told was about addressing a meeting in rural Saskatchewan, when Grits were even less popular than Tories had been in John Diefenbaker's youth. The subject of LaMarsh's speech was the agriculture policy of the Pearson government, and during one pause for breath she heard a farmer on one side of the hall mutter: 'Bet she's never been behind a plough!' And from the other side of the hall came the response: 'Looks like she should be in front of one!'

It was Judy, too, who claimed to have heard a woman get up at a western rally where bilingualism was being discussed, and shout: 'If English was good enough for Jesus, it's good enough for me!'

Charles Lynch, A Funny Way to Run a Country, 1986

Later [1967] there was a flare-up between Trudeau and me, which also stemmed from a judicial appointment of a man I had known years earlier, and to whom I objected on the basis of that knowledge. Our exchange got pretty heated, and he lost his temper when he saw me doodling on my note pad. I was, and am, an inveterate doodler. I let words falling on my ears flow through my mind to my pencil and onto paper. Usually the doodles are pretty harmless, often sketches. This time I wrote: 'Arrogant bastard.' He inquired to whom the words referred, and I suggested he was bright enough to deduce the answer to that. He went ahead and made the appointment anyway.

Judy LaMarsh, Memoirs of a Bird in a Gilded Cage, 1969

Then the [1968] convention. I had no intention of appearing at it except to cast my vote for Leader. The call went out for all the ministers to be present together to listen to Pearson's farewell speech. On my entry into the hall I ran into the Hellyers and was invited to sit with them. The rest is history and pretty well documented on film and tape and in endless newspaper reports. The public has the erroneous impression that I called the Prime Minister a bastard in public, on television. I did not do that. Not even I am that plain spoken. I was asked to go to try to convince Hellyer that he should pull out before the third ballot and swing to Winters although he knew as I did that most of his supporters would refuse to vote for Winters no matter what. The crush of people was unbelievable, I had to fight my way over to an aisle filled with bodies. I suppose most of them were reporters; I have no idea. I couldn't get closer than the row of seats ahead of Hellyer's. I leaned over and hollered in Paul's ear. Out of the corner of my eye, I saw a man (so far as I know I never saw him before, and don't know his name) bend to his notebook as I said, 'Get out now and we'll go on to stop the bastard.' I knew that remark was likely to come to the public's attention. I could not know that a directional microphone had also picked it up for the world to hear. In the noise and crush and heat and confusion, I was interrogated on a report that I had said I would never serve under Trudeau. I confirmed that. What I didn't add was that I had no intention of serving anyone, ever again.

Ibid.

PETER REILLY

A lively TV journalist, Peter Reilly was a member of the House of Commons from 1972 to 1974.

My seatmate was Peter Reilly, the Conservative MP from Ottawa West. He was a former broadcaster, and the two of us made a scrappy Irish pair, offering a running commentary about the scene around us. He revelled in his own colourful past and told stories on himself, escapades that usually involved women—and always liquor. Once, at a campaign meeting, a bristling question came from an older woman: 'Mr Reilly, is it true that you have a drinking problem and have been married three times?' Reilly faced it head on. 'Madam,' he said coolly. 'If you'd been married three times, you'd have a drinking problem, too.' On another occasion when he'd been out on a bender, he returned home late and tried to sneak in quietly. He shed his shoes and his clothes on the way to bed and crawled under the covers, congratulating himself for not waking anyone. He was ready for sleep when he suddenly realized that he'd come to the wrong house and had climbed into bed with a previous wife.

Sean O'Sullivan with Rod McQueen, *Both My Houses*, 1986

GORDON AIKEN

Rules, even Parliamentary rules, are made to be bent. Gordon Aiken, Conservative MP from 1957 to 1972, reports the example of an artful MP, one Clancy, exasperated by taunts from across the floor, making his point without breaching the proprieties of the House.

'Mr Speaker,' he asked, properly addressing the Chair, 'would it be out of order if I called the honourable Member a son-of-a-bitch?' The Speaker nodded his head. 'I thought so,' said Clancy, resuming his seat.

Gordon Aiken, *The Backbencher*, 1974

Several correspondents report that this story was often embellished in the re-telling,
with the aggrieved MP muttering: 'Nevertheless, when the Hon. Member goes home
tonight, I hope his mother crawls out from under the porch and bites him.'

EUGENE FORSEY

After teaching from 1929 to 1941 at McGill, Eugene Forsey was research director
of the Canadian Labour Congress. He twice ran as a CCF candidate, but refused to
join the NDP in 1961 because of its 'deux nations' policy. Dr Forsey sat in the Senate
as a Trudeau Liberal from 1970 to 1979, but broke with the party in 1982 over
constitutional amendments.

Forsey attended McGill, where he studied economics and political science.

At first his home-grown conservatism was reinforced by Leacock, the head of
the department, whom Forsey recalls as a masterful teacher. ('He could have
done absolutely anything. He could have been Prime Minister.') Then there
was the equally powerful example of Meighen, whom Forsey had often heard
in the House of Commons, speaking in flawless sentences for two or three
hours at a stretch, without a single note. ('He was far and away the most
brilliant parliamentarian this country has ever produced.') Soon, however,
Forsey was being swayed by Leacock's deputy, Joe Hemmeon, who called
himself a Communist, and by the minister of Forsey's church, an English
Wesleyan in the radical tradition. Forsey began to consider himself a socialist
in 1926. As he recalled it, the turning point came when the old guard Conservatives began conspiring to remove Meighen from the leadership. 'The
business establishment, especially in Montreal, thought that Meighen was a
dangerous radical. When I wrote an article for the student newspaper, defending
Meighen as a progressive, I was called on the carpet by the principal, Sir Arthur
Currie. He spent one whole hour accusing me of "Bolshevism". Imagine that—
I was a Bolshevik because I supported the leader of the Conservative party!'

Charles Taylor, Radical Tories, 1984

Back in Canada in 1929, Forsey began a twelve-year stint as a sessional lecturer
in his old department at McGill. As he recalls the period, he was always in
trouble for his socialist views. ('I was a constant headache to the authorities.')
Although the quarrel was later patched up, Leacock was aghast at his star
pupil's apostasy. ('He told Hemmeon he wanted to shoot me.') Regarded with
suspicion by Sir Arthur Currie and other members of the university establishment, Forsey never received a promotion and never achieved tenure. When
he finally sought an explanation from the Dean, he was told that he was
'injudicious'. Pressed for an example, the Dean replied: 'You have been heard
in this building speaking in an excited tone of voice.'

Ibid.

That Canada was a nation of two cultures he had no doubt; but he was equally certain that this fact did not justify the use of the ambiguous phrase 'two nations'. Canada, he insisted, was politically and legally one nation and the adjective 'national' was the proper word to describe its collective policies and enterprises. It was his emphasis on this vital distinction that led him to break with the New Democratic Party, the successor to the CCF, the party which he had served faithfully for almost thirty years. In the new party's constitution, which was presented to the founding convention in the summer of 1961, the word 'national' had originally occurred no fewer than seventy-six times; but on the curious ground that it 'hurt and offended our French-Canadian fellow citizens', this exactly appropriate adjective was deleted, and in many cases, though not all, the innocuous word 'federal' was substituted instead. Disgusted with this ludicrous exercise in appeasement, Eugene quickly resigned from the new party. As he said later, the NDP founding convention was probably the only occasion in history when some thousands of people gathered to found a new national party and began by agreeing that there was no nation to found it in!

D.G. Creighton, Introduction to Eugene Forsey, *Freedom and Order*, 1974

All the pundits came on [television] and explained with great elaboration just how large Pearson's [1965] over-all majority was going to be. I am a very poor judge of election prospects, but I sat there saying to my wife, 'They're all wrong, he is not going to get a majority at all.' The pundits were particularly strong on the gains he was going to make in Nova Scotia. Well, I am part Nova Scotian. I had just been down there, and I said, 'They're crazy, he is not going to gain in Nova Scotia at all. He is going to lose seats in Nova Scotia, mark my words.'

Then on came John being interviewed by Norman DePoe. Norman DePoe in his most blustering and heckling fashion said, 'Mr Diefenbaker, what have you got to say about the argument that the government needs a clear majority to strengthen it?' John, looking more avuncular and benign than I could have believed possible, replied, 'I have always heard that it is no use adding spokes to the wheel when the hub is gone.'

'Well,' I said to my wife, 'There is the perfect description of the Pearson government.'

Forsey, quoted in *Diefenbaker: Leadership Lost*, ed. Peter Stursberg, 1976

When the St Laurent government began to replace the title 'Dominion of Canada' with the simple 'Canada', an exasperated Forsey charged: 'The rot in our national life has gone so far that government thought it could safely unveil its treason.' On other occasions he has indulged in heavy sarcasm. To proposals that the provinces receive sweeping powers at the expense of Ottawa, Forsey responded that the reconstituted nation would need 'a distinctive flag, which would surely stir the blood of every citizen of the 10 mini-states: 10 jackasses eating leaves off a single maple tree.'

Charles Taylor, *Radical Tories*, 1982

Recently, there have been suggestions that when Ed Schreyer retires as Canada's high commissioner to Australia he might re-enter active politics. It must be asked, therefore, if it is proper for a retired governor general to do such a thing. Some journalists have said, 'Why not?' Indeed, Mr Schreyer himself has seemed to countenance the notion. 'There is nothing written, nothing even understood, about the constitutional propriety or inadvisability of a former governor general's entering or re-entering politics,' he said over three years ago.

Of course there is nothing written, for the very simple reason that until Mr Schreyer raised the possibility no-one had ever thought of such a thing. There is nothing written, though perhaps there has hitherto been something understood, about the propriety of a governor general's opening Parliament in his nightshirt.

Mr Schreyer's statement betrayed a fundamental failure to grasp the responsibilities and limitations of the viceregal office. The limitations are imposed by the fact that its occupant must be absolutely free of even the slightest suspicion of partisanship. This he cannot be if Rideau Hall is accepted as a stopping place on the road to 24 Sussex Drive.

Eugene Forsey, *Saturday Night*, Jan. 1988

MITCHELL SHARP

After a career as a senior civil servant, Mitchell Sharp was Minister of Trade and Commerce and then of Finance in the Pearson cabinet. From 1968 to 1974 he was Minister of External Affairs.

His [1968 leadership] campaign ended suddenly when, as finance minister, he introduced a tax-increase bill that was defeated on third reading in the Commons owing to a blunder he still regrets.

But rather than dropping out quietly, Mr Sharp announced loudly that he was throwing his support behind the then justice minister, an eccentric Montreal intellectual named Pierre Trudeau who was already the object of a curious and unCanadian excitement soon to be known as Trudeaumania.

This gave the sandal-wearing, philosophy-spouting lawyer the Bay Street credibility that only a Toronto minister of finance could deliver in those days.

Mr Sharp recalls that business people would ask him whether 'that fellow Trudeau isn't a little queer?'

Invariably, Mr Sharp would reply that, on the contrary, 'he's a very rich man and a conservative in financial matters', and that was usually enough to gain their support, he said.

Richard Cleroux, *The Globe and Mail*, 11 March 1988

GÉRARD PELLETIER

With Trudeau and Jean Marchand, Gérard Pelletier was one of the 'three wise men'
from Quebec who joined Pearson's Liberals during the election of 1965. He held the
portfolios of Secretary of State and later External Affairs in the Trudeau cabinet
(1968–75), and then was appointed Canada's Ambassador to France.
Here Pelletier reflects on why the three went to Ottawa.

The reasoning was very simple. I remember at my house—Marchand and
Trudeau were there one night—I summed up the situation. I said, 'You see,
the separatists will win by default, because there's nobody in Ottawa with
whom they can identify as Quebeckers.'

It's no reflection on any of the ministers but the fact is that nobody in
Quebec identified with them. It was not only because they had had this trouble
with the Dorion inquiry and the furniture deal, which seems pretty picayune
when you look at it with the benefit of hindsight, and all these things. But
Lamontagne was a university professor. He had no deep roots within the
population; he was not very widely known. Tremblay was a university professor. Favreau was a very highly competent lawyer, but not known generally.

So we said, 'If people look in the direction of Quebec city for everything all
the time and they have no counterbalance in Ottawa—I mean people with
whom they can identify because they've known them in labour, on television,
heard them over the radio and in journalism—separatism will win by default.'
This was the basic reasoning, really.

I must say also that we had been sympathetic towards the NDP but always
at odds with them on their approach to Quebec. At every election, they came
to us and they said, 'Well, you'll help us?' We said, 'Yes, we'll help you if you
concentrate on five or six ridings. You have very few resources. We might get
one or two members elected if you want to concentrate.' But the national
direction of the party, the national authorities, always said, 'No, no, we must
have at least' (I think it was) 'thirty candidates, because you need that if you
want to be on radio and television between elections. We need to say in the
rest of the country that we have a chance of forming a government because
we run forty candidates,' which was total nonsense. Then, every time the
language question, for instance, came up, one of their members from Vancouver
or Manitoba would say exactly the wrong things. And they were giving in to
a kind of special status for Quebec in which we didn't believe.

We didn't just change our minds in 1965. We had been at odds with them
on very, very many questions, but particularly on the question of the approach
to Quebec and separatism. It wasn't a sudden change of mind. It was a process
that took us to this position: 'We have a choice to make. Either we want to
build now and see the country change in twenty-five years, and that would be
with the NDP'—and I don't think we were very wrong because it's ten years
later and they certainly have another fifteen years to wait—'or we want to do
something right now, and the only answer to that is that Liberal party.' The

Liberal party opened the door, and we knew very well that we could eliminate what we didn't like in Quebec about the way the machine was run and so on.

We did a pretty thorough job of housekeeping. I remember what they called 'the old guard' at that time in Montreal published a pamphlet to say how the old guard was betrayed and eliminated. The newsmen went to Marchand and said, 'What comment do you have to make on this?' He said, 'Mission accomplished.' That's what we wanted to do.

Pelletier, quoted in *Diefenbaker: Leadership Lost*, ed. Peter Stursberg, 1976

JEAN MARCHAND

A Quebec union leader who (with Pelletier and Trudeau) ran for Pearson's Liberals in 1965, Jean Marchand held several cabinet posts from 1965 to 1976 and was then called to the Senate.

Marchand was street-smart and tough as a longshoreman. He knew who had to be controlled and who had to be flattered and who had to be elbowed aside. He was earthy, vivacious, fearless, funny, and charming. When he was asked what he liked best about Ottawa, he answered in a flash, 'The fast train to Montreal', and the Anglos, far from being affronted, were delighted at the insult.

Christina McCall-Newman, *Grits*, 1982

PIERRE ELLIOTT TRUDEAU

The fifteenth prime minister of Canada, Pierre Elliott Trudeau held office from 1968 to 1979 and 1980 to 1984.

After Pierre Trudeau became prime minister, Grace Pitfield—the mother of his régime's most prominent public servant, Michael Pitfield, who had been born into one of the old English-Canadian Montreal families and had relatives married into half the others—reminisced about French-English relations in her youth and early married life. 'We didn't talk to the French Canadians very much in those days [the 1920s and 1930s],' she said. 'Except for a few people like Georges Vanier [later the governor general] and his wife Pauline, they just didn't go to the places we went to or do the things we did. I mean, you never even *saw* them at the Ritz. Some of my friends had been at school with Grace Elliott [Trudeau's mother, who had been educated at Dunham Ladies' College in the Eastern Townships and was the daughter of an English-speaking businessman said to be descended from United Empire Loyalists]. They heard later that she had married a Frenchman. But nobody knew who he was and of

course they never saw her afterwards.' In brief, the Trudeaus were not 'just
like the Molsons', they weren't just like the old-rich French-Canadian families
like the Simards or the Taschereaus either. They were the Outremont new
rich, members of a small, recently prosperous urban middle class. Grace Elliott
may have been gently reared, but her father had made his money in tavern-
keeping and her husband in selling gas.

Christina McCall-Newman, Grits, 1982

*In the election of 1963 Trudeau was no Liberal. He attacked Pearson's 'hypocrisy' on
nuclear policy and denounced the PM as 'the defrocked Priest of Peace'.*

Back in Canada once more, he was invited, with Marchand and Pelletier (who
had become considerable political figures, plugging away while Trudeau flitted),
to join the Liberal party. The three men spurned the offer. They were supporting the NDP and, in the pages of *Cité Libre*, Trudeau poured terrible scorn
on Prime Minister Pearson for accepting nuclear weapons for Canada. . . .
(Trudeau's article in the April 1963 edition of *Cité Libre* was called 'The
Abdication of the Spirit', and contained this passage: 'I would have to point
out in strongest terms the autocracy of the Liberal structure and the cowardice
of its members. I have never seen in all my examination of politics so degrading
a spectacle as that of all these Liberals turning their coats in unison with their
Chief, when they saw a chance to take power. . . . The head of the troupe
having shown the way, the rest followed with the elegance of animals heading
for the trough.')

Walter Stewart, Shrug: Trudeau in Power, 1972

*As a Liberal MP in 1965, Trudeau became parliamentary secretary to Pearson and
then Minister of Justice (1967–8). In December 1967 he introduced a bill to expand
the grounds for divorce in Canada.*

Abruptly, the press began to write about Trudeau. They wrote more two
weeks later, when he brought down the Omnibus Bill to reform the Criminal
Code—legalizing lotteries and therapeutic abortions, and decriminalizing a
variety of acts, the most contentious being homosexuality when 'performed in
private between consenting adults'. To justify this, Trudeau tossed off the most
resonant of all his phrases: 'The state has no place in the bedrooms of the
nation.'* The entire nation sat up and took notice.

*This is the way the phrase always is quoted, although Trudeau actually said, in an
interview on December 22, 1967, 'The state has no place in the nation's bedrooms.'
The original author of the phrase was *Globe and Mail* editorial writer Martin O'Malley.

Richard Gwyn, The Northern Magus, 1980

At the federal Liberal convention of 1968 that selected Trudeau, Joey Smallwood tried to guide his province's delegates.

Newfoundland had been thought to be securely in Bob Winters' camp; Winters was himself a Maritimer and a long-time friend of both Newfoundland and Smallwood. But a few days before the convention, Trudeau made a flying trip to St John's and the word went out that Joey, ever the political opportunist, had defected. But there were reports of dissension in the delegation over the switch, and this led to what could have been the most hilarious gaffe in Canadian broadcasting history.

I was in the midst of presenting a round-up of reports from the floor. Each reporter was at standby with the representative of some region by his side. One of them, Henry Champ . . . was with a burly, beery Newfoundland delegate. Mistakenly thinking he had been given a cue and not realizing he wasn't on the air, Champ began his interview:

'There are rumours of a major split in the Newfoundland delegation,' he said. 'As I understand it: Joey Smallwood wants the entire delegation to declare for Trudeau but some of you aren't prepared to go along. Are you one of those? Tell me what's happening.'

The delegate paused a moment to gather his thoughts, his mind unfocussed after a long night of partying and politicking. 'Well,' he said, 'here's the way it is. I'm a Bob Winters man myself and they're tryin' to get me to switch. I'm not sure exactly what's happenin', but I'll tell you this: Joey can point my cock but he can't tell me when to piss.'

Charles Templeton, An Anecdotal Memoir, 1983

Anyone who was paying attention to such things could also have been aware of two Trudeau faults that later were greeted with apparent surprise: his capacity for cutting nastiness when attacked, and his occasional insensitivity to things that are important to other people. . . .

The insensitivity was displayed right at the beginning of his prime-ministerial tenure. First, to maintain the option of calling an election for June 17, he advanced the date of his swearing-in by two days, thereby depriving Pearson of the sentimentally important opportunity to step down exactly five years after taking office. Much worse, he then handled the announcement of his election call in Parliament in such a way that he cut off the opportunity for party leaders to pay tribute to the outgoing prime minister. Instead of leaving time for the tribute before he made his announcement, or asking MPs to remain in the chamber afterward, he was coldly logical: Since the governor general had already granted dissolution, it was inappropriate for anyone to speak. The result was that Pearson, who had chosen not to run in the election, found himself leaving Parliament for the last time, without a formal word of farewell.

George Radwanski, Trudeau, 1979

What was not accepted . . . was the Prime Minister's attitude towards the House, a place where his contemptuous shrugs and pointed refusal to answer questions crystallized around two disturbing events. The first came when, during the debate on rules, some opposition MPs began to file out of the House, and the Prime Minister called out, 'I think we should encourage members of the opposition to leave. Every time they do, the IQ of this House rises considerably. . . . When they get home, when they get out of Parliament, when they are fifty yards from Parliament Hill, they are no longer honourable members—they are just nobodies.' The second incident occurred in February 1971 when, under consistent heckling because of his inability to deal with questions on unemployment, Trudeau told two Conservative MPs, one after the other, to 'fuck off', carefully mouthing the words so that they would not appear on the Hansard record, and he could claim later that what he had said was 'fuddle duddle'.

Walter Stewart, Divide and Con, 1973

Trudeau allowed his ministers a fairly free hand in the running of their departments, but cabinet authority was dispersed into so many committees that only the PM and his immediate entourage could exercise any real influence on overall government policy. He conducted cabinet meetings like Jesuit seminars, encouraging ministers to criticize each others' proposals, not imposing his views on others but allowing them instead to find their own way to his convictions.

These mental gymnastics muffled the effectiveness of progressive politicians in the room, notably Robert Andras and Eric Kierans, and rendered totally silent other ministers unsure of their dialectic ability. 'You were always listened to with great respect, but nothing would ever happen,' Kierans complained after he resigned in the spring of 1971. 'You know, when the Pope gets down off the altar at St Peter's and walks down the aisle, the one thing you're sure of is that he's going to get to the other end. You can argue and argue, but the procession always goes on its way.'

Peter C. Newman, Home Country, 1973

The 'October Crisis' of 1970 involved the FLQ (Front de Libération du Quebec) and the use of the War Measures Act.

Finally, at 12:45 P.M. on October 15, after long discussions between Montreal, Quebec City and Ottawa, Jérôme Choquette, as attorney-general, signed an official request under the National Defence Act asking for troops. The army, whose military intelligence wing had been on top of the Quebec situation from the days the first bombs had begun to go off in the early sixties, had a full-scale plan ready to go. . . .

It was a terrible shock to most Montrealers, like waking up in a foreign country. Suddenly fast-moving convoys were rumbling through the streets of Montreal. Voyageur and Huey helicopters came clattering between the skyscrapers. Suddenly troops with camouflage nets on their helmets, wearing all the paraphernalia of war, with FN semi-automatic rifles carried at the port arms position, were everywhere throughout the old metropolis. . . .

There is still some mystery surrounding exactly who drew up the list of 468 Quebecers who were arrested and detained under the awful powers of the War Measures Act, beginning in the dark hours before dawn on Friday, October 16. But in the end, there can be little doubt that the final list of names was approved by city lawyer Michel Côté from his position deep in the heart of the command hothouse at CAT headquarters. It included all the street radicals of the Swiss Hut era, as well as poets like Gérald Godin, Trudeau's former friend, and journalists like the ubiquitous Nick Auf der Maur, who was summoned from his desk at the CBC and taken off to the cells of Parthenais to join old friends from the battlegrounds of the sixties such as Michel Chartrand, Pierre Vallières, Charles Gagnon and hundreds more. It has since become a badge of honour among Quebecers to have been jailed during the War Measures Act, but the romance of the time as it is seen retrospectively blurs the real hardship caused to people who lost jobs or whose names were smeared with respect to employers and their more conservative family members. The police also used the powers of the War Measures Act to wreak revenge on the underground newspaper *Logos* which had mocked them for so long. The police descended on the newspaper offices in the student ghetto near McGill in the dead of night and systematically destroyed every piece of equipment and seized every file. The newspaper was never heard from again. Drapeau used the powers directly to close down the film *Quiet Days in Clichy*, a harmless exercise in soft sex based on a Henry Miller book which outraged the mayor's Victorian sensibilities.

But most disturbing, the powers of the War Measures Act suddenly became a factor in the Montreal municipal election. The opposition movement was almost torn apart with internal dissension on how to respond to FLQ and the opposition's leading candidate was arrested and thrown into jail. Dr Henri Bellemare, a physician operating a clinic in the ghetto area, was one of the few candidates actually considered to have a chance of unseating one of Drapeau's councillors. With his name smeared by the tarring brush of the Act, that possibility quickly evaporated.

Michel Côté says now that Jean Drapeau played only an indirect role in the day-to-day decisions during the October Crisis: 'He was busy running an election campaign', observes Côté. Côté is right. The October Crisis *became* Drapeau's election campaign. Despite a rising chorus of pleas that the campaign be postponed until some sense of serenity descended upon the city, Drapeau was skilfully using the enemies of the crisis to reinforce the hammer he already wielded. Any restraint the mayor felt in that direction evaporated forever on the afternoon of Saturday, October 16 when the strangled body of Pierre Laporte was discovered in the trunk of a battered old car on the South Shore near his home. Politicians everywhere in the country expressed a deep horror and revulsion at the act, Trudeau an icy resolve that the terrorists would be hunted down and made to pay. Drapeau, with tears welling in his eyes, appeared on camera and spoke about the dangers facing men in public life, and how this danger must be accepted even to the . . . but he never finished. He simply stopped, covered his face, shook his head and walked away overcome.

In Montreal, as in Quebec City, the politicians suddenly began to believe the wildest plots and most incredible scenarios that their police force had been pushing. Premier Bourassa called aside Guy Joron, an old friend and one of six Parti Québécois members elected in April 1970 to the National Assembly. Joron remembers Bourassa so scared that he was in tears, repeating over and over again: 'I have only a few days to live.'. . .

Trudeau himself remembers the scene with considerable astonishment, observing to biographer George Radwanski that instead of being the producer of a drama to 'sock it to the separatists', as he was later accused, he was an actor in it:

> 'When I went to Laporte's funeral, I said, "Look, I want to walk from the helicopter to Notre Dame Church. I want the people to see me." And then we had a meeting, a secret meeting with Drapeau and Bourassa, and I suddenly found myself in a bullet-proof car being driven from the Champs de Mars to Notre Dame with cordons of police everywhere. . . . Montreal, as you know, was seized in a reign of terror.'

Trudeau insists that the crucial event that had spurred him to action was a petition drawn up by *Le Devoir*'s editor, Claude Ryan, CNTU president Marcel Pépin, Laberge of the Quebec Federation of Labour and Charbonneau of the Teacher's Union as well as others calling for the government to negotiate the release of Laporte and Cross in exchange for political prisoners.

Brian McKenna and Susan Purcell, Drapeau, 1981

In the election of 1972 the Liberals slipped to a minority government position, only two seats ahead of Stanfield's Tories.

Instead of strategy and issues, the Liberals had a slogan, THE LAND IS STRONG, coined by George Elliott [of MacLaren Advertising]. It reflected perfectly the lulling effect Trudeau's campaign was intended to have. Probably no Canadian party has ever fought an election on a less meaningful slogan—though that might have been the case if Elliott's first version, A DIRECTION FOR CANADA, had been adopted. When he presented the gem to the campaign committee one of its right-wing members passed a scribbled note to a friend suggesting an alternative: FROM THOSE WONDERFUL FOLKS WHO GAVE YOU BENSON, BASFORD, AND MACKASEY. Although few Liberals took THE LAND IS STRONG theme seriously (Alberta campaign chairman Blair Williams even refused to use it in his advertising campaigns), only John Turner had the courage to question it in public. 'I've used it once in the whole campaign,' he told a group of students at the University of Winnipeg on October 20, 'and that was to see if I could get it out without breaking up.'

Peter C. Newman, Home Country, 1973

One of the few changes Trudeau made when he first moved into 24 Sussex was to hang in the stairwell, where he would see it first thing in the morning and last thing at night, a banner with a strange device: a quilt, made for him by the artist Joyce Wieland, on which she patch-worked the phrase: '*La Raison avant La Passion.*'

Trudeau's personal motto is Reason over Passion. Between 1968 and 1972, he made it the motto of his government. Not so much a motto, really, as a cry from the heart: years of solitary study and thought compressed into a single epigrammatic and idealistic phrase. The idea failed. To be rational about something as irrational as politics, Trudeau discovered, is to be irrational. 'My faith in politics, my faith in the democratic process, has changed a bit,' he said later, after Canadians had rejected both him and rationalism in the 1972 election.

Richard Gwyn, The Northern Magus, 1980

Ontario leader Bob Rae's private assessment: 'Trudeau makes Judas Iscariot look like a team player.'

Allan Fotheringham, Look Ma . . . No Hands, 1983

It is an odd footnote to history that Bob Rae, presently leader of the Ontario NDP, put motions of 'no confidence' that brought down two governments, Joe Clark's in 1979, and Frank Miller's Tory administration in Ontario in 1985.

The 1974 campaign had an added dimension.

It was the morning of the magician, all over again. 'In 1972, my campaign never really got off the ground. But this year, I've found the secret. I have a train, and I have Margaret,' he said, and everyone knew it was true. He could do nothing wrong: while Stanfield fumbled his famous football, Trudeau scrambled over a six-foot wrought-iron fence and looked graceful doing it. Reporters grumbled that Trudeau's policy announcements all were issued just before their deadlines, so that they had no time to make more than headlines out of them; no matter, the headlines appeared and the rest of the time reporters had all the colour and anecdote they needed to feed the Goat.

Above all, there was Margaret. She'd made up her own mind to campaign. Davey and Coutts were appalled and urged Trudeau to stop her; he tried and luckily for him he failed. 'He's a beautiful guy,' she said, gauche and nervous, to a crowd of 2,500 in West Vancouver. 'He taught me a lot about loving.' The crowd tittered at the unintended *double-entendre*. Davey and Coutts winced, and despatched an aide, Joyce Fairbairn, to hold Margaret's hand and, if possible, to close her mouth. Reporters giggled, then discovered the next day that the whole country had fallen in love with her. Overnight, Margaret had become a magician in her own right.

Richard Gwyn, The Northern Magus, 1980

His marriage to 23-year-old Margaret Sinclair in 1971 gave his image a boost, though his approach to married life was unconventional, to say the least. Within Margaret's hearing, he lectured us on how she should be assumed not to have a political idea in her head. He humoured her and put fetters on her at the same time. He told us she was publicity shy, and it was years before the awful truth became clear.

Once, when he abandoned her at an official dinner to attend an unexpected vote in the Commons, Margaret came directly to me to take issue with a column I had written saying her ambition to be a press photographer was impractical for a newsmaker of her impact. She defended the practicality of her plan, and when I chided her for having such political naiveté, considering that she had grown up in the house of a politician father, she looked me right in the eye and said she had hated her father and had left his house as soon as she was old enough to walk out, and that she had never respected or agreed with any of his ideas until after her marriage. (Father James Sinclair had told both Pierre and Margaret that the marriage was a mistake, and he lamented privately that since he had four daughters, why did the prime minister have to pick the crazy one?)

Charles Lynch, You Can't Print That!, 1983

In 1974 a fund was created by private donors to build an indoor pool at 24 Sussex Drive, the residence of the PM.

Bill Teron was believed to be the largest contributor of all: at least $60,000, his original estimate for cost of the pool. He ceased to be Trudeau's architectural adviser and soon vanished from the government scene in Ottawa. The amount of Trudeau's contribution was not known, but was believed small. As a millionaire, he never carried money on his person. When representatives of charities went to his office for the standard publicity pictures, Trudeau instructed an aide to make a donation because he didn't happen to have anything on him. The aide was never repaid. Trudeau's Christmas gifts to his staff were his own unwanted presents from foreign embassies in Ottawa. The press secretary usually got the Bulgarian vodka.

Dave McIntosh, Ottawa Unbuttoned, 1987

Among Marshall McLuhan's many correspondents was his friend Trudeau. This letter is included as a reminder of Trudeau's mastery of TV and of McLuhan's lively interest in politics.

24 February 1977

Dear Pierre:
Everybody I know has been deeply thrilled by your recent performance and reception in the US. That was a really imaginative and masterly approach, which you brought off superbly.

It was while I was trying to explain *charisma*, as manifested by Jack Kennedy and also by Jimmy Carter, that I raised the fact of *your* very powerful charisma. Jack Kennedy looked like the all-American boy, the corporate, inclusive image of American ideals. Nixon, on the other hand, looked like himself alone, a private image, fatally defective in the TV age. In contrast, Jimmy Carter has the charisma of a Huck Finn, a Southern boy, and he also has the vocal rhythms and corporate power that got him the black vote. It was while I was explaining these things that the interviewer asked: 'What about Pierre·Trudeau?' I replied that your corporate mask, your charisma, is both powerful and very popular with the young, in part because of the subtle hint in your image of 'mask' of the native Indian. As you know, the Red man is very powerful with the TV generation since he is Third World, and they are also Third World. He was *always* Third World; but they, the young, are having their first experience of it. Naturally, pulled out of the context of this image discussion it sounds very different, and even derogatory. You know me well enough to know that I would never say anything derogatory about you.

In the case of Carter, it became clear during the election that the image has supplanted the policy. A political point of view is not practical on TV since it is a resonating, multi-positional image, so that any moment of arrest or stasis permits the public to shoot you down. Maybe that is the meaning of the old gangster quote: 'Talk fast, Mister!', and also, '*Smile* when you say that!' I have yet to find a situation in which there is not great help in the phrase: 'You think my fallacy is all wrong?' It is literally disarming, pulling the ground out from under every situation! It can be said with a certain amount of poignancy and mock deliberation.

I am doing a piece about separatism and media in collaboration with Barrington Nevitt. He's the management consultant with whom I did the book on *The Executive as Dropout*. Our piece draws attention to the hidden *ground* that underlies all the many forms of separatism in our time. I refer to the *ground* of instant information that extends to the entire planet, and the effect of which is not centralism but decentralism. Any form pushed to its limit, as is pointed out by Aristotle and Aquinas, flips into the opposite form. Whereas hardware communication is a kind of transportation which centralizes organizational structures, electric communication is simultaneous and confers autonomy on every part of a structure. That is why the executive drops out of the old organization-chart patterns at electric speed. At electric speed, which is the speed of light, we are disembodied beings. On the phone, or 'on the air', we are instantly present, but minus our bodies. Politically, discarnate man may have an image, but not a physical body. There is a corresponding loss of personal identity and responsibility which creates separatism in private life and family life and in all institutional existence. When one becomes aware of this hidden *ground* and its effects, one should be better prepared to cope with, and to counteract, these effects. Ours is surely the first human generation that has ever encountered such an undermining disease which afflicts us at all levels of church and state.

Letters of Marshall McLuhan, ed. Matie Molinaro, Corinne McLuhan, and William Toye, 1987

Trudueau had announced his retirement, but Clark's minortity government lasted only until December 1979.

Then Clark spoke. 'I rise on a point of order. The Government has lost a vote on a matter which we have no alternative but to regard as a question of confidence. I simply want to advise the House that I will be seeing His Excellency the Governor General tomorrow morning.'

When Clark sat down, the Commons erupted. MPs threw paper in the air in the traditional salute to the end of a Parliament and the onset of an election. They shouted across the aisle at each other, laughing at the huge mistake the other side had just made.

Trudeau, however, remained in his seat for about ten seconds while those around him stood and headed for the door. His head rested on his hand and his shoulders were hunched forward. Throughout the roll call vote, he had gazed downward, lifting his head only to listen to Clark's announcement. Then he dropped his head again and kept it there. When he looked up again, he had a quizzical, thin smile on his face.

Secretary of State David MacDonald walked across the aisle to Trudeau's seat. He and Trudeau were members of the Class of 1965, having entered the Commons together in that year. MacDonald said simply that they both had been in Ottawa for nearly fifteen years and they might not see each other again. He wished Trudeau well. 'Being in politics, Pierre, is a bit like eating peanuts. Once you start, it's hard to stop.'

Trudeau smiled and replied: 'Yes, and it's not very good for you, either.'

Jeffrey Simpson, Discipline of Power, 1980

As a fillip to his joy, Trudeau began competing with the members of the media in games of poetry identification in the final week [of the 1980 campaign]. He inserted lines of poetry into his speeches, inviting the reporters to guess the poem. The reporters, in turn, tested him with quotations when he returned to his campaign plane. Seventy-two hours before the election returns were known, he broke free from his speech before a thousand Liberals in Scarborough, peered down at the members of the media in the front of the hall, and tossed off four lines of poetry, slightly amended:

> Turning and turning in the widening gyre
> The falcon cannot hear the falconer;
> Things fall apart; the centre cannot hold
> And mere anarchy is loosed upon the Tory Party.

He was paraphrasing William Butler Yeats' poem 'The Second Coming'.

Ibid.

Pierre Trudeau succeeded in giving Feb. 29 new meaning. Now, along with being Leap Year Day, hockey hero Henri Richard's birthday and Sadie Hawkins

Day, it is remembered as the day he told Canada he was resigning as prime minister.

The decision had been made the night before, during an Ottawa blizzard that had brought the city to a standstill.

'I went home, discussed it with the boys, put them to bed,' Mr Trudeau told reporters on Feb. 29, 1984. 'I walked until midnight in the storm, then I went home and took a sauna for an hour and a half. It was all clear.'

Thus a new phrase—'going for a walk in the snow'—entered Canada's political dictionary. Mr Trudeau made fun of it even as he recounted how he had made the decision: 'I listened to my heart and saw if there were any signs of my destiny in the sky, and there were none—there were just snowflakes.'

Graham Fraser, *The Globe and Mail*, 29 Feb. 1988

EDWARD R. SCHREYER

The NDP Premier of Manitoba from 1969 to 1977, Edward Schreyer was appointed by Trudeau to be Governor General (1978–84).

When Ed Schreyer was premier of Manitoba in 1972, he maintained a close friendship with author Farley Mowat, both sharing a deep interest in protection of the environment.

Mowat appeared with me on my open-line radio program, CJOB Winnipeg, one day in January. He was pushing his latest book, wearing a kilt and obviously suffering the effects of too much celebrating the night beforehand. It was 31°below F.

'God, it's cold Warren. What the hell am I doing in Winnipeg in January?' Mowat shouted into the microphone at 8:30 A.M. on a Monday morning. 'Get Schreyer to send me a bottle of rum.'

We continued with the interview. Within 15 minutes, a courier arrived at the studio with a 60-ounce bottle of dark rum. The card was signed simply: 'Ed and Lilly'.

Contributed by Peter Warren, Winnipeg

JAMES CROSS

During the 'October Crisis' of 1970, British diplomat James Cross was more fortunate than Pierre Laporte, the other FLQ hostage, who lost his life.

I was dressing in the bathroom when I heard a ring at the door bell downstairs. I heard a second ring a few minutes later, and I heard voices. I took no notice as I thought the maid was answering the door.

Then a man came into the bedroom and pointed a pistol at me and told me to get down on the floor. He made me turn, lie on my face. He called downstairs to one of his friends and a second man came up armed with a sub-machine gun, driving in front of him the maid who was carrying her child.

The first man kept the maid and child and my wife under control in the bedroom. I might add that our dog had jumped up on to the bed and he told my wife to hold the dog. Otherwise, he would shoot it.

The second man took me into the dressing room, dressed me, allowed me to say goodbye to my wife and took me downstairs, where there was a third man also armed with a sub-machine gun.

They threw a raincoat over my shoulder, took me out down the steps to a car which had a taxi sign on the roof, and there was a fourth man sitting at the wheel of the car. I was pushed into the car down between the seat at the back and covered up with a rug. We drove for about five minutes, then we stopped at a garage or building of some sort. I was taken out of the car, told to keep my eyes closed and a gas mask was put on my head, in which the eye pieces had been painted out.

I was then driven for approximately 20 minutes and taken out of the car in the garage, led upstairs into a room, where I spent the next 60 days.

James Cross, quoted in The Globe and Mail, 10 Dec., 1970

ROBERT STANBURY

From 1972 to 1974 Robert Stanbury was Minister of National Revenue. ·

Stanbury . . . was inspecting Customs facilities at Vancouver airport. Three jets had just landed and there was a heavy crush at the Customs counters. One traveller yelled, 'Who in hell is in charge here?' Stanbury stepped forward and announced, 'I am the minister.' The traveller kicked Stanbury in the shins.

Dave McIntosh, Ottawa Unbuttoned, 1987

MICHAEL PITFIELD

Closely associated with Trudeau and his cabinet, Pitfield was Secretary to the Cabinet and later Clerk of the Privy Council. He was appointed to the Senate in 1982.

Michael Pitfield, when secretary to the cabinet, didn't even bother to call the cabinet minister concerned, let alone seek his approval, when he shuffled the minister's deputy to another post. In his brief reign, Prime Minister Clark managed to fire Pitfield, but he had to give him $100,000 in severance pay to do it. When Trudeau came back in 1980, so did Pitfield. He tried like hell later but couldn't find a job in the private sector and had to settle for a Senate appointment. Then he put in a huge bill for overtime as clerk of the privy

council. The treasury board paid him a handsome, if not the full, amount, though nobody has been able to find out how much. Only one politician ever stood up to Pitfield: Allan MacEachen. When Pitfield protested appointment of a defeated Cape Breton Conservative to a government board, MacEachen told him sharply: 'When you've been elected in Cape Breton, come and talk to me.'
                                                            Ibid.

RENÉ LÉVESQUE

Journalist, broadcaster, minister in Premier Jean Lesage's Liberal cabinet (1960–6), René Lévesque founded the Parti Québécois in 1968 and was Premier of Québec from 1976 to 1985.
   In his Memoirs, *Lévesque comments on the character of Trudeau and on their first meeting.*

How can one define the undefinable? He was extremely cultivated, certainly, but almost exclusively only in matters of jurisprudence and politics. I had the impression that, except for show, the additional baggage he had accumulated from studies in the humanities left him supremely indifferent, like seed fallen on rock. Even in conversation his thought constantly took on a dialectical twist, and to have the last word he would stop at neither sarcasm nor the most specious argument. In its written form his thought was dry and typically technocratic, as exemplified in the pages of *Cité libre* where he recommended 'borrowing from the architect his concern for "functional" discipline'. It was thanks to this little review he masterminded that we first met, some time in 1954 or 1955, I think. I had gone along with Pelletier to meet Trudeau in the cafeteria of Radio-Canada and offered to contribute the occasional article.
   'Very good,' he said in that drawling tone he affected, 'but allow me one simple question: Can you write?'
   You'll have guessed by now that we didn't exactly hit it off.
                              René Lévesque: Memoirs, trans. Philip Stratford, 1986

On the ballot slip all the candidate was allowed to have after his name was his profession, so I appeared as 'René Lévesque, journalist'. One can well imagine my stupefaction on discovering that right after my name came a 'René Lévesque, artist'! In those days all anyone had to do was supply a list of names and pay the deposit—it helped, obviously, to be on the right side—and a phantom candidate was thereby created. As a result of this fraud the last days of the campaign were spent driving around with this insistent message flying from every one of our automobiles: 'Vote for the *real* Lévesque—Lévesque, journalist.'
   But voters are such a distracted lot that on the morning of the 22nd [June 1960] one of our staunchest party militants, who had been very upset by these

tactics, confessed to us, a little late: 'O my God! It's not possible! I think I voted for the artist!' And she burst into tears. . . .

Over on rue Dante in the Italian quarter a bunch of hoodlums had started raiding the polls. As soon as I heard about it I jumped in the car and went over. Luckily, Rougeau was with me. When they saw this living legend, the mobsters backed off a little, hesitating to bite even though they still showed their teeth. It seemed a long time before the municipal police got around to coming and hauled all these fine birds off to the station. Thank God our SOS had been sent to the municipal force, for one of the first crooks to be picked up turned out to be, under his black shirt, none other than a captain in the Provincial Police.

Then all evening long and part of the night we were constantly thrown up and down a roller coaster: a few votes ahead, a few behind, sliding hour by hour from elation to depression until finally the official result was announced: I had won by 129 votes. By drawing off nearly a thousand votes that animal of an 'artist' had almost done us in!

Ibid.

As Lévesque [in 1963] clawed desperately through his pockets for cigarettes and rasped out arguments in a voice that turned syllables into wheezes and consonants into coughs, the warm night beyond the kitchen doors was disturbed by a muffled report. Lévesque's monologue continued but Laurendeau raised his head suspiciously. Lévesque rejected his suggestion that it might have been a bomb and plunged ahead with his argument, interrupting himself only long enough to curse the fact that all the cigarettes in the universe seemed to have disappeared.

In a few minutes, there was another roar that rattled the windows.

Laurendeau started to insist that bombs were exploding nearby. Lévesque impatiently said something about underground blasting for the city's new subway and was just picking up the threads of his argument again when a third explosion shook the house. This brought Pelletier's wife downstairs. Police sirens could now be heard in the distance.

The Pelletiers, Laurendeau and Lévesque piled into Pelletier's car and drove toward the sound of the sirens, Lévesque still grumbling about not being able to find any cigarettes.

Soon they happened on the scene of one of the explosions. A few dazed men and women in dressing-gowns were edging from doorways near a street-corner where the front of a small restaurant had been heavily damaged. The first thing that Lévesque and the others noticed, as they drove past, were the packs of cigarettes lying among the shattered glass. Lévesque groaned in frustration.

By this time they had heard another explosion only a short distance away. On one of the upper avenues above Sherbrooke Street, where Westmount climbs toward the mansions of Summit Circle, they came across a large crowd at the scene of an explosion near a church. By now Lévesque was worrying that a bystander might identify him. Any connection between the bombings and the 'radical' of the Quebec cabinet could have been dangerous for him. Pelletier parked his car some distance from the crowd, leaving Lévesque with his wife while he and Laurendeau went to investigate.

As they walked toward the scene of the explosion, Pelletier recalled that one of his associates at *La Presse* had informed him recently about loose talk in the news room, something about exploding bombs along Sherbrooke Street.

Most of his younger reporters were sympathetic to separatism and cultivated contacts in the *Rassemblement pour l'indépendance nationale*, as well as among more extreme groups. Strange faces drifted through the editorial corridors of the newspaper from time to time.

All at once, Pelletier realized that he was staring at one of those faces, pale and bearded, across the empty space where the mailbox had stood. My God, he thought to himself, he's come to check the work of his friends.

As the two men returned to the car where his wife waited with Lévesque, Pelletier noticed something that had escaped his attention a few minutes before. He had parked his car beside another mailbox.

It was the mailbox, he still insists to this day, that contained the bomb that exploded the next morning in the hands of an army explosives expert, maiming him for life.

Peter Desbarats, René: A Canadian in Search of a Country, 1976

An incident in 1965 revealed the sense of isolation that Lévesque felt in the cabinet even at a time when he was working closely with Kierans on various programs. He was attending a conference in Newfoundland when he read speculation about the candidacies of Pelletier, Marchand and Trudeau in the approaching federal election. Maurice Sauvé, who was also at the conference, telephoned Marchand in Ottawa with Lévesque hovering over his shoulder. Marchand explained that the Pearson Liberals were anxious to recruit himself and Gérard Pelletier but had strong reservations about the 'socialist' Pierre Trudeau. After Sauvé had talked with Marchand, Lévesque took the phone to warn Marchand to 'avoid the mistake that I had made' and to insist that all three enter federal politics together.

Ibid.

Lévesque wrote of De Gaulle's visit to Quebec in 1967.

As soon as [the General] appeared in the little square where the whole of Quebec seemed jammed, you could feel a current running through the acclamations of the crowd, a current that had been intensifying from village to village along the King's Highway, le Chemin du Roi, leading to Montreal, nourished by the sure escalation of his rhetoric. So when he strode forth into

that other square packed with people where the mayor of Montreal was waiting
for him in front of his city hall, everyone was saying, 'If he goes on at this
rate, something's going to happen that our grandchildren will still be talking
about!'

The same presentiment must have been haunting Jean Drapeau, so when the
General expressed a desire to step out on the little balcony to greet the wildly
enthusiastic crowd, the Mayor hastily excused himself, saying the microphone
wasn't hooked up.

'But Monsieur le Maire,' said my good friend Bouchard, the devoted technician who was always with the Radio-Canada team, 'it's no big deal', and
added with his customary obligingness, 'I can fix that for you in a jiffy.'

'Then do so, my friend,' said De Gaulle, 'do so.'

And off they went, the three of them, the technician glad to be of service,
the Mayor rather apprehensive, and the General exuding an air of lofty serenity.

Behind the city hall, among the guests waiting patiently on a large terrace,
two MNAs, Yves Michaud and I, he elected for the first time, I re-elected the
previous year, stood regretting the fact that we were no longer journalists at
this historic moment and watching in some frustration as De Gaulle appeared
on a TV set, stepping onto the balcony on the other side of the building. When
he began speaking 'confidentially' of a certain climate of liberation, in one
instinctive movement we drew closer to the screen, crouched low so as not to
block other people's view.

It was in this posture that his 'Vive le Québec . . . libre!' held us paralysed
a few instants. Then, hearing the deathly silence that reigned behind us, we
turned around to face the rest of the guests. It is rare to have such an opportunity
to see the two Montreals so clearly. In a state of shock, frozen in a fury that
as yet was only emitting a few anticipatory rumblings, stood the Anglophone
city. As for French Montreal, except for those constrained by office or acquaintance to reserve, they did not hide broad, complicit smiles, or even, in the
background, gestures more discreet but just as enthusiastic as those of the
crowd in the street.

René Lévesque: Memoirs, trans. Philip Stratford, 1986

*In 1968 Lévesque founded the Parti Québecois. It won the provincial election of 1976,
but the election of 1970 was hard going.*

Lévesque's campaign expressed the interplay of fear and hope within the
French-Canadian spirit. He spoke frankly and movingly to his audiences about
their 'fear of independence, fear of the flight of capital, fear of the attitude of
the English-speakingCanadians and Americans'; but he also held out the hope
that 'if we want it to be, this can be the beginning of the normal history of
Quebec.'

'Do you believe that it can be?' he asked the 12,000 people who crowded into his opening election rally at the Maurice Richard Arena in east end Montreal.

'Oui!' roared the audience, in a response that sounded 'like a clap of thunder' to one of the journalists at the meeting.

Lévesque presented various forms of this verbal catechism to many audiences during the campaign. When more than 1,000 people came to hear him speak in Hull, across the Ottawa River from the national capital, Lévesque reminded them that 'many people on the other side are watching you'.

'Does that make you afraid?' he asked.

'Non!' shouted his audience.

More than mass professions of faith were needed to overcome the traditional insecurity and conservatism of French-Canadians. The 'Brinks' affair' showed this as it quickly became one of the symbolic and memorable episodes of the campaign.

A few nights before the election, in an efficient and well-publicized operation, a convoy of eight armoured trucks was loaded with securities at the main office of the Royal Trust in Montreal, and dispatched to points outside Quebec. Lévesque claimed that the incident was 'dramatized for electoral purposes', that the transfer of securities was a normal procedure and that it had no significance for the province's economy. Once the stories and photographs had been published, officials of the trust company also played down the importance of the transfer, but no one really underestimated the effect of the 'Brinks' affair' on the vote a few days later.

Peter Desbarats, René: A Canadian in Search of a Country, 1976

From an interview of René Lévesque by Peter Gzowski:

P.G. In the section of your *Memoirs* on your experiences as a correspondent in Europe during World War II, you say good things about Paris, but it almost seems as though you enjoyed living in London more.

R.L. Oh yes, I love London. It's a truly marvellous city. I hope my wife doesn't hear me say it, but if I had to live in Europe, I'd rather live in London than even Paris.

P.G. (laughing) Not too good for the old image, eh René?

R.L. Well, I've always been consistent. You must understand, I've *always* said, the English—AT HOME—are wonderful.

Interview, CBC radio, Morningside, 4 November 1986

DAVID LEWIS

National Secretary of the CCF after 1936, and a key figure in the creation of the New Democratic Party in 1961, David Lewis entered Parliament in 1965 and led the NDP from 1971 to 1975.   As a student at McGill in 1932, he won a Rhodes Scholarship.

I joined a number of other hopefuls in a waiting-room outside a large board-room on one of the top floors of Windsor Station, the CPR terminal in Montreal. Presumably, this was the locale of the interviews because Sir Edward Beatty, President of the CPR and Chancellor of McGill University, was chairman of the selection committee. When summoned, I sat in the chair intended for the victim, crossed my legs, and lit a cigarette, determined to be self-controlled and nonchalant. I remember fully only one exchange, but I have always carried with me the impression of an exhausting forty-five minutes of probing and wide-ranging interrogation. Much of the questioning concerned my socialist ideas and activities. At one point, Sir Edward Beatty turned to me and, with a quizzical sparkle in his eyes, asked, 'Lewis, if you became the first socialist prime minister of Canada, what would be the first thing you would do?' I could not suppress a defiant glint in my eyes when I answered with emphasis, 'Nationalize the CPR, sir.' Sir Edward smiled with amusement and the other members exchanged silent glances which I could not interpret.

On my way home in a streetcar which moved slowly through heavy snow, I chided myself for treating the interview so cavalierly. Even if I didn't expect to be picked, I shouldn't have been so brazen. I arrived home into Sophie's arms. She was sitting with my parents around the kitchen table waiting impatiently for my return. I told them a little about what had transpired. My mother was shocked at my behaviour, but Sophie and my father chortled. I lay down to have a nap and was awakened by a phone call from Colonel Stairs, Quebec secretary of the Rhodes Trust, who asked me to come for another interview the next morning. This changed the complexion of things, especially since the next day was Sunday. Obviously, I would not be brought before the committee a second time, on the members' Sabbath, unless they were giving my candidature serious consideration. For the first time all of us became anxious, and Mother expressed her indignation that her son should again be put through a painful ordeal when nothing might come of it.

Minutes after the second interview began, it became clear that I had to satisfy the committee members that I was not a communist. This presented no difficulty; not only was I not a communist, but my father's lessons and my experiences in Svisloch and Montreal had made of me a strong anti-communist. None the less, I was troubled by the inquisition. It seemed to me contrary to academic freedom to make a candidate's political views a consideration in the choice of Scholar. My answers were therefore not conciliatory. This meeting produced another exchange for which Beatty won my respect and gratitude.

Some members of the committee shot questions at me which could only be described as tricky. The natural response to such a challenge is to show that two can play at the game. Thus, when one of the members asked me softly, in the tone of a cross-examining lawyer who is about to tighten the net around the witness, 'Lewis, what is your opinion of the Russian Revolution?' I took my time answering. It was obvious that if I said that the important thing was to free the Russian people from Czarist oppression, without a long speech about the evils of Bolshevism, my inquisitor would have the answer he wanted. And the occasion did not lend itself to a lecture on capitalism, socialism, and communism. So I answered in equally soft tones, 'I am in some difficulty, sir, because the question is so broad. The Russian Revolution had political, economic, cultural, religious, and moral aspects; which of them would you like me to comment on?' Whereupon the questioner slammed the table in front of him and said angrily, 'I asked a civil question and I expect a civil answer.' I was somewhat taken aback, but before I could stammer anything, Sir Edward said, with the firm authority of a chairman, 'I think Lewis's answer was entirely civil; your question *was* very broad.' And that was that. I have never felt as grateful to anyone as I did to Beatty at that moment.

The weather was worse on Sunday than it had been the day before, and the journey home by streetcar took hours. No sooner did I enter the house than the phone rang. Colonel Stairs informed me that I had been chosen a Rhodes Scholar.

David Lewis, *The Good Fight*, 1981

David often follows a phrase such as 'If one may say so without arrogance' with something arrogant: 'Anyone who attended that convention knows it was run by one man—David Lewis.' But on one occasion, his self-assurance faltered. That was in 1961, when the NDP was being formed, and a leader had to be found. Many CCFers thought Lewis was the natural choice, and at first he was inclined to agree. But there was the matter of his Jewishness: would Canadians accept a Jew? David thought not, at least not yet, so he declined to run. They party turned to T.C. Douglas, then the Premier of Saskatchewan, and when Douglas accepted, a celebration was held at the home of Andrew Brewin, now NDP MP for Toronto Greenwood. David took up a commanding position near the fireplace and told the story of the campaign of persuasion. 'I flew out to Regina and spoke to Tommy. Then I met with the cabinet, and his riding association. I told them they had to give Tommy up. . . .' At this point Brewin burst in, 'For God's sake, David there were five of us out there! It was a committee!' David didn't miss a beat. 'Yes, yes, of course, When I say "I", I mean "we". Then I talked to members of the provincial council. . . .'

Walter Stewart, *Divide and Con*, 1973

1969 looked like the end of the beginning when Ed Schreyer swept to power in Manitoba. Schreyer, who openly confessed to a jaded CBC interviewer that his view of social democracy was on a par with Roosevelt's New Deal, did, in Manitoba-miniature, what Lewis dreamt of nationally. Schreyer had carried the city labour vote, the province's rural vote and a very considerable slice of Manitoba's right-thinking upper and middle classes.

But alack, alas, as fall followed summer, 1969 began to look like the beginning of the end. What Trudeau had failed to do to Lewis, the Waffle seemed to accomplish effortlessly. Their strident cry for Quebec self-determination and the nationalization of 'the commanding heights of the economy' were plunging the Lewisites into the political lower depths. The Waffle mastery of socialist in-fighting, namely mike-control, delegate discipline and *zitsfleisch* (the ability to sit on your ass in a hot convention hall until hell freezes over and your opposition gets bored and leaves) were making a mockery out of the Lewis family's vaunted political cunning. Given the traditional socialist belief in openness and faith in the public, the TV cameras and mikes were everywhere. The public disembowelling of the NDP was soon to become one of Anglophonia's favourite spectator sports.

In the spring of 1971, Lewis had to endure the humiliating TV spectacle of a fight-to-the-finish with a mere post-war baby stripling for the leadership of a party he had himself founded. In that NDP convention, Jim Laxer was the Waffle David who almost knocked the bloated Goliath of Canadian socialism off his very wobbly feet. (The Lewis victory celebration was the quietest one that the Jaded Observer could recall in over a decade of covering these peculiar rites. The Lewis quest for revenge seen by that same Jaded Observer in a quiet tête-à-tête with the Lewis family that evening was certainly one of the bloodthirstiest his collective memory, conscious or unconscious, could recall.)

Larry Zolf, *Dance of the Dialectic*, 1973

Lewis ran a particularly effective national campaign in the 1972 election.

Lewis was blooming; . . . it had to do with three little words—corporate welfare bums.

The history of those three little words is interesting, and a far cry from the orderly process usually ascribed to political parties in search of programs. (Just to set the record straight, the official NDP slogan, the product of its more orderly party process, was 'Canada Needs More New Democrats'; the number of voters who were galvanized by that slogan into taking the plunge for socialism is not on record; it may safely be estimated as small.) During a meeting in Lewis' office in Ottawa—an anxious meeting, dominated by an almost frantic search for some new club with which to belabour the wicked Grits—somebody (memories are hazy on this point) mentioned that he had read a story in *The Toronto Star* complaining that Shell Canada Limited had made huge profits but had paid almost no Canadian taxes. Wasn't that worth exploring? You just bet your NDP handbook it was and minutes after the meeting ended, Murray Weppler, Lewis' executive assistant, was on the telephone to *Star* columnist Alexander Ross, who had written the article in question.

The Ross column, which appeared on April 27, 1972, under the heading 'Big Business pays less tax than people do', ought to be cast in bronze as an historical monument. . . . Ross began by wondering aloud why no opposition party had picked up the tax ripoff issue, and went on to lay down some startling examples. 'Although the corporate tax rate is around 50 per cent,' Ross wrote, 'the effective rate of taxation in many industries and for many companies is much less. The metal mining industry—and here we're talking about 268 large firms—declared a pre-tax profit in 1969 of $610,882,000, and paid total taxes of $68,740,000. This works out to an effective tax rate of a shade less than 12 per cent.'

Well, sir, that was a paragraph likely to make anyone, especially a socialist or a nationalist (the metal-mining industry is mostly foreign-owned) in search of an issue, sit up and take notice. But Ross went on to name a series of huge and profitable companies that appeared to be getting away with murder. Shell Canada Limited declared profits between 1964 and 1969 of almost a quarter of a billion dollars, and did not pay one dime of tax; Falconbridge Nickel Mines made $216 million between 1964 and 1970 and paid less than $15 million in income tax; Cadillac Development Corporation, one of the largest land developers in the nation, saw the value of its holdings increased by 500 per cent between 1964 and 1969, and its profits soar by 1,400 per cent, but Cadillac had never paid any federal income tax.

In a sense, the entire NDP campaign consisted of mining the implications of that single newspaper column, and the process began with Weppler asking Ross where in tunket he had got the figures. Easy, the columnist replied; the general figures are carried in the Federal government document *Corporation Financial Statistics*, and the company figures appear either in annual reports or in information filed in *The Financial Post* annual surveys of Industrials, Oils and Mines (Ross had been a columnist for *The Financial Post* before moving to the *Star*); anyone who cared could work out what any corporation listed in the surveys had made and what taxes it had paid.

And that's how the issue was born. Boris Celovsky, the director of the NDP research staff, researchers Peter Sadlier-Brown and Veronica Seale and members of the office staff began to pull together a dossier on corporations who had made large profits and paid low taxes. The phrase 'corporate welfare bums' was a joint effort; in preparing Lewis' first speech on the issue, Veronica Seale wrote 'the real welfare recipients are the corporations'; in reading this, Lewis changed it to 'the real welfare bums are the corporations', and Weppler suggested shortening it to 'corporate welfare bums'. Funnily enough, the party didn't realize what a hot property it had in that phrase until it began to appear in headlines, and then they exploited it to the full. At first, the researchers thought they were working on a single speech, but it soon became clear that the issue constituted a major scandal, enough to become the primary theme of the campaign.

Walter Stewart, *Divide and Con*, 1973

Though [the Liberal] government barely survived that election, the period from 1972 to 1974 was an exciting and productive term. It was a good test for Trudeau, because it taught him the flexibility and ability to compromise that I saw in cabinet and in caucus. At least he seemed to have grown and changed, and in politics perception is everything. What saved him in the long run was the pride of David Lewis, the leader of the NDP. The Liberals could only stay in office with the support of the NDP because we were in a minority position, so Lewis was forced to vote with us in the House of Commons in order to prevent an election that no one wanted. He did that for two years, but he was a rather proud and doctrinaire man, and he couldn't stand being accused of keeping Trudeau in power. Finally he decided to side with the Tories in a non-confidence vote and force an election.

Immediately after Lewis's announcement, Réal Caouette jumped to his feet and said, 'The NDP will drop from thirty seats to fifteen and Lewis will be defeated in his own riding, because he has failed in his responsibility to the Canadian people to maintain the government.' That proved to be correct.

If Lewis had held on and made the minority government work, Trudeau probably would have gone to the polls in 1976 and won another minority. But when the people saw that the minority didn't work, they wanted a majority government and gave it to Trudeau over Stanfield. It was part of the luck that gave Pierre Trudeau nine lives.

Jean Chrétien, Straight From The Heart, 1986

STEPHEN LEWIS

A CCF-NDP organizer from an early age, Stephen Lewis led the Ontario NDP from 1970 to 1978. In 1984 he was named Canada's Ambassador to the United Nations.

The NDP makes a practice of loaning its people around the country at election time, and on one occasion Stephen had been sent to Prince Edward Island to help organize a provincial campaign there. Here's his account, based on my memory:

> When I arrived there I began by examining the old election results in Charlotte-town. I was going to try and build from strength and so I selected a polling subdivision where the NDP had done reasonably well at the last election. Once the campaign was over I of course wanted to be in on the count on election night, and so I went round to the polling station, but they wouldn't let me come in. So I went downtown and got a press pass, and then they let me in. And this is what happened. The DRO turned the ballot box upside down and emptied its contents on the table, and the count began. First a ballot for the Tory, and then one for the Liberal, then another Tory, and then he picked up a ballot clearly marked for the NDP. He turned it over, and examined it distastefully, and then gingerly put it in a third pile. The count went on. One for the Tory, one for the Liberal, another Tory, and then—lo and behold, there was another ballot marked for the NDP. The DRO picked it up, looked at it suspiciously, and then a gleam of understanding shone into his eyes as he said: 'Some son of a bitch voted twice.'

Contributed by Professor John Wilson, University of Waterloo

This one was told to me by Stephen Lewis. In the Waterloo South by-election of 1964 the successful NDP candidate, Max Saltsman, owned a dry-cleaning business. Stephen was canvassing there one day and introduced himself by saying that he was working for Max Saltsman. The woman at the door looked a little puzzled but excused herself for a moment and returned with a huge bundle of dresses and suits which she deposited in Stephen's arms.

Contributed by Professor Garth Stevenson, Brock University

JEAN CHRÉTIEN

'Le petit gars de Shawinigan', Jean Chrétien occupied eight different cabinet posts in the Pearson and Trudeau governments.

I've always joked that Pearson noticed me because of his love of baseball. I have never been a star at sports but I have always been able to play most positions reasonably well. If a short stop was needed, I was just good enough to be a short stop. If a catcher was needed, I was just good enough to be a catcher. Like my career in the cabinet, I was good at plugging holes. I wasn't a sports star because I lacked practice more than agility, but it was more fun to be a goalie one day, a centre the next day, and a defenceman the day after that. Anyway, Pearson asked me to pitch a softball game between the politicians and the press. He was our coach and Charles Lynch of Southam News was theirs. Lynch had bushy hair and made lots of noise. He surprised me because I had the notion that anglophones were rather dull and subdued. We won the game, and I think Pearson was so pleased that he made me his parliamentary secretary.

Jean Chrétien, *Straight From The Heart*, 1986

I got into trouble with the first speech I made as a minister. It was to the German Association of Canada in Toronto on the subject of whether Quebec should have a special status as a province. That was an important debate at the time. Because I was to speak in English, I enlisted the help of my assistant, John Rae, an extremely bright, perfectly bilingual kid and older brother of Bob Rae, now leader of the Ontario NDP. I had spotted him in 1965 in Switzerland, where his father was Canadian ambassador, and I had said to my wife, 'If ever I become a minister, I will have a guy like that as my assistant.'

When I offered him the job, he had just earned the right to vote because he had just turned twenty-one years old. . . . Eventually he became a vice-president of Power Corporation in Montreal, and he was the manager of my leadership campaign in 1984.

Anyway, in this first speech I said, 'Those who are in favour of special status are often separatists who don't want to admit that they are separatists.' Because the subject fell under the prerogatives of the minister of justice, I showed my draft to Trudeau, who said, 'You are absolutely right. It's going to hurt, and you'll have some problems, but you're right.'

Being full of bravado I thought, 'If that's what I believe, that's what I'll say.' So I went off to Toronto with my speech under my arm and John Rae at my side. When we arrived at the hotel, Rae went up to the desk and said, 'I'd like the keys for the rooms of the Honourable Jean Chrétien and his assistant.'

'Who are you?' the clerk asked. You have to remember that Rae was twenty-one and looked fifteen.

'I'm the assistant.'

'Go away, kid,' the clerk said.

Rae came back, very embarrassed, but I said, 'Don't worry about it, John, I'll fix it up.' So I went up to the desk and said, 'I'd like the keys for the room of the Honourable Jean Chrétien and his assistant.'

'Who are you?' the clerk said. You have to remember that I became a minister when I was thirty-three.

'I'm the minister.'

But the clerk wouldn't give me the keys either. It wasn't an auspicious start.

Ibid.

If his officials got over their initial doubts, much of the public didn't. Jean Chrétien didn't look like a Minister of Finance was expected to look. He hated reading the long, technical speeches that came with the job. Often he just told his jokes, summarized the text, and swung into his usual patriotic rhetoric. The clarifications that followed from his officials increased the suspicion that he didn't comprehend the material. While the bankers heard the skeptical naïveté of the people in his voice, the people heard the cold-hearted mumbo-jumbo of the bankers. As a result, everyone was rather confused about Chrétien's real principles. He became a prisoner of his own creation, his political image. He had worked so hard to seem ordinary that no one could believe he wasn't.

'The first day I came into Mitchell Sharp's office,' he often told his audiences, 'there was a big meeting there, the Governor of the Bank of Canada, the Deputy Minister of Finance, all those big shots, you know. For an hour and a half they discussed bond issues, interest rates, balance of payments, and what not. At the end of the meeting Mitchell came to me and said, "Jean, this meeting was very secret and you should not talk to anybody about what you have heard." I said, "Mitchell, don't be worried, I have not understood a goddamn thing at all!"'

Ron Graham, One-Eyed Kings, 1987

In his best-selling memoir Straight From the Heart, *Chrétien offered his views on Brian Mulroney, the US, and free trade.*

Brian Mulroney is a man who knows that one of the great weaknesses of people is flattery. They like a pat on the back, just as he himself likes to be patted. So he's done that all his life, very successfully. During his first two years in office that characteristic has turned him into a 'groupie' of Ronald Reagan: 'Yes, yes, Mr President, I love you, Mr President, you're the greatest, Mr President.' It seems he'll do anything to please Reagan.

During the Tory leadership campaign in 1983, for example, Mulroney warned against the effects of free trade on Canadian interests. In office, in the absence of any other policies, he has seized the business community's slogan that Canada needs a free-trade deal. I find it strange that the same businessmen who came to my office when I was a minister and begged for protection for their industries are now demanding free trade. In private they qualify their stance with nuances and exceptions, but publicly they follow each other with the same set speech and without asking too many questions.

I am a trader, I believe in trading, and I think that Canada is the greatest trading nation in the world. But getting under the protectionist umbrella of the United States goes against the traditional wisdom of Canadians. . . . Political annexation would be the next practical step.

If that is the wish of Canadians, fine with me. I'll fight it, but I'm a democrat. But I'm afraid that we'll go down that route without knowing it, that there will come a point beyond which we cannot turn back or change our mind, that Canada will disappear without a debate or a decision. In some ways the situation is the reverse of what I describe in the book about Quebec separation. I write that the old strategy of the Quebec separatists was to separate link by link, a little bit at a time, until nothing remained to keep Canada together. Now, with the Americans, we'll add links, one by one, until the cable becomes so long and strong that we're dragged into a political union.

A good example of the effect happened in the summer of 1985 when the United States decided to send a ship, *Polar Sea*, through Canada's Arctic waters without asking for our permission. It was a way for the Americans to assert their case that the Arctic passage was an international one, though the American ambassador to Ottawa stated plainly that it was an international passage for the United States but not for the Soviet Union.

The Americans had tried the same thing with the *Manhattan* when I was Minister of Indian Affairs and Northern Development. I personally flew to the North, visited the *Manhattan*, and requested that it raise the Canadian flag. Fortunately our flag was raised (for I wasn't sure what the hell I could have done if it wasn't), and it was my judgement as a lawyer that Canada's position had prevailed. No Canadian flag was raised on the *Polar Sea*, however. I had brought up the issue in the House of Commons in June, two months before the voyage, but the Secretary of State for External Affairs merely accused me of making something out of nothing. By the time the government acted in September, the damage had been done.

Afterwards I had an opportunity to meet with some representatives from the American Departments of State and Defense, and I gave them hell. 'Why did you come to humiliate us?' I asked. 'For fourteen years when Trudeau was Prime Minister, you didn't do that. So why did you quickly humiliate a Prime

Minister who wants to be your friend? Next summer, for the fun of it, you should go to the waters north of Siberia to demonstrate that they are international too.'

It was clear to me that the Americans had taken advantage of Mulroney. They wouldn't have dared try such a provocation under the Liberals, but Mulroney was trapped by the fact that he was trying to get his business deal with Washington. He had to be nice.

Jean Chrétien, *Straight From The Heart*, 1986

ROBERT STANFIELD

'Silent Bob' or 'Big Thunder', Robert Stanfield was Premier of Nova Scotia from 1956 to 1967 and led the federal Conservatives from 1967 to 1976. He is proof of Stephen Lewis's dictum that 'The surest route to affection and esteem is defeat and retirement'.

One of the policies that cemented the early popularity of the Stanfield Government and of Stanfield himself was the special effort concentrated on road building. In Nova Scotia this was probably the biggest vote getter in the Stanfield arsenal. With its widely scattered population and its poor County roads and side roads, the Province was a road builder's paradise.

Stanfield was very fortunate in having G.I. Smith as his first Minister of Highways. They not only worked perfectly as a team, they were both dedicated to the rebuilding of as many miles of road as possible, as cheaply as possible. Ike Smith was not only tireless and energetic but thoroughly immersed in highway problems and he must have made the lives of the engineers interesting, to say the least. Every effort was made, as Stanfield and Smith used to put it, 'to get the people out of the mud'. And to a surprising extent they did. The one cause of discontent was the conviction on the part of some elected members that their particular constituencies were not 'getting as much new paving' as some other favoured constituencies.

There were accusations that 'every rabbit run' was paved in Pictou West, while in Kings South we had to be content that the main highway ran through its most populous parts. Some constituencies were rich in main highways or had many miles of Trans Canada Highways and some had none. The member for Guysboro, Tando MacIssac, was sometimes very bitter because his County, a large and sparsely populated area, was not getting the roads he thought it deserved. On one occasion he 'brought the House down' with a speech in which he compared the dearth of highways in his County with the proliferation of highways, Trans Canada and Provincial, in Cape Breton.

'People driving on a main highway in that little Island' he asserted, 'could stand up in their cars and wave their bonnets at people driving on at least three other paved highways, all going to the same place.'

E.D. Haliburton, *My Years With Stanfield*, 1972

In comparison with Trudeau, Bob Stanfield seemed like a man for the season of yesterday. His candidates were as good as Trudeau's, but he lacked the organization, and he appeared at times to lack the will to win. Stanfield lumbered from city to city in a decaying old DC-7C that had spent its best years lugging American tourists to Japan and Canadian Legionnaires to London. Leased from Transair, the plane was christened 'The Misajumax' (after the Stanfield children, Mimi, Sarah, Judy, and Max), but everyone called it the 'Flying Banana'. It had a cruising speed of three hundred miles per hour—barely half the speed of Trudeau's DC-9—and Stanfield always seemed to be an hour or more behind schedule. He scheduled an open-air rally in Victoria Park in London, but no one thought to approach the city fathers. A municipal bylaw forbade political rallies in public parks, and the city enforced the bylaw. The organizers showed more foresight one memorable day in Quebec City. Knowing there was no passenger ramp that would fit the DC-7C, they ordered one built. But no one thought to measure the plane and the hastily-built wooden ramp was three feet too high for the plane door. The passengers had to hoist themselves up onto the ramp and scramble out on all fours. In Rivière-du-Loup, the streets were teeming with people an hour before Stanfield arrived, but when his motorcade passed through, they were deserted. It was as though the people had fled the city in terror. That night, they took Stanfield into Matane, a community of eleven thousand people in the Gaspé, to campaign for one of his star candidates, Julien Chouinard. Though the arena held fifteen hundred people (not an impossible number of seats for any half-competent organization to fill), only two hundred turned out for Stanfield, despite the added attractions of a free dinner of lethal-looking baked beans and the 'music' of quite possibly the worst rock-and-roll band the country had ever produced. Not that it mattered. The sound system failed and no one could hear a word Stanfield said. A local Tory worker, much pleased with the night's work, kindly offered to drive two reporters back to the airport to catch the Stanfield plane. 'How many people do you think were there to hear M'sieu Stanfield?' he asked. 'No more than two hundred,' the reporters replied. A heated auction ensued, with the organizer refusing to accept any estimate below fifteen hundred and the newsmen refusing to go above three hundred. The organizer resolved the dispute by the simple expedient of driving in the opposite direction from the airport and dumping his passengers on the road on the far side of Matane.

Geoffrey Stevens, *Stanfield*, 1973

'Silent Bob' did not light many fires at Conservative rallies during the 1968 campaign.

The audience was full of open, hearty westerners ready for laughter; the leader was a taciturn, close-mouthed easterner, ready for responsibility.

The obvious point of the evening was to boost Conservative solidarity by showing off its regional strength. There were six leading provincial Tories on

the platform, three of them premiers. 'Ike' Smith, Stanfield's successor as
the premier of Nova Scotia, gave a routine speech about regional economic
disparity and after praising his predecessor made an unconscious blunder by
saying, 'Now let me turn to one or two other Canadian problems besides Mr
Stanfield. . . .'

Peter C. Newman, Home Country, 1973

The public never saw Stanfield's emotions on display—and assumed he had
none. A glimpse was seen, however, on the final day of the futile 1968
campaign, when an exhausted Stanfield boarded his lumbering campaign plane
in Belleville, Ontario, for the flight home to Halifax and the obvious results
from the ballot box. He had travelled forty thousand miles in fifty-one days in
an increasingly useless crusade while the press and the public went ga-ga over
this rich, sexy bachelor called Trudeau.

While reporters filed their last stories, Stanfield settled into a bottle of Scotch.
Once aloft, he marched into the press section, sat down beside the *Globe and
Mail*'s Geoff Stevens and took off on a bitter attack on the press. The scribes,
astounded and delighted at the passion of a Stanfield they had never seen
before, gathered in stunned awe.

The Tory leader ripped into Trudeau with great contempt. Robert Stanfield,
in truth, was swacked. To show that Trudeau was not the only politician who
had ever read a book, Stanfield quoted lengthy passages from De Tocqueville
and talked knowledgeably about music and theatre. There was one stop in
Moncton, where Stanfield staggered from the plane to deliver a few words for
the local candidate—except he couldn't remember his name.

When he reached Halifax, he was driven home and the accepted version is
that when Mary Stanfield opened the door of The Oaks, her husband fell flat
on his face at her feet. 'That's the last thing the country needs,' she cracked,
'another Sir John A. Macdonald.'

Allan Fotheringham, Look Ma . . . No Hands, 1983

The Old Chief was a constant critic of his successor as Tory leader, Bob
Stanfield, and one day in the fall of 1968 something came up in the House on
which Diefenbaker felt a statement was needed. 'This is a subject,' he told me,
'on which Stanfield should be saying something. Instead of which, he is taking
a two-week immersion course in Montreal, in FRENCH! Eugene, we Baptists
know all about immersion. But we know enough not to stay under for two
weeks!'

The Hon. Eugene Forsey, interview, Ottawa, 19 Feb. 1987

Stanfield is also a genuinely funny man, but his humour is so wry and so self-
deprecating that it is lost on large public gatherings. He would far rather laugh

at himself than at others. . . . Finlay MacDonald, Stanfield's chief of staff, likes to tell the story of a dinner party in Halifax where the host left the liquor out on a table so that his guests could help themselves before dinner. Stanfield finished his first drink and wandered up to the table to help himself to a second Scotch and water. He poured three fingers of Scotch, then filled his glass from a pitcher of clear liquid. Returning to the sofa, he sipped the drink thoughtfully. When MacDonald went to pour himself another drink a few minutes later, he was startled by the reduced level of the gin in the pitcher. He looked suspiciously at Stanfield's nearly-empty glass. 'Did you just drink a Scotch and gin?' MacDonald spluttered. Stanfield looked amused. 'You know,' he said, 'I thought it was rather strange, but I was just getting to like it.'

Geoffrey Stevens, Stanfield, 1973

The number-one drinking event in Ottawa, about which the public never hears, is the off-the-record parliamentary press gallery annual dinner. Each year that he was there, Stanfield's droll speech from the head table completely overshadowed Trudeau's. His self-deprecating wit ('Am I speaking too fast for you?'), adroitly timed one-liners and perfectly chosen insults made Trudeau, woodenly reading his gag-filled script, sound like a Rotarian.

At the dinner following his 1974 defeat, Stanfield rose and began his ponderous introductions. 'Your Excellency,' he said, turning to Governor General Jules Léger, 'Prime Minister, Mr Broadbent, Mr Chairman, ladies and gentlemen—and Doug Ball.' The place collapsed. It was an in-joke of magnificent self-deprecation, since Doug Ball was the photographer who took that famous campaign shot of Stanfield fumbling a football, a devastating cameo that was widely credited with encouraging his defeat. There are Tories still bitter over the selective way newspapers played that picture, since Ball had supplied Canadian Press (which distributed the photo) with other shots of a surprisingly graceful Stanfield catching and passing the football.

Allan Fotheringham, Look Ma . . . No Hands, 1983

Although Stanfield rarely displayed it in public, he had a rich sense of humour. From a farewell roast at Halifax, 1976:

Who ever heard of [Charles] Lynch before I drew national attention to him by sharing the spotlight in starring roles with the National Ballet in Ottawa, in the *Nutcracker Suite?* Before that, he was just wandering around the country looking for opportunities to play 'O Canada' on his mouth organ. He is unique among Canadian journalists. He's the only columnist I know who's made a good thing out of being wrong all the time.

Following the 1974 election I was sitting in Halifax, pondering my political future, when Judy LaMarsh wrote a column saying some very kind things about me. I knew then that my fate was sealed, that I was finished. Have you ever been embraced by Judy LaMarsh?

Remember what C.D. Howe once said, that he was as busy as a happy hooker working two beds?

At the Variety Club, Toronto, 1971:

I knew Trudeau would never marry Barbra Streisand, because I heard him say so many times that 'the States has no place in the bedroom of the nation'.

    They say Trudeau has no respect for the past. It is obvious he has a great feeling for our history as a nation of pioneers who slaved and starved to maintain this country when Canada was a wilderness. If he didn't have this kind of affection for us, why would he be trying so hard today to restore those conditions?

    Trudeau says the Liberal Party is the kind of organization that you can join freely, and leave freely. I guess it's only between joining and leaving that there's no freedom at all.

To a convention of broadcasters, Toronto, 1971:

I know the CBC will give me the full treatment when I'm history. I resent the fact that CBC has been covering the Diefenbaker years and calling them 'The Tenth Decade'. This series should have been called 'The Pre-Stanfield Years'.

In the immortal words of Cleopatra, I didn't come here tonight to talk politics.

To the American Association of Cartoonists, Ottawa, 1975:

I don't resent being caricatured. Cartoonists get no less pleasure carving me up than they would get carving their own mother. But nobody would pay them to carve up their mothers.

    A couple of cartoonists, years ago, tried to prevail on me to enter national politics, and I was flattered until they told me that I had the kind of bony anatomy that they could really do a job on. They said I owed it to my country! . . .

    Some cartoonists are still doing cartoons of me with one drooping eyelid. I've had it corrected, and in the interest of those cartoonists who have a passion for symmetry, I've had the other eyelid lowered, and some of you haven't noticed. . . .

    You can never allow your work to be confused by the facts, and I assume that is why your cartoons appear on the editorial pages.

Charles Lynch, A Funny Way to Run a Country, 1986

A letter to the editor of The Globe and Mail:

February 11, 1977

In his column this morning, Geoffrey Stevens attacks my competence as a driver, saying: 'He has the reputation among his friends of being the worst driver this side of Hull.'

This assertion has a false ring because my friends would never use my name in such a racist manner. Furthermore, I resent having my driving ability questioned by a columnist who, from time to time, uses the nominative case after a preposition.

I am considering suing *The Globe and Mail* and Mr Stevens for several millions of dollars, and I most certainly will if his irresponsible comment should cause an increase in my insurance rates.

I wish to assure the people of Ottawa who may read *The Globe and Mail* that they are perfectly safe with me on their streets. I drove a car long before Geoffrey Stevens was born and my accident record is spotless.

I quite agree with Mr Stevens, however, that Joe Clark should not drive a car. He obviously has things on his mind from time to time. I have never been accused of that.

Robert L. Stanfield
Ottawa
Shocked and Appalled, ed. Jack Kapica, 1985

RICHARD HATFIELD

New Brunswick's Conservative Premier from 1970 to 1987, Richard Hatfield was no stranger to controversy.

Any discussion of the outstanding eccentrics of the Tory story must include Richard Hatfield, the quite remarkable premier of New Brunswick, the only bachelor among our provincial leaders. Stories about him fuel the late-night sessions. The most popular one currently delighting the cocktail circuit is the one about the night Dick Hatfield baked his cat.

The story, which has been circulating and gathering credence for some years now, has Hatfield coming home late one rainy night to his beautifully decorated home in Fredericton to find his loving cat wet and bedraggled on the doorstep. Thinking to warm it, he turned on the oven and lowered the door to let out a shaft of heat. Being forgetful, he went to sleep, but was awakened in the middle of the night by an acrid smell. The cat, seeking warmth, had leaped upon the oven door, which snapped shut. Fricasséed pussy, as we say.

Hatfield, defensive about the wide circulation of the story, says it is not true—although he does concede there is faint source for the true story. The celebrated tale, he explains, comes from when he was a boy. He didn't bake his cat. He did, though, put his pet rabbit in the deep freeze.

Allan Fotheringham, *Look Ma . . . No Hands*, 1983

When criticised for expensive travel to New York, and once having spent 168 days of a year outside the province, Hatfield replied: 'I was elected to run New Brunswick. No one said I had to *live* there.'

Colombo's New Canadian Quotations, 1987

WILLIAM DAVIS

Ontario's Premier from 1971 to 1985, William Davis was known as 'Brampton Billy', leader of 'The Big Blue Machine'.

Around Davis, after the mad dash for a majority [1981], there was a sense that he'd achieved the goal and couldn't imagine what to do next. The legislature lost its excitement. With a seventy-seat Tory majority, there was no possibility of a political upset—even should the Opposition combine, as it had only occasionally dared to do during the six previous years of minority government. When New Democrat or Liberal MPPs protested their inability to use the committees or the legislature to press issues, Davis repeatedly reminded them in the House that 'the realities of March 19' had freed him from the trammels of the Opposition. The beaming faces on the crowded Tory benches provoked cries from the Liberal and NDP seats against the bland self-satisfaction of the government. But Davis, rising in his seat, held out his arms as if to embrace his majority and crowed, 'Bland works'.

Rosemary Speirs, *Out of the Blue*, 1986

The Conservative Government of Ontario made an election promise to plant two trees for each one harvested and to regenerate every acre logged. Soon after the election, they introduced Bill 77 (1979), an Act to amend the Crown Timber Act, without any reference to their promise.

Mr Elie Martel (Sudbury East NDP) asked why the Minister of Natural Resources had not written the Conservative Party's election promise into the Bill, 'because that's what the Premier told Ontario it could expect'.* Failing to receive a reply to his question, Mr Martel moved an amendment to the Bill, adding the words: 'shall provide for the yield to be sustained on the basis that at least two trees are planted for every tree cut under the agreement and to regenerating every acre harvested.'** He claimed that he had no choice but to move the amendment to enshrine Premier Davis's noble words in a piece of legislation.

This plunged the Government into a quandary. Premier Davis and his colleagues had to vote for the NDP amendment, because it was written with the Premier's own words. Yet they could not vote for it, because it committed the Government to plant every acre harvested, including those in new roads and campsites, and those regenerating naturally. Other options available were to hope that Mr Martel would withdraw his amendment, after the laughter had subsided, or to let the Bill die.

The Minister of Natural Resources and some of his colleagues approached Mr Martel later, and asked what they could do to encourage him to withdraw the amendment. On reflection, Mr Martel asked the Government to consider ways to provide the people of Ontario with much better information on the status of Ontario's forests.

So by mutual agreement on December 10, 1979, NDP member Mr Martel withdrew the Conservative Premier's words, and the Government of Ontario committed itself to report annually on forest regeneration, and on the relationship between growth and harvest, on the licensed Crown forests dedicated to sustained yield management. The important concept of providing the Legislature with audited statements on the effectiveness of forest management in Ontario was thereby laughed into law.

*Ontario, Legislative Assembly Debates, 31st Legislature, Session 3, November 6, 1979, p. 4279.
**———, November 13, 1979, p. 4415.

Contributed by Professor Paul Aird, University of Toronto

FLORA MACDONALD

Flora MacDonald was national secretary of the Progressive Conservative Association from 1966 to 1969, was elected MP for Kingston in 1972, and made an unsuccessful bid for the Tory leadership in 1976. Minister of External Affairs in the Clark government (1979–80), she is currently Minister of Communications in the Mulroney cabinet.

When she headed for Ottawa in 1956, seeking a job with External Affairs on the principle that it would probably lead to a lot of travelling, she got off the train, went in search of a YWCA and happened to go by the Conservative national headquarters. She wandered in, was put to work and stayed nine years.

Flora as secretary eventually ran the Tory office and developed an invaluable network of contacts across the country. When the increasingly eccentric Diefenbaker abruptly fired her in 1965, that solidified in the membership's mind that he had to go. It was Flora and her Maritime Mafia, Dalton Camp and the others, who engineered the dramatic leadership review that finally ousted him.

Camp and MacDonald were quite a team. Dalton, the acerbic, debonair Toronto ad man by way of New Brunswick, with his scheming and elegant speech-writing. Flora, the indefatigable organizer, with her fingers on key Tories in every province. They masterminded Duff Roblin's win in Manitoba, Stanfield's victories in Nova Scotia and a Tory win over the Liberals in Prince Edward Island.

Bell Canada almost sabotaged another Flora coup when Camp gathered his anti-Dief plotters in Kingston to lay the strategy for the overthrow of the Chief. Flora's job was to contact Tories across the land to determine how many delegates Camp could count on.

Bell Canada, however, grew quite alarmed when this unmarried woman who had taken an apartment in Kingston immediately ran up bills of $500 to $600 in long-distance calls across the country. It took some explaining to convince the telephone snooper that Flora was not involved in another type of business.

(Dief, the master of the heavy-handed *double entendre*, delighted in describing her, after he fell out with her, as 'the finest woman ever to walk the streets of Kingston'.)

Allan Fotheringham, Look Ma . . . No Hands, 1983

When Stanfield called an election in Nova Scotia in 1960, Flora was dispatched from national headquarters to work with Rod Black on organization and with Camp on strategy and speech-writing, and to run the provincial headquarters for the duration of the campaign. She remembers all too clearly being summoned to a meeting with Stanfield, his cabinet, and his key organizers: 'I think the whole thing was put on for my benefit, though I was too naive to know it at the time. They were discussing candidates and campaign managers, and as they talked they were drawing up a calendar of dates. They were going to allow John Jones that week for his drunk and that would mean the rest of the campaign would be on solid ground because so-and-so would fix it up. The next week would be allowed for someone else's drunk. These were all crucial people, some of them sitting at that very table, and I sat there thinking, "Oh, my God".' Stanfield was delighted with her reaction and chuckled later: 'You know it was worth that meeting just to see the startled look on Flora's face.' And, as Flora quickly discovered, Nova Scotia politics being what they were, some of the drunks planned in jest occurred right on schedule.

Geoffrey Stevens, Stanfield, 1973

[Tory MP James] McGrath admits he was inadvertently the cause of getting Flora rattled one day when she caught the Speaker's eye and rose to ask a question on Indian affairs. Mistakenly thinking his desk microphone was turned off, he whispered to her, 'Sock it to them, Flora baby!' All hell broke loose.

The Conservatives gave her a round of desk-thumping applause which lasted several minutes. When it finally died down, a blushing Flora put her question and the proceedings resumed.

Alvin Armstrong, *Flora MacDonald*, 1976

JOE CLARK

A Conservative MP from Alberta since 1972, Joe Clark became leader of his party in 1976. He defeated Trudeau's Liberals in 1979 and became Canada's sixteenth prime minister, holding office for eight months.

Clark's advisors had discussed a lengthy foreign trip for nearly a year before Clark left for Japan, India, Israel, and Jordan on January 2, 1979. Clark acknowledged his inexperience in foreign affairs. A long trip was considered to be an essential part of his own 'preparing to govern'. . . . The itinerary offered no coherent theme, except for the education of Joe Clark, whose party stood poised to form the Government of Canada. This fact alone allowed Clark to meet the leading political figures of the countries he visited, and it attracted more journalists than the Conservatives had reckoned might be interested in Clark's travels.

The trip was a public-relations disaster. Clark was exceptionally nervous and only met journalists at infrequent 'scrums', at which he sounded ill-briefed. He looked uncomfortable throughout the trip: wearing an eggshell-blue suit and an ascot while side-stepping the cow patties on the earthen streets of an Indian village; asking ludicrous questions—'What is the totality of your land?'—or making ridiculous statements—'Jerusalem is a very holy city'. King Hussein of Jordan kept Clark cooling his heels for seventy-five minutes, perhaps in retaliation for Clark's having spent twice as much time in Israel as in Jordan. Organizational foul-ups plagued the trip: Clark's Egypt Air flight from Tokyo to Bangkok arrived too late for Clark's luggage to be loaded on a connecting flight to New Delhi; his flight back to Canada was four hours late. Some of the accompanying journalists, devoid of 'hard news', took to writing more about Clark's gaffes than about the rest of the trip. When Clark returned to Canada he was known as the man who could not keep track of his own luggage.

Jeffrey Simpson, *Discipline of Power*, 1980

Joe Clark, when I ask how he expects to win with a name like Joe and hasn't he another name, says, 'Sure. It's Charlie. But you wouldn't expect me to run on that, would you?'

On CBC's 'As It Happens' I say that Clark will fight off his foes 'because he's got an ace up his hole', and in the shocked silence that ensues I add, 'Sure. That's why he walks that way.' And Flora MacDonald, hearing this on her car radio, swerves into the ditch.

Charles Lynch, *You Can't Print That!*, 1983

Nancy Jamieson was Clark's legislative assistant in December 1979.

She hurried down to Parliament Hill for a 7:30 A.M. breakfast meeting with middle-ranking staff from Clark's office in a private dining room adjacent to the parliamentary dining room. William Neville, Clark's chief-of-staff, had called the meeting to allow members of Clark's staff to talk about the Government's priorities for the coming weeks with Conservative Party officials such as national director Paul Curley, communications director Jodi White, and Walter Gray, head of the party's research bureau. Midway through the meeting, Neville turned to Jamieson and asked her to outline the parliamentary timetable for the period until Christmas.

'I think you're a little premature,' she replied. She explained to her startled audience that she now believed the Government would probably be defeated that night. Throughout Wednesday, Jamieson had been observing the disturbing signs from the Opposition parties. Jock Osler, Clark's press secretary, had called her Wednesday night after hearing reports from the Liberal Christmas party. Maybe the Liberals were serious after all, Osler said. On Wednesday night, Jamieson made several other calls and satisfied herself that the Government was headed for defeat. No one at the breakfast table believed her. Her warning was treated as a minor joke, an excessively skittish reaction to a tight but manageable parliamentary crisis.

At 8:30 A.M., Jamieson walked over to Conservative whip Bill Kempling's office. Kempling had not yet arrived, but Jamieson learned after talking to an assistant and making several phone calls that six Conservative MPs were out of town, sulking, or ill. She could scarcely believe it: six Conservative MPs missing on the day of a non-confidence vote in a minority Parliament!

Fifteen minutes later, Jamieson took her seat at one end of a U-shaped table in Clark's office for the Prime Minister's daily staff meeting. Beside her sat Senator Lowell Murray, Clark's closest political confidant and chairman of the Conservatives' 1979 campaign. He did not always attend the morning staff meeting, but he had risen that morning and watched a television program on which Liberal and NDP spokesmen repeated their intention to vote against the budget and Créditiste Eudore Allard said his party would abstain. With that jolt, Murray hustled down to Clark's office for the staff meeting. As usual, Clark called on Marcel Massé, Clerk of the Privy Council, to open the meeting. For about twenty minutes, Massé ran through a list of items of routine government business. When he finished, Clark went slowly around the table, asking those present if they had anything to raise. . . . Some raised routine matters, others passed. No one mentioned the budget vote. With about ten minutes left in the meeting, Clark turned to Jamieson.

'Sir, the Government is going to be defeated tonight,' she said.

'Why?' Clark asked.

Jamieson bluntly replied: 'Because we don't have the numbers.'

Jeffrey Simpson, Discipline of Power, 1980

Clark lost the Tory leadership to Brian Mulroney at a party convention in Ottawa in 1983.

'He just didn't deserve this,' said one sobbing organizer.

He was still disconcertingly ordinary as he stood at the podium in the final moments of the convention and urged his party to be loyal to Brian Mulroney. His body was still stiff and funny-looking, his voice slightly irritating, his very generosity and fortitude like weaknesses. Abused and mocked, betrayed by his own colleagues and discarded by the party that had been his life, he had come back for another whipping, until one hoped he would be himself at last, release his emotions in a fury of disappointment, and send all the schemers and liars and traitors to hell.

But he *was* himself, now singing 'O Canada' with his arched back at attention and his hands finally at rest. His face was cauterized by pain and his mouth was determined not to tremble on the lyrics. He was an awkward kid from High River at the end of his big dreams.

Ron Graham, *One-Eyed Kings*, 1987

JOHN TURNER

Having entered the House in 1962, John Turner served in the cabinet of Mike Pearson from 1965 to 1968. Unsuccessful in a party leadership bid in 1968, he was Minister of Justice (1968–72) and Minister of Finance (1972–5), under Trudeau. After an absence from politics, he became Liberal leader in June 1984, and Prime Minister from June to early September of that year.

In the Pearson cabinet of 1967, Trudeau and Turner were obvious rivals.

The appointment of Trudeau to the prestigious Justice portfolio was the only real surprise. The press described him as 'a colourful, free-thinking intellectual', and wrote stories about his taste for sandals, bright shirts, and casual ascots. At the swearing-in ceremony Pearson quipped that everybody knew Trudeau was going to be appointed to the cabinet because he had shown up in the House wearing a tie. 'And shoes too,' John Turner added. It was the last time he ever joked publicly with or about Pierre Trudeau.

Jack Cahill, *John Turner: The Long Run*, 1984

As Minister of Justice in Trudeau's cabinet, it fell to Turner to guide through the House changes in the Criminal Code relating to abortion and homosexuality.

Turner, who had come so close to becoming a Catholic priest, had to examine his conscience closely before proceeding on both issues, but particularly on abortion. He sought theological advice from two separate church sources, one in Quebec City and one in Toronto, one in French and one in English, on the duties of a Catholic legislator in a pluralistic society. . . .

Turner received thousands of letters, mostly from Catholics, protesting the proposed relaxation of the abortion legislation. His own riding president in Ottawa-Carleton, Dr Dalton J. McGuinty, a staunch Roman Catholic and father of eight children, resigned after pronouncing that the abortion law would be 'a dark day for our country', and at one stage a delegation of concerned Catholic bishops called on him. 'I asked the boys', Turner says, 'whether they had a legal opinion as to what the bill really meant, and they didn't have one. So I said to them, "Here's what it really means", and I told them what it meant. And I said, "Gentlemen, I happen to have two theological opinions as to what my duty is." I had them and they knew it.'

Turner personally abhors homosexuality also, and on that issue he told the Commons: 'The nub of the matter is who is to decide what moral behaviour or conduct is to be reflected in the Code? That is the point. In a pluralistic society there may be different standards, differing attitudes, and the law cannot reflect them all. Public order, in this situation of a pluralistic society, cannot substitute for private conduct. We believe that morality is a matter for private conscience. Criminal law should reflect the public order only. Despite the fact that most of us in our personal convictions have a complete repugnance to the conduct from which we are lifting the taint of criminal law, this does not to my mind interfere with the validity of the principle we are trying to submit to the House. The bill does not endorse such acts. It does not popularize such acts. It does not even legalize this kind of conduct,' he insisted. But his arguments were questioned at length and strongly opposed by many Conservatives and all Créditistes. The opposition could be summed up in one exchange:

> John Diefenbaker (PC, Prince Albert): 'What has the government done for the people of Canada since December 13 last?'
> George Muir (PC, Cape Breton-The Sydneys): 'Made them all homos.'

The Catholic Quebecer Créditistes filibustered the bill for twenty-one days, claiming, among many other things, that it was 'a Communist plot to prevent us from reproducing ourselves so as to be able to seize the country without any trouble.' But eventually, on May 14, 1969, almost eighteen months after Trudeau first introduced it, after the Créditistes had no talk left in them, and after forty-four attempts at amendment, Turner secured passage of a slightly redrafted version of the omnibus bill, with the abortion and homosexual sections unscathed. The vote was 149 to 55. Former Prime Minister John Diefenbaker voted against it along with forty-two other Conservatives, one Liberal, and eleven Créditistes, while Conservative Party Leader Robert Stanfield voted in favour. It was by far the most massive law reform in over fifteen years.

Ibid.

As Minister of Finance in a minority government, in 1973 Turner presented a budget that was an eclectic success.

Turner had to bring down a budget on February 19 that the Conservatives could support and that also dealt with the corporate tax cuts and fast write-offs to which he was personally committed and which had died on the order paper when the previous Parliament was dissolved. These were absolute anathema to the NDP. In addition, he had to consider it an election budget with some measures popular to the public because the government could fall at any time. Turner was walking in a political, fiscal, and monetary minefield. . . .

The budget was a political masterpiece. It stole, almost holus bolus, a Stanfield plan for the indexing of income tax to the cost of living, which many Liberals had been ridiculing. It declared that the Trudeau government remained committed to the business tax concessions and fast write-offs, but that they would be dealt with in separate resolutions later on. It reduced income taxes 5 per cent and eliminated 750,000 lower-income Canadians from the tax rolls altogether. It increased old-age pensions across the board to $100 a month and abolished sales tax on children's clothing and candy bars and pop in an effort to control prices. As Turner read the budget speech, New Democrat Stanley Knowles presented David Lewis with a congratulatory flower, and at the point when Turner claimed credit for the tax indexation, the Tories cried, 'Author, Author', while Stanfield rose to take a mocking bow. It was a raucous evening and even Trudeau got into the spirit of things, shouting at Stanfield: 'Look out, we may even steal your underwear.' But it worked. The NDP was neutralized. The Conservatives were sewn up. The people were pleased.

Ibid.

[During the 1984 campaign] the Liberal leader was subjected to a rash of headlines about his pants.

The scene was the Martinet restaurant, in Trois Rivières, where Turner was having dinner with local dignitaries, hosted by the Quebec hatchetman of the Liberal cabinet, Privy Council President André Ouellet.

In the midst of the festivities, a waiter dumped coffee on Turner's lap, staining his grey flannels.

Ouellet led Turner to a nearby washroom, trying to avoid campaign reporters who were gathered at the bar. Turner and Ouellet disappeared into the washroom and, in a few moments, Ouellet emerged, carrying Turner's trousers.

Ouellet walked down the hall and sidestepped into the women's washroom with Mrs Geills Turner, who set to work to clean the stain from the PM's flannels, which were duly returned to Turner by Ouellet, back in the men's room.

A photographer and a technician who were in the men's can when Turner and Ouellet entered, reported that Turner had peeled off his pants saying: 'Take them down to Geills, and she'll take care of them.'

She did, indeed. And the resulting national debate almost equalled in intensity the earlier bruhaha about Turner's bum patting tendencies. Was it demeaning to expect the wife to clean the pants? Couldn't Turner clean his own?

Truly, Murphy's Law was working overtime against Turner, and the incident cost him with men and women alike. Worse, it made him a laughing stock, and if there is anything a political leader is not supposed to be in an election, it is that.

Charles Lynch, Race For The Rose, 1984

EDWARD BROADBENT

NDP MP from Oshawa since 1965, Ed Broadbent became his party's national leader in 1975.

Mel Watkins, political economist at the University of Toronto . . . had gained a reputation as a liberal continentalist, but in the late 1960s he shifted rapidly to a radical nationalist position. His highly publicized 1968 report to the federal government on foreign ownership had helped to popularize the term 'branch-plant economy'. In April 1969 Watkins began to organize informal talk sessions with Ed Broadbent, the MP for Oshawa, and James Laxer, who was then a graduate student at Queen's University. Laxer's network of allies in the universities of Ontario and the West would form the core of the Waffle—a name allegedly coined by Broadbent when he insisted, 'If we're going to waffle, let's waffle to the left.'

Thomas H. McLeod and Ian McLeod, Tommy Douglas: The Road to Jerusalem, 1987

The more mainstream members of Watkin's group—Broadbent, Charles Taylor, Gerald Caplan—gradually drifted away as it became clear that Laxer planned to set up an ongoing dissident caucus. In September [1969], Watkins and Laxer issued their manifesto, 'Towards an Independent Socialist Canada'. It set out the 'development of socialist consciousness' as the first priority of the NDP. . . .

The manifesto proposed that the NDP bring about socialism through public ownership combined with worker control of industry, and not through regulation. The party should pursue its strategies not only through Parliament but through a broad range of popular organizations. The manifesto insisted at the same time that Canada should break from the American empire and the NATO alliance, and align itself with the Third World.

Within a month, the 125–member NDP National Council issued a counter document, 'For a United and Independent Canada'. It offered many of the short-term proposals put forward in the Waffle statement, such as stricter controls on foreign investment in Canada and public ownership of resource industries. Broadbent observed a 'curious overlapping' of the two papers; he and Charles Taylor had taken a hand in drafting both.

Ibid.

At the end of 1979 he worked with adviser Lawrence Wolf to improve his TV image for the 1980 campaign.

Broadbent's schedule was so arranged that he spent most of the time between Christmas and the new year working on the commercials. To get just the right shots of Broadbent, Wolf used long-range cameras and even knocked out the wall of a room during the hours of filming. The Toronto home of Stephen Lewis, former NDP leader in Ontario, was used for one location; the historic Grange House in Toronto for another. Poor Broadbent nearly melted filming a commercial in Grange House, where the central heating, television lights, and roaring fire in the fireplace combined to make the set unbearably hot. To ensure that the viewer focused on nothing but Broadbent in the five-minute, free-time commercials, Wolf blacked out everything else on the screen and shone a light only on Broadbent's face, while the leader talked earnestly about NDP policies in response to set-up questions asked by Wolf, sitting off-camera.

Wolf, a friendly, gregarious man, was delighted with the negative advertising produced for the Liberals by Red Leaf and for the Conservatives by Media Buying Services, whose offices are two throws of a stone from Wolf's in the sandblasted chic of Toronto's Yorkville district. Wolf may have built part of his reputation on 'competitive advertising', but the ads he saw from the Liberals and Conservatives went too far. They had crossed the line from competitive advertising to negative advertising. As Wolf said one afternoon during the campaign:

> . . . Look at all the Liberal commercials, the subject is Clark. When you look at the Conservative commercials, the subject is Trudeau. That's really an ass-backwards way to advertise. We're proud of our leader. We think he has something to say. He's a positive, rather than a negative option. We feel he's the best of three choices, rather than the worst of three evils.'

Jeffrey Simpson, Discipline of Power, 1980

DAVID PETERSON

Following forty-two years of Conservative rule in Ontario, David Peterson became Liberal Premier in 1985.

For the time being at least, the Liberal ministers were acutely conscious of their origins in Opposition. Peterson had promised a new openness in government and free access to information that his researchers had so often demanded and never got from the Tories. On the day of the swearing-in, the premier had invited the public into his office to see the inner places of government, but there were limits to his offer.

During cabinet the next day, Peterson noticed a middle-aged woman whom he didn't know. There were lots of new faces around these days, however. He'd supplied cabinet with a seating plan so newcomers could identify who was speaking. Peterson leaned back in his chair between treasurer Bob Nixon and education minister Sean Conway and inquired quietly behind his hand just who the woman was. Conway replied that she was probably with the cabinet office. So Peterson signalled Ed Stewart and asked him to make the introduction. 'I thought she was with you,' Stewart said in surprise. He then asked her business and was told: 'I came to see the open government.' She was politely, but firmly, ushered out.

Open government, it seems, was not to be taken that literally.

Rosemary Speirs, Out of the Blue, 1986

WILLIAM VANDER ZALM

A member of the British Columbia Socred cabinet since 1975, William Vander Zalm became Premier in 1986.

On December 22, 1975, after his swearing-in ceremony, Human Resources Minister Vander Zalm was sipping champagne when he made the most important remark of his political career, 'If anybody is able to work, but refuses to pick up the shovel, we will find ways of dealing with him.' (This quote was also recorded as: 'If they don't have a shovel, they should get one, because otherwise we're going to give them one.')

Vander Zalm said he did not know what criteria should or would be used to decide who was employable. This was clearly one of his haphazard, off-the-cuff remarks. But the press eagerly picked it up and went looking for responses. Alderman Darlene Marzari, vice-chairman of the Vancouver Resources Board, half-jokingly wondered if Vander Zalm might consider building 'internment camps for single employable males'.

Vander Zalm took no steps to defuse this situation.

He did just the opposite.

Bill Vander Zalm ordered hundreds of tiny sterling silver shovel-shaped lapel pins. He sprayed short-handled shovels with gold paint. He proceeded to auction these 'shovel packages' to add to the Social Credit Party coffers. The shovel would become his emblem, his totem.

Like the merchandiser who uses a logo to distinguish his product from all others, Vander Zalm, with his training in sales, seized upon the shovel as a selling tool for himself. Soon shovels of various shapes and sizes decorated his office. The shovel, a symbol of unpretentious hard work and contact with the earth, a symbol of Vander Zalm's own past and his success in industry, was the perfect symbol for Vander Zalm to use in reaching out to the grass roots of the Social Credit Party.

He began to sign notes, 'Happy Shovelling'. His campaign for self-promotion was based upon his instinctive marketing knowledge that the secret of propaganda is repetition. In years to come shovels auctioned by Bill Vander Zalm at Social Credit functions would sell, in some cases, for almost $1,000.

Alan Twigg, Vander Zalm: From Immigrant to Premier, 1986

JOHN CROSBIE

A member of Smallwood's Newfoundland cabinet from 1966 to 1969, John Crosbie joined the Conservatives in 1971 and entered the cabinet of Premier Frank Moores. Elected to the House of Commons in 1976, he was Minister of Finance in the Clark government from 1979 to 1980, challenged Mulroney for the Tory leadership in 1983, and became Minister of Justice in 1984.

Newfoundlanders seem to require salt, blarney, and steel in their political leaders, so it took awhile for other English-speaking Canadians, accustomed to more anodyne political performers, to appreciate the mixture. After a hesitant start in his portfolio, Crosbie's political stock soared when Canadians heard more of his Newfoundland twang and spicy comments. They might not have liked his message, but it was hard not to be entertained by a minister who called Trudeau's Cabinet 'Disco Daddy and the Has-beens'; told an audience at the Canadian Tax Foundation, 'You won't believe this, but there's a move afoot to move our interest rates to Jerusalem'; called himself 'Canada's first ethnic Prime Minister'; and sported mukluks instead of the traditional new pair of shoes worn by a finance minister on budget night. Shortly after his election to the Commons as MP for St John's West in a 1976 by-election, he criticized those opposed to the seal hunt, especially French actress Brigitte Bardot, who 'did a lot of twitching over here—twitching in ways you wouldn't believe; then again, you might'. In jesting retaliation, he moved in the Commons to ban the importation of French wine 'because [the French] brutalize the grapes when they pound them with their feet'. He delivered his cascade of one-liners with the twang of the Newfoundland outports, thicker in public than in private, that turned 'barrels' into 'burr'ls', 'tough times' into 'toof toimes', 'Conservatives' into 'Consarrvatives', and 'budgets' into 'boogets'. 'With a Polish Pope and a Newfie finance minister, you mainlanders had better watch your jokes,' he told a Toronto audience.

Jeffrey Simpson, Discipline of Power, 1980

During his run for the leadership in 1983,

Crosbie, of course, killed himself (if there was any doubt he was a Tory, he removed it here) by his casual slur in Quebec. He had been making rather good progress with the point that he 'like 22 million other Canadians' was unilingual. No one else had ever had the guts to say that in public before: that nowhere near the five million people in Quebec were bilingual and he shouldn't be regarded as 'a criminal' because he wasn't.

It was a fair comment, gaining him a lot of points from sensible people who had never quite had the courage to say that themselves. We can't leave the running of the country completely to a 'bilingual élite', he said, pushing his advantage just a trifle bit further, an interesting concept that had been bothering a number of Canadians for years.

That was the casual, sensible, honest Crosbie at his best. Pushed even further, nagged by basically anglophone reporters who sniffed a little blood, the unfortunate aspect of the Brahmin Crosbie burst forth, testily. Out came the fatal riposte that he couldn't speak 'Chinese or German either', but that didn't prevent him or other Canadians from communicating with those nations.

Allan Fotheringham, *Look Ma . . . No Hands*, 1983

The House of Commons is an unforgiving place with a long memory, as Transport Minister John Crosbie showed Liberal leader John Turner last week.

Turner asked Crosbie 'why the minister does not get off his butt and protect the fishermen in Newfoundland'—a jab at the continuing Canadian problems with French fishing rights on the East Coast.

'The Hon. Leader of the Opposition knows all about butts,' retorted Crosbie. 'He has had his hands on more butts than there are Members of this House.'

Crosbie was referring to Turner's ill-starred 1984 election campaign exposure on TV when he was seen slapping Iona Campagnolo's rump in a pally manner that enraged many women.

Toronto Star, 1 Nov. 1987

BRIAN MULRONEY

Despite never having run for public office, Brian Mulroney contested the Tory leadership in 1976. In 1983 he tried again, and won. He entered the House of Commons later in 1983, and the election of 1984 made him Canada's eighteenth prime minister.

It is important to remember that Ronald Reagan did not actually sing 'When Irish Eyes Are Smiling' onstage at Quebec City's posh Grand Theatre with Brian Mulroney on March 17, 1985, at the glitzy $550,000 black-tie finale to the Shamrock Summit.

Oh sure, he and Nancy were up there on the stage, even mouthing a few words, but Reagan had said beforehand that he wouldn't sing and didn't want a microphone near him. Mulroney had asked him to go on stage at a wrap-up of the Gala Soirée, so he went as a favour. But he didn't sing.

Brian Mulroney did sing, however. He has a splendid baritone singing voice, the result of a lifetime of singing for assorted American audiences.

He used to delight in telling the story himself. As a boy soprano in Baie-Comeau, he would sing 'Dearie' for American newspaper tycoon Colonel Robert McCormick whenever McCormick came to town to check his paper mill. 'He'd give me fifty dollars a crack,' said Mulroney. 'I remember standing on top of the piano singing the song with Jack Dempsey sitting right in front of me. The colonel had brought him in for some fishing. I just about had a heart attack. I was eight, maybe nine.'

Mulroney grew up to be a baritone, and after the Tories weren't buying his song and dance at the 1976 leadership convention, Hanna Mining Company of Cleveland, Ohio, asked him to come and sing the praises of their Canadian affiliate, the Iron Ore Company of Canada. In return, they offered to make him a millionaire and gave him a mansion in Westmount, membership in the best clubs, a fishing camp in Labrador, and four box seats directly behind the Montreal Canadiens' bench at the Forum. He did well by them, too. He ended labour strife and turned a profit, and when it came to a choice between sending dividends south of the border or propping up the mine at Schefferville, Mulroney did right by his American masters—he closed the town.

Claire Hoy, *Friends in High Places*, 1987

'There's too cozy a relationship between economics and politics,' says David McQueen, economics professor at York University. 'Canada's biggest businessmen have entry to the highest policy-making circles, and this means a secrecy and centralizing of decision-making and fixing things up between the old boys.' . . .

[The] power is very much on the political foot, not the financial, maintains Hal Jackman. Mulroney went to the Palm Beach, Florida, home of his former 'employer', Conrad Black, whose companies are the largest shareholders of the Iron Ore Co., where Mulroney was president. The purpose of the 1983 visit was to garner Black's blessing for an inevitable leadership test of former prime minister Joe Clark, whose support was beginning to crumble. 'Black asked him, "Why do you want to run?"' says Jackman, a Clark supporter. '"The prime minister is not that powerful. The job doesn't pay that much and there's no security. You're not interested in country-governing, are you? I guess it's because you don't want to kiss ass, you want other people to kiss your ass." Brian agreed.'

Diane Francis, *Controlling Interest*, 1987

A group of Mulroney's Quebec backers tried to force Clark to call a leadership contest after the 1981 general meeting, where Clark got only 66.4 per cent, but Clark refused, thinking that having just lost his brief minority government in 1980, much of the vote against him at the 1981 meeting was a result of that. With two years until Winnipeg, he could turn it around in his favour. In their book *Connections*, authors Allan Gregg, Patrick Martin, and George Perlin argue . . . that from 1980 until the 1983 Winnipeg meeting, Mulroney worked hand in hand with some of his most trusted friends and advisers to undermine Clark, while at the same time continuing publicly to pledge allegiance to the leader. (The most memorable example is the dramatic show of unity with Clark in Montreal, on December 6, 1982, a little over a month before Winnipeg.)

'That was an incredible display,' says *Gazette* reporter Claude Arpin. 'He had Joe over at the Ritz. It was unbelievable. They had forty people crammed into a tiny room and Brian actually put his arm around Joe and said "He's my leader, he always will be." And a lot of us knew that Mulroney's guys were out there with thousand-dollar bills buying delegates who were going to go to Winnipeg later to vote against Joe.'

Claire Hoy, Friends in High Places, 1987

'In a political campaign the only reality is perception, part expectations, part feelings,' said [Mulroney adviser] Tom Scott. 'After seeing Turner in the debates, everyone was asking, "Is there a Prime Minister anywhere?" So, knowing that Mulroney was a superb television performer, we decided to put him in the window.'

'Putting him in the window' meant featuring him up front in the ads, in which he did nothing fancier than talk straight into the camera about a series of issues. What he said about those issues wasn't the substantial message. The substance was in the lead, 'I need help with . . . ', and the finish, 'Together we can do better'. Besides being vehicles for getting the basic slogan out to the electorate, the ads also spoke to the two major reservations people still had about Brian Mulroney, his glibness and his trustworthiness. The format let him look like a Prime Minister, sound deep and concerned, and take the high road in contrast to the Liberals' muddy route. Suppressing his usual highly partisan, highly exaggerated, highly facile style, which was at the root of the 'trust factor', he projected himself as earnest, informed, caring, and very sincere. . . .

Gregg and Scott took Mulroney to a hotel north of Toronto and spent a day perfecting his sincerity. Mulroney videotaped the scripts in one room, then went into the room where Gregg and Scott watched the takes on a television, and the three of them went over the details of what was right, what wasn't right, and what he should do the next time. 'I don't know what those poor fuckers in the hotel thought we were doing with the leader of Her Majesty's Loyal Opposition,' Gregg said, 'but his progress was remarkable. He started off all pumped up and full of himself, like all politicians do—it's less them than their vision of what a politician is—but Mulroney was a quick study, and though he doesn't like anyone else criticizing him, he can be very self-critical.

He could see the problems for himself on the TV set, and in effect he became his own director.' Twenty-five good tapes were finished by four o'clock, then rushed to Kitchener where focus groups sat waiting to judge them at six. The almost instantaneous feedback was favourable, on the whole, and eight scripts were selected for airing. As Atkins once said, 'Brian Mulroney can perform and do a script very well.' Thus, the candidate was able to lay to rest the doubts that he was untrustworthy and all surface.

Ron Graham, *One-Eyed Kings*, 1987

He gave up smoking, and, more recently, reading all the newspapers and watching almost every national news broadcast—no mean feat for a media junkie.

This was a man who read everything, and was always catching me out because I'd missed some item somewhere. Once, when we were about to leave Ottawa for a goodwill trip, I made sure I'd read everything there was to read in Canada that might interest him. This time, I'd survive the quiz. No sooner were we strapped in the Challenger than he asked me, 'Have you read this story in *Le Figaro*?' A French paper. I could have strangled him. . . .

For it is a fact that rivalling his obsession with Trudeau was his obsession with the media. Every morning at dawn, the major dailies were delivered to the prime ministerial residence at 24 Sussex Drive, and he'd have read them all before his senior staffs' morning meeting. In the evenings, he was forever fiddling with a TV channel selector to make sure he didn't miss anything. When he wasn't there, he'd have someone record newscasts for him, and when we were overseas, he'd sometimes have the cassettes flown over. (Contrary to rumour, we never went as far as satellite feeds; the cost was simply prohibitive.)

I paid the price for The Boss's obsession one memorable night during the winter of 1986. We were staying at the Ritz Carlton hotel in Montreal, where, on Friday January 24, Mulroney gave an excellent interview to *Le Devoir*. The story appeared early Saturday, and Canadian Press put an item on the wire. That was fine; we had scored a small coup. All was peaceful as we settled down that night at the Ritz.

Normally, I would have left the hotel to savour the downtown joys of Montreal night-life, but a kindly fate kept me in my room like a good little Ontario boy. I was snuggled into bed at 12:30 A.M. when the phone rang. The Boss wanted to see me. At once. Good Lord, what could be coming down on our heads now?

When I got to his suite, he was sitting on the couch wearing a dressing-gown and a put-upon expression. Sitting in a nearby armchair in his pajamas was his principal secretary, Bernard Roy, looking just antsy. Mulroney had been listening to the radio, as usual, and had picked up a report that was making him lose sleep. I no longer remember exactly why, but he was certain that the newsreader had dangerously misrepresented what he'd said to *Le Devoir*. I told him the announcer was probably reading from the CP story, and that he'd added a little something, as announcers often do.

'Get on the phone to Canadian Press,' he ordered. 'I never said that.'

I turned to leave for my room, but he wanted me to make the call right there, in front of him. After speaking to the CP desk, I told him that, as far as I was concerned, the story that was read to me had been eminently correct.

'Then call the radio station.'

There was, naturally, no one at the station but the wretched announcer, who played me a tape of his report. There wasn't anything terribly wrong with it, but, as I'd expected, he'd given the item a bit of topspin. I chewed him out, telling him that I'd been there for the intereview, I knew what was in the CP story, and he had no right to put such distortions out on the air. When I hung up, the Prime Minister was looking at me anxiously.

'And . . .' he said.

'I think I scared him, but you never know.'

Then he did something that will remain forever engraved in my memory. From the pocket of his dressing gown, he pulled out a small shortwave radio and began fiddling with the dial. I was so dumbfounded that I couldn't help blurting to Roy, 'Isn't someone going to unplug him?'

Mulroney found that very funny, but he kept at the radio until he satisfied himself that the offending item had been dropped from the next newscast.

'Well,' he said, 'you must really have scared him.' Then, almost shyly, he added, 'I'm sorry I disturbed you.'

Michel Gratton, 'So, What Are The Boys Saying?', 1987

Somehow a statement of Mulroney's missed being the 'Quote of the Day' in the Globe and Mail, *but it was later nominated by a reader, in a letter to the editor, as 'Quote of the Year':*

'I am not denying anything I did not say.'

The Globe and Mail, 18 Sept. 1986

As a place to stop, and think, that may be as good as any.

ACKNOWLEDGEMENTS

IRVING ABELLA and HAROLD TROPER, *None Is Too Many*. Copyright © Abella and Troper 1983. Reprinted by permission of Lester & Orpen Dennys Ltd, Toronto.

KEN ADACHI, *The Enemy That Never Was* (1976), used by permission of McClelland and Stewart, the Canadian Publishers.

ALVIN ARMSTRONG, *Flora MacDonald*. Used by permission of J.M. Dent & Sons (Canada) Limited.

ED ARROL, 'When Pot Hole Kellie kidnapped the premier', 'Canadianecdote' *Maclean's* 1 July 1961. Used by permission.

JEAN BANNERMAN, *Leading Ladies Canada* (1977). Used by permission of Mika Publishing Company, Belleville.

CARL BERGER, *The Sense of Power* (1971). Reproduced by permission of University of Toronto Press.

CONRAD BLACK, *Duplessis* (1977), used by permission of McClelland and Stewart, the Canadian Publishers.

ALLAN BLAKENEY, 'The Early Years' in *NeWest Review*, special issue on 'Tommy and His Legacy', Saskatoon, May 1987.

PAUL BILKEY, *Persons, Papers and Things* (1940), used by permission of McGraw-Hill Ryerson Limited.

ROBERT BOTHWELL and WILLIAM KILBOURN, *C.D. Howe: A Biography* (1979), used by permission of McClelland and Stewart, the Canadian Publishers.

RUSSELL BRADDON, *Roy Thomson of Fleet Street* (Collins, 1965). Used by permission of John Farquharson Ltd, London.

MICHAEL BRADLEY, *Crisis of Clarity* (1985 Summerhill Press Ltd). Used by permission.

JACK CAHILL, *John Turner: The Long Run* (1984). Used by permission of the author.

J.M.S. CARELESS, *George Brown and the Mother of Confederation*, Canadian Historical Association, Report of the Annual Meeting 1960 and *Brown of The Globe* (Macmillan 1963) are reprinted by permission of the author.

FLOYD S. CHALMERS, *A Gentleman of the Press* © 1969 Floyd S. Chalmers. Published by Doubleday Canada Ltd. Used by permission of Doubleday Canada Limited.

JEAN CHRÉTIEN, excerpted from *Straight from the Heart* by Jean Chrétien, Key Porter Books, Toronto. Copyright © 1985 by Jean Chrétien. Used by permission.

JOHN ROBERT COLOMBO, *Colombo's Canadian Quotations* (1974) and *Colombo's New Canadian Quotations* (1987). Reprinted by permission of Hurtig Publishers Ltd and the author.

DONALD CREIGHTON, *John A. Macdonald, The Old Chieftan* © 1955, *John A. Macdonald, The Young Politician* © 1956, reprinted by permission of Macmillan of Canada, A Division of Canada Publishing Corporation. From *Towards the Discovery of Canada: Selected Essays* (Macmillan, 1972). Used by permission.

BRIAN C. CUTHBERTSON, *The Loyalist Governor: Biography of Sir John Wentworth* (1983). Used by permission of Petheric Press.

R. MACGREGOR DAWSON, *William Lyon Mackenzie King* (1958). Reproduced by permission of University of Toronto Press.

HUGH A. DEMPSEY, *The Best of Bob Edwards* (1975). Reprinted by permission of Hurtig Publishers Ltd and the author.

PETER DESBARATS, *René: A Canadian in Search of a Country* (1976). Reprinted by permission of the author.

VINCENT DURANT, *War Horse of Cumberland: The life and times of Sir Charles Tupper* (1985). Used by permission of Lancelot Press Limited.

OLIVE ELLIOTT in the *Edmonton Journal* 24 April 1976. Used by permission.

JOY E. ESBEREY, *Knight of the Holy Spirit* (1980). Reproduced by permission of University of Toronto Press.

ALLAN FOTHERINGHAM, excerpted from *Look Ma . . . No Hands* by Allan Fotheringham, published by Key Porter Books. Copyright © 1983 by Allan Fotheringham. Excerpted from *Capitol Offences* by Allan Fotheringham, published by Key Porter Books. Copyright © 1986 by Allan Fotheringham. Used by permission.

ARTHUR R. FORD, *As the World Wags On* (1950). Used by permission.

DIANE FRANCIS, *Controlling Interest* © 1986, reprinted by permission of Macmillan of Canada, A Division of Canada Publishing Corporation.

R. DOUGLAS FRANCIS, *Frank H. Underhill: Intellectual Provocateur* (1986). Reproduced by permission of University of Toronto Press.

JOHN FRASER, exerpted from *Telling Tales*, Collins Publishers, Toronto. Copyright © 1986 by John Fraser.

WALTER GORDON, *A Political Memoir* (1977), used by permission of McClelland and Stewart, the Canadian Publishers.

RON GRAHAM, excerpted from *One -Eyed Kings*, Collins Publishers, Toronto. Copyright © 1986 by Ron Graham.

MICHEL GRATTON, *So What Are The Boys Saying?* (1987), used by permission of McGraw-Hill Ryerson Limited.

RICHARD GWYN, *The Northern Magus: Pierre Trudeau and Canadians* (1980), *Smallwood: the unlikely revolutionary* (1968), used by permission of McClelland and Stewart, the Canadian Publishers. Excerpt from 'Pearson' *Saturday Night*, Sept. 1960, used by permission of the author.

SANDRA GWYN, excerpted from *The Private Capital* by Sandra Gwyn, McClelland and Stewart, Toronto. Copyright © 1984 R. & A. Gwyn Associates. Reprinted by permission of the Colbert Agency Inc.

E.D. HALIBURTON, *My Years With Stanfield* (1972). Used by permission of Lancelot Press Limited.

D.J. HALL, *Clifford Sifton*, vol. 1, *The Young Napoleon 1861–1900*. Used by permission of the University of British Columbia Press.

W.G. HARDY, 'The Orangemen who made the duke see red', 'Canadianecdote' *Maclean's* 1 August 1959. Used by permission.

W.A. HARKIN, *Political Reminiscences of The Right Honourable Sir Charles Tupper* (1914 Constable & Company Ltd).

ROSS HARKNESS, *J.E. Atkinson of the Star* (1963). Reprinted with permission of The Toronto Star Syndicate.

ARNOLD HEENEY, *The Things that are Caesar's* (1972). Reproduced by permission of University of Toronto Press.

CLAIRE HOY, excerpted from *Friends in High Places* by Claire Hoy, published by Key Porter Books. Copyright © 1987 by Claire Hoy. Used by permission.

CHARLES W. HUMPHRIES, *'Honest Enough to Be Bold'* (1985). Reproduced by permission of University of Toronto Press.

BRUCE HUTCHISON, *The Far Side of the Street* (1976), Macmillan of Canada, Toronto. Used by permission of the author.

GEORGE IGNATIEFF, *The Making of a Peacemonger: The Memoirs of George Itnatieff* (1987). Reproduced by permission of University of Toronto Press.

JACK KAPICA, *Shocked and Appalled* (1985), Robert Stanfield's letter to the editor, used by permission of *The Globe and Mail.*

WILLIAM KILBOURN, *The Firebrand* (1960) by William Kilbourn. Reprinted with the permission of Irwin Publishing, Toronto, Ont.

JUDY LAMARSH, *Memoirs of a Bird In a Gilded Cage* (1969), used by permission of McClelland and Stewart, the Canadian Publishers and the Estate of Judy LaMarsh.

PIERRE LAPORTE, *The True Face of Duplessis* (1960), used by permission of Harvest House Limited, Montreal.

RENÉ LÉVESQUE, *Memoirs* (1986), trans. Philip Stratford, used by permission of McClelland and Stewart, the Canadian Publishers, and Québec/Amérique.

DAVID LEWIS, *The Good Fight* © 1981, reprinted by permission of Macmillan of Canada, A Division of Canada Publishing Corporation.

CHARLES LYNCH, *A Funny Way to Run a Country* (1984), *You Can't Print THAT!* (1983). Reprinted by permission of Hurtig Publishers Ltd and the author. *Race for the Rose: Election 1984* (Methuen 1984), used by permission of the author.

CHRISTINA MCCALL NEWMAN, *Grits* © 1982, reprinted by permission of Macmillan of Canada, A Division of Canada Publishing Corporation.

DIANA MCCANDLESS, 'When the Speaker shot Sir Robert's cat', 'Canadianecdote' *Maclean's* 6 May 1961. Used by permission.

E.M. MACDONALD, *Recollections Political and Personal* (1938), used by permission of McGraw-Hill Ryerson Limited.

THAD MCILROY, *Personal Letters of a Public Man* © 1985 Arcadia House Inc. Published by Doubleday Canada Ltd. Used by permission of Doubleday Canada Limited.

DAVE MCINTOSH, *Ottawa Unbuttoned* (1987) by Dave McIntosh. Reprinted with the permission of Stoddart Publishing, Toronto, Ont.

BRIAN MCKENNA and SUSAN PURCELL, *Drapeau* (1981). Reprinted with the permission of Irwin Publishing, Toronto, Ont.

THOMAS H. MCLEOD and IAN MCLEOD, *Tommy Douglas: The Road to Jerusalem* (1987). Reprinted by permission of Hurtig Publishers Ltd and the authors.

C.B. MACPHERSON, *Democracy in Alberta* (1962). Reproduced by permission of University of Toronto Press.

PAUL MARTIN, *A Very Public Life*, vol. 1 (1983), vol. 2 (1985). Used by permission of Deneau Publishers & Company Ltd.

DAVID J. MITCHELL, *W.A.C. Bennett and the Rise of British Columbia* (1983). Used by permission of Douglas & McIntyre Ltd.

ALBERT and TERESA MORITZ, *Leacock: A Biography* (1985). Reprinted with the permission of Stoddart Publishing, Toronto, Ont.

DESMOND MORTON, *A Peculair Kind of Politics* (1982). Reproduced by permission of University of Toronto Press.

JOHN A. MUNRO and ALEX I. INGLIS, *Mike: The Memoirs of the Right Honourable Lester B. Pearson*, vol. 2, *1948–1957* (1973), vol. 3, *1957–1968* (1975). Reproduced by permission of University of Toronto Press.

HUGH BINGHAM MYERS, *The Quebec Revolution* (1963), used by permission of Harvest House Limited, Montreal.

PETER C. NEWMAN, *Renegade in Power* (1963), *Home Country* (1973), *The Distemper of Our Times* (1968), used by permission of McClelland and Stewart, the Canadian Publishers and the author.

GRATTAN O'LEARY, *Grattan O'Leary, Recollections of People, Press, and Politics* (1977). Used by permission.

SEAN O'SULLIVAN, excerpted from *Both My Houses* by Sean O'Sullivan with Rod McQueen, published by Key Porter Books. Copyright © 1986 by Sean O'Sullivan and Rod McQueen Communications. Used by permission.

FRANK W. PEERS, *The Politics of Canadian Broadcasting 1920–1951* (1969). Reproduced by permission of University of Toronto Press.

MAURICE POPE, *Public Servant: The Memoirs of Sir Joseph Pope* (1960), used by permission of Oxford University Press Canada.

HERBERT LENCH POTTLE, *Fun on the Rock*, used by permission of Breakwater Books, Ltd, the original publisher of this material.

LOUISE REYNOLDS, *Agnes: The Biography of Lady Macdonald* (Samuel Stevens, Toronto, 1979). Used by permission.

CHARLES RITCHIE, *Diplomatic Passport* © 1981, reprinted by permission of Macmillan of Canada, A Division of Canada Publishing Corporation.

ABRAHAM ROTSTEIN, *The Prospect of Change: Proposals for Canada's Future* (1965), used by permission of McGraw-Hill Ryerson Limited.

JOSEPH SCHULL, *Laurier: The First Canadian* © 1965, reprinted by permission of Macmillan of Canada, A Division of Canada Publishing Corporation.

OSCAR DOUGLAS SKELTON, *The Life and Times of Sir Alexander Tilloch Galt* (1920), used by permission of Oxford University Press Canada.

ROSEMARY SPEIRS, *Out of the Blue* © 1986, reprinted by permission of Macmillan of Canada, A Division of Canada Publishing Corporation.

C.P. STACEY, *A Very Double Life* © 1976, reprinted by permission of Macmillan of Canada, A Division of Canada Publishing Corporation.

DELLA M.M. STANLEY, *Louis Robichaud: A Decade of Power* (1984). Used by permission of Nimbus Publishing Limited.

GEOFFREY STEVENS, *Stanfield* (1973), used by permission of McClelland and Stewart, the Canadian Publishers.

WALTER STEWART, *Shrug: Trudeau in Power* (1972) and *Divide and Con* (1973), used by permission of the author.

LLOYD STINSON, *Political Warriors* (1975). Used by permission of Queenston House Publishing.

PETER STURSBERG, *Lester Pearson and the Dream of Unity* © 1978 Peter Stursberg. Published by Doubleday Canada Ltd. Used by permission of Doubleday Canada Limited. *Diefenbaker: Leadership lost 1962–67* (1976). Reproduced by permission of University of Toronto Press.

A.J.P. TAYLOR, *Beaverbrook* (1972 Simon and Schuster). Used by permission.

CHARLES TEMPLETON, *An Anecdotal Memoir* copyright © 1983 by Charles Templeton. Reprinted by permission of McClelland and Stewart, the Canadian Publishers and JCA Literary Agency Inc. as agents for the author.

DALE C. THOMSON, *Louis St Laurent: Canadian* (Macmillan 1967). Reprinted by permission of the author.

E.A. TOLLESFON, 'The Battle for Medicare' in *NeWest Review*, special issue on 'Tommy and His Legacy', Saskatoon, May 1987.

TORONTO STAR, 'Turner Made Butt of Crosbie Memory' *Toronto Star* 1 November 1987. Reprinted with permission of The Toronto Star Sydicate.

ALAN TWIGG, *Vander Zalm: From Immigrant to Premier*, Harbour Publishing Co. Ltd., 1986. Quoted with permission of the publisher.

THOMAS VAN DUSEN, *The Chief* (1968), used by permission of McGraw-Hill Ryerson Limited.

BERNARD L. VIGOD, *Quebec Before Duplessis: The Political Career of Louis-Alexandre Taschereau* (1986). Reprinted by permission of McGill-Queen's University Press.

PETER B. WAITE, *Canada 1874–1896* (1971), used by permission of McClelland and Stewart, the Canadian Publishers. From 'Between Three Oceans: Challenges of a Continental Destiny' in *The Illustrated History of Canada*, edited by Craig Brown. Copyright © by Lester & Orpen Dennys Ltd 1987. Reprinted by permission of Lester & Orpen Dennys Ltd, Toronto. From *Oliver Mowat's Ontario*, ed. Donald Swainson (Toronto, Macmillan of Canada, 1972). *The Man from Halifax* (1985) and *The Life and Times of Confederation 1864–1867* (1962). Reproduced by permission of University of Toronto Press.

NORMAN WARD, *Her Majesty's Mice* (1977), used by permission of McClelland and Stewart, the Canadian Publishers and the author.

ELIZABETH WANGENHEIM, 'The Ukrainians: A Case Study of the "Third Force"' in Peter Russell, *Nationalism in Canada*. Reprinted by permission of the University League for Social Reform.

EUGENE WHELAN, *Whelan: The Man in the Green Stetson* (1986) by Eugene Whelan with Rick Archbold. Reprinted with the permission of Irwin Publishing, Toronto, Ontario.

WALTER YOUNG, 'M.J. Coldwell' *Journal of Canadian Studies*, vol. 9, no. 3, 1974. Used by permission.

ROLAND WILD, *Amor De Cosmos* (1958), used by permission of the author.

Every effort has been made to determine and contact copyright owners. In the case of any omissions, the publisher will be pleased to make suitable acknowledgements in future editions.

INDEX OF NAMES

INDEX OF AUTHORS